"Matthew Ingram has not only investigated a huge amount of material and talked to many people, he also has an ability to bring it all together in a way that makes sense and is fun to read."

Charles Dowding, author of *No Dig*

"A fascinating and detailed account of the extraordinary people prepared to counter the march of depletive systems. Matthew Ingram beautifully describes the alarm bell ringing for hippies and far-sighted visionaries prepared to stand up for soils and sustainable practices. The Garden *sheds light on the characters and events that have shaped the use of our land. For those of us searching for sustainable solutions to complex and overlapping problems, this book provides forgotten information and lessons from the past for the dilemmas of the present and the future."*

Ian Wilkinson, FarmEd

"The idea of gardening and farming as acts of revolution and dissent may be unfamiliar to many of us, so it's great to have Matthew Ingram's brilliantly readable book celebrating the unexpected ways that individuals, communities, and movements have, simply by growing their own food, found green-fingered ways to stick it to the man."

Hugh Fearnley-Whitingstall, River Cottage

"I admired Retreat. *Fluid and intelligent and... I could go on! The new Matt Ingram is even better... With* The Garden, *Ingram recuperates an even more transgressive gesture: the counterculture's attempted rethinking of our first culture: agriculture."*

Jay Stevens, author of *Storming Heaven*

"Matthew Ingram has preserved and enlarged a corner of history which few have visited or are even aware of. He narrates, with the page-turning excitement of a mystery novel and the first-hand accounts of those who witnessed it, a pivot point that had enormous implications. If we get through the converging crises of this decade, our future will be profoundly better as a result of the shift he describes."

Albert Bates, The Farm

"Matthew Ingram has done all of us who care about ecological growing and a better world a big favour in this compendious but highly readable history of the gardening counterculture and its personalities. His in-depth, warts-and-all account of these past efforts will be endlessly informative for new generations wrestling with the demons of agricultural change, cultural change, and climate change in our present, sobering times."

Chris Smaje, author of *A Small Farm Future*

THE GARDEN

THE GARDEN

Matthew Ingram

Published by Repeater Books
An imprint of Watkins Media Ltd
Unit 11 Shepperton House
89-93 Shepperton Road
London
N1 3DF
United Kingdom
www.repeaterbooks.com
A Repeater Books paperback original 2019
1

Distributed in the United States by Random House, Inc., New York.

ISBN: 9781915672681
Ebook ISBN: 9781915672698

The manufacturer's authorised representative in the EU for product safety is eucomply OÜ - Pärnu mnt 139b-14, 11317 Tallinn, Estonia, hello@eucompliancepartner.com,www.eucompliancepartner.com

Printed and bound by CPI Group (UK) Ltd, Croydon, CR0 4YY

TABLE OF CONTENTS

VISIONARY GROWERS AND FARMERS OF THE COUNTERCULTURE

In nature, four things are required to grow healthy plants: air, sunlight, water, and soil. What's important about soil is that it's decayed organic matter alive with microorganisms. Put this simply, one might infer that it shouldn't be a problem to manage this. Surely human beings could see to it that such a simple scenario, a vitally important one which is the basis of all our food, could be tackled in a straightforward way? Not a bit of it.

In what amounts to a combination of some of our worst traits — ignorance, greed, pride, vanity, laziness, and impatience — we have messed it up. Messed it up along so many vectors that not only our food, but also our environment has suffered to the extent that civilisation is imperilled.

It's one thing to offer practical solutions, but the real problem lies with us as individuals. To change our behaviour, we first need to change who we are. Modern societies have seen precious few large-scale attempts to adapt our ways of living. The ones that are forced upon us by wartime conditions or epidemics tend to result in temporary adjustments that are quickly undone.

In contrast, voluntary shifts — like the one which preoccupies me here, the counterculture — have resulted in more durable transformations. The counterculture offers us many models of what kind of culture we need to survive as a species. The forms of ecological farming which relate to the counterculture — that were either adopted by it or that it popularised or invented — offer us a viable agricultural framework. These farming methods point to a way to strip away the muddled and maladjusted actions that get in the way of that essential simplicity to which we need to return. And as Joni Mitchell put it in her song "Woodstock", "We've got to get ourselves back to the garden".

The cultural ferment of the late 1960s and '70s was the cradle for many forces which led to positive transformations of the dominant model of Western society. We can argue that the well-documented phenomenon of sexual liberation, the increased consumption of whole foods, the personal computer revolution, and the introduction of wellness modalities have all led to a better world. These currents' their presence was faint before the counterculture — the preserve of eccentrics, cranks, and hobbyists at the fringes. The counterculture's dramatic interrogation of society thrust them into the mainstream. As we will see in the pages of this book, the counterculture's approach to growing and farming *also* embraced the peripheral and derided, bringing to these niche concerns a whole generation's youthful energy.

We will see how the hippies were entranced by the nonconformists of the early twentieth century who dared to question the new dogma of scientific agriculture. The Austrian mystic Rudolf Steiner, England's organic movement, and Japan's philosopher-farmer Masanobu Fukuoka were to them adopted parents who showed them a way to manifest their urge to act in accordance with nature, rather than just dream wistfully about it. The example of the pioneers of self-sufficiency and the foundational ecology movement gave a context to the strivings of the back-to-the-land impulse. The post-war world — open for exploration by backpackers and overland travellers — and a West newly permeated by those proselytising Eastern philosophy primed them to examine the holistic practices of Indigenous agriculture. They took influence from, among others, the Mayan peoples, the Native Indian Americans, the Aborigines of Australia, the farmers of West Africa, and perhaps most appropriately given the period's fascination with Hinduism, India.

BIODYNAMICS AND BIOINTENSIVE

You want cosmic? Rudolf Steiner (1861-1925), the founder in the early twentieth century of the esoteric new religion anthroposophy, was cosmic. He writes: "In earthly existence I live within my soul and bear in my Spirit the forces of the starry heavens." Far out, man! The most devoted and orthodox biodynamic growers, those who cleaved to the very word of anthroposophy, thought the hippies unworthy of "serious" consideration (just as they disdained even renegade biodynamic luminaries like Alan Chadwick), but even if the feelings weren't mutual, the hippies loved Steiner. In the back-to-the-land-era scripture *The Whole Earth Catalog* (1971), its oracle, Stewart Brand, describes biodynamics in shorthand: "They plant by the moon." "Some European mystic is behind it." "A lot of weird theories. Nothing proven." "They surely know their plants." Brand becomes slightly more expansive: "I have yet to see a 'respectable' formal evaluation of the 'biodynamic gardening' inspired by Rudolf Steiner. All I know is, the most sensational gardens I've ever seen all claim they owe something to biodynamic notions of soil nutrition, companion plants and the year cycle." Of Steiner's book *Agriculture Course* (1924), Brand says, "With the farthest out illustrations (in color) ever seen in a garden book". Psychedelic!

Throughout the hippie literature, there are trails that lead back to biodynamic concepts. In the countercultural milestone Jeanie Darlington's *Grow Your Own: An Introduction to Organic Gardening* (1970), Darlington comments, "If you like to work in conjunction with the moon, it is best to turn sod and work soil when the moon is in the barren signs, such as Leo, Virgo, Gemini and Aquarius." In the joyous *Country Women* (1976) compendium, Sherry Thomas writes, "Companion planting makes for physically & symbolically beautiful gardens. A little private dabbling in herbal magic, a return to the Medieval woman's lore."

Stewart Brand, somehow uncharacteristically soft, pointed the longhaired hordes to Anthroposophic Press's *Gardening for Health and Nutrition* (1971) by the Reverend John Philbrick and his wife Helen, describing it as "the most practical entry into biodynamic gardening". In their book, whether by accident or design, the Philbricks struck just the right tone for the hippies:

> When I step out into the garden, I go to meditate and commune with what's there. Every morning when the weather is decent, I get up at sunrise, take a mugful of coffee and go into the garden just to look. You see, I am aware that God walked in the Garden in the cool of the day. Time and time again I find Him there. Often he opens my eyes to see things that I wouldn't otherwise see. From the outset I began to recognize that the most important things surrounding me in the garden are the Forces of Life. That life is the key to existence on the planet.

Ministering Episcopal congregations in Massachusetts and Missouri, the Philbricks connected strongly to the Christian aspect of Steiner's thought. They write:

> I feel it is important for every Christian farmer or gardener to have at least a little patch of wheat as well as a grapevine on his place, because in the night in which He was betrayed, our Lord took bread, which is the essence of the wheat, and after supper He took the cup that contained the essence of the grape, and when we have both of these plants together,

> we have the Presence of the Light of the World, the Light which is the Life of Men.

When it came to biodynamic gardening, "it has to do with the inter-relatedness (dynamics) of these life forces (bio)". What they liked best was companion planting:

> Now, if you go to a dog show and buy a highly bred cocker spaniel puppy, I guarantee that you'll spend most of your time at the vets, not because the animal itself is sickly, but because it's so highly bred that if there is any disease near it, it just picks it up. This is what happens in your rose bed. The answer is that we must find a plant that is just as opposite and just as primitive as it can be to plant with roses. In this particular instance, the plant is garlic. Immediately someone wants to know if the rose bush will smell like the garlic and I say, 'No, and you'll never get a garlic that smells like a rose,' because it's not this that transfers. You're not thinking on the right level, so see. You should be thinking about these intangible dynamic forces.

The classic book *The Secret Life of Plants* (1973) by Tompkins and Bird, the archetypal hippie growing volume, only touched lightly on biodynamics. We follow the progress of Glenn Graber of Ohio who, noticing parasitic nematodes appearing on his land, switches from chemical agriculture to organic, driving the pests away, before finally graduating to biodynamic compost. At the end of *The Secret Life of Plants*, which in 1979 received its own spin-off documentary replete with all-synth soundtrack by Stevie Wonder, the authors announced that their next book was going to be called "The Cosmic Life of Plants". This sequel to the blockbuster eventually saw the light in 1989 and was instead called *Secrets of the Soil*. With this volume, a slightly more sensible book than its predecessor, Tompkins and Bird leaned heavily on biodynamics. Chapter after chapter concerns itself with biodynamic agriculture: there are sections on burying the preparations in cow horns; mixing the BD 500 solution; on the Koliskos' research on lunar planting; Pfeiffer's foray into municipal composting; on scaling up the use of preparations to industrial proportions (sprayed from crop-dusting planes); with appendixes dedicated to Steiner's work. More thoroughly assembled and deeply researched than its predecessor, one can't help but wonder whether this meticulousness came at the cost of speed. By 1989, after eight years of the Reagan administration, hippie ardour had largely been extinguished, with countercultural impulses forced to society's peripheries. With its market dried up, the book was less popular. Some people, however, were paying attention. I noticed a copy on no-dig legend Charles Dowding's bookshelf when I visited his Homeacres market Garden in May 2022.

Ehrenfried Pfeiffer

In the Philbricks' book, there is an account of a visit by the great sage Ehrenfried Pfeiffer (1899–1961). Pfeiffer diagnoses a sick peach tree by pointing to a fence post at the other end of the garden, declaring, "See that shelf fungus on the side of the fence post... Either get rid of the fence post, or spray it with crankcase oil and get rid of the fungus..." John Philbrick says, "After that I began to look around to see what other things might be related."

Ehrenfried Pfeiffer is an important bridge between Steiner and younger generations of growers in both Europe (he was the star turn at the UK's first biodynamics conference organised by Lord Northbourne in 1939) and America, where he moved to live. A student of Rudolf Steiner's, he was the motivating force behind Steiner's Agriculture Course lectures. Pfeiffer gently cajoled the magus to turn his attention to the matter of farming at what turned out to be right at the end of Steiner's young life. In 1922 a group of farmers went to ask Steiner's advice about the degeneration they had noticed in seeds and in many cultivated plants.

They gave the example of a crop of lucerne which once would have grown in the same field for thirty-year stretches; now the soil needed to be rested after seven years. Where farmers had used their own seed or barley, oats, wheat, and rye, now they had to switch to new strains every few years to maintain vitality. Animal sterility and diseases were also on the rise. Steiner informed Pfeiffer that the issue lay not with the seed or stock, but with diseased conditions in the environment, "especially in the soil".

In 1923, Steiner gave Pfeiffer instructions on how to make the compost amendments, "preparations", for which biodynamic agriculture is at once famous and, sadly, ridiculed. BD 500 was made by filling the fresh manure of pasture-fed cows into the animal's horns and burying the horns for six months. In the early summer of 1924, Steiner was present when the first batch of horns was dug up. Initially the team, digging where they thought they had buried them, struggled to find them. Steiner was getting impatient and was making his excuses to go when they struck the first horn. He showed them how much of the fermented manure was needed in a pail of water, and using Pfeiffer's walking stick, stirred it in, vigorously emphasising "the forming of a funnel or crater, and the rapid changing of direction to make a whirlpool". Steiner then indicated to them how the resulting preparation was to be sprayed and how much of an area a certain amount would cover. Pfeiffer summarises of the fleeting exchange: "Such was the momentous occasion marking the birth-hour of a world-wide agricultural movement."

Pfeiffer quite rightly took pride in the remarkable clairvoyance of Steiner's intervention: "Facts recognised as early as 1923–24 in bio-dynamic circles — the significance of soil life, the earth as a living organism, the role played by humus, the necessity of maintaining humus under all circumstances, and of building it up where it is lacking — all this has become common knowledge." The Swiss Pfeiffer moved to the USA at the outbreak of the Second World War, where he settled at Three-Fold Farm in Spring Valley, New York. Steiner had asked Pfeiffer to find a reagent which would reveal the "etheric formative forces" in living matter. After months of experiments, using a solution of copper chloride, Pfeiffer developed a "sensitivity crystallization method" which produced a chromatograph unique to each plant. The principle is similar to the classroom experiment of separating individual dyes from ink. Pfeiffer would examine the resulting concentric rings and, as Tompkins and Bird put it in *The Secret Life of Plants*, "disclose new secrets of life". For instance, testing rose hips (a natural source of vitamin C), Pfeiffer concluded that its pattern of vitality revealed in his test was far greater than that of the alternative chemically produced vitamin C, pure ascorbic acid. This concurs with recent trends in nutrition which seek to create supplements in "food" form on the basis that their vitamins are more bioavailable than in lab-concocted chemicals.

Pfeiffer wisely toned down the more obviously superstitious notes of biodynamics, but was not shy of making more cosmic pronouncements. Apparently no fan of dairy products, in his book *The Earth's Face* (1947) he points to cows' sacred status in Ancient India, Athenian civilisation, and as they are represented in both Egyptian and Roman mythology. "As long as cows were sacred no one thought of drinking milk for nourishment. It was a ceremonial drink solely." Taking a very Jungian perspective on the loss of mankind's spiritual dimension, he remarks:

> For milk to become a food, this rich symbolism had to be forgotten. In effect the spiritual world had to be denied. What a mighty fall of humanity took place when the holy emblem of deathlessness, of the passing of the threshold at birth and death, became mere nutriment and even — during the Roman decadence — a beauty ointment to enhance the lustre of the body.

Agreeing with many critics of industrial agriculture and its mechanistic thinking, he writes, "Man must be perceived as both a material and spiritual entity."

Steiner

But what of Steiner himself? Dying aged sixty-four in 1925 (it's conjectured of exhaustion), agriculture and plants might be seen as little more than a side-show to his career. In 2024, biodynamics celebrated its centenary, and as of 2020 its techniques were being used on 251,842 hectares in fifty-five countries, finding notable success in the cultivation of vineyards. Although biodynamics has subsequently become a central plank in his legacy, as we've pointed out, the Agriculture Course lectures happened just before his death in 1924 and weren't translated into English until 1958. They are included in Volume 327, nearly at the end, of the 360 volumes of Steiner's works. Steiner himself was much more preoccupied with meditation; with education and the Waldorf schools; with his ideas for social reform and the concept of the "Threefold Social Order", which captured the public's imagination after the First World War; with architecture; with the performing arts; with his plays; and with the Eurythmy form of dance.

In his *Autobiography*, one of the more easily readable of his many books, Steiner gives us a snapshot of the central idea that motivated him, one which we can see puts him in sympathy with the etheric impulses of the countercultural generation:

> I must acknowledge that my relationship to geometry was the beginning of a view that took shape gradually within me. During childhood it lived in me more or less unconsciously; by my twentieth year it had assumed a definite, fully conscious form. I would have said that the objects and events seen by the senses exist in space, the space outside the human being; but a kind of soul-space exists within as the setting for spiritual beings and events… I differentiated

between things and beings that are visible and things that are invisible.

He shares with the heaven-ascendant counterculture of the late 1960s a love of this spiritual world over and above the material plane: "I must add, however, that I loved living in that world. I would have experienced the sensory world as a surrounding spiritual darkness if it had not received light from that other world."

In Neudörfl in Austria, where Steiner lived as a child, he was surrounded by nature. The young Steiner would harvest blackberries, raspberries, and strawberries in the woods; with the local children, he would pelt nut trees with stones so they might each establish their own store for the winter; he would annually gather grapes from vineyards with the cottagers. He recollects, "My parents had been assigned a small garden near the station. It had fruit trees and a small field for potatoes. My sister, brother and I picked cherries, looked after the garden, prepared potatoes for planting, readied the ground, and then dug the ripe potatoes."

Felix the herb-gatherer

Unbeknownst to his history teacher, instead of paying attention in class, Steiner was secretly struggling through Kant's *Critique of Pure Reason* (1781). This budding philosophical inclination was, unusually, connected to the world of plants through an encounter with "a simple man of the people" he met on the train to Vienna. Felix Kogutzki earned an income by gathering medicinal plants in the countryside and selling them to pharmacies in Vienna. Steiner was able to talk to Kogutzki about the spiritual world as someone of experience in that sphere. "He carried on his back a bundle of healing herbs; in his heart, however, he carried the results of what he had gained from nature's spirit while gathering them." Throughout his life, Steiner was a practical philosopher seeking to illuminate the world itself with spiritual insights made manifest in cultural forms like dance, education, and farming. To this extent, he maintained a distance from the entirely metaphysical world of books. Kogutzki — unlike the teachers or priests he encountered who introduced him to mathematics, literature and philosophy — might be seen to be his first true spiritual teacher, or guru: "From our first meeting I had a deep affinity with him. Gradually it seemed as though I were in the company of a soul from ancient times — one untouched by civilization, science, and modern views — who brought me the natural knowledge of ancient times".

The tremendous importance of Felix Kogutzki to Steiner, who Steiner immortalised as Felix Balde in his play *The Soul's Probation*, allows us to appreciate how the ideas which lead to biodynamics, although seemingly at the periphery of his scholarship, are in fact a neglected core to his thinking, which have only over time acquired a commensurate standing. One of Steiner's disciples, Emil Bock, tracked down Kogutzki's heirs. The story was recounted in *The Search for Felix the Herb-Gatherer* (1958):

> In Vienna, on the following day, the problem was to find Richard Kogutzki, Felix's second youngest son. We finally discovered him in Floridsdorf, an out-of-the-way industrial suburb, to which he had moved just under a year previously. The people of Trumau had always referred to him jokingly as the 'doctor of the left' (der Linken), because he had tried unsuccessfully as a young man to study law — i.e., to become a 'doctor of the right' or 'of law' (der Rechte). We found a pathetic little man of 76, emaciated and bent with worry, but with bright eyes. At first I had to support him with my arm, as he had difficulty in moving about. But it was quite an experience to see how he livened up in the course of conversation, and finally, when I had shown him the passage about his father in Dr. Steiner's *Story of My Life*, he pranced about the room like a small child.

Bock goes on,

> Finally I read to him what Dr. Steiner had written and said about the herb-gatherer. This led to the transformation I have already mentioned. There was no holding him. He kept jumping up and repeating: Isn't what you have just read exactly the same as I was telling you? Only it is all expressed much better. That is the kind of father we had. If only we had seen it as clearly when he was still alive! We loved our father—and how we enjoyed being with him! But it is only now, after all this long time, that at last I understand everything!

Goethe

Besides Kogutzki, Steiner's other "plant" influence was the polymath and author of *Faust* (1808), Johann Wolfgang von Goethe. In one of Steiner's early jobs in 1882, he was invited to edit Goethe's then deprecated works on natural science. Steiner's view, as he processed Goethe's work, was that the then novel mechanistic trend in scientific thinking was inadequate for comprehending Goethe's insights: "His ability to recognize the special spiritual relationship between humankind and the world also enabled him to recognize the true position of science within the larger realm of human achievements." Goethe, he believed, did not fall into science's trap of isolating fragments for scrutiny. Steiner wrote that "to attain ideas that mediate knowledge of the organic, it is first necessary to bring life into the intellectual concepts that are applied to the inorganic. For me, those ideas appeared dead and, consequently, were suitable only for understanding what is dead."

Goethe's idea of the *Urpflanze*, transfixed Steiner. Goethe's observation, which pioneered the principle of homology in 1843 — one which took thirty years before it was accepted by biologists — was that a plant's various organs evolve from the leaf. They progress flexibly from cotyledons (the seed's embryonic leaves), to photosynthetic leaves, to flower petals. The process, as these forms metamorphosise from one to the other, conveys the impression of some vital sentience hovering behind the canvas skein of our normal reality; as Tompkins and Bird put it in *The Secret Life of Plants*, "a supersensible force capable of developing into myriad different forms". In his own introduction to the anthroposophical edition of Goethe's essay "The Metamorphosis of Plants", Steiner writes, "One must keep clearly in mind most of all the fact that here the external manifestation is determined by an inner principle; that in every organ the totality is active", and that "from this he [Goethe] drew the conclusion that the nature of the plant is not to be found in these characteristics, but must be sought at a deeper level... since those characteristics are not constant, what is constant must be sought in something else which lies beneath changeable externalities."

Goethe, who saw the "proliferous" carnation as the most perfect and remarkable manifestation of the phenomenon, is actually very matter of fact and methodical in the essay, not even touching on any philosophical ramifications in the conclusion. Although, if we consider it carefully, even though the supersensible ramifications are apparent, the first impression conveyed is that Steiner is over-egging it with his "spiritual" take.

However, Goethe's original realisation of the principle of homology has about it the whiff of *satori* (the Zen Buddhist concept of a sudden awakening to universal truth). Goethe had gained an insight central to his concept of metamorphosis while walking in the Sicilian gardens at Palermo. He says that "it came to me in a flash that in the organ of the plant which we are accustomed to call the leaf lies the true Proteus who can hide or reveal himself in all vegetal forms. From first to last, the plant is nothing but leaf, which is so inseparable from the future germ that one cannot think of one without the other." With these two — Kogutzki the herb-gatherer and Goethe — in his intellectual background, the brilliance of Steiner's interventions in agriculture become a lot more understandable.

Agriculture Course

Because its ideas are so important, influencing as they do the principles of organic agriculture, it seems justified to try and summarise and recount some of the insights of Steiner's Agricultural Course here. Introducing the talks to the landowners who gathered to hear it at Count Keyserlingk's estate at Koberwitz near Breslau, Steiner says, "The Course itself will show us how intimately the interests of Agriculture are bound up, in all directions, with the widest spheres of life." He explains to the assembled group of landowners his ability to comment on the subject:

> I grew up entirely out of the peasant folk, and in my spirit I have always remained there — I indicated this in my autobiography. Though it was not on a large farming estate such as you have here [Count Keyserlingk's estate], in a smaller domain I myself planted potatoes, and although I did not breed horses, at any rate I helped to breed pigs. And in the farmyard of our immediate neighbourhood, I lent a hand with the cattle. These things were absolutely near my life for a long time; I took part in them most actively. Thus I am at any rate lovingly devoted to farming, for I grew up in the midst of it myself, and [referring to a demonstration of the preparations] there is far more of that in me than the little bit of 'stirring the manure' just now.

Steiner approaches the subject, as he puts it, as though wider cosmic forces are at play within the local sphere:

> Everything that lives in the silicious nature contains forces which come not from the Earth but from the so-called

> distant planets, the planets beyond the Sun — Mars, Jupiter and Saturn... everything that contributes to the sequence of generation after generation in the plants — works through those forces which come down from the Cosmos to the Earth: from Moon, Venus and Mercury via the limestone nature.

The most elegant and compelling analogy Steiner uses to explain this idea, and one which he used often also in different contexts, is that of the compass: "Anyone who thought of the magnet-needle alone — anyone who looked in the magnet-needle itself for the causes of it always turning northward — would be talking nonsense."

On the other hand, modern science, as he sees it, seeks to completely ignore this wider context. This is the impulse he identifies in chemical, industrial agriculture, which, as we can acknowledge in the damage it does in the wider ecological context, is ignorant of anything apart from that which is intensely local to the plant itself, using only the plant's size, not its health, as its metric. Steiner says, "What does science do nowadays? It takes a little plate and lays a preparation on it, carefully separates it off and peers into it, shutting off on every side whatever might be working into it." The role of the preparations is to mend this rupture, as he puts it. The purpose of the most famous preparation, BD 500, is, when sprayed over tilled land, "to unite it with the earthly realm"; this is his prescription "for one who likes to see Nature as a whole and not only as in the Baedeker guide-books".

In the fourth lecture of the Agriculture Course in which Steiner described the creation of BD 500, he also gave details of another preparation, BD 501, this time mixing finely ground silica to a paste, filling a cow-horn with it, burying it in the spring, and digging it up in the autumn. This is diluted in a weaker solution than BD 500 and sprayed externally on plants, as if it were a stimulant. Steiner remarks, "Why should it not be possible to make machines able to extend over whole fields the slight sprinkling that is required." The homeopathic amounts of the active ingredients in the preparations are often mocked by cynics, but "just as 1 g of rich soil has a billion microorganisms, a biodynamic spray will have microscopic amounts of bacteria and fungi," suggests Kai Lange, diploma coordinator of the Biodynamic Agricultural College in the UK. To this extent, just as faecal microbiota transplantation, from a donor with a healthy gut, is used in establishing a healthy gut biome in a sick person — so, potentially, could the preparations be effective in the soil beyond any theoretical, or spiritual benefit.

As Steiner explained it, the use of these preparations is not a substitute for the spreading of cow manure in the fields. Steiner favoured cow manure over any other, and in fact was a little contemptuous of horse shit! "You must remember that cow-horn manuring is not intended as a complete substitute for ordinary manuring. You should go on manuring as before. The new method should be regarded as a kind of extra, largely enhancing the effect of the manuring hitherto applied. The latter should continue as before." The preparations took many forms and came as part of a whole array of interventions: sewing yarrow in the bladder of a stag, hanging it up in the sunshine for maximum exposure to the sun; placing chamomile into bovine intestines, oak bark into a skull, and dandelion into a bovine mesentery (the membrane which surrounds the intestines). Steiner suggested planting by the moon, as "the old Indians used to do until the nineteenth century", burning weed seeds, and creating a "theoretical herbicide" preparation with a dilution of the ash, "just as you create one from the burnt skin of a field mouse caught 'when Venus is in the sign of Scorpio' as a deterrent of mice". The same principle was used to deter nematodes and fungal rust.

The importance of connecting the local with the wider mattered to Steiner not just at the cosmic scale, but also within the environment of the farm itself. Steiner believed that a healthy farm should be conceived as an individual entity, and that whatever was needed for agricultural production should come from within the farm. Only when sick and in need of remedy, for instance, would you bring in manures from outside. He writes:

> Inasmuch as these things are so, your farm is in truth a kind of individuality, and you will gain the insight that you ought to keep your animals as much as possible within this mutual interplay — and your plants too. Thus, in a sense, you mar the working of Nature when you take your manure not from your own farm animals, but get rid of the animals and order the manure-content from Chile. Then you are playing fast and loose with things — neglecting the fact that this is a perfect and self-contained cycle, which ought to be maintained, complete in itself.

Alan Chadwick

Fascinated by the topic, I spent a large amount of time researching Steiner. I visited Rudolf Steiner House near Regent's Park in London twice. I went on a countryside ramble with the amazing herbalist Kirsten Hartvig, who works out of the Rachel Carson Centre at Emerson College in Forest Row. At Forest Row, the spiritual home of Steiner thought in East Sussex, I visited Tablehurst Farm *and* Plaw Hatch Farm. I was treated to a one-on-one tour of the vegetable garden at the Michael Hall Waldorf School by biodynamic grower Laurie Donaldson. In Gloucestershire, I was shown around Ruskin Mill by horticulturalist Jason Warland. I spoke to Rachel Phillips, director of Devon's Apricot Centre. I interviewed Patrick Holden, once a back-to-the-land hippie who studied biodynamic agriculture at Emerson College in 1972 and who is now the patron of the UK Biodynamic Agricultural Association — more on which later in the Sustainability chapter. I read several of Steiner's books (details of which you can find in the Bibliography). In Stroud, I visited what was once the home of

Lili Kolisko, the Steiner disciple who researched the effects of the moon on planting and growing. I also interviewed a very senior English anthroposophist specifically about the counterculture and Steiner on condition of their anonymity.

All of which research gave me the impression of an organisation that, while once cautious of outside influence, is striving to connect to the groundswell of interest in biodynamics. On the subject of this, its patron, Patrick Holden, in an interview with Richard Swann in biodynamics' flagship magazine *Star and Furrow*, takes a faintly critical view of this former insularity. Talking of the Agriculture Course lectures Rudolf Steiner gave, Holden remarks:

> It is an irony that his lectures were given in response to a recognition by farmers... who recognised that they needed to do something [to stem] the loss of vitality of their crops. I think he might have been rather surprised to see how the biodynamic movement has become so separate from mainstream agriculture.

Not surprisingly, therefore, it has been down to maverick outsiders (of which there was no shortage in the countercultural era), to bring biodynamics' insights and charm to wider use. The pre-eminent example is Alan Chadwick (1909–1980), the thespian turned master gardener who in California, late in his fascinating life, pioneered the biointensive form of gardening. This combined the disciplines of biodynamic growing with that of French intensive gardening. Chadwick was described by E.F. Schumacher as "the finest teacher of intensive horticultural, agricultural methods that I think the world possesses today".

In *The Last Whole Earth Catalog* (1972), in the section on "Land Use", there is a captioned photo of a couple of hirsute, blond young men sowing seedlings in a vegetable garden. The caption reads, "Transplanting cabbage seedlings in Chadwick's incredible biodynamic garden at UC Santa Cruz, the main reason a lot of longhairs are attending the school." Chadwick's influence at the university was such that at the height of the counterculture, numerous students, rather than simply "attending the school," were in fact dropping out of their regular courses to go and work with him in the garden. Inevitably, this created friction in the university.

Chadwick was raised a vegetarian and pacifist by his mother, a Theosophist who upon the organisation's schism followed Steiner and his camp into anthroposophy. As a young man, one summer, his mother, Elizabeth, dispatched Alan and his brother Seddon to the Goetheanum, Steiner's Swiss headquarters, where they were schooled on biodynamic horticulture. In an interview in the film *An Introduction to the Biointensive Method*, Chadwick recounts in his theatrical way:

> All of those people that I studied with, and I was very, very much a youth — I mean I was terribly young, I was a child — when I studied with them, they were the great thinkers of the day, the really great thinkers. And they were all — one and all — looked upon as errant cranks, except by the few that were very observant.

At Dornbach, when Chadwick was a teenager, Rudolf Steiner himself had talked to him about the biodynamic preps. He once again met him on one of Steiner's speaking tours in London in the early 1920s. After a full life as a respected stage actor, a naval officer in the war, and a professional grower, Chadwick was charged by his friend Freya von Moltle (who had first connected Chadwick to professor Paul Lee at UC Santa Cruz) to "help offset the dehumanizing forces of the technological age by sharing his love and knowledge of nature with others". Chadwick believed that gardening was the only way to prevent another world war by bringing active peace on Earth by working with healthy, creative, positive life forces. It is meaningful to view Chadwick's garden at UC Santa Cruz as the spiritual centre of what the hippies called Flower Power.

When he arrived in the spring of 1967, his teaching methods were unconventional. To his gardening charges he also gave lessons in mime, mien, and deportment. They were expected to memorise the Friar's speech from *Romeo and Juliet* on the power of medicinal herbs. Chadwick's disciple Wendy Johnson describes (in her book *Gardening at the Dragon's Gate*) the UC Santa Cruz garden in its transformation from a ragged slope:

> Birds never seen before on the campus called and cooed from the thick shrub borders of the garden. Sweeping cascades of Old World and modern roses from 'Sombreuil' to apple-scented eglantines festooned the garden arbors. Vines of the green-fleshed Malta winter melon cascaded across the path twining toward raised hills of 'Rose Fir Apple' fingerling potatoes. A groaning abundance of food spilled forth from this garden, free to all for the taking.

Chadwick was always loyal to the spirit of biodynamic growing. In a video, *The Vision of Biodynamics,* from a lectern which seems in the context more like a pulpit he declaims, "The vision of biodynamics in agriculture and horticulture is the great science, the knowledge, the understanding of the operation of those laws of God." Later he insists, "The whole attitude of biodynamics is in no way negative, it is in no way saying, 'You must not use machinery!' 'You must not use chemicals!'... It is completely disinterested in that... It is completely positive. It is reverence and obedience by the total laws by which everything in this world has ever lived." As conventional as this sounds within the dogma of biodynamics, Chadwick was nagged by dogmatic anthroposophists for not using the preparations, sprays which might be described as the obvious hallmark of the technique. He thought they made people think the gardens' health was attributable to potions. On one occasion, Chadwick avoided a biodynamic delegation which had travelled to his final garden in the Shenandoah Valley in Virginia all the way from Spring Valley in New York. If you can find the wonderful documentary *Garden*

Song (1979) which Bullfrog Films have very generously made freely available for the online resource of the Alan Chadwick Archive, you can see how the biointensive method works. As the voiceover explains, "Closely spaced planting means a green canopy stifles weeds and keeps moisture in the soil. Influenced by Steiner's theories, chemical pesticides and fertilisers are never used."

Sixties social philosopher and professor emeritus Norman O. Brown (Jim Morrison of the Doors' favourite, and whom we met in my previous book, *Retreat*) was resident at UC Santa Cruz when Chadwick was working there. The two collaborated on the film *The Garden* (1971), in which Brown reads selections from his poem "My Georgics", a meditation upon agriculture and spiritual practice, against the background of Chadwick's organic garden, where flowers were one of the principle crops. When Brown's friend the avant-garde composer John Cage visited the campus in 1968, where he was designing a curriculum for the nascent art department, he was encouraged by Brown to introduce himself to Chadwick. The pair shared a fascination with mushrooms, Chadwick being an expert at identifying the poisonous from the edible. In his diary, Cage, who was enchanted, remembers how "when we went mushrooming with his student-helpers, Chadwick, half-naked, leapt and ran like a pony". Of Chadwick's hippie underlings, Cage said, "Students had defected from the university or had come especially from afar to work with him like slaves. They slept unsheltered in the woods. After the morning's hunt with him and them, I thought: These people live; others haven't even been born." Chadwick discussed Steiner's ideas with Cage: "Chadwick described magnetic effect of moon on tides on germination of seeds. 'Moon inclining draws mushrooms out of Earth.' We talked of current disturbance of ecology, agreed man's works no matter how great pygmy compared with those of nature." Cage specified that his mushroom books and pamphlets, of which there were over three hundred, should be left by his estate to Chadwick, a "gardener who knows how to hunt and who is surrounded by youth he's inspired." Sadly, this stipulation was never honoured.

Dr John Jeavons

Chadwick had many followers who were inspired by him. Most well known are the following: Green Gulch Farm's gardener and Buddhist lay-entrusted teacher Wendy Johnson, author of the wonderful *Gardening at the Dragon's Gate* (2008) and a columnist for *Tricycle*, the leading Buddhist journal; Santa Cruz flower-farmer Nancy Lingemann; USC apprentices Beth Benjamin and Jim Nelson, who founded the organic farm Camp Joy; and California winemakers Jim Fetzner and Katrina and Jonathan Frey. But it's likely that Chadwick's most significant disciple is Dr John Jeavons.

Jeavons currently runs the Ecology Action organisation, which has worked for over fifty years to refine their method. He explained to me, "We have over 10 million people using successfully Grow Biointensive closed-loop, sustainable mini farming in 152 countries in the world." Hereafter, for the sake of simplicity, we will refer to Grow Biointensive as biointensive. The reason for this massive global reach — of special significance in developing countries like Kenya, Mexico, Nicaragua, Ecuador, and Peru where Ecology Action has a strong presence — is the global success of Jeavons's book *How to Grow More Vegetables (and Fruits, Nuts, Berries, Grains and Other Crops) Than You Ever Thought Possible On Less Land with Less Water Than You Can Imagine* (1974). For many years, as far as Jeavons is aware, it was the only book available of its kind. *HTG* is now in its ninth edition, and has been translated into nine languages including Spanish (in its sixth edition), Arabic (in its fifth edition), French, German, Hindi, Brazilian Portuguese, and Russian. It has sold 600,000 copies. Eighty-two years old, Jeavons is a busy man, corresponding daily with colleagues in his global charity Ecology Action's network, every year teaching eight-month-long internships, managing their growing list of publications, working in the experimental gardens in Willits, California, as well as being in the last stages of writing another book with, he assures me, an even longer title than *How to Grow More Vegetables*...

He is no stranger to life's travails. Jeavons's father — of whom he has two memories from when he was one and two — was killed in Belgium in the conflict preceding the Battle of the Bulge in the Second World War. Jeavons's widowed mother vowed that the world should be brought to peace. Then, aged five, Jeavons suffered a serious injury. Two years later, finally feeling better, he remembers lying on the floor and speaking to God. In gratitude, he said to the Almighty, "If there's anything you would like me to do, please let me know." Jeavons connects this event to another, twenty-two years later, when he first visited Chadwick's four-acre site at UC Santa Cruz. The minute he saw it, he knew that was his instruction.

After visiting the garden, Jeavons subsequently went to the last three of four lectures, arranged over a month, that Chadwick gave at Villa Montalvo Arts Center in Saratoga, near Chadwick's base in UC Santa Cruz. He then took a six-week teaching course with Chadwick's senior apprentice Steven Kaffka in the Palo Alto Community Garden behind the public library. Kaffka is now a professor emeritus at UC Davis in the department of plant sciences. Jeavons, as I discovered in our three-hour-long interview, is astonishingly focused. As he puts it to me, "You can see that I somewhat rigorously, conceptually, and mathematically study things." A political science graduate at Yale, at the time of his visit to Chadwick's garden he had also worked for the US Agency for International Development. This scientific bent is apparent in the work he's done both as a systems analyst for Stanford University and at the Motorola Aerospace and Electronic Centre in Scottsdale Arizona, where he learnt about sample testing. He believes it's a mathematical and strategic trait he shared with his military father.

Jeavons studied Chadwick's work, work Chadwick himself portrayed as somehow intuitive, and in 1972 turned it into a scientific system. Jeavons wrote the first edition of the *HTG* book in three days straight, and then spent a whole year editing what he had written. Using his connections to Stanford, in the middle of the night they printed five hundred copies on a Xerox machine loaned by the nearby Xerox Corporation facility. Ecology Action had already been written up in an article in Rodale's *Organic Gardening* magazine describing their preliminary research, so Jeavons used the mailing list he'd drawn up from respondents to that to market this homemade first edition. It differs from the latest version: "It's more poetic and has less numbers, but it's the same stuff."

Chadwick was not amused: "Well, he didn't like my quantification; that's an understatement." Someone gave Chadwick a copy at a meeting in San Jose, California. "He looked at it and he took it, and he threw it on the floor as hard as he could. He says, 'Rubbish!'" In time, however, Chadwick actually read the book and loved it. He wrote to Ecology Action, and Jeavons recounts, "He called what we're doing *a masterpiece*. In the classical tradition." In the documentary *Garden Song*, Chadwick talks about Jeavons's book *HTG* and how, with it, Jeavons will bring Chadwick's own ideas to a wider audience. Chadwick says, "And the little man who's got a window box in New York, or the little man who's got twenty feet by twenty feet in a dirty smelly plot where a bus fumes blows over it, is discovering how to grow things and compete." Jeavons referred to this commentary and said to me, "I'm getting goosebumps thinking about it."

The testing ground for *HTG* was a four-acre plot in the middle of a Stanford Industrial Park. Jeavons had convinced the Syntex Corporation, famous for their birth control pill, to let him use the site. He invited Chadwick to inspect the land; his view of it was that "there was nothing worse that you could have gone to literally on this earth. If you went to the middle of the Sahara, it really couldn't have been much worse." Chadwick told Jeavons, "Here is going to be the exemplative, if you can do it here..." Over nine years, Jeavons carefully measured the input and output of the garden and found Chadwick's method produced four to six times the US commercial average yield of grains, fruits, and vegetables using dramatically less water, fertiliser, and energy.

The biointensive method

Biointensive is, as the name implies, a combination of some of the ideas (and crucially the spirit) of Steiner's biodynamic techniques with the ideas of French intensive growing. From biodynamics it takes the ideas of companion planting — planting to divert pests, to encourage pollinators, to enrich the soil, and with intercropping to allow harvesting at different times or for other complimentary reasons. Also, from biodynamics it borrows an interest in lunar planting. A truncated explanation of this is that biodynamics specifies that you should plant root crops on the waning moon and leaf crops on the waxing moon. The idea being that the contraction of the waning moon effects an undertow current beneath the soil, benefiting growth, and the waxing moon draws that current upwards, drawing leaf growth upwards. Jeavons described to me how one year they planted six potato beds: "The three that were planted in the root period did the best. So that was right." However, despite "Planting by the Phases of the Moon" being charted in the edition of *HTG* that I have, Jeavons tells me, "Trying to juggle all that got too complex, even for us. But it worked!" Like Chadwick, he doesn't use the biodynamic preps but has experimented with them and, although he has no idea why, they did increase the yield.

From the techniques of French intensive growing, biointensive took other techniques. French intensive is the style that was developed, beginning in the 1500s, by French master gardeners in the market gardens which ringed Paris. The technique has had its own brush with progressive thinking, as it is celebrated in the anarchist Peter Kropotkin's book *Fields, Factories, and Workshops* (1912). Kropotkin is more famous for writing about the phenomenon of "mutual aid" in evolution, where it is pitted in contrast to the typically savage Darwinian idea expressed in Tennyson's maxim, "Nature, Red in Tooth and Claw". In *Field, Factories, and Workshops*, Kropotkin writes in the context of anti-capitalism extensively about the "striking" French-inspired intensive technique:

> They have created a totally new agriculture. They smile when we boast about the rotation system, having permitted us to take from the field one crop every year, or four crops each three years, because their ambition is to have six and nine crops from the very same plot of land during the twelve months. They do not understand our talk about good and bad soils, because they make the soil themselves, and make it in such quantities as to be compelled yearly to sell some of it: otherwise it would raise up the level of their gardens by half an inch every year... This is where agriculture is going now.

These employed a whole range of ingenious techniques to wring high yields in unpromising situations. Jeavons describes in *HTG* how "during the winter, glass jars were placed over seedlings to give them an early start. The gardeners grew up to nine crops each year and could even grow melon plants during the winter." A crucial innovation of the method is to pack plants very tightly together so that when they are mature their leaves nearly touch one another. Chinese growers of antiquity are described employing the same technique in F.H. King's *Farmers of Forty Centuries* (1911). In biointensive, firstly, seedlings grown from seeds in seed trays they call "flats" are "pricked" out. Ingenious planting then executes the intensely close spacing by transplanting the seedlings into four-to-five-foot-wide raised beds *in triangular formation.*

Normally seedlings are planted squarely in rows — but think what a waste of space there is in the centre of those squares. Jeavons says of the approach, "The close spacing provided a mini-climate and a living mulch that reduced weed growth and helped hold moisture in the soil." French intensive also shares with biodynamics an interest in companion planting, if understood with rigorous practicality.

Double-digging

In French intensive, the soil is improved by deep preparation, which results in the method's characteristic raised beds. This occurs in part as a result of the soil being fluffed up as well as enriched with more compost. The raised bed itself creates a microclimate. This practice, called double-digging, is at the heart of the biointensive technique. Because it's so important, we need to accurately describe it. In the "initial double-dig" method, firstly, half an inch of compost is spread over the bed. Secondly, the first foot of soil is removed by spade. Thirdly, the second foot beneath is loosened by fork. According to the biointensive method, this improves drainage, allows air into the soil, and means roots grow deep and densely. Finally, the first foot of soil, sometimes kept in buckets while the subsoil is being loosened, is replaced back on top. In the "ongoing double-dig" method, the compost is added as a layer on top at the end, not at the start of the process. Biointensive has a tool, a "U-bar", which makes subsequent digging easier. The end result of the fluffing up of the top two feet, is a gently raised bed.

These days, *any* form of digging is greeted with tremendous disapproval. Double-digging is certainly the most extreme example of the procedure, with what Edward Faulkner called "trash farming" — discing-in green manures — somewhere in the middle. However, over the years researching this book, within the biological field alone I have heard delivered with passion, and sometimes venom, just about every argument for and against almost every approach to growing and farming. I've concluded that as long as organic matter is being returned to the soil (and in the case of animal manure, preferably composted, and not in excessive quantities) and chemicals are not used at all (but if so, in the most minimal amounts), then one is hard pushed to criticise. In the entirely wonderful documentary series *In Our Hands* (2021) (on YouTube), Jeavons himself says, "The goal of double-digging is good soil structure, *it's not double-digging*. Once you have it twenty-four inches deep, you don't double-dig anymore."

If double-digging were all that was on offer to growers, all that was endorsed by biointensive, then the potential damage to soil structure it effects might warrant conversation. But Jeavons sees the technique taking its place among a wide range of others: "Sustainable approaches in the future will probably be a synthesis, a sustainable collage of Grow Biointensive methods, agroforestry, no-till Fukuoka food-raising, traditional Asian blue-green algal wet rice farming, natural rainfall 'arid' farming, and Indigenous farming." Jeavons is a vocal fan of the Japanese "farming philosopher" Fukuoka: "I love the guy... a really special dude". Fukuoka's technique, which we examine in the "Natural Farming" chapter, is the only one besides his own that Jeavons endorses. However, with a hint of mischief, he says that Fukuoka's apprentices who went on to study with him revealed that they "spent 100% of their time weeding", something which, as close-planting suppresses weeds, apparently doesn't trouble biointensive so much.

Biointensive composting

Hand-in-glove with this deep soil preparation is biointensive's own specific techniques of composting. The process of rebuilding the world's topsoil, which we are merrily destroying and washing into the ocean, is a daunting one. By Jeavons's reckoning, it's estimated that in California it can take as much as twelve thousand years to build up six inches of topsoil, which is the amount you need to grow food. However, at the Syntex site, Jeavons's team was able to create an inch of topsoil in nine and a half years.

Jeavons is captivated by compost. They've been researching it in great detail for twenty-three years, and in his view, most of us are doing it wrongly. Compost, a substance made *only* by people, is the result of an aerobic process (one occurring in the presence of oxygen). The biological action takes place on a combination of nitrogenous or "brown" material like the stalks of grain, woodchip, or paper, and carboniferous "green" material like grass, vegetables, or (confusingly brown) manure. A standard mixture of the two substances is in the ratio 30 nitrogen to 1 carbon — but in Jeavons's experiments, a 60 to 1 ratio might more easily produce compost.

Jeavons, like Fukuoka, who he snitches on for sometimes using chicken shit, is against the use of animal manures: "They're full of salts." After a number of years, he claims that soil is ruined by toxic deposits of Potassium. If they are vegans however, it is purely at the behest of sustainability, because livestock *can* fit into the biointensive system. However, according to his calculations, growing animals to eat takes a much larger area than growing a vegan diet.

Where animal waste is not ok in biointensive compost, human waste may soon be. Rudolf Steiner would not approve. Jeavons laughs that "he'd go shrieking off into the forest and tell you you're going to die". In *Agriculture Course*, Steiner says, "Human faeces should be used as little as possible. It has very little effect as manure, and it is far more harmful than any kind of manure could possibly be." Jeavons tells me a joke: "Why do people use chemical and organic fertilizers? Because they don't have their shit together." Through Ecology Action as the affiliated non-profit, they are running a trial in Kenya at the moment, approved by the Kenyan Ministry of Agriculture and the Ministry of Health. "It started in 2023. It's going to complete in 2026. And it's showing how you can recycle all human waste. Properly, safely, and legally. Now into its sixteenth month, and so far, it's looking very promising. But we're not talking about it until the four years are up." We should know for sure by February 2027. Ecology Action has already published a book on the subject, *Future Fertility: Transforming Human Waste into Human Wealth* (1995) by John Beeby. We chatted about Joseph Jenkins and Jenkins's famous *The Humanure Handbook* (1996). There's the inevitable slight difference in opinion, but Jeavons rates Jenkins and admires his work. Jenkins has visited Jeavons, and they had tea together.

Ecology Action are "on" everything it seems, Jeavons having even prepared an extensive water "rap" for me which went deep into the data on biointensive's incredible water efficiency. This is a result of the combination of the protective canopy closely spaced planting, and the water-absorbing "sponge-like" efficiency of healthy soil rich in humus, the decomposed organic matter.

Biointensive in the developing world

It is double-digging that has caused biointensive to be such a massive hit in the developing world. Jeavons points out that a lot of the world's soils, where conditions aren't as clement as in North America and Europe, are compacted. As an example, in the In Our Hands films, we see in Mexico the destitute "hard pan" remains of a chinampa, once-fertile land originally reclaimed from the edge of shallow lakes by the Aztecs. You just try and grow anything on what is the equivalent of concrete! The soil structure needs to be rebuilt from scratch, it's no good throwing compost on top of it and vowing not to till. Plant roots would never penetrate downwards through it. Double-digging also apparently plays a role in leaching salts from damaged soils — another problem in the developing world.

The challenge of how the developing world was going to feed itself was an especially pressing one at the end of the

1960s. Jeavons, like Frances Moore Lappé, author of the counterculture-era classic *Diet for a Small Planet* (1971), was aware of former Stanford University professor Paul Ehrlich's book *The Population Bomb* (1968). This sketched out the imminent future in apocalyptic term;, early editions began, "The battle to feed all of humanity is over. In the 1970s hundreds of millions of people will starve to death in spite of any crash programs embarked upon now." Jeavons's background was, as we've seen, at the US Agency for International development, so therefore he was primed to make the connection between global food productivity and the techniques Chadwick used. He's still as worried today, writing in the latest edition of *HTG*, "At the rate the world has been becoming desert since 1977, the planet may be predominantly desert in just 70 years." When we spoke, Jeavons was troubled by ominous premonitions.

As early as the *Garden Song* film, biointensive was described as being suitable for third-world application because: "it's labor intensive, low tech, and uses minimal amounts of water and energy." Its greatest appeal is its efficient use of land. In comparison to the US, where it was estimated that four people could be fed per acre, the biointensive method feeds fifteen people per acre." Talking in *Mother Earth News* in May 1976 in an article titled "Biodynamic Farming Methods Lead to Bigger Harvests", the young Jeavons explains:

> Our findings thus far indicate that the method may soon make it possible to grow an entirely balanced human diet on 1/4 to 1/20 of the area presently required by conventional means... and that such yields can be accomplished using as little as 1/2 to 1/16 the nitrogen fertilizer, 1/2 to 1/16 the water, and 1/100 the energy expended today by mechanized agriculture.

This is "grassroots" global intervention. It's not directed from above, but laterally. Watching the In Our Hands films, we find that the Ecology Action teachers we meet in Kenya, Mexico,

Nicaragua, Ecuador, and Peru are local people. And it amazed me to find out that the day we spoke, Jeavons had been talking to a team from Latin America who were visiting the G-Biack community organisation in Kenya to help with the teaching *there*. He's still aware, though, of how his work can resonate with Indigenous peoples. Although he didn't teach at all for the first twenty-one years, wanting to be 100% confident of his offering, he remembers the earliest talks he gave in Vancouver, Canada. "There's this group of people, but one third of the audience was Native Canadians. Canadian Indians. They heard me pitch sustainability and they were just sitting there grinning [he gestures] from here to here." It's fitting that Jeavons has a Doctorate, an honorary PhD in Agroecology, not from his alma mater, Yale, but from the Universidad Nacional Agraria (UNA) of Nicaragua.

The activist Vandana Shiva, for whom the relationship of the developed world to the developing is a key topic, describes the effect upon the Punjab of the chemical agriculture of the Green Revolution in her book *The Violence of the Green Revolution* (1989):

> Two decades of rapid transformation of the economy, society and culture of Punjab had generated an ethical and moral crisis. The overriding culture of cash and profitability disrupted old social ties and fractured the moral norms that had governed society. Circulation of new cash in a society whose old forms of life had been dislocated led to an epidemic of social diseases like alcoholism, smoking, drug-addiction, the spread of pornographic films and literature, and violence against women...

With regard to the legacy of sowing peace that Jeavons inherited from Alan Chadwick, time and again, with their global horticultural projects, he and his partners in Ecology Action have witnessed how the adoption of their biointensive growing methods have soothed local hostilities. Kenya's

Samuel Nderitu, working in Sierra Leone, one of Africa's most impoverished countries, found over three consecutive charitable procurement contracts that discord between men and women, Christians and Muslims, was greatly diminished in the community. Likewise, Mexican Juan Manuel, working with small communities in his own country, found that over time, gender relations were markedly more harmonious after adoption of the biointensive method.

And the counterculture?

Yes, I got more useful information than I could have dreamed of in our interview. But, no, Jeavons doesn't do answers. I asked him only seven questions in the three hours we spoke. One of his favourite replies, which he trotted out with great mirth, was "Yes. No. And maybe." I really wanted to know whether he considered himself radicalised by then current events like the rest of his generation. As that question also disappeared in the rear-view mirror, I wondered to myself whether the Beach Boy Brian Wilson considers *himself* a product of his era? And my own answer to that was "No he probably doesn't." Wilson might even be happiest talking technically, but about microphones, harmonies, and orchestration; like Jeavons is about growing.

But equally, Jeavons's frame of reference in this field is entirely consistent with his generation's. He talked to me of Alan Chadwick, Frances Moore Lappé, DDT (Rachel Carson), Richard St. Barbe Baker, Masanobu Fukuoka, and Larry Korn; of Paul Hawken (who marketed the tools Jeavons pioneered with the Smith & Hawken tool company), of New Alchemy, of Vandana Shiva, and Wendell Berry — all people you will meet later in the pages of this book.

Still, I did get what seemed might be one *answer.* I asked Jeavons why, of all people, he became so involved in this question of global sustainability, and became so effective within it? It turns out to have more to do with insatiable curiosity than altruism: "Because I wanted *to know*. It's just like when I wanted to find out about the three types of compost: 30 to 1, 45 to 1, and 60 to 1." And with that he's off again; recommending woolly pod vetch for its ability to fix three times the amount of nitrogen as other legumes; discussing the writing of William Albert Albrecht; informing me how sorghum does well with wet and dry feet because of its incredible root system; explaining how French breakfast radishes grown for four months are the best carbon-producing crop; revealing how hot compost takes as long to cure as cold; confiding that tree crops won't in fact feed the world; and quoting Gandhi.

ORGANIC

Time and again through my research, I encountered excellent summaries of the history of the organic movement written by Tompkins and Bird, Michael Pollan, Charles C. Mann, Craig Sams, and Philip Conford. I myself took the trouble to read many of the foundational texts. F.H. King's pioneering *Farmers of Forty Centuries* (1911) is a Wisconsin University agricultural scientist's travelogue through the scenery of Chinese, Korean, and Japanese agriculture early in the twentieth century. King witnessed the thriftiness and, as he puts it, "the almost religious fidelity with which they have returned to their fields every form of waste". G.T. Wrench's *The Wheel of Health* (1938) follows up the observations of nutritionist Sir Robert McCarrison of the diet, health, and cultivation techniques of the Hunza people of what is today Northern Pakistan. Lord Northbourne's *Look to the Land* (1940) is a high-minded and philosophising text most famous for its coinage of the term "organic": "The farm must be organic in more senses than one." Both Sir Albert Howard's *An Agricultural Testament* (1940) and his *The Soil and Health* (1947), we will return to shortly. Some of the later texts, Soil Association founder Lady Eve Balfour's highly technical and perhaps surprisingly popular *The Living Soil* (1943) and the American organic authority J.I. Rodale's recapitulation of the organic idea for the US audience, *Pay Dirt* (1945), are themselves summaries of the work of King, McCarrison, Wrench, Northbourne, and Howard. "Organic" as a phenomenon both in its own time and years later when the counterculture discovered these texts, owes everything to books.

The argument that is at the heart of this literature is thus: healthy soil produces healthy crops, which create healthy animals and people. The health of the soil, a living organism, is established principally through what was called by Sir Albert Howard "the Law of Return" — the return to soil of organic matter. Throughout the book you are reading, we will meet individuals (whether they represent themselves as organic or not) who make the case for very different methods of managing soil. Usually, these manifold differences of opinion are tempered with a respect for other perspectives, but sometimes they aren't. However, all are united around the Law of Return — it is the unifying principle for all agriculture which prioritises the vitality and preservation of soil.

The early organic movement has in recent years been incorrectly characterised as somehow being Nazi. Philip Conford, in openly discussing the presence of fascists and Nazi sympathisers in the British organic movement in his classic book *The Origins of the Organic Movement* (2001), led a few people to leap to the conclusion that in its early years organic represented a pseudo-Nazi "blood and soil" ideology peopled entirely with eugenicists and racists. In fact, Conford lays out a rich landscape of different groups and individuals from a spectrum of disparate political and social backgrounds of which the far right were but a fraction: guild socialists, distributists, anarchists, Theosophists, anthroposophists, Christians, nutritionists, environmentalists, and gardeners.

Organic and chemicals

The real ideology of the organic movement radiates outward from this principle of "the living soil". Over the years, however, this has consistently been misconstrued and misrepresented as a simplistic opposition to chemicals. If you ask most people what characterises organic food, they will tell you that it has been grown without chemicals. It hasn't helped the clarity of the organic movement's message that organic fertilisers, fungicides, herbicides, and pesticides have become increasingly important – and have been sanctioned with organic certification. In the strictest theoretical terms these outside "inputs" are not necessary if the soil, and the ecology around it, is healthy. Notwithstanding all this, certainly in historical terms, the animus towards chemicals can't be underestimated. When Sir Albert Howard railed against their use, there would not have existed the full range of inputs that modern organic growers have available to them. At that time, there would have only existed the historic methods of growing sometimes referred to as "organic by default". The change happened with the escalation in the use of guano, seagull shit from small islands off the desert coast of Peru, which exploded in popularity in Europe after 1840. Hardcore organic growers like Eliot Coleman assert that, even before industrial nitrate and ammonia fertilisers took off, this was the birth of the chemical impulse in agriculture.

The fertiliser industry, which picked up the slack of the guano craze, got its scientific approval from the work of pioneering German organic chemist Justus von Liebig. Liebig dismissed ideas of a vital force's role in plant growth. Plants, he argued, sourced carbon and hydrogen from the air and water, and he identified nitrogen (N), phosphorous (P), and potassium (K) as the surplus required minerals. This is known as the NPK hypothesis and held that inorganic sources could provide minerals just as effectively as organic. Liebig believed that plants were able to get their own nitrogen well enough, which in fact applies only to legumes, and therefore produced a fertiliser of his own which didn't work. Thanks to their foreign influence and empire, the British had access to large deposits of sodium nitrate in Chile and India, and had no need to resort to chemistry to produce it. Post-war, the Haber-Bosch process was turned to the task of producing ammonia for fertilisers.

NPK fertilisers are effective at making plants grow big. However, their use comes with a whole range of problems. Using them causes the biology, which is naturally implicated in plant growth, to die off. They contribute nothing to soil structure, and the outcome is soil that can't support beneficial insects or earthworms.. It can't function as a sponge to absorb rainfall and lock in valuable moisture. Plants grown in it are susceptible to illness and attack by pests, nature's censors, and require fungicides and pesticides. These plants don't have the same sophisticated profile of nutrients and micronutrients that, grown in tandem with soil biology, organically grown plants do. Therefore, they are less nutritious and tasty, and the associated pesticides used in their production are harmful when ingested. Dead soil compacts or is blown and washed away, and surplus fertiliser finds its way, in the process of eutrophication, into ponds, lakes, and the ocean. This supercharges algae and bacterial growth, and the demand for oxygen kills off marine life. NPK is a hazard for human health and, being both made of and produced using fossil fuels, is a significant driver of greenhouse gas emissions.

Since the 1920s, the critics of industrial agriculture have fought a losing battle with its wealthy and powerful institutional advocates. Only now, with the evidence of the damage it has caused becoming horribly apparent, and with modern science finally reaching a degree of sophistication such that the arguments in favour of abstaining from it are understood in the context of biochemistry, has there arisen something of a shift in consciousness. In the meantime, mankind has backed itself into a corner. The growing demand for meat, inefficient as a source of protein in terms of its land use, further compacts the problem. Population levels are such that the volume of food which industrial agriculture can produce, even at these steep environmental costs, appears on the face of it to be an attractive option. Its very low manual labour requirements work hand in glove with the convenience that chemical agriculture allows. Still, industrial agriculture's antagonists argue that with careful management they are capable of equalling or even bettering this productivity.

Biodynamic pioneer Ehrenfried Pfeiffer pointed out in his preface to Steiner's *Agricultural Course* that Justus Von Liebig wasn't the cynic he was supposed to be, quoting the following passage: "Inorganic forces breed only inorganic substances. Through a higher force at work in living bodies, of which organic forces are merely the servants, substances come into being which are endowed with vital qualities and totally different from the crystal." In his wonderful *The Little Book of Food* (2003), former Soil Association chairman and hippie Craig Sams quotes the penitent Von Liebig, aged sixty-five, when he was disillusioned with his attempts to help farming:

> I have sinned against the creator and, justly, I have been punished. I wanted to improve His work because, in my blindness, I believed that a link in the astonishing chain of laws that govern and constantly renew life on the surface of the Earth had been forgotten. It seemed to me that weak and insignificant man had to redress this oversight.

Organic and spirituality

A vital part of the original organic message — which has at once been a sustenance and guiding principle for the movement and something which it has been chastised for — is spirituality. This is most famously summarised in the classic put-down that it's all about "muck and mystery". This hinges on the assumption that organic was not sufficiently scientific. Ironically, historians of the organic movement ascribe this phrase to Sir Albert Howard, who used it as a put-down of biodynamic techniques. Lady Eve Balfour was particularly a target of this, as much as she seemed oblivious to the insult. Balfour had decidedly spiritual leanings, believing as she did in the principle of communication with spirits of the deceased. In *The Living Soil* she writes:

> The chief need in the world to-day, far transcending all others, is the need for a spiritual and moral revival involving the adoption of a different standard of values. If the farming profession were to be reorganized so as to fulfil its true function of serving the community, then the land could play an important part in this revival.

Elsewhere Balfour states, "Our world must be conceived as a kingdom of life, wherein the performance of vegetation is recognized and respected."

What is popularly understood as spirituality has always been used as a stick with which to beat organic agriculture. The historian Conford unearthed as series of adverts taken out by ICI in 1945:

> At the top of each would be a mythological symbol: the Egyptian key of abundance, the pine cone, the bull, the rain-god or the sun. Then the ignorance of the past would be contrasted with the enlightenment of the present: 'the pine was "thought to be the home of the tree spirit"; early man "did not know" that human life depended on the soil's fertility...' Each advertisement concluded with the proud boast that myth and superstition had now been vanquished by science: 'To-day science holds the key to the mysteries of growth'; 'Instead of magic there is science.' In each case, the concluding sentence was 'To-day the symbol of fertility is ICI.'

Another important early organic spiritualist was the landowner and thinker Lord Northbourne. Northbourne wrote, "The spiritual value of contact with reality, of feeling oneself part of nature, like all the most valuable things, is not statistically measurable, but is no less real for that." Sir Albert Howard took a more measured view, not believing in the potions of Steiner's biodynamics and calling their whole approach, "organic-plus" — with the suggestion that the "plus" was an unnecessary addition.

Sir Albert Howard

Sir Albert Howard's legacy is slightly eclipsed by that of the magnificent Lady Eve Balfour. She founded the United Kingdom's marvellous Soil Association and so, to some extent, has therefore been immortalised. Howard was not a founder member of the Soil Association because he disapproved of test farms, and specifically of Balfour's Haughley Experiment, which was arranged on two adjoining farms in Suffolk, England. Because of Howard's time in India and connections there, the technical originality of his Indore composting method, his importance to J.I. Rodale's work in America, his exhumation by Wendell Berry in the pages of *The Last Whole Earth Catalog* (with F.H. King and no one else), and Vandana Shiva's more recent celebration of him, we are going to explore Howard further here.

Howard, a Shropshire farmer, was an implacable foe of what he called the "NPK mentality" of chemical farming. A first-class graduate of the Royal College of Science and a foundation scholar of biological sciences at Cambridge, Howard precisely knew the world of the laboratory, which he unremittingly criticised as having no grasp of the practicalities of farming. His attitude upon visiting the scientific Broadbalk wheat trials at Rothamsted gives us a snapshot of his attitude towards them: "I can truthfully say that never in my long experience have I seen arable land in such a hopeless and filthy condition."

Describing criticism of his ideas by the chemical lobby, Howard writes, "I had no difficulty in pulverising the objections these specialists advanced to my thesis that insects and fungi are not the real cause of disease and that pests must be carefully treasured, because they are Nature's censors and our real professors of agriculture." At Cambridge, at the School of Agriculture, when faced with arguments put forward by the lecturers, he remarks, "I felt I was dealing with beginners and that some of the arguments put forward could almost be described as the impertinences of ignorance." Howard proceeded to thoroughly embarrass them in front of their delighted students.

Howard's first wife, Gabrielle Matthaei, was an accomplished botanist in her own right, being the first to discover the role of temperature in photosynthesis. She abandoned what was to be a glittering career to marry him and support him in his work. As her sister Louise — who was to marry Howard after Gabrielle's early death aged fifty-three — comments of her sibling, she was the "inspirer of a pioneer in science, one on a level with himself, as Sir Albert never ceased to emphasize". Louise Howard herself made in a letter to Howard what she thought was an influential observation on his work, encouraging him to think holistically of the plant "as a live thing, knowing no divisions of science".

The Indore method

In 1905, after a spell lecturing in agricultural science in the West Indies and Kent, Howard moved to India, where he remained for nearly thirty years. His first post there was as imperial economic botanist to the Government of India, but it is his subsequent work at Indore, in the state of Madhya Pradesh, that was to make his reputation. Running a government research farm, Howard was full of admiration for his colleagues the Indian farmers:

> As my understanding of Indian agriculture progressed and as my practice improved, a marked diminution of disease in my crops occurred. At the end of five years' tuition under my new professors — the peasants and the pests — the attacks of insects and fungi on all crops where root systems suited the local soil conditions became negligible.

When it came to the lackadaisical techniques of the modern form of farming, the Indians had it licked:

> When we compare these results [from chemical agriculture] on nitrate accumulation with what the Indian cultivator is

> doing, we are lost in admiration of the way he sets about his task. With no help from science, and by observation alone, he has in the course of ages adjusted his methods of agriculture to the conservation of soil fertility in a most remarkable manner... He does not over-cultivate or cultivate at the wrong time. Nothing is done to over-oxidise his precious floating nitrogen or to destroy his capital of humus. He probably does more with a little nitrogen than any farmer in the world outside China. For countless ages he has been able to maintain the present standard of fertility.

Between the years 1924 and 1931, and informed by the influence of these teachers, Howard devised the Indore method of composting. Although composting as a process can be dated back to the early Roman Empire — Howard's Indore method, even if not followed with the rigor he specified, served as an organisational principle for the organic movement as it spread from Europe to North America. Although Rudolf Steiner advocated it, there are no descriptions of composting in *Agriculture Course*, only the injunction to use manure directly on the fields. Howard had remarkable success in convincing large farms, plantations, and estates around the world to adopt his method.

The clearest and simplest description of the Indore method comes in Howard's wonderful book *The Soil and Health*. He writes:

> For those not familiar with these accounts it may be briefly stated that the process amounts to the collection and admixture of vegetable and animal wastes off the area farmed into heaps or pits, kept at a degree of moisture resembling that of a squeezed-out sponge, turned, and emerging finally at the end of a period of three months as a rich crumbling compost, containing a wealth of plant nutrients and organisms essential for growth.

It might not be entirely obvious what the benefits are of taking organic matter to one side, away from the fields, and processing it on its own before then returning it. Indeed, the Japanese philosopher-farmer Masanobu Fukuoka ridiculed this carting around of material, opting instead to leave organic matter decomposing on the ground where it lay, and by that simpler method replenishing the soil's humus content. Fukuoka thought composting was a waste of time. However, to the contrary, Howard explains that the principle value of compost is that the process of its manufacture happens separately from cultivation and therefore time is *gained*: "Everything being ready and the humus being regularly renewed at frequent intervals [from the compost heap], the soil is able to feed an uninterrupted succession of plants". This ability to constantly renew the beds, and therefore maximise production, is exactly what benefits the French intensive method we have studied. Legendary organic gardener Leonard Wickenden, accorded the greatest respect owing to his background as a professional chemist, explains in his wonderful *Gardening with Nature* (1954) another benefit of composting separately. Wickenden argues that organic matter decaying in situ for a time leaches nitrogen in the process of its breakdown before the microbes involved in that process themselves die and become an available source; "But for a time, any crop surrounded by fresh organic matter will almost certainly suffer."

Refreshingly, in a field where everyone is clamouring that their method is more sustainable than the next man's, Howard never claimed that agriculture was not an interference in the natural order. However, the interruptions and intrusions need to be balanced with "definite duties to the land which are best summed up in the law of return". And Howard must have picked up more than just soil science from his gracious hosts; he understood the composting process itself within an entirely unsuperstitious cosmic framework: "An eastern religion calls this cycle the Wheel of Life and no better name could be given to it. The revolutions of this Wheel never falter and are perfect. Death supersedes life and life rises again from what is dead and decayed."

India itself was delighted with the compliments Howard lavished upon it. Vandana Shiva — critic of the folly of the Green Revolution, seed activist, and firebrand ecologist — writes of him, "Howard believed that the cultivators of the East had a lot to teach the Western experts about disease and pest control and to get Western reductionism out of the vicious and violent cycle of 'discovering more and more new pests and devising more and more poison sprays to destroy them.'" She describes when Howard came to Pusa in 1905, where there were no pests and therefore no insecticides, and applauds his conclusion: "I decided that I could not do better than watch the operations of these peasants and acquire their traditional knowledge as rapidly as possible." After five years of education, he learnt how it was done. Shiva writes, "Howard could teach the world sustainable farming because he had the humility to learn it first from practicing peasants and Nature herself."

Howard on chemical agriculture

Howard is often described as "thundering", and there are no more stirring condemnations of the foolishness of chemical agriculture than the ones he penned. In *An Agricultural Testament* he writes, "The slow poisoning of the life of the soil by artificial manures is one of the greatest calamities which has befallen agriculture and mankind." And why would anyone want to eat these vegetables? Howard can spot them a mile away: "It is an easy matter to distinguish vegetables raised on NPK. They are tough, leathery, and fibrous."

Because the methods of chemical agriculture mistakenly placed volume of productivity above anything else, Howard clarifies:

> Many of the things that matter on the land, such as soil fertility, tilth, soil management, the quality of produce, the bloom and health of animals, the general management of livestock, the working relations between master and man, the esprit de corps of the farm as a whole, cannot be weighed or measured.

Rather he talks about the sacred duty of handing fertile soil to the next generation.

> The earth's green carpet is the sole source of the food consumed by livestock and mankind... The consequence of abusing one of our greatest possessions is disease. This is the punishment meted out by Mother Earth for adopting methods of agriculture which are not in accordance with Nature's law of return. We can begin to reverse this adverse verdict and transform disease into health by the proper use of the green carpet — by the faithful return to the soil of all available vegetable, animal, and human wastes.

As the writer Wendell Berry points out in a classic countercultural-era review of *An Agricultural Testament* printed in *The Last Whole Earth Catalog*, "The scientific respectability of organic methods has been obscured for us both by those who have insisted upon making a cult of the obvious and by the affluence and glamor of the technological agriculture — the agriculture of chemicals and corporations."

J.I. Rodale

Writing in hippie bible *The Last Whole Earth Catalog*, Gurney Norman comments of the North American organisation Rodale's *Organic Gardening Magazine*:

> More central to organic gardening as a movement is a monthly magazine published by the same Rodale's... called

> *Organic Gardening and Farming*. It has occurred to me that if I were a dictator determined to control the national press, *Organic Gardening* would be the first publication I'd squash, because it is the most subversive. The whole organic movement is exquisitely subversive. I believe that organic gardeners are in the forefront of a serious effort to save the world by changing man's orientation to it, to move away from the collective, centrist, super-industrial state, toward a simpler, realer, one-to-one relationship with the earth itself.

The approval was total. Not one but four Rodale books — *The Basic Book of Organic Gardening, How to Grow Vegetables and Fruits by the Organic Method, The Encyclopedia of Organic Gardening,* and *The Organic Way to Plant Protection*, as well as the magazine *Organic Gardening and Farming* — were listed in *The Whole Earth Catalog*. In particular, their encyclopedia was one of the iconic books of the back-to-the-land movement. Wherever I turned in my research within the United States, Rodale's was at the root.

J.I. Rodale was born in Manhattan in 1898 and was the son of an Orthodox Jewish grocer who had immigrated from Poland. As a young man he was preoccupied with his health, suffering heart murmurs, and was rejected by the military on account of his poor eyesight. Rodale's travails are set against the background of his working in the heavily polluted city of Pittsburgh. Upon investigating methods to improve his health, he discovered the writing of Sir Albert Howard. According to the decentralist Mildred Loomis, this came courtesy of their movement via the library of fellow decentralist Ralph Borsodi:

> J.I. Rodale visited Borsodi at the Suffern, New York, School of Living. Borsodi showed Rodale his library of which Rodale commented, 'For me, your library is a gold mine! Scores of books which I need. That one book by Dr. G.T. Wrench,

> [*The*] *Wheel of Health*, fantastic! All about the remarkable people in the Himalayas, the Hunza! Sturdy at more than a hundred years of age, mostly because of their natural food grown in such good soil.'

At lunch, Rodale savoured Borsodi's beans, carrots, apples, and cream from their cow, Nellie, with their own honey added. Afterwards, he returned to the library to take notes and marvel at Eve Balfour's *The Living Soil*, Sir Albert Howard's *An Agricultural Testament*, and F.H. King's *Farmers of Forty Centuries*. The work of Howard in particular was electrifying. Of it, Rodale said, "The impact on me was terrific! I decided we must get a farm at once and raise as much of our family's food by organic methods as soon as possible." Rodale's own American conveyance of the ideas of the English organic pioneers, *Pay Dirt* (1945), was anointed with an introduction penned by Howard himself.

Originally, Rodale's audience was small but devoted, but then, at the turn of the decade, the counterculture caught up with them. By 1971, *Organic Gardening and Farming* was selling 720,000 copies a month. In a cover story that year, the *New York Times Magazine* described J.I. Rodale as "the Guru of the Organic Food Cult." The magazine profiled the Rodale audience in a smarty-pants cynical tone typical for the day:

> Loosely clustered under the movement's antichemical umbrella is a wide variety of food cultists, from old-line vegetarians to youthful Orient-oriented 'macrobiotic' dieters with their emphasis on whole grains, especially rice, plus reactionaries yearning to turn back all clocks, dropouts in search of simpler, more natural life styles, ecologists who are worried about the long range environmental effects of some chemicals, Dr. Strangelove paranoids who read poison plots on the ingredient labels of pancake mixes and, increasingly, rather ordinary folk to whom pronouncements about the perils of cyclamates, DDT, mercury, monosodium

glutamate, phosphates, etc., have stirred a wariness about all man-made chemicals, particularly those that get in their food, or that they think do.

At the height of his fame, a day after this article was published, Rodale died of a heart attack during the recording of a television show on the couch of talk show host Dick Cavett.

Jeanie Darlington

In the US towards the end of the 1960s, the countercultural logic of the times pointed unwaveringly towards organic growing. At this point in its history, before the total alienation which today urban people have from rural life, and before organic's current interpretation as "expensive food for rich people", organic growing was understood as a partisan means to fight the industrial complex. Early stirrings are evident in a 1967 issue of the *San Francisco Oracle*: the cover is resplendent with a photographic collage tableau depicting Timothy Leary, Allen Ginsberg, Alan Watts, and Gary Snyder as Buddhas. Inside, Elsa Gidlow writes an article, "Notes on Organic Gardening", which is characterised by its practical information. However, Gidlow still manages to strike an effectively cosmic tone: "We are returned to mystery and the power of cooperating with life — rather than, as so often now, working against it." She concludes, "Who feels called to the war against processed nonfood for processed nonpeople, and to the creative work of production for health and sanity without which there is no dance or song, music or joy?"

One who heeded this call was the author Jeanie Darlington, who wrote *Grow Your Own*, which was published in 1970. It might be the earliest truly countercultural intervention on the subject. The cover — a photo of Jeannie cradling a newborn baby, she and her partner decked in floral hippie clothes, their long hair-flowing against a wall of wildly growing Ivy — is worth a thousand words. Gurney Norman gave it a rave review in *The Whole Earth Catalog*:

> There's a new book out now called *Grow Your Own*, by Jeanie Darlington, that to my mind comes closer to being the first word... *Grow Your Own* is for gardeners who are absolutely just beginning, and not only beginning, but beginning in a city at that, right up there on the very front lines where conditions come closest to impossible... by a young Berkeley, California woman who did the whole organic trip in a plot ten feet by ten feet outside her home, paid close attention to what was going on, did careful homework, and turned it all into a lovely little paperback book. It's an extremely personal book, sort of like a letter to close friends, charming and informational... She's a freak, but she's a competent freak, and competent freaks just may be the most important people in the entire culture at this nervous point in its development. *Grow Your Own* is a solid achievement that everybody in the community can not only benefit from, but feel proud of.

Darlington explained in its pages, "I haven't been a mad gardener all my life. In fact, I really only began in the spring of '68 with a vegetable garden." She describes how her journey began:

> I was working at a nursery at the time, so I had plenty of knowledge about all the super fertilizers and magic bug killers. And I was pretty good at selling these to the customers. One spray company even paid employees dividends each month according to how much of their product we sold. Naturally I pushed it. Fortunately, it was the least toxic spray we carried and was safe (?) to be used on vegetables within one day of harvest. It didn't contain DDT. But I wondered, 'If it kills all the bugs it says, how come one day will make it safe for me?'

All this was to change. "Luckily, I happened to pick up from the floor one day an introductory offer to 10 months of [Rodale's] *Organic Gardening and Farming* magazine at half price. It dawned on me then that I wanted to learn how to garden with natural fertilizers and without poisons. I could hardly wait to receive my first issue." Darlington had "thought Organic Gardening was something weird old spinsters in Marin County did, like saving seed from year to year for the past 35 years and things like that". The bibliography of *Grow Your Own* lists a slew of the Rodale books.

At around this time, in a remarkably principled way, she quit working at the nursery. "A third of the products I was selling were only making Standard Oil richer and the air and earth more polluted. I felt rather guilty." The negative perception of growing organically as somehow cranky and old-fashioned still persisted:

> Some people still wonder why go to all the trouble to do it organically. I think it's much simpler to garden organically, at least on a backyard scale. People are beginning to be aware of ecology. Organic gardening is something each of us can do to help. I'm quite sure it's cheaper to garden organically than with synthetic chemicals. You don't have to buy five different types of poison sprays and several different fertilizer mixes. Compost can be made for free or for a very little bit of money.

Darlington explains:

> Most importantly, it's better for your soul to garden organically. If you use chemical fertilizers, you are disregarding the fact that soil is a living, breathing thing. Soil becomes only a medium which supports plant upright; chemical fertilizers destroy many life forms such as beneficial soil bacteria and earthworms. Poison sprays not only pollute the atmosphere, but also kill many harmless

> insects and many helpful predators, this destroying the balance of nature. Gardening organically is working in harmony with nature.

Particularly interesting in the context of the times is Darlington's conjecture that "chemical fertilizers put your soil on a speed trip. The normal component balance of the soil is disturbed by the availability of more plant food than can be accepted." This comparison of fertiliser to the stimulants we abuse as people is underrated. On the addictive "NPK mentality", Lord Northbourne writes, "It seems that they are like many, or most, drugs or remedies, in that the more you use the more you have to use..." A review of the book written in 2013 on Amazon reveals Jeanie, then aged seventy-one, checking in to buy a copy to give to friends. She reveals that Sandy, the man on the cover, died in 1989. "This book sold at least 175,000 copies way back then. I made 10% — $1.75 for each one. And believe me, in 1970 that was wonderful."

Craig Sams

I first interviewed Craig Sams five years previously at his home in Hastings, when we mainly discussed the macrobiotic diet. Macrobiotics, the vehicle of charismatic Japanese food guru George Ohsawa, was described as both "the Diet that's Killing Our Kids" and "Hippie Kosher". A convert, Sams and his brother Gregory ran a restaurant in Notting Hill called Seed where the leading lights of the day — most notably John Lennon and Yoko Ono, with whom they would form a close bond — would gather and eat brown rice. At that meeting in 2018, Sams said a couple of things to me which at the time I didn't understand. Talking of his family's background in Nebraska, he told me that in the Midwest, in a few generations, the colonising European farmers had destroyed soils that had taken thousands of years to build. I didn't get this at all! Surely all the farmers had to do was dig a little deeper into the ground and start again? Wasn't soil — simply dirt, as I then understood it — just *there*?

I had come to talk to Sams about the health modalities that emerged against the background of the counterculture. At one point, he began talking about something called the Peckham Experiment, run by George Williamson and Innes Pearce. Between 1926 and 1950, 950 families in South London were given access to a range of sporting, social, and cultural activities. They were also fed organically grown food. The subject's health outcomes were remarkable. I was confused. What did organic food have to do with wellness? What did it have to do with hippies? As the saying goes, "Ontogeny recapitulates phylogeny"; unaware of the role of soil as it related to health, the evolution of my own understanding as I wrote *Retreat* was pitched somewhere at the tail-end of the 1960s, before that disembodied generation came to terms with the importance of biological farming techniques. Having the opportunity to talk to Sams, and having to work out these two riddles, was the seed of this book.

This time I met Sams in Central London at his members' club in Soho. Just shy of eighty, he is very tall, stands upright, and has a tan and a head of white hair. Most well-known for launching Green & Black's chocolate with his wife Josephine, he's serious but at the same time kind and patient. Inspected from either end, Sams's career seems improbable, but follow it from step to step, and it has its own inexorable logic. He explains:

> People in the restaurant would say, 'Look, I can't come here every time I want brown rice! And I've tried to get it shopping. I can't find it anywhere.' So, we started bagging up stuff and selling it. So, you'd pay your bill, and the guy who took your money would sell you a pound of brown rice or a pound of buckwheat or some Kombu seaweed or something like that.

Running Seed Restaurant led the Sams brothers to start their own food shop, Ceres Grain. As well as importing and selling macrobiotic staples like tamari soy sauce and umeboshi plums, Ceres sold organic produce sourced from British farmers. Their own brand, Harmony Foods, also specialised in organic produce, like their pioneering organic wholegrain cornflakes (made the way John Harvey Kellogg intended them) and organic peanut butter. In organic circles at this period, he describes himself as labouring under the reputation of being at "the capitalist end of the spectrum; you know, I wasn't a good wholesome, big farmer or something". However, as Soil Association founding member Mary Langman would have counselled, there need be no threat to organic principles from the food's commercial propagation.

In 1971, the Sams brothers sat on a Soil Association committee as it drew up the first guidelines for organic standards. The resulting document took up only two sides of a single A4 sheet of paper. Sams explains, "Lady Eve was rattled by us." She and Brigadier Vickers had sought to distance themselves from such hippies, as Lord Kitchener had just tabled a motion in the House of Lords that MAFF, the Ministry of Agriculture, Fisheries and Food, should develop a policy for organic farming. However, by supplying produce to the novel organic shop, Wholefood, which Mary Langman had set up in Baker Street (Langman who had been PA to Innes Pearce of The Peckham Experiment), they established contact with Lillian Scofield, the manager there. Scofield took the whole range of the Harmony Foods products and was their main customer for years.

Sams sees his role as an organic distributor in this era as being akin to that played by a broadcasting corporation like the BBC. It didn't interfere too much with his path into the Soil Association. Because he was so into organic food, first, he worked as its treasurer: "And I wormed my way into the hearts of the membership because, you know, one of them said, at one of the AGMs, 'It's the first time I've actually understood a treasurer's report because normally it's very dry.'" When Charlotte Mitchell, the chair, retired he became the chairman of the Soil Association between 2001 and 2007.

I asked Sams what his take was on the sudden shift at the end of the 1960s between "the electric, urban, and chemical" to "the acoustic, rural, and natural", and he credits the influence of the macrobiotic diet: "It said, always buy food that is grown near to you, always buy food that is in season, always buy food that is grown without chemicals. Always eat whole grains." Sams wants to play down this "always", as macrobiotics, followed correctly, isn't prescriptive like a normal diet. As we will see, its influence, especially in the American back-to-the-land communes, was immense, even as that influence is today being downplayed somewhat. For instance, for whatever reason, a pivotal macrobiotics figure such as Paul Hawken dials back any mention of it in his extensive resume.

Sams also credits the influence of LSD to this shift to the more natural:

> Acid and dope created an awareness because like [with food it's] something you're consuming... you connect to nature. And you connect to your own nature as well... [you do] a full body scan of yourself. And you realise, 'I'm not physically healthy in this way' or that 'I'm not mentally healthy in this way or that', and so you address those issues... Where are we? Sixty, fifty years later, [and the] psychiatric profession is going mad about psilocybin.

Biochar

Today, Sams's main focus is the Carbon Gold fertiliser business. He arrived at biochar, as it were, from a number of different directions. On a professional level, he had investigated the carbon footprint of Harmony Food's cornflakes and discovered that — because the corn had been grown organically, thereby increasing the biomass in the soil — they were practically offsetting their own distribution footprint already. This prompted him to encourage the Soil Association to promote its positive climate contribution. This bore fruit in a large report the organisation published in 2001.

Although he doesn't describe himself as a farmer, Sams has always been a gardener. He looks after an extensive garden at Hastings, where he lives, has an orchard whose apples he bottles into juice, and even cultivates a mesh-protected dandelion patch. Already having an interest in "carbon and farming", he describes the moment he got "the biochar bug" as being the result of reading a book. "I read a book called *1491* by a guy called Charles Mann. 1491 was a year before Columbus discovered America... and it described what it was like before the Spanish and the English and the Portuguese all turned up..." Mann's exhumation of an alternate ecological history didn't just prick up Sams's ears; as we will see, it also profoundly influenced original counterculture warriors such as Tennessee mega-commune the Farm's Albert Bates. The organic movement in particular has repeatedly turned to the wisdom of Indigenous techniques of agriculture as a reserve of wisdom. It forms the opening chapter in the lore of biochar.

Author Charles C. Mann's blockbuster *1491*, which was published not in the countercultural heyday but in 2005, brought new information on the history of the Americas to a wider audience. Mann's research, which we follow here, revealed that before Columbus landed in 1493, rather than a wilderness, there was in fact half an entire world of peoples and their cultures there. Mann picked at the still-dominant idea that the main influx of humans into the Americas was across the Bering strait, believing instead that ocean navigation was more common than we now imagine. Unlike Europeans, the Native Americans did not live in close contact with animals, only the dog and the llama, and were therefore vulnerable to many diseases (measles, for instance, being a variant of cattle's rinderpest virus). As a result, as Mann writes, "it is widely believed that between 1500 and 1600, nine out of ten Native

Americans died." He supposes that Cortes's success rested on this. Most fascinatingly for growers of an exploratory mindset, Mann brought to global attention the phenomenon of *terra preta* — meaning "black earth" in Portuguese.

Anthropologists had found that large sections of the Amazon had terrible, often poisonous soil, but they also discovered regions of rich, fertile, dark earth covering a total of a few thousand square miles that they believe was man-made. Usually one or two feet deep, it is sometimes as much as six feet deep. Not a product of slash and burn "swidden" agriculture, which does not produce enough charcoal, on the one hand it's theorised that the farmers had evolved a technique of partial burning dubbed "slash-and-char", before stirring the resultant charcoal into the soil. On the other, the frequent presence of shards of pottery, and the very high bacteria levels in terra preta — as much as a hundred times more than in adjacent soils — suggest the charcoal had been primed with excrement and food waste. This suggests closer, "hands-on" management. Mann represents a credible body of scientific evidence when he ascribes to the Indians a high degree of agricultural management. Prairies were likely to have been forested before, and forests were carefully cultivated with tree crops (he wittily describes the Amazon rainforest as "a lot of old orchards"). These were innovations invisible to invaders from the East who marvelled at the supposedly "untouched" Edenic landscapes they encountered. Mann concluded of the ingenious processes behind terra preta and its ecological sagacity that

> it suggests that for a long time clever people who knew tricks that we have yet to learn used big chunks of Amazonia nondestructively. Faced with an ecological problem, the Indians fixed it. Rather than adapt to Nature, they created it. They were in the midst of terraforming the Amazon when Columbus showed up and ruined everything.

Craig Sams implicitly saw the relevance of biochar, and the way it creates something of a coral reef, to the needs of a living soil:

> The worms are the sign of healthy soil. I remember Paul McCartney once saying, 'I know I've got organic certification, but to me I'm really organic when every time we plough, we just see worms everywhere.' When a worm eats a mouthful of soil, for every Actinomyces bacteria going in its mouth, nine or ten come out of the other end. So, worms actually increase the microbial population of soil. Now, if you're a conventional farmer, you don't have worms. They died long ago because you sprayed herbicides, and fungicides and all the rest of it. This is where biochar becomes so important. Because if you are one of those microorganisms, the next guys up, the saber-toothed tigers, if you like, the lions, are the nematodes, the mites, the protozoa, the amoeba. Those are the larger life forms. Protozoa need to eat 50,000 bacteria a day to stay alive. That's fine, that's the food chain in the soil! If you have biochar in the soil, the pores of the biochar are filled by the biology. And the organisms that eat them can't get at them because they're in this honeycomb structure, because it keeps the fine cell structure of the original wood [from before it was turned into charcoal]. That's why your soil microbiome becomes so much more densely populated and resilient when you have biochar in the soil.

Regarding carbon, when I mention to him that this book is called *The Garden* after Joni Mitchell's lyric from the song "Woodstock", Sams points out that in Mitchell's own version the whole verse runs, "We are stardust, we are golden, *We are billion-year-old carbon*, And we've got to get ourselves back to the garden."

SEED Magazine

Craig Sams, together with his partner and brother Greg and their father Ken, was also instrumental in the creation of *SEED* magazine. *SEED* magazine was a vehicle of their organic and macrobiotic empire, which comprised the Ceres shop on the Portobello, their restaurant, Seed, and their wholesale distributors, Harmony Foods. It is, however, much more than this, providing a vivid snapshot of the zeitgeist as the preoccupations of the countercultural generation meshed with an interest in natural food, growing, and the countryside.

There are almost too many examples to pick from that illustrate this, but a favourite of mine is an article, "How to Win Friendship and Respect When You Move to the Country" (1976) which touches on the back-to-the-land movement as it was experienced in the UK. The editorial intro runs as follows:

> For years now, people have been reading *SEED* and inspired with our beautiful message have been leaving the cities and seeking the natural life in the countryside. Jeremy Sandford (who confesses to having made most of these mistakes and worse) provides the following precepts for those who plan to help in rebuilding the rural Albion.

The instructions themselves have about them the feel of true stories from the frontline redacted to spare the embarrassment of the perpetrators: "Tell the farmer that you'll build him a first-rate pig sty. Put it up without foundations (nobody told you). Feel very hurt when he's angry. When he pays you short, threaten to sue him." "The first evening of your arrival, announce in the pub that you like the place so much that you'll get some friends to help you hold a festival there for a few thousand groovers in the summer. Point out that this should bring some pretty far-out vibes to the neighbourhood." "Just as he starts to castrate the first of a dense herd of 500 lambs, move in to make sure the farmer fully appreciates the vegetarian position." "When discovered screwing your lady midst the dung of farmer Jones' cow byre, explain that it's because the spirit paths there are especially propitious." "With friends, indulge in a touch of transcendental chanting to celebrate the summer solstice; your neighbours' mares and colts, unused to the subtle rhythms of the East, stampede into barbed wire and become entangled." "Persuade the farmer to lend you half an acre for growing organic vegetables. Get him to plough it up for you and dung it. Don't plant the vegetables. When the land plants itself with nettles, point out that the nettles have as much right to be there as any other vegetation."

Another *SEED* regular column was entitled "Organic Gardening" and had a series of guest writers: Stephen Barnett, Chris Patton, and Jasper. *SEED* also covered the self-sufficiency aspects bubbling under in the UK. Philip Brown describes his shock at trying to cope as a new arrival on the Isle of Skye. Bobbie Barrett tells her story of aiming for a Scottish croft, a stone cottage in Wales, or a smallholding in Wiltshire, but settling for a small garden where previously they had none, and an allotment. John and Maureen Plowman read John and Sally Seymour's *Self-Sufficiency* (1973) and use their bungalow's thirty-by-one-hundred-and-fifty-foot garden to grow "basic fruits and vegetables". John Seymour himself is interviewed in 1975 where he tells *SEED* that:

> I can't stand — and never could — modern Western cities. I think towns and cities are necessary, but to serve the countryside, not as ends in themselves. I think civilization should be rural, as it really was in Periclean Greece and Elizabethan England. Although much went on in towns, most men had their roots in the country.

John Butler

One of *SEED*'s signature offerings was the "Changing Seasons" column by organic farmer John Butler, which ran from June 1972 to May 1976. The magazine itself ceased publication in 1977. In 2023, Butler, aged eighty-six and now retired from farming but passionate about the living soil, runs a YouTube channel, "Spiritual Unfoldment with John Butler", with 223k subscribers and a few videos having over a million views. Many followers remark upon the ASMR quality of Butler's very peaceful delivery of speech. Butler's not from a farming background; his father was an organic grocer and landscape painter who instilled in him the importance of paying attention in the present moment. Butler, who had trained to be a farmer, accepted stewardship of a thousand hectares to grow food in Bolivia to support a local community there, but instead met a Peruvian woman and went to work in Peru. He experienced what he describes as a feeling of surrender there while trekking in the jungle. On his return to farming in the UK, he attended the School of Meditation, which had been set up in 1961. There, he refined his ability to connect with "stillness".

Butler encountered Craig and Gregory Sams because he sold produce to their Ceres shop in Notting Hill, ultimately leading to his *SEED* column. This was presaged by an interview conducted for the April 1972 issue. He had been working his farm for six years. Even at this stage of his life, his approach to farming was metaphysical in intent:

> If we study virgin soil, we see what can be described as a perfect organic situation. If a farmer manages to maintain his land at that potency, he's doing quite well. But he can do a lot better, because man has access to spiritual subtleties that he can transmit to things he comes in contact with... Man can take something like a carrot or a cabbage and put

> something of a spiritual quality into it if he so wishes. This to me, is the real direction of organic food.

In the main, however, the column takes a very practical angle. His view on farm animals, for instance, is that they should never be competitors for available food supplies but rather should be used to utilise by-products and land that cannot be used for anything else. Butler gives the example of cattle converting straw — the stalk residue of wheat — into strength, warmth, meat, leather, and manure. They can also, he suggests, become extensions of our own capabilities to digest, thereby providing us with products like milk and wool. They can give us companionship too.

Butler pulls no punches about the difficulties of farming, and indeed there is something of a downward-bearing arc to the mood of the column. January 1975 is especially bleak:

> I am finding this the most difficult year yet to sell my produce. I have not been able to increase my prices with inflation. In fact I've had to sell cauliflowers at the same price I was charging five years ago. Organic vegetables always were a luxury trade and it seems people are now less prepared to pay that extra premium for them… A couple of years ago I was enthusiastically saying 'Yes, I can farm organically and make a living off three acres.' Now that is not so. Of course, we are more or less self-sufficient for food — that's quite easy. What seems almost impossible is making enough cash from our produce to anything like pay for the work going into it.

Although Butler was the object of hippie fascination, he was oblivious to them. When I wrote to him and asked what he made of that generation, he replied in good humour, "I never made anything of them, being more interested in farming, but I was familiar with Findhorn (the story of which is told in Chapter 6) and knew a bit about anthroposophy." He also pointed out that "self-sufficiency for me was a by-product, not a primary aim, of good farming." Indeed, organic historian Philip Conford, who has written about Butler in his capacity as a farmer, points out that they were practicing self-sufficiency some years before John Seymour's books came out. In many respects Butler's trajectory through growing and farming is the inverse of that of the counterculture. Where the counterculture, disorientated and disconnected from the axis of life, both sought comfort and found wisdom in going back to the land; Butler, on the other hand, whose motto is "Feel your feet on the ground," used the soil as a solid base from which to explore what is described in Eastern philosophy as non-dualism, the experience of consciousness outwith the boundaries of the ego.

Although these currents are regularly found in the "Changing Seasons" column, they are perhaps nowhere more evident than in his very long, double-page, penultimate column for the magazine. It is reproduced in the wonderful collection *Mystic Apprentice* (2020), which goes more intensely into what will become his lifelong preoccupations.

> Well, as I was turning my compost heap, I realised that what I was doing was creating the conditions for an increase in life. Composting was the process of raising matter to a higher level of consciousness, and all those millions of bugs and bacteria which we are told exist in good compost, were that extra increase in life, made manifest. Consciousness was what pulled me out of my worldly troubles, and consciousness worked the same on the land. Compost was a vehicle for giving spiritual food to the land. One could forget everything else. Consciousness was what mattered. The consciousness of worms and bugs and birds and of plants and of me, the farmer, all lifting the soil, lifting each other, lifting ourselves up towards God.

WWOOF

Sue Coppard had been working as a secretary at the Textile Research Unit at the Royal College of Art in London. She liked the job but missed the countryside. As a child she had loved staying on her cousin's farm: "Pure bliss for me". She wanted to learn about organic farming and decided the best way to go about that was practical experience. She had just heard about organic farming, reasoning, "It occurred to me — correctly — that such places might be more inclined to use unskilled labor than a big, commercial farm". Organic farming, she believed, was "surely the only conceivable possibility for the future".

A friend of a friend, Michael Allaby, editor of the Soil Association's journal, put Coppard in touch with the Steiner organisation's Emerson College in East Sussex, located a short trip south of London. At that time the college ran the two-hundred-acre biodynamically farmed Tablehurst Farm beside it. The vice-principal, John Davy, encouraged his sceptical farm managers to give them a shot. Coppard placed a hasty advert in the then nascent *Time Out* magazine for "Working Weekends on Organic Farms". That magazine, which was founded in 1968 and had countercultural beginnings in the underground press, received fifteen enquiries. Their assembled group of three people took the train down from London with their work clothes and sleeping bags and spent the weekend clearing brambles and unblocking ditches to the sound of birdsong. Pleasantly surprised, the farmers invited them back. Allaby ran an article in his journal entitled "Coppard's Land Army", which brought forth from the hedgerows both more WWOOFers like themselves, and hosts looking for help. A job working for the Sams family's Portobello-based journal *SEED* also followed, where she started as a secretary before in time becoming its editor, all the while acquiring a deeper organic education and connections.

Sue Coppard wrote an article herself in *SEED* in February 1973. By this stage she could claim that the WWOOFers had "worked on farms, market and 'ecological' gardens, and have contacts as far away as Scotland and New Zealand". And this was just the beginning. WWOOF started as an acronym meaning "Weekend Working on Organic Farms"; today it stands for either "Willing Workers on Organic Farms" or "World-Wide Opportunities on Organic Farms". Nowadays, WWOOF enables you to help out in over 130 countries around the world and is a truly global network. The wonderful WWOOF organisation has been an omnipresent thread in my research for *The Garden.* I visited the Steiner Michael Hall School's walled garden in Forest Row by way of answering an advert on their online portal. At Findhorn, I interviewed the CSA's (Community Supported Agriculture) resident WWOOFer, the highly skilled grower Veronica Caldwell. In upstate New York, when I visited the legendary Soul Fire Farm, I found that the site director Jonah Vitale-Wolff started out with WWOOF working on farms throughout New Zealand, Spain, and Central America.

WWOOFers have long been a valuable asset to many farms, in his self-sufficiency classic *Living on a Little Land* (1978) Patrick Rivers writes:

> Shirley and I could never have achieved what we have without the help of scores of 'wwoofers' who have come to us — most of them for weekends, some for stretches of several weeks... I can recall none who have not shared our views on living more simply, and on the need to bring about a gentle revolution by setting an example.

Rivers also remarks, "Besides helping both farmer and learner, WWOOF plays a small but valuable role in bridging the gap between city and countryside and reviving interest in the land."

Coppard — who I would have loved to have been able to interview, and tried to with some persistence and the enthusiastic support of WWOOF themselves — is now sadly very old. In an earlier interview, she describes the phenomenon in decidedly cosmic terms: "The way I see it now is that WWOOF was hanging about in the stratosphere looking for a way to manifest, and picked on me as a suitable channel: a London secretary with modest organizational skills who needed to get out into the countryside!"

The Real Organic Project

One of my most important pathways into the landscape of growing and farming was through the American Dave Chapman's Real Organic Project, which shares a fascinating and dizzyingly comprehensive series of interviews on YouTube and Spotify. These are conducted by Chapman and his co-director, Dr Linley Dixon, and now number nearly 150. They speak with leading global advocates for what his friend Eliot Coleman would call biologic farming. The subjects hail from all manner of industries: of every race, age, and gender, they are growers and farmers, yes, but also chefs, scientists, businessmen, journalists, bureaucrats, politicians, and theorists. Although it is an awe-inspiring educational resource, one tooled so as to convincingly substantiate the argument for the importance of the integrity of the organic standard, the work has an explicit political function.

The Soil Association, a charity registered in 1946, is the custodian of the organic label in the UK and is responsible for certification. In the USA, the National Organic Program is run by the United States Department of Agriculture. The NOP came into existence much more recently, when Congress passed the Organic Foods Production Act in 1990. At the time, it probably felt like a tremendous idea to America's organic producers. After all, what better guardian of a standard than the government itself? While some organic standards such as German's Naturland are, as in the UK, overseen by a trade body, other organic standards, such as Japan's, *have* been equitably handled by the state.

In the USA, however, the label has been deprecated. As Chapman's friend, the farmer Eliot Coleman puts it, "Ever since the USDA was given control of the word, the integrity of the USDA CERTIFIED ORGANIC label has been on a predictable descent..." Giant agricultural businesses have eyed the profits made by small organic producers and have determined to capture that market. This has partly been achieved through lobbying government, a subtle form of reeducation and manipulation of lawmakers who it seems don't understand the issues, and a bending of the regulatory framework. In 2022 in the US, $166.9 million was spent to this and other related ends, outstripping even the $124.5 million spent on lobbying for defence. A recurring analogy in the Real Organic Project is that of the playground swing: the organic movement in the USA built the swing themselves, and the bully boys of corporate agriculture pushed them off it. As we say in England, "It's just not cricket."

Central to this hustle has been the organic certification of (1) crops grown hydroponically, (2) animal products like beef, poultry, and eggs produced in concentrated animal feeding operations (CAFOs). With regards to hydroponics, whereby plants are grown, not in soil, but in nutrient solutions, "organic", as it is often erroneously assumed, does not mean food grown without chemicals. It is not enough that the solution, the growing medium, is comprised of organic ingredients. It is axiomatic, rather, as Sir Albert Howard defines it, that, "it must be grown in fertile soil, that is to say in soil well supplied with freshly prepared, high quality humus". Much as organic hydroponic is, after a bitter defeat for the Real Organic Project, now allowed by the USDA, strictly speaking it does not conform to the principles of organic. Indeed, European organic regulations insist on soil, the outlier being organic hydroponic growers in the Netherlands who supply the American market but not their domestic one.

So far as the quality of life of confined animals is concerned, here the Real Organic Project honours the spirit rather than the letter of organic. Howard's formula for human health, enshrined by Lady Eve Balfour in the tenets of the Soil Association, is that healthy soil creates healthy plants and animals, and in turn healthy humans. To keep animals in degrading conditions, quite apart from ethical concerns about their welfare, does not create healthy animals. The Real Organic Project, having tried but failed in the task of reforming the USDA, set about the creation of an add-on label. Those farms that have already passed NOP organic certification can add it to their produce. Over one thousand farms have joined the programme.

As an itinerant Englishman, dutifully attending day-long Real Organic online conferences and numerous book club events, I've been keenly aware of being the only European in the room. What is obvious to me, however, is that the difficulties that Chapman is tackling in America will soon be visited upon the rest of the world. Organic, as a brand, has been attacked from all sides. Certainly, organic has its flaws, the most notable being its inability to account for the climate cost of transportation and for the ecological sense in eating seasonally. But its critics unwittingly play to commercial interests when they claim that, by supporting soil tillage, organic is not climate-friendly. Some regenerative agriculture commentators have inferred that organic methods damage the soil, seemingly without realising that organic's true emphasis is positively in favour of soil health, not negatively in opposition to chemicals. Though, certainly, these two emphases are interconnected.

"No-till" is the ecological method of growing without digging or ploughing. Alongside the use of cover crops it is the hallmark of the viable new ecological trend in modern agriculture: *regenerative*. No-till has ended up being promoted in tandem with herbicide use by chemical manufacturers. This is because tillage is the conventional method of clearing away weeds, and without its action the easiest thing to do is apply herbicides. No-till is also implicated in the preservation of mycorrhizal fungi networks, which tillage disrupts. Amid a tsunami of media commentary about the importance of mycorrhizal fungi, there is suddenly academic dissent. Professor of Biology at the University of British Columbia Melanie Jones and Associate Professor at the University of Alberta Justine Karst have recently attempted to put the brakes on Dr Suzanne Simard's idea from 1997 of what has been dubbed the "wood-wide web". Nature magazine summarised the pushback thus:

> The review laid out what the authors regard as the three key claims underlying the popular idea of the 'mother tree': that networks of different fungi linking the roots of different trees — known as common mycorrhizal networks (CMNs) — are widespread in forests; that resources pass through such networks, benefiting seedlings; and that mature trees preferentially send resources along the networks to their kin. The scientists concluded that the first two are insufficiently supported by the scientific evidence, and that the last "has no peer-reviewed, published evidence".

Once the proof of the significance of mycorrhizal networks in forests is questioned, by extension the importance of their being undisturbed in other environments is less clear. What ought to be manna for the argument made throughout this book for mutualism and interconnectivity is, in this instance, not currently backed up by science.

Another argument popularly made in favour of no-till is that it facilitates the drawdown of carbon dioxide from the atmosphere and its accumulation as carbon exudates. These exudates are the carbon secretions with which plants feed soil microbiota in a reciprocal arrangement to influence nutrient availability, soil pH, and recruitment of bacteria and fungi. There is broad agreement, as soil scientist Dr Christine Jones emphasises, that root exudates, a plant's underground carbon outputs, are a critically important factor in creating soil, driving life in the root zone which creates the soil structure.

However, with regards to a plant's carbon drawdown, some such as Dr Will Brinton of Woods End Laboratories in Maine, assert that the rhizosphere doesn't extend far from the plant into the soil, that oxidation after tillage is overemphasised, and that, in terms of its contribution to carbon sequestration, a plant's accumulating biomass (its flowers, leaves, stem, and roots) dwarfs the significance of its exudate deposits. None of this is to diminish no-till's advantages, such as decreasing soil erosion or increasing soil respiration (a marker of the abundance of microorganisms). But these challenges suggest that in some circumstances tillage's negative ecological impact can be overestimated. In light of the claims of no-till, it's worth remembering, too, that a vital plant *can* be grown in a container in healthy soil.

The current criticism of organic extends further. It is supposedly only for rich people (organic costs more for the consumer for a number of reasons: in spite of possessing greater value, as it is a more nutritious product, the process is usually less productive in terms of yield — but the principle reason it is more expensive in the shops is that, farcically, it is not propped up by government subsidies like chemical agriculture is); it uses too much land (intensively farmed in smaller plots, it can be highly productive); and the old chestnut: if the world was to farm in this manner, it would mean starvation (a battle wages on about which percentage of the world is fed by small farms, but it is reckoned by some to be as high as 80%).

Sadly, regenerative agriculture — which currently exists only as an adjective without an organisational body to police a regulatory framework — is often used as a stick with which to beat organic, and threatens, if not carefully watched, to be a Trojan horse for the conventional agriculture infrastructure. Dr Will Brinton playfully describes regenerative as the three Cs, "chemicals and cover crops". For many years, the Soil Association and Lady Eve Balfour resisted organic certification, before eventually Patrick Holden and Peter Segger introduced it, causing Balfour herself to step down. Craig Sams describes it as "a sad end to her role as founder, but within a couple of years, the organic market boomed because you could trust the organic claim". Sams has some concerns that without certification, regenerative will be subject to inevitable scandals which will damage the organic market by implication. However, in the wings there are schemes such as the Sustainable Food Trust's 'Global Farm Metric', again with Patrick Holden at its helm, which seek to create, if not a framework of certification, then an unequivocal method of measuring and stating a farm's footprint; more on which in the "Sustainability" chapter of this book.

Dave Chapman

I visited the tall and rangy Dave Chapman, who looks ten years younger than his seventy, at Long Wind Farm in the wooded valley in Vermont where he grows tomatoes. Chapman has, strategically, made a virtue of his own self-effacement in his intense cooperation with others. He has conducted a gloriously never-ending series of interviews for the Real Organic YouTube channel, in which he graciously defers to the knowledge of his peers. Simultaneously, he has drawn around himself a movement as he works hand-in-glove with his senior colleague, the legendary farmer Eliot Coleman. To this extent it's sometimes hard to know where the intensely modest Chapman starts and ends. He's pulling strings, but you wouldn't know it.

Chapman showed me past the acre-size compost lot into one of his immense greenhouses and gave me the lowdown on the finely honed cultivation techniques they use. Later, we sat on his adjacent verandah and ate blueberries from Hugh Kent's ROP-certified farm with local yogurt and honey. Getting Chapman to talk about himself is an uphill battle: "I have to say, I try to walk a fine line... I don't think it's helpful for me to be invisible, but I really don't think it's helpful for it to be about me or my farm, because that's not the point... I don't generally talk much about me, and I hardly ever mention Long Wind Farm."

There's so little information available about Chapman, the driving force to what is effectively a movement — in keeping with his roots, a rebellion even — that I wasn't even aware of his background in the back-to-the-land movement. Growing up in Lancaster County in Pennsylvania on a dairy farm, graduating in 1971 in the last year of the draft lottery, he escaped being sent to Vietnam because they only went up to number fifty that year, and he had been allocated a higher number. To his mother's chagrin, although expected to attend college (and in spite of being accepted), he deferred indefinitely, taking a string of different jobs. He lists his favourites as working as a grill cook and at an Army and Navy surplus store. In the early 1970s, living in the Northwest in Washington State, Chapman was dreaming of being a horse farmer. This led to him going to horseshoeing school to learn more about the animals. He wound up in Vermont in 1976, after the first wave of re-settlers in 1968. Of the back-to-the-land movement, he says, "It's not like we were inventing it; we were, but it was something that we were being swept along by and we were swimming, you know, and in this direction or that direction." In Vermont he bought and raised two oxen. While his oxen were growing, he went, by way of an education, and worked for a year with Jake Guest, one of the first wave, who had left the commune he had joined — called Wooden Shoe, in New Hampshire — and was starting to farm on his own.

Chapman's first mentor, Jake Guest

In one of Chapman's many interviews, he speaks to his friend, the slightly more senior Jake Guest, who is still farming organically. In some respects Guest's views are an articulation of Chapman's own, albeit shifted backwards a few years. An anti-war protestor, and an employee at Dartmouth College,

Guest was thrown in prison after his group took over the administration building in New Hampshire. Out of jail, and fired up, the fifty-two of them decided to set up a country retreat. Guest describes the climate of the times and how agriculture moved centre-stage as a cultural activity:

> Corporate America was making money off Vietnam — their kids weren't going to Vietnam! What else were they doing? Well, there's no farmers around here. Where did they all go? They were taken over by the big corporations who took over the food industry. It was all connected, Vietnam, corporate America — these are not nice corporations. They don't give a shit about you.

Deciding that it was a "no-brainer" that they grow their own food, Guest taught himself from books:

> We had no idea what we were doing. We had the Rodale's *Encyclopedia of Organic Gardening*, but it was typically for somebody who was 65 and retired... there were no young people who were organic farmers... not that I knew of... and then I started bumping into these biodynamic people... whatever the hell that was... anthroposophy or some shit... but it has a resonance. This around the time of *Silent Spring* — that was an incredible event.

Guest remembers reading the Rodale tomes, F.H. King, Edward Hyams's awesome survey *Soil and Civilization* (1952), and Peter Henderson's positively antique *Gardening for Profit* (1874) by kerosene lantern at night with a pack of Lucky Strikes. He reflected, "The British have a whole bunch of practical farming books... they tell you *exactly* how to plough a field..."

Chapman meeting Eliot Coleman

Around this time in the late 1970s, Chapman, oxen in tow, met Eliot Coleman at a gas station. Chapman has nothing but praise and affection for his old friend:

> Eliot, of all the visionary farmers in America, and there are definitely other great ones, he really led something. He's very much a contrarian, is very independent-minded. He's a very talented human being, just bright and driven... Well, we spent a lot of time together... I never put it this way, but we were soulmates. He was a mentor for sure. He's thirteen years older than me. And with a wealth of experience in those thirteen years. So, he was very generous with it. We were fascinated by the same things. I love to read. He loves to read. So, he shared his library with me, and I read a lot of it. And we discussed it, and we still do. I haven't talked to him today, but I certainly talked to him yesterday, so we call a lot, and we're talking about tillage and practical things like that.

Between his "teachers" Coleman and Guest, and with the two Guernsey cows providing labour, discing and spreading manure with them, Chapman set about raising mixed vegetables on a single acre for market:

> The other thing... is that when I did start to farm — and I was gardening before I was farming — I loved it. I loved the smell of the soil. I love working in that way with my body. I loved watching plants grow. It was all pretty much, you know, as they say, as much fun as you could have with your clothes on. It was really great, and then it's, like, well I wonder if I could possibly make a living at this?

He moved to the site of Long Wind Farm in 1984, where he built two little greenhouses out of two-by-four timbers, and by which time he had the crude brushstrokes of market gardening worked out. Today it seems like he is defined by the farming work he loves and the struggle he is engaged with in the Real Organic Project. Although Chapman is a Tai-chi practitioner (explaining that they started doing it as a family), and in the past practiced Vipassana meditation (but evidently doesn't anymore), about the undercurrents of holism that often travel with organic agriculture, he says:

> I'm not religious in the traditional sense, the common sense of that word... And I don't talk about this a lot with people, because I don't want to weird them out. But I do think that it's the truth that... it's not just about farming, it's not just about food, that we as a species have got to come up with a more mature way of dealing with the world than we have had.

I'm wary of taking up any more of Chapman's time. The phone is ringing. Meetings are piling up. Even if he couldn't seem more modest, friendly, and relaxed about it, he has important things to do.

Eliot Coleman

Coleman is a foundational figure in the organic food movement. He is a living bridge between the Old-World organic pioneers of England, Germany, France, and Switzerland and the New World. Coleman organised American trips to Europe in the 1970s and was involved in the background in drafting the proposals for the creation of the US Government's USDA organic certification (too important a matter to be left in the hands of government). What's more Coleman, who possesses one of the world's finest personal libraries of books relating to growing, is also a custodian of the movement's intellectual heritage. Coleman's writing in dazzling, technical books like *The New Organic Grower* (1989), makes liberal use of quotations from the historical doyens of organic agriculture, often in their florid nineteenth-century English. As a grower he is legendary for his pioneering use and design of new tools, for his use of soil blocks, for examining the crops willing to grow at the same latitude around the world, innovating by growing in the winter in the sub-zero temperatures of Maine, and for pioneering no-input farming through the ingenious use of green manures and discing.

I'm seated at a large wooden kitchen table in the Coleman residence, a big house but only just large enough to hold his and his wife Barbara Damrosch's enormous library of books on growing and gardening. It is set in fourteen farmed acres of what is normally land unsuitable for agriculture, near the Atlantic coast in the far northeast corner of America. It's a mere two-and-a-half-hour drive to the Canadian border. Eliot Coleman is now eighty-five years old but possesses an almost brutal energy. I flinch as, with relative frequency, Coleman pounds his fist on the table to drive home the urgency of certain finer points in his argument. Damrosch, who joins us, is obviously more used to it than me.

There's an expression in gardening for plants which appear out of the blue. They might be unexpected perennials, seeds sown elsewhere in the garden which have germinated in unusual places, or perhaps exotic weeds. They are called "volunteers". It's a splendid expression which captures a "have-a-go" spirit. I liked the term so much that I toyed with it as title for the book because so many of the growers and farmers I interviewed did not come from agricultural backgrounds. Eliot Coleman is one such "volunteer". With no farming in his family, Damrosch explained how a tenure teaching Spanish literature and the athletic programme (think outdoor activities) at Franconia College — a radical liberal arts institution — in the mid-1960s, affected Coleman. "It changed his life. I mean, he had had a very square, straight upbringing. WASP kind of Republican, you know. He was just overnight exposed to a different world." Coleman explained:

> It was started in this huge, abandoned resort hotel in the mountains of New Hampshire… by a bunch of investors from New Hampshire, and New Hampshire at that time was the most conservative state in the country. And they thought, okay, we'll start a little college and make use of this building, and they made a mistake of hiring people with imagination, and it took about only three years before they took over.

Exposure to the ideas at the college led Coleman to resist the draft to the Vietnam War on principle: "The idea of objecting to war and objecting to the draft, you know, I knew absolutely nothing about. So, the minute I learnt about this, I went down to my draft board in New Jersey and signed up as a conscientious objector." The board weren't having anything of his gesture and, since he was a teacher, simply gave him the teaching deferment he was entitled to. He recalls that they were unpleasant to deal with, and still expresses antipathy to that war.

As a young man, Coleman's passion was the outdoors and extreme sports. This might seem out of place in someone who describes himself proudly as an old hippie, however it's worth recalling Jack Kerouac's description in *The Dharma Bums* — the 1958 book in which Gary Snyder is immortalised as Japhy Ryder, and which is often seen as a prophesy of the countercultural hippie revolution — of "a vision of a great rucksack revolution, thousands or even millions of young Americans wandering around with rucksacks, going up to the mountains to pray, making children laugh and old men glad, making young girls happy and old girls happier, all of 'em Zen lunatics…" As a mountaineer, a rock climber, and a kayaker (making the first American kayak-racing whitewater team), Coleman "was always going and putting myself in places that were difficult. You had to work your way out of it." As he puts it in his book *The New Organic Grower*, "I wanted to grow food not with artificial industrial aids but in harmony with the same natural systems I had come to know so intimately during my adventures in the wilderness."

Eliot Coleman and the Nearings

It was his passion for extreme sports that drew him into the orbit of the Nearings (whom we meet in depth in the "Self-Sufficiency" chapter) and their book *Living the Good Life* (1954) (from which we in Britain ultimately derived the title of the famous TV show *The Good Life*). It is a foundational text of the American back-to-the-land movement. Cycling across the US west to east ("We heard that the wind blew that way"), as they were crossing Idaho, a huge truck pulled over. The driver was impressed to see their ten-speed bikes, which he himself raced, and asked Coleman and his friend to stop for dinner with him and his mother in the next town. At dinner, the man sized up Coleman, then a skinny kid, and advised him to eat yoghurt, in those days a niche health food product, to bulk up. Soon finding himself cross-country skiing, Coleman followed up a tip that he could buy a yoghurt-maker in the town near Franconia College. The store proprietor, a "really weird guy and in a one piece of workers' overalls", also loaned out books, suggesting one written by the vegetarian health-food fanatic Murray Rose, the Australian swimmer (aka "the Seaweed Streak"). Rose had raced in three Olympic games when such a thing was unheard of. Coleman was transfixed by the possibilities and returned the next day to return the book "and to buy seaweed and sunflower seeds and all this stuff", whereupon the owner recommended he borrow another book, the Nearings' *Living the Good Life*.

At odds with the new management, which had set about trying to convert Franconia back into a regular college, Coleman was fired from his job. In 1966, he and his first wife visited the Nearings at their Maine homestead. On their return home, they immediately started a garden where they were living in New Hampshire. They returned to visit the Nearings in 1967, still early in the story of Helen and Scott Nearing's burgeoning hippie adoption, whereupon Helen said, "'I hear you're looking for land. Why don't we just sell you the back half of our place? We're not using it.' So that's how that came about. So, I arrived here in the fall of '68." In a deal driven by their socialist principles, they sold Coleman sixty acres for an astonishing $33 an acre. Since that time, Coleman himself has sold three pieces of the land to friends for the same price. Coleman's wife, Damrosch, herself a well-known gardening author whose *The Garden Primer* (1988) was a bestseller, was also drawn into the homesteading sphere by the book: "That's why I left New York. That's why I gave up. I had become a full-time writer in New York, and I figured I can do that in Connecticut and grow my own food, just like Helen and Scott, you know? So, I did." In subsequent years, the Nearings have had their critics, but Coleman's loyalty to them both carries weight and is touching. He credits them with teaching him the ropes of economic survival, and the paramount importance of meticulous, efficient planning. "They were without a doubt the most practically organised country people I have ever met. In fact, I remember marvelling that Scott was the one nonagenarian I knew with plans for the future farm project he would be working on ten years hence."

The land Coleman had bought was poor and totally bereft of the topsoil necessary for growing vegetables. It was scrubland covered by low spruce trees and fir forest and was scattered with rocks. He asked the soil conservation service in Maine to come and profile it, and their report said that nothing he had was suitable for agriculture. It's a common statement one hears from people who know *a little* about farming, that some land is "good" and others "bad". Especially on market-garden-sized plots around three acres in size, but more time-consumingly on larger expanses of land, (whether clay, sand, or chalk), a topsoil can be built. Coleman tells people that the truly significant thing about what they achieved at Four Season Farm, if the world is concerned about starving in the future, is that if they could "turn this piece of shit into what it is now by just tilling-in locally available organic matter", then there's hope.

While he was building a house, they lived in a camper Coleman had built on the back of his Volkswagen pick-up truck. Working the land into shape appealed to his tastes for extreme sports. Chopping a stump out of the ground, he remembers being approached by a neighbour:

> 'Eliot isn't that a lot of work?' And I said, 'Well, Berwyn, let me tell you what I used to do before I decided I would be a farmer. I used to go on mountaineering expeditions, and I would be living in a tent eating freeze-dried food. And during the day, I would have a seventy-pound pack on my back chopping steps into a vertical ice cliff, so I could pack supplies up to camp four.' I said, 'Compared to that, this is easy', and it really was!

Coleman studies

Although he had the example of the Nearings' organic gardening next door, like other back-to-the-landers at that time, Coleman found a lot of information in books. An early favourite was the retired chemist Leonard Wickenden's *Gardening with Nature* (1954), an informed rebuttal of the NPK dogma. Even so, at the time, he explains how "every University Ag professor and everybody at the USDA, all said that what I wanted to do was impossible. [Thumps table] 'It's impossible to grow vegetables, without the chemicals!'" Discovering the works of Sir Albert Howard was for him like happening upon Copernicus. Coleman found in Howard, and in his own practice, that "the thing that blows my mind from the start was that if I did it right, there were no pests. And if you grow the plants correctly, they have all their immune systems together, and I thought that was the most fascinating idea in all of this."

The failure of agriculture to systematically embrace this "plant-positive" approach has a lot to do with the commercial interests behind the chemical model seizing the narrative to the extent of embedding their ideas into agricultural education. Coleman explains: "I've always said the greatest problem with organic farming is that it only makes money for the farmer... If I do it correctly, I'm not buying anything." As for any institutional publicity he might get, "There's no reason for any Ag industry to tell people what I'm doing — because there's nothing to sell." Done properly, "everyone can grow bounteous yields of vigorous plants that are free from pests by using homemade compost and age-old biological techniques; there is no market for fungicides or pesticides or anhydrous ammonia".

Enshrined in Howard's *The Soil and Health* is the idea of the benefits of healthy soil being passed down through healthy plants to healthy people and animals. This is an important topic for Coleman. When he compares the plight of the unhealthy plants to that of human beings, he's alarmed that people don't get it. "'Oh absolutely not!' 'Oh, there's sickness out there, it'll get you, no matter what you do!'" A favourite text of his is the Peckham Experiment coordinators Williamson and Pearce's *Science, Synthesis & Sanity* (1965):

> They talk about the difference between pathology and their new word ethology. And with ethology you're working to keep sickness at bay — and with pathology you're studying and treating how to ameliorate sickness... When I talk to people about that, vis-à-vis my farming, I say I have no interest in palliatives. I only have an interest in how I can grow things so they don't have problems. Correcting the cause rather than treating the symptom.

The self-fed farm

However, it's fair to say that Coleman's thinking has evolved. In his view, J.I. Rodale, who informed the first wave of American organic farmers, didn't get the glorious simplicity of the original organic idea, and placed too much emphasis on inputs. They replaced the NPK model of chemical inputs with purchased organic fertilisers and crushed rock minerals. He thinks that early editions of his *own* book, *The New Organic Grower*, didn't correct this. "I'll admit it allowed us to produce obviously fantastic food. So, the organic-with-inputs worked. But what fascinates me now, is how much better soil fertility I am able to create with growing really serious amounts of green manures and mowing them and tilling them in." In this respect, Coleman's hero today is Edward H. Faulkner, author of *Plowman's Folly* (1943) and *A Second Look* (1947):

> The interesting thing is, all of these people today who are into no-till will often cite Edward Faulkner as the father of the no-till movement, which means that all of these PhDs only read the title of books. They don't read the book, because if you read the goddamn book, he was against the way the [mouldboard] plow buried all the green in an airless pile at the bottom of the furrow. He wasn't against tillage; he was a hundred percent in favour of tillage. In fact, he thought you could create fertility with tillage.

Tillage is one of the hot topics in today's regenerative agriculture. The current orthodoxy of no-till can play into the hands of chemical manufacturers who provide products which kill back unwanted plant growth to prepare the soil for sowing seed. This is a problem tillage has always dealt with without herbicides. In drier climates, where soil structure is even more precarious, Indigenous farming cultures have never tilled very deeply. How deep does Coleman till?

> Four inches is what we aim at. And Faulkner explained, and it was a well-known fact when he explained it, that when organic matter decomposes in the soil, it gives off that stuff that everybody is against these days called CO2. And the carbon dioxide mixes with the soil water right there to create carbonic acid... Faulkner was against heap composting because he wanted the CO2 given off to stay on in the soil. And when you do that, the carbonic acid is extremely effective at etching minerals out of the soil particles, which are nothing but pieces of rock. And so, his theory, and I think I agree with it 100%, is that you could almost farm forever, because every time you've tilled under green matter into the top few inches of the soil, the carbonic acid was creating nutrients for you.

Organic America

In the early 1970s, organic farming in America was in its infancy. The Chinese agriculturalists — who Wisconsin Professor F.H. King studied for his *Farmers of Forty Centuries* — experienced population density and limited land, making sustainable farming essential. The North Americans were different; the seemingly endless vistas of virgin land ripe for farming played a part in deterring interest in care for the soil. The experience of the dust bowl in the 1930s, fictionalised in John Steinbeck's novel *Grapes of Wrath* (1939), was a wake-up call. Sir Albert Howard describes the American situation:

> In 1937 the condition and needs of the agricultural land of the U.S.A. were appraised. No less than 253,000,000 acres, or 61 per cent of the total area under crops, had been either completely or partly destroyed or had lost most of its fertility. Only 161,000,000 acres, or 39 per cent of the cultivated area, could be safely farmed by the present methods.

American writer and conservationist Aldo Leopold's idea of the "land ethic", a responsibility described in his *A Sand County Almanac* (1949), which "enlarges the boundaries of the community to include soils, waters, plants, or collectively: the land," was a notable stirring of American soil consciousness. There had been organic farming in the US before the arrival of chemical agriculture, and there were stubborn farmers who continued to farm in the old ways, ignoring the hype around chemical agriculture. The Amish had always farmed in a way that was effectively organic, and there were examples like the homesteading practiced by Ralph Borsodi and his School of Living in the 1920s. However, even though there were prominent American voices (in King, Faulkner, and English émigré Wickenden), America's most important populariser, J.I. Rodale, looked to Europe, and especially the England of Sir Albert Howard and Lady Eve Balfour, for inspiration. Not surprisingly, thrilled by these legendary personalities, the young Coleman was eager to travel there:

> I went there first time in 1974. And I met [Lady Eve Balfour] and all the European organic types at an organic conference in Paris. And then I was there in '76 and '77 for... the early IFOAM [International Federation of Organic Agriculture Movements] meetings in '76, '77 and '79. I put together tours of European organic farms for American farmers. Nobody was aware that they were so far ahead of us back then.

Bob Rodale, J.I. Rodale's son, went on the tour Coleman organised in 1979 as a fact-finding mission researching the creation of the USDA organic standard. What sound almost like historic events were in fact very homespun. The first was organised when Coleman was still living without electricity out of a log cabin near the road, close enough to have a telephone line reach it. However, Coleman coordinated his affairs largely by airmail letters. He rented three VW buses, capable of seating nine persons per vehicle, and rounded up twenty-seven Americans. Bob Rodale liked to be behind the wheel and so drove one.

Unlike many of her peers in the organic movement, Lady Eve Balfour, the legendary founder of the UK's Soil Association and author of the bestselling *The Living Soil*, was open to the new generation of hippies fascinated by organic growing. Of people we encounter later in this book, Patrick Holden was well-acquainted with Balfour and indeed spoke at her memorial service, and Paul Hawken met and interviewed her on the subject of Findhorn. Eliot Coleman encountered Balfour too. Coleman confided to me that she was a total badass — "She was a piece of work." I pressed him for a story; was she wearing the eye patch?

> She usually had a beret on and everything, but the eye patch was later in life. That didn't come on until the late '80s, I think. But anyway, the Soil Association used to help us and set up meetings, and I can remember a number of times we'd be sitting around a pub in London and there'd be a bunch of the British growers there, and Lady Eve Balfour always used to come to those things and meet the crew I'd brought. And back then you didn't get the upper classes in organic agriculture [in the USA]. You got the hippie leftists... And on one of my tours, one of the people who came along, because he was running an organic gardening programme for people in Denver, Colorado, was a guy who was a veteran of the Abraham Lincoln Brigade [the American volunteers who fought Fascism in Spain]. So, he was a hardcore old-time leftist. He was sitting at the table where I was, and Lady Eve Balfour was moving around the room from table to table, talking to all of us. And she came and sat at our table. And everybody was just blown away by how knowledgeable she was. She really knew what she was talking about. And then, after a while, she got up to go and talk to people at another table. And this hardcore old leftist, who was sitting next

> to me, he turned to me and said, 'Damn,' he said, 'If that's the aristocracy, I think there should be more of them!' He was so impressed. And so was everybody else. She was just incredible.

Of these European jaunts, Damrosch wanted to point out that in that era, as Coleman had said, Europe was way ahead of the US, especially in using the right scale of tools for small farms. "All of his movable greenhouse ideas were influenced by places like France and Holland. And then after about ten years, I would talk to people here about that and they'd say… well, you know that it's really shifted around because now we're really looking to the US for this movement." She credits the Rodale organisation for that evolution. In terms of innovation, Coleman is renowned in gardening circles for devising innovative tools for small-scale production like "the Tilther", which is driven by a battery-powered electric drill, his moveable greenhouses, and for his experiments growing vegetables used to certain latitudes at radically different longitudes. Coleman worked out that, although Maine was a lot colder, as cold as –20 °C in January, because it was on the same latitude of 45° and received the same sunlight as Bordeaux in France and Genoa in Italy, logic dictated that they would be able to grow the same vegetables. Together, he and Damrosch took a trip to Europe following that latitude. This, and especially a visit to the Parisian market garden of Louis Savier, opened the door to an investigation into growing vegetables in the cold.

I put it to Coleman that the idea of growing in the winter has got non-conformism written all over it and asked him why he pursued it so doggedly?

> Because, well, it wasn't impossible to do. I'm surprised nobody had done it before, because there were plenty of unheated greenhouses; nurseries were storing their potted shrubs in over winter, just to keep them alive. And nobody

> thought of actually using them to protect stuff that was growing, that you were going to eat. And it inspired me because when I first started here, we were very successful. We had crowds coming to the farm stand, but every October, I would turn my business over to the Californians... These people are all beautiful. They hang out with movie stars, and they know how to surf. What's not to dislike? But why am I giving them my business? So, we just started trying to go later into the fall, and earlier in the spring.

However, as Damrosch describes, there was a eureka moment: "The way he really discovered it was kind of by accident... he had a greenhouse, and somehow he had a cold frame inside it, and he noticed that stuff was regrowing in there." Coleman elaborates, "It's a greenhouse within a greenhouse. And in my book [*The Winter Harvest Handbook* (2009)] I show the difference between 20 degrees below zero outside... about 8 degrees above zero in the greenhouse, and 25 degrees under the inner layer." And all of the plants they are growing, spinach and carrots and scallions (spring onions), are fine as long as the temperature doesn't go below 25 °C. A surprising benefit emerged: because the temperatures were colder, the vegetables were sweeter.

Many of the countercultural growers and farmers I spoke to had spiritual inclinations. Coleman's benefactor Helen Nearing certainly did. These matters are definitely not everyone's cup of tea. However, I take from the Swiss analytical psychologist Carl Jung the idea that there lies tremendous value in entertaining these concepts. A favourite of the movement, Jung appeared on the cover of the Beatles' *Sgt. Pepper's Lonely Hearts Club Band* (1967) — (note to self: not Walter Evans-Wentz, as I stated in *Retreat*.) As he put it, "We moderns are faced with the necessity of rediscovering the life of the spirit; we must experience it anew for ourselves." Although Coleman is nothing if not intensely grounded and fiercely practical, and is not at all religious in any respect, he does register awe and delight at the beauty of the natural world. On an earlier occasion he told me that

> I often look at some of these things, especially the descriptions of the soil microbiome and how the plant is giving off exudates to stimulate the type of bacteria... providing the nutrients it needs. I tell people that's almost enough to make me believe in God. This is such magical stuff... and the life in the soil... All those little organisms in the soil are in charge and they are actually my livestock and I'm feeding them organic matter... I don't know if you could call that spiritual, but I think it's merely a deep appreciation of the planet we're fortunate enough to live on, and how its systems function.

As I'm heading off to wander around the autumnal Four Season Farm, he adds, "Just the fact that that tiny little seed turns into a cabbage that you can store and eat all winter... I don't need people laying hands on people to have miracles. That's a total miracle and blows my funky mind anyway!"

SELF-SUFFICIENCY

Self-sufficiency in the USA

In his classic book *The Gift of Good Land* (1981) Wendell Berry gives us a thumbnail sketch of what self-sufficiency looks like:

> What is required for the production of this $2,000 to $4,000 worth of subsistence? Well first of all, a vegetable garden... This can be accommodated easily on half an acre of ground... Next in importance, I think, is a milk cow — or, more exactly, what you might call a milk cow economy: the cow for milk, cream, and butter; her calf for beef; a meat hog to consume the surplus of skimmed milk (also kitchen scraps, residues from the garden, etc.). The economic value of one family milk cow, used in this way, is most impressive. (I say one cow, because the value of the second cow will be a great deal less...) Cow and garden, then, would require at most two acres of good ground.

So goes the dream!

Before the total transformation that occurred at the very end of the 1960s, and which ran through the 1970s in the form of the radical back-to-the-land movement, practitioners of self-sufficiency were analogous to beatniks, those countercultural precursor to the hippies. Just as beat visionaries like Allen Ginsberg, Jack Kerouac, and Gary Snyder were the first wave before the flood, so Mildred Loomis, the Nearings, and John Seymour presaged the communal living experiments of the following decade. In this era, self-sufficiency wasn't just a practical economic solution, or even a socialist statement as it had been in the 1930s; there's the sparkle of something transcendental to it.

Henry Thoreau

I'd been advised by the Walden Pond State Reservation that, as Sundays were their busiest days, I should arrive early as "sometimes we have more people that want to come than can actually visit at one time." This spooked me. To fly to Massachusetts and be turned away from Walden Pond seemed unthinkable. I suggested that I might show up at 8am, and was reassured that that was a good time: "No one is here yet."

And so it was that on a cool, damp, late September morning I took the Pond Path for half a mile around Walden Pond to the site of Thoreau's hut. I was entirely alone apart from some chipmunks, a red squirrel, and — in the clear pond, in the distance — a swimmer or two. At the site of the cabin, marked out by granite posts connected by a chain, there is a cairn on which visitors have left stones to mark their pilgrimage. For coming to Walden is a pilgrimage. If there is a symbolic moment in Western history when we can pinpoint a fork in the road in the inexorable march towards technological materialism, this is it.

The tiny house that Henry Thoreau (1817–1862) built by the pond in 1845 would have been surrounded by sparse vegetation and would not have been amongst such tall trees as it is today. It would have even further lessened the impression that the cabin was in the wilderness. This was most definitely not isolated countryside, situated as it is, not far from the notable town of Concord. Thoreau's biographer Laura Dassow Walls, whom we will follow here, clarifies that:

> Thoreau is often said to have turned to 'Nature,' but what he actually turned to was, more exactly, the 'commons' — spaces back then, were still open to everyone; woods, fields, hilltops, ponds and blueberry thickets, rivers, meadows,

trails up nearby mountains, the long open beaches on the Atlantic shore.

The countryside around Concord had drastically changed since the arrival of the English. Wild animals such as cougars, bears, moose, deer, porcupine, wolves, and beavers had all gone by 1855. By this time, traditional subsistence farms nearby were failing and being wiped out by the global marketplace.

I took the opportunity to walk behind the site to the train tracks where an MBTA commuter train, #1706D, sailed past me, blowing its horn. When I visited the Walden Museum, the attendant there assured me that, yes, the tracks were there in Thoreau's day. Dassow points out that "by the time he left Walden, at least twenty passenger and freight trains screeched past his house daily." Thoreau's contemporary in Concord, Ralph Waldo Emerson, believed that the arrival of the railroad in 1844 changed everything. At once, many local farms were broken up and sold as house lots. It was Emerson who had purchased fourteen acres on the shore of Walden Pond and encouraged Thoreau to "build yourself a hut, & there begin the grand process of devouring yourself alive".

Thoreau's early life

The March day when Thoreau borrowed an axe and strode into the woods was preceded by a series of events, some remarkable, others small but resonant, which together shaped his unique personality. As a child, on his mother's instruction, Thoreau planted a potato which had sprouted in her kitchen garden. It grew a crop which was "dug by myself and yielded a dinner for the family". In 1841, Henry's brother, John Thoreau, died from a shaving injury to his finger. The wound, it's believed, incubated tetanus bacteria from animal droppings in manure, which as part of John's daily chores he would have been exposed to.

An exacting student of the Bible, Thoreau's interest spilled beyond it into research into the scriptures of other major religions — Hinduism, Islam, and Buddhism — in his search for spiritual truth. In 1854, an English traveller, Thomas Cholmondeley, boarded in his mother's house. Striking up a friendship, the following year he sent Thoreau forty-four volumes of the sacred texts of India's Vedic tradition. You can still see some of these books at the Concord Museum, where they keep Thoreau's actual desk and bed.

In 1844, while camping along the Concord River, Thoreau's fire where he was cooking fish caught the grass. The grass being tinder-dry after a spectacularly warm and rain-free April, the blaze quickly raced out of control. Thoreau frantically tried to get local farmers to help put it out, but recounted six years later, "What could I do alone against a front of flame half a mile wide?" The newspaper at the time said three hundred acres were burned and set the financial loss at an exorbitant $2,000; Thoreau's own estimate was a hundred acres or more. The local people were enraged, calling him "a damned rascal", and for years afterwards they would taunt and shout "Burnt Woods" behind his back. Thoreau at once reflected on his "shame and regret", but simultaneously thought that this process was a natural one: "I have set fire to the forest — but I have done no wrong therein — & now it is as if the lightning had done it..." His biographer Walls reflects, "From that day forward, Thoreau knew a truth few others fully understand: human beings are not separate from nature but fully involved in natural cycles..." Beyond this awareness of the Anthropocene, we can see how the experience both separated him from the community and reinforced within him a defiant attitude towards social norms.

This defiance was born out in his famous incarceration. Towards the end of July 1846, the subject of Thoreau's refusal to pay the yearly dollar-and-a-half poll tax levied on every man from the age of twenty upwards came to light. He'd avoided paying this since 1842. The local tax collector, Sam Staples, even offered to pay it for him, but Thoreau asked him not to because, as he had told Staples many times before, "he didn't believe in it and shouldn't pay". Staples therefore had no choice but to accompany him to jail. Once there, later in the evening, he realised the implications of society's coercive power, "the State in which I lived". This experience formed the basis of Thoreau's book *Civil Disobedience* (1849), an influence upon Leo Tolstoy, Mahatma Gandhi and Martin Luther King Jr, and which principles ennobled him with a generation of young people facing the Vietnam War draft, just as they were enchanted by *Walden* (1854). At some point that same evening, someone, scholars believe it was his Aunt Maria, paid Staples the necessary sum, and Thoreau was released the following morning. In his own words, he was annoyed that "some one interfered and paid that tax". However, he'd seen the same happen to others when a family member stepped in. Thoreau seemed to have an uncanny knack for grasping the symbolic power of gestures, and this very slight event has come through in his writing — just as his two years, two months, and two days at Walden Pond did, both elevated to iconic stature.

Thoreau at Walden

Not only close to a town, Walden had also been frequented for a century by hunters, fishermen, swimmers, boys, people looking for firewood, and the other residents of the woods, of whom a number were former slaves. Indeed, reliable witnesses described escaping slaves being brought to the house for Thoreau to look after until dark, when he would escort them to a safe shelter. Walden woods was one of the two places around Concord where the poverty-stricken and forsaken were able to locate. It was a relatively busy place, and Thoreau, a young man aged twenty-eight, would have been the subject of a lot of attention and many opportunities to explain his ideas. His bean field was visible from the main road:

> It was the only open and cultivated field for a great distance on either side of the road, so they made the most of it; and sometimes the man in the field [Thoreau himself] heard

> more of travelers' gossip and comment than was meant for his ear: 'Beans so late! peas so late!' — for I continued to plant when others had begun to hoe...

Popping home for dinners and to get his laundry done have laid him open to the charge of hypocrisy — but mostly the mechanics of his life were extremely simple. He had no toilet, cooked in a hole in the ground, and baked dough made from lake water and flour on a stone beside it. When later he installed a stove, the sum total of his kitchen equipment was a kettle, two pans, jugs for oil and molasses, three plates, two knives, two forks, one spoon, and a cup. Famously, he owned three chairs, "one for solitude, two for friendship, three for society".

Indian philosophy played an important part in the fantasy. In June 1845, when he was living by the pond, the Bhagavad-Gita arrived in Concord. Fascinated by it, the summer he was jailed he copied into his notebook: "He cannot be a Yogee, who, in his actions, hath not abandoned all intentions." As the New England ice industry harvested from the pond for delivery to India, he reflects of the process:

> In the morning I bathe my intellect in the stupendous and cosmogonal philosophy of the Bhagvat-Geeta... I lay down the book and go to my well for water, and lo! there I meet the servant of the Bramin, priest of Brahma and Vishnu and Indra, who still sits in his temple on the Ganges reading the Vedas, or dwells at the root of a tree with his crust and water jug. I meet his servant come to draw water for his master, and our buckets as it were grate together in the same well. The pure Walden water is mingled with the sacred water of the Ganges.

Thoreau's farming

Absolutely central to the legend of Thoreau at Walden is his growing there. It was not promising land. "One farmer said that it was 'good for nothing but to raise cheeping squirrels on.'" He writes, "Before I finished my house, wishing to earn ten or twelve dollars by some honest and agreeable method, in order to meet my unusual expenses, I planted about two acres and a half of light and sandy soil near it chiefly with beans, but also a small part with potatoes, corn, peas, and turnips."

In fact, Thoreau did not plan to subsist on his beans. "Not that I wanted beans to eat, for I am by nature a Pythagorean, so far as beans are concerned, whether they mean porridge or voting, and exchanged them for rice." The first year, Thoreau hired a man with an ox and plough to prepare the land, but held the plough himself. Afterwards, he did not spread manure, "not being the owner, but merely a squatter, and not expecting to cultivate so much again" — in other words, because he saw no need to care for its future productivity. Altogether he grew "twelve bushels of beans, and eighteen bushels of potatoes, beside some peas and sweet corn. The yellow corn and turnips were too late to come to anything." Thoreau details the farm's outgoings and revealed a profit of $8.71. That doesn't sound great, but he reassures us,

> All things considered, that is, considering the importance of a man's soul and of today, notwithstanding the short time occupied by my experiment, nay, partly even because of its transient character, I believe that that was doing better than any farmer in Concord did that year." Even though "Mine was, as it were, the connecting link between wild and cultivated fields...

However, during the process the penny drops for Thoreau regarding the possibilities inherent in self-sufficiency; that's to say, if he grew what he actually planned to eat rather than sell it as he did,

> if one would live simply and eat only the crop which he raised, and raise no more than he ate, and not exchange it for an insufficient quantity of more luxurious and expensive

> things, he would need to cultivate only a few rods of ground, and that it would be cheaper to spade up that than to use oxen to plow it, and to select a fresh spot from time to time than to manure the old, and he could do all his necessary farm work as it were with his left hand at odd hours in the summer...

Thoreau grew quite a lot of beans this first year: "My beans, the length of whose rows, added together, was seven miles already planted". The process delighted him:

> I came to love my rows, my beans, though so many more than I wanted. They attached me to the earth, and so I got strength like Antaeus. But why should I raise them? Only Heaven knows. This was my curious labor all summer — to make this portion of the earth's surface, which had yielded only cinquefoil, blackberries, johnswort, and the like, before, sweet wild fruits and pleasant flowers, produce instead this pulse.

He busied himself:

> Removing the weeds, putting fresh soil about the bean stems, and encouraging this weed which I had sown, making the yellow soil express its summer thought in bean leaves and blossoms rather than in wormwood and piper and millet grass, making the earth say beans instead of grass — this was my daily work.

He distilled what he learnt of the experience:

> This is the result of my experience in raising beans: Plant the common small white bush bean about the first of June, in rows three feet by eighteen inches apart, being careful to select fresh round and unmixed seed. First look out for worms [by which he means pests], and supply vacancies by planting anew. Then look out for woodchucks, if it is an

> exposed place, for they will nibble off the earliest tender leaves almost clean as they go; and again, when the young tendrils make their appearance, they have notice of it, and will shear them off with both buds and young pods, sitting erect like a squirrel. But above all harvest as early as possible, if you would escape frosts and have a fair and salable crop; you may save much loss by this means.

This last bit of advice was hard won because, the following year, a hard frost on 12 June killed everything that he had planted: beans, tomatoes, squash, corn, and potatoes. In September 1847, Thoreau loaded up his books and furniture and left the house. He was answering a request to keep Lidian Emerson company while her husband Ralph toured Europe on the back of interest in transcendentalism. Emerson, who owned the land, bought Thoreau's cabin, and leased it to his gardener. Thus, came to a close this tiny, simple event which has become so pregnant with symbolism.

Thoreau and the hippies

Thoreau comes up again and again in the literature. Self-sufficiency guru John Seymour jokes, "Thoreau did nothing most of the day but just sit around and think. He did not require much food. If I were a bachelor, I should want to do just that. I think that his was the perfect mode of existence — for a bachelor."

Scott Nearing and his wife, Helen, the most famous homesteaders in the US, and who regard Thoreau as their most important role model, make a habit of quoting him: "Thoreau said on cutting one's own fuel: 'It warms us twice, and the first warmth is the most wholesome and memorable...'" and "Shall we forever resign the pleasure of construction to the carpenter?"

Back-to-the-land hippie Raymond Mungo, author of the commune classic *Total Loss Farm* (1970), "botches up"

Thoreau's itinerary in North America; he writes, "'Stay home,' Henry again, 'and see the world.'" Writing in *The Whole Earth Catalog*, Stewart Brand recommends the latest cheap edition of *Walden*: "This edition is the one, I believe, that Thoreau would have bought. It costs sixty cents. The prime document of America's 3rd revolution, now in progress."

Ralph Borsodi, Mildred Loomis, and the School of Living

Self-sufficiency has a long and rich history in the United States. Its roots are documented in books like David Shi's *The Simple Life: Plain Living and High Thinking in American Culture* (1985). As much as there are precedents to the hippie urban exodus and their aspirations to farm, the historian Dona Brown points out with regard to Thoreau that, prior to the hippies, earlier generations of back-to-the-landers rarely made any use of his example: "One can search in vain among those texts for even a mention of his name". As tempting as it is to look for historical continuities, as much as the results might appear to be similar, there seems to be a fundamental difference between the aims of earlier movements and that of the hippies. In *Back to the Land* (2011), Brown remarks,

> Though it is natural to view earlier back-to-the-landers through the lens of the 1970s, I have found that it can be misleading. Ever since the 1970s, to be sure, back-to-the-landers have expressed a profound attachment to the natural world, along with a commitment to environmentalism. Earlier back-to-the-landers, however, generally articulated different priorities... In fact, earlier literature dwelt comparatively little on the joys of rural life and a great deal more on the rising cost of food, job insecurity, and the desire for independent work.

A precious few earlier examples were drawn on by the hippie generation. The School of Living is one which passed the acid test. Its father, Ralph Borsodi (1888–1977), began as a marketing consultant to large companies. In spite of his success in this field, Borsodi was dissatisfied. He didn't like his family's crowded neighbourhood, the precariousness of renting, monotonous commuting, his work helping his clients sell more material goods, and the widespread growth of consumerism. The Borsodi family's domestic life was also troubled: the children suffered from constant colds, and his wife struggled with anaemia. A friend, Hereward Carrington, turned Borsodi onto literature with novel ideas of nutrition, which resulted in the family changing their diet. Then, in 1919, they bought a rundown seven-acre property in Rockland County at the southernmost tip of the state of New York. With no prior experience, Borsodi repaired and remodelled the house. Borsodi's partner in the School of Living, Mildred Loomis (1905–2000), describes in the collection of her writings *Decentralism* (2021) how the Borsodis "gardened, produced and preserved food, and were delighted at the reduction of cash needed for their food budget".

Their ambitions growing, and convinced of the economic efficiency of their new lifestyle, the Borsodis built on sixteen wooded acres their new Dogwoods Homestead, including outbuildings for chickens, two goats and a pig, and a pair of stone cottages for their sons. This became Borsodi's "homestead laboratory", from which he wrote America's first full critique of modern industrialism, *This Ugly Civilization*, in 1929. In the book, Borsodi laid out the processes of the homestead. in his essay in *Decentralism* (2023), Loomis summarises:

> They made organic compost by layering vegetable and animal waste, kitchen refuse and good earth. They tilled the resulting humus, full of living bacteria into their soil. They planted and harvested green beans, peas, corn, tomatoes, carrots, potatoes, squash and pumpkins. They cared for

> a small flock of chickens and two goats. They pruned old grape vines, berry canes, aging apple and pear trees. They were rewarded with bushels of fruit, although not always of the first grade. 'It is better to find a worm [pest] now and then, than to spray with chemicals.'

Borsodi's subsequent book, *Flight from the City* (1933), was, like Helen and Scott Nearing's *Living the Good Life* (1954), successfully reissued to the back-to-the-land audience as a paperback in the early 1970s. Ralph Borsodi writes in the 1972 edition's introduction, "Perhaps the human animal will wake up before it is too late. Perhaps the fact that so large a number of young people are repudiating what the establishment is offering them is a hopeful sign of the times." Both books feature a preface by darling of the counterculture, and *Gestalt Therapy* (1951) co-author, Paul Goodman. Goodman writes in his preface, "There is a rich irony in the re-issuing of this book at the present time. To many young people, the Borsodis must seem to have been the squarest of the square, and yet *Flight from the City* has become part of the hippie counter culture."

Borsodi subsequently founded the School of Living in 1936. In Suffern, New York, he and friends bought forty acres of land, called their community Bayard Lane, and set to holding seminars and informal lectures based upon Borsodi's ideas. When the Second World War broke out, Mildred Loomis — formerly a teacher and a social worker — and her husband John moved to Brookville Ohio, where they lived entirely off the land, keeping their income below taxable level and producing up to 95% of their food. From that time, Loomis herself carried on the educational activities of the School of Living out of the Heathcote Community in Maryland and published a magazine called *The Green Revolution*. Even John Seymour in Wales, the British Self-sufficiency guru whom we meet later in the book, was aware of this. He writes,

> Way back in 1960 I found that there were a lot of people living like us in the United States, and that they even published a paper: *The Green Revolution* (nothing to do with that other upstart, 'green revolution' which consists of breeding wheat and rice that would grow large yields if fed with even larger quantities of scarce nitrogenous fertilizer).

Although she continued to spread Borsodi's ideas, his "17 Major Problems of Living", arguing that economic democracy depended upon a widespread return to self-sufficient homesteading, the parting of ways was probably for the best. Countercultural historian Jonathan A. Bowdler expresses alarm that Borsodi, who had like many intellectuals in the 1920s supported the ideas of eugenics — the belief in the refinement of human genetics — continued to advocate for it after the Second World War, despite the Nazi atrocities of the holocaust, when more perceptive thinkers abandoned it. Bowdler claims that Borsodi's list of undesirables, "the paupers and dependents, the hemophiliacs and other bearers of hereditary handicaps, the criminals, the prostitutes and perverts, and the irresponsible pursuers of pleasure (even from the good families)", was racially coded.

Loomis has been referred to as the "grandmother of the counterculture" which reputation rested on her embrace of the younger generation. Richard Fairfield, the most important then contemporary chronicler of the alternative communes of the 1960s and '70s, his work being published in the journal *The Modern Utopian*, established an early connection to Loomis which evolved into a collaboration. Fairfield, writing at the time, described her as "being sensitive to the new community movement emerging in the '60s. She has been sympathetic and encouraging to the young dropouts and hippies, seeing in the young the only hope for a rural revival toward which she has so fervently worked all her life."

In an essay in *Decentralism*, Loomis writes of the oil shocks of the day and relates them to their movement's preoccupations:

"In the 1970s, people everywhere awoke to an energy crisis — to the fact that all are earthbound creatures, 'that we live fully only as we keep wholesome reciprocal contact with the soil.'" As we know, it was Borsodi's library which turned J.I. Rodale onto the ideas of Sir Albert Howard. The importance of healthy soil and organically grown food is at the centre of the healthy life that the School of Living advocated.

The Nearings

Staying in Harborside, Maine, next-door to Eliot Coleman's Four Season Farm, after paddling at noon in the freezing water of Ames Cove, I wandered over in the warm sunshine to Scott and Helen Nearings' final house of Forest Farm. Forest Farm is home to the Good Life Center, a trust established by Helen Nearing, which serves as a distributor for the Nearings' publications and a venue for talks and workshops. I was very grateful to be shown around by the then current resident stewards, Ron and Susan Corl. Thinkers, they have been living self-sufficiently for twenty years and build tiny houses.

In as decent a summary as we are liable to find, Helen and Scott Nearing are described on the Good Life Center website as "pioneers of American socialism, as revolutionaries, as enemies of social injustice, and as godparents of the sustainable living and organic agriculture movement". Not as widely known outside of North America — in the UK, John Seymour sits upon the throne of self-sufficiency — within the United States, their story is fundamental.

Visiting Forest Farm was a long-cherished ambition of mine. Ron guided me around the stone-built house, their small lean-to greenhouse, and the exquisitely kept, walled vegetable garden. There, Ron pointed to a lone "volunteer" sunflower and explained he had let it grow because it was Helen's favourite plant. Then we walked up, through a wood, to the hilltop and the Nearings' previous residence next-door, a wooden house now owned by Ned Reynolds, who, with his dog Scout, showed us around the grounds. In the Nearings' shared library, with its huge window looking out over Penobscot Bay, Susan showed me treasures like a copy of *Alice's Adventures in Wonderland* dedicated to Helen by Krishnamurti in 1921 with the inscriptio, "Curiouser and curiouser!", and a copy of Ruth Stout's gardening classic *How to have a Green Thumb without an Aching Back* (1955), dedicated "For Scott, who helped me make my garden grow, When I was ignorant and didn't know..." There's a whole wall of Helen's spiritualist books built around a plinth resplendent with Theosophical symbols and the text "There is no Religion Higher Than Truth", and a shelf of her books on UFOs.

Scott Nearing

Born to a relatively wealthy family in Pennsylvania in 1883, Scott Nearing followed a path into academia. Nearing was dismissed from Wharton School of Economics at the University of Pennsylvania for openly condemning the conditions created by industrial capitalism. Then he was fired from the University of Toledo as a traitor for pacifist speeches against America joining the First World War. He was indicted under the Espionage Act by a federal grand jury on charges of insubordination, disloyalty, mutiny, and encouraging resistance to the First World War draft. To top this all off, Nearing — who is interviewed in Warren Beatty's movie *Reds* (1981) — after publishing a critique of Vladimir Lenin in 1930, was expelled from the Communist Party.

Nearing has attracted controversy for his views on eugenics. These are explored in his book *The Super Race* (1912). The context of eugenics was for Nearing, like for Luther Burbank (1849–1926), the world of plants. He writes, "Modern society is a garden of which the products are men and women. The sowing, weeding, cultivating — carried forward through social institutions — determines by its character whether the race shall decay, as other races have done, or progress toward the Super Man." In his doctoral thesis, *The Countercultural Back-*

to-the-Land Movement, the academic Jonathon A. Bowdler accuses Nearing of taking the position that "more Americans of western European descent needed to be encouraged to go back to the land in order to create an American super race" — this does carry with it the interesting subtext that a component of the countercultural back-to-the-land impulse was a kind of "White flight". This was the exodus starting in America in the 1950s and '60s whereby Whites abandoned the inner cities, leaving areas that were more racially diverse, for the suburbs. Unlike Ralph Borsodi, who failed to adjust to the intellectual landscape after Nazism, eugenics had disappeared from Nearing's writing by his 1960s works.

Just as Thoreau attracted the counterculture with both *Walden* and *Civil Disobedience*, Nearing's *The Conscience of a Radical* (1965), a riposte to works like Barry Goldwater's *The Conscience of a Conservative* (1960), was a hit among the New Left. As a result of his radical ideas, Nearing never stopped being snooped on by the state. Comically, he was under surveillance by the Harborside Post Office in Maine. Its proprietor, Dorothy Crockett, was set up and installed with the explicit purpose of monitoring the Nearings' mail — the evidence, in an only partially redacted 794-page file, was acquired by their neighbour Jean Hay Bright after the Nearings' death through a freedom of information request from the FBI.

Nearing had some experience with farming and building with stone from when, between 1908 and 1915, he lived at the Arden community in Delaware, founded by social reformers in 1900, incorporating the principles of Henry George's Single Tax and William Morris's Arts and Crafts philosophy. Any kind of academic career he might have had was in tatters. In the deepest part of the Great Depression, in 1932, he moved his young second wife, Helen Knothe, from New York City to a farm in the Green Mountains of Vermont. There, he suggested the couple "could at least grow our own food".

Helen Nearing

Helen Knothe was born in 1904, was twenty-one years younger than her husband Scott, and grew up a vegetarian in a family of Theosophists. In *Loving and Leaving the Good Life* (1992), she describes Theosophy as

> not a religion; it is described as a universal brotherhood without distinction of race, color, sex, caste, or creed. It purports to be the ancient wisdom, the philosophy that underlies all religions. It integrates the esoteric aspects of Buddhism, Hinduism, Mohammedanism, Judaism, and Christianity — all religions being paths to the truth and no one religion containing the whole.

The Knothes kept a large garden from which the family was provided with "fresh, organic, wholesome food". Knothe describes how, as a child, she kept teddy bears, not dolls, and preferred to canoe on the lake while other girls "frolicked and socialized".

Leaving America for Europe in 1921, she was brought to an international Theosophical convention in Paris and introduced to the president, the Englishwoman Annie Besant, and from a box overlooking the stage, watched the young Jiddu Krishnamurti, who was being promoted by the organisation as the World Teacher-Elect. Of their eventual relationship, she says it was "passionate and compelling and professed to be eternal. It lasted, full of protestations of undying devotion, for half a dozen years, then sank into cool acquaintance, finally to nonrecognition." The young Krishnamurti sent her letters, some of them as long as twelve pages.

In 1923, she was persuaded every evening through the summer to assist as he was "undergoing intense spiritual ordeals involving his physical body as well as his psyche", she would be called into the house by his brother to find him "sometimes unconscious, sometimes moaning and groaning, with apparently intense pains in his spine and head". Krishnamurti volunteered that "it must be the kundalini energy coiled up like a serpent at the base of his spine, which burns its way to the top of the head". However, following the death of his brother Nitya in 1925 from influenza after tuberculosis, Krishnamurti became "older, colder, more restrained". Helen was never sure why he lost interest in her and severed connections, reflecting sadly that (although a very gifted, concert-level violinist) she had "no magnificent talent, no overwhelming beauty or distinction, no great intellect, no fame, no monetary contribution to make". While he, on the other hand was a "star performer" whose life was orchestrated by the famous and well-to-do. Visiting India on her own many years later, she was able to book an appointment to see Krishnamurti after a lecture he was giving in Madras. She waited amongst half a dozen other appointees before being ushered in and greeted formally, "How do you do?" She remarked that "the conversation was trivial and soon my allotted time was up".

She had encountered Scott before, but the second time they met, in 1928, he was at the nadir of his previously brilliant career. Expelled from academia, she describes him then as a "social leper, alone and outcast even from his family". Falling under his influence, she worked the winter of 1928–29 at various factories, a paper mill, a box factory, and as a candy packer. When he invited her by cable to join and help him work on his book *War* (1931), she "quit suitors and the high life, cut off my long hair, distributed my best clothes and fancy jewelry and fancy belongings to girlfriends, and made ready to go". Her parents, in Holland at the time, who had hoped for an "advantageous marriage", were not best pleased as she headed to Vermont with a much older man. However, the break from her privileged upbringing was not total, and she writes that in 1933, "a former Dutch suitor of mine died and left me a small legacy".

The Nearings in Vermont

Their life and work together in Vermont are chronicled in the brilliant and cranky *Living the Good Life* (1954). Upon its first release it was self-published, but Schocken books republished it in 1970 with an introduction by Paul Goodman; just as Goodman would provide one later for Ralph Borsodi's aforementioned *Flight from the City*. It became a hit. Selling fifty thousand copies in its first year, it would go on to sell 170,000 copies and be translated into five languages. It is, apparently, still on the curriculum in South Korea, from where tourists still come to visit the Good Life Center. In 1995, the *New York Times* described it as a "modern day *Walden*". Writing together in *Living the Good Life* they state, "The society from which we moved had rejected in practice and in principle our pacifism, our vegetarianism, and our collectivism." They claimed to be turning their back on the world of money. "Farmers and home owners by the thousands lost everything they had during the Great Depression because they could not meet interest payments. We decided to buy for cash or not at all." As they put it, "We considered dry wood under cover better than money in the bank."

Because of their many connections, the Nearings, even before the crowds who would descend upon them in Maine, would have many visitors. But as they point out, "Most of them were in for a shock. No coffee, no cereal, no bacon, no eggs, no toast, no pancakes or maple syrup. Just apples, sunflower seeds, and a black molasses drink. Such a fare sent many a traveler on his way soon enough." They stuck with this ascetic lifestyle to the end of their long lives. Helen describes it in her book *Loving and Leaving the Good Life*:

> Here are some factors for health and a long life which we have put into practice: positive, optimistic thinking; a good conscience; outdoor exercise and deep breathing; no smoking; no alcohol or drugs, including coffee and tea; a simple diet — vegetarian, sugar-free, salt-free, low in

calories and fat and 55% raw. These will vitalize the life span. Avoid medicines, doctors, hospitals.

Nearings growing in the cold

Vermont is cold, and especially so where the Nearings had moved, which had an elevation of 1,800 feet above sea-level, was in a valley surrounded by mountains, and had a frost-free growing-season of only eighty-five days a year. They write:

> We knew our climatic limitations. If we were careful, there would be a chance for tender vegetables such as squash and tomatoes to grow and mature. Hardier crops like potatoes, beets and carrots surely would get by. Apple trees would survive most winters. Plum and pear trees might frequently freeze. Cherries and peaches were out of the picture. The trees that did survive would bear fruit perhaps two or three years out of five, because late frost might catch the blossoms. Among the nut trees only beechnuts and hazels could be counted on, and they bore crops, about one year in three. Our food raising, if food raising we did, must be concentrated in a brief period of each year and even then we would be compelled to pick our vegetables with care.

They describe at least two occasions when the thermometer touched 25 °F below zero (equivalent to –31 °C).

Coping with this extreme climate took careful planning: "After the snows, when the gardens were white and frozen, we turned to our vegetable cellars with their winter roots, cabbages, winter squash, potatoes, beets, carrots, turnips, onions, rutabagas, celery root, parsley root and pears and apples." About 1 July, they removed the summer vegetables and planted the hardy frost-free plants: beets, endive, Chinese cabbage, kale, and collards. They extended their growing season by means of a small sun-heated greenhouse in which they wintered many plants and started others for spring planting: "We continued to eat this lettuce until January 5th... We had not dreamed that lettuce would last so long in an unheated greenhouse under sub-zero weather conditions." In the "Organic" chapter the reader has met their neighbour, Eliot Coleman, "who maintained an organic market garden next-door to us for several years". Coleman took these techniques of growing in the cold to the next level.

Another crop which is ready early in the season, between February and April, is maple syrup. Helen had the idea to package and market the maple syrup they were harvesting from their trees. They sold it in the pages of the *Free America* magazine in the 1940s for a decent profit, allegedly covering the costs of seeds, taxes, and garden expenses. On the back of this enterprise, the first book they wrote together was *The Maple Sugar Book* (1950). This explains their process. In it, they comment that "our experience has convinced us that maple production is one of the means of family and household rehabilitation. It offers occupational variety and a modest source of cash income." The book also contained their own brand of insight: "The average urbanite is like any ant in any anthill — a helpless creature of circumstances set up by landlord, merchant, factory owner and banker."

Nearings on the soil

The Nearings arrived in Vermont with their land in a state: "The farmers who had preceded us in the valley had... left the unprotected soil to the mercy of sudden showers, driving rains, melting snows and high winds. Consequently, most of the top soil had been swept off the hills and a good deal of it flushed down the West River and the Connecticut into the sea." But there were options available to them: "Must we turn our depleted soils back into forest and wait thousands of years until they are restored to wholeness? Certainly not. We can build whole, living, balanced soil by composting."

And the couple were hardcore composters, stating that

> our compost making followed the general lines laid down by Albert Howard in his *An Agricultural Testament* and *The Soil and Health*. By Ehrenfried Pfeiffer in *Bio-Dynamic Farming and Gardening* and *Soil Fertility, Renewal and Preservation*, by Eve Balfour in *The Living Soil*, and by J.I. Rodale in *Pay Dirt* and *The Organic Front*. We modified their patterns somewhat to meet our particular needs.

They relate the details as follows:

> In our early experiments with compost making, we used animal residues — chiefly manure. Later we changed our practices and made compost as it is made in the forest, with the products of vegetation. We supplemented this vegetation, much of which came from depleted soils, with ground limestone, ground phosphate rock, ground potash rock, marl, or colloidal earth.

Like many before and after them, they say, "we regard the untouched forest floor as the most extensive and most successful experiment in mulching."

In the magical Bullfrog Films documentary *Living the Good Life* (1977), talking in Maine, Scott explains their refusal to use animal residues:

> We take no animal residues. No bone meal. No tankage. No dried blood. None of these things. Because as vegetarians we're against the slaughter business and we don't want to participate in it. As a matter of fact, we've been here twenty-four years on this place and no animal residues have been used on the place during those twenty-four years.

Later in the same film, and together with Helen he goes on:

> Scott: The important thing for you is to live a good life yourself, and living a good life, a part of living a good life, is

learning to live with other creatures who are also inhabiting the planet at the same time that we are. Not exploiting them, not using them, not overriding them.

Helen: Not preying on them.

Scott: Not preying on them, not eating them, not enslaving them, of course.

Helen: And not being slaves to them.

Moving from Vermont

Ultimately, the Nearings grew increasingly bitter in Vermont. They were frustrated that their neighbours weren't interested in their collectivist endeavours, finding them, as they put it, too "sovereign". After having lived there for fifteen years, paper interests started to cut the forests to make way for development. The Stratton wilderness disappeared, and in its place came the Stratton ski slopes. They complain, "We were not happy in surroundings that were becoming a center for trivial activities and purposeless living".

Helen, a water diviner, is described as being able "to sense vibrations more diverse than those reported by the five senses". They put her to task to find them a new location. They explain how in *Continuing the Good Life* (1979):

> Taking a detailed map of Maine, Helen went back and forth fixing her mind on the kind of place that we wanted and asking the pendulum to indicate that place. Consistently the pendulum circled the Penobscot area, at the head of the bay. We set aside a week, crossed the 350 miles that separated Jamaica, Vermont, from Penobscot Bay, Maine, and began our search by visiting two organic gardeners, who lived very close to the point on the map indicated by Helen's pendulum.

The Nearings in Maine

By the time they were living in Maine, the Nearings had somehow settled into their stride. They had the whole self-sufficiency thing down pat. They describe in *Continuing the Good Life*:

> We produce 85 per cent of our food and all our fuel, except gasoline for the car. We must pay cash for spare parts, replacements, hardware. We pay our rent when we pay local taxes. Some of our clothes we make, some we buy in thrift shops and at rummage sales; a few clothes we buy new. We use and buy no habit-forming drugs, including alcohol, tobacco and caffeine. Our supply of printed matter, postage and stationery comes to us via our Social Science Institute, to which organization we hand over all royalties and lecture fees. Our travel expenses are paid by those who ask us to talk. Surrounded as we are by a cash-credit economy, we need a certain amount of cash income each year.

This cash income was provided in Vermont by maple syrup. In Maine, the idea was to sell their blueberries.

Scott continued to express a passionate concern for the soil. In the *Living the Good Life* documentary, he is filmed lecturing a crowd of what mainly looks like hippies in the vegetable garden:

> We're trying to build up the soil, not to wear it down. And the way to build it up is to get every smidge of material that you can get your hands on, and put it back into the soil. The Chinese do this, they do it in other parts of Asia. They've been doing this, Professor King said, for 4,000 years, and their soil remains good, viable, productive, soil. And we've been here in this country for only 250 years. I mean, we White Western Europeans, and we've lost about 40% of our topsoil during that time. It runs down the Penobscot River,

> and the Hudson River, the Mississippi River, into the ocean. And every time you let the water run across the land and come out, yellow and murky, and full of silt, full of compost, full of humus, every time you do that, you're impoverishing the soil. It doesn't make any difference what your bank account is, if you don't have topsoil, you can't raise wheat and onions.

And as he goes on, they don't plough: "This ground here was ploughed in 1952. And it hasn't been ploughed or harrowed since. It's been worked a little with hand tools."

The Nearings and the hippies

As Paul Goodman writes in his 1970 preface for *Living the Good Life*, "the eccentric ideas of the Nearings and others are no longer out in left field". Goodman says that "the disgrace of the cities and the degeneration of the high technological culture have been such that just to survive and maintain one's personal integrity has become for the hippies a life's work." The book, he believed, best functioned as a guide: "What the young can get from this book is know-how. They are, understandably, inept farmers; the Nearings are, famously, superb farmers." In a 1971 article, "The Weavers of Maine" reissued in the excellent *The Modern Utopian* (2010), we can see this education happening before our eyes:

> During their first few autumns in Maine, the Weavers spent long hard hours canning all their vegetables, apples and peaches. Someone finally bought them one of Scott Nearing's books about living off the land and they began to learn about storing cabbages, carrots and parsnips in leaves and sand in the root cellar.

The Nearings themselves were not exactly enchanted by the younger generation and were confused by their motives. By the 1970s, the number of visitors ranged between 2,000 and 2,500 in the course of a year. It often reached dozens in a day:

> Hundreds of people came to see us and our farm in Vermont. The thousands of young people who now come to our farm in Maine are the same type of seekers... Increasingly they are turning their backs on a world community that has tolerated war and is preparing for the contingency of one in the future. They are ardently in favour of peace in a broad sense but are not ready to accept a commitment to any organization that works collectively for the cause. Almost universally they favor 'freedom': that is, the pursuit of their personal goals and fancies. They are not joiners and generally not members of any group more specific than is implied by the adoption of a specific diet or the practice of some yoga exercises... Never before in our lives have we met so many unattached, uncommitted, insecure, uncertain human beings.

Goodman tries to offer some insight:

> What did these people want? They describe with dry humor their methods of coping with the attractive plague. But to the hippie farmers in the present historical dispensation, this gathering of the tribe is the whole point, the proof and the fruition. It is the counterculture. Like the old monasteries, the little farms are way stations on pilgrimages, and they provide havens for runaway kids that are far better than Haight-Ashbury or the East Village.

As their neighbour Jean Hay Bright put it in her book *Meanwhile, Next Door to the Good Life* (2003), "After *Living the Good Life* was reissued, the Nearings suddenly became cult figures. Spontaneously and mysteriously, the Nearing homestead at Harborside became part of The Tour, one stop on a national, and sometimes international, pilgrimage to find one's soul."

Eventually, they had to restrict visiting hours to between three and five in the afternoon only. But there was, certainly with Helen, empathy. She describes her parents, Theosophists, as the "flower children" of their time. "We would like to take every opportunity to help young people in their serious search for a lifestyle that would make sense to them. All are possible recruits for a general effort now under way to stabilize and improve man's earthly living space." In a series of incredible acts of generosity, at phenomenally low prices, they sold a large slice of land to Susan and Eliot Coleman, "a promising young couple, for what they could afford to pay", another slice to Jean and Keith Heavrin (Jean who became Jean Hay Bright), and "the tip-end away from the water to Greg Summers".

As for the underground journalism of the back-to-the-land era, the Nearings were welcomed with open arms at *Mother Earth News,* who described them as "exactly the kind of folks that 'made this country great.'" They were the sole subject of eight articles between 1977 and 1979. A number of these were in a question-and-answer format. In one, they responded a little testily to an enquiry about their income from maple syrup in Vermont, blueberries in Maine, and through book sales: "None of the money comes to us personally. We've arranged for all royalties and speaking fees to go to a publication fund that uses the income to get out our economic and political books, which most commercial publishers reject out of hand."

Living the Good Life was praised in *The Last Whole Earth Catalog*: "Lots of savvy advice in here, and a good picture of how it works in practice to turn your back on advantages that you know are right out there waiting for you." Stewart Brand himself reviews the reissue of their *The Maple Sugar Book*:

> My family had a sugar bush in Michigan, so we always had a cellar-room full of gallon cans of pure maple syrup, which solved most Christmas-giving problems and saddled me with an early addiction. This book by the Nearings (of *Living the Good Life*) continues their fine philosophical rap and

> lays out the definitive information on maple-sugaring. You don't have to have maple trees to enjoy it, but if you do...

No doubt archetypal hippie Raymond Mungo, author of *Total Loss Farm* (1970) used the manual for his own sugaring:

> The syrup of March is pure natural energy, it slides down our throats with the ease of the atmosphere. A big round storage tank sits in the clearing, dumbly awaiting the sap, which flows down to the road and into a second tank through several thousand feet of clean hardware store pipe.

The Nearings' rejection of meat, refined flour, and processed sugar brought them right up to date with the trendy ideas of macrobiotics. And they rubbed shoulders with the coolest people of the day. Alicia Bay Laurel recounted to me:

> We were on a television show together, and we hit it off right away. But it wasn't because I was such a great gardener, because I was really just a beginner. It was because we were all socialists, you know, *rabid socialists*. And we started talking about it on television and naming the names of the 1% of that time. The Fords, the Mellons, and the DuPonts, and immediately, the television station cut to a commercial... I stayed in touch with them for, well, really till they died. You know we had letters back and forth and [Helen] knitted me a wool poncho in my favourite colour, which is purple... She also introduced me to Juliette de Baïracli Levy, who was a friend of theirs of their generation... one of the pioneers of herbalism in the hippie era for the pre-hippie era.

In the Nearing library, I spy a copy of Alicia Bay Laurel's *Living on the Earth* (1970) that she had left there in 2000 for the Good Life Center.

Jean Hay Bright

In the "Organic" chapter, we met Eliot Coleman, the Nearings' most famous neighbour, and perhaps protégée is not too strong a word for it. But Coleman and his wife Damrosch are not the only ones in the Nearing orbit to have written books about life in Harborside. Jean Hay Bright's observations in the chunky 370-page book *Meanwhile, Next Door to the Good Life* (2003), now in its second edition, are sometimes pointed. For all that, Hay Bright communicates some extremely valuable information which — on some occasions more affectionately than others — takes the shine off the Nearings.

Jean and her husband got *Living the Good Life* through their Book of the Month Club. Keith, her husband, was a Vietnam vet who had come back "jumping at every noise, his eyes darting into the dark corners of every room, acting for all the world like a hunted animal". Driving up from Rhode Island in the autumn of 1971 to Maine and a landscape covered in old snow, they slept a freezing night in their VW camper before knocking on the Nearings' door. Keith was roped into chopping wood with Scott, and Jean was welcomed into the kitchen, where she helped Helen, who explained to her that visitors were scarce at that time of year. Helen said that the Colemans were doing well, but they were hoping some people with children would move into the neighbourhood soon so that the Coleman's daughter Melissa wouldn't be so lonely. Encouraged to return by Helen, and not to buy land elsewhere without speaking to them first, they were overwhelmed when the Nearings offered them a cabin in the backwoods between the Coleman's and their house for $2,000. Helen insisted on a ten-year right of first refusal. If they decided to sell within ten years, she could buy back their property "for the same price and on the same terms". This was a very kind and generous offer.

In *Continuing the Good Life*, the Nearings remark of visitors that they did not remember

> one daughter or son of a coal miner, nor do we recall young people whose parents worked in textile factories or steel mills. We had daughters and sons galore of merchants, or doctors, teachers, lawyers, bankers and public officials — people who had been born into affluence of a sort, raised in comfort if not pampered in luxury.

Well, in fact, Hay Bright's father worked in a steel mill, and it turns out that she was well-placed to see clearly into the truths behind the Nearings' lifestyle.

Nearing hypocrisy

The problem with the prophets of self-sufficiency, a situation still pertinent today with YouTube videos of people claiming to depict their own lives "off-grid", is that it's tempting for some people to avoid full disclosure. The trouble really starts when people who don't have any kind of financial safety net follow the example of those who do. This was a massive problem in the back-to-the-land era. In the UK, the likes of John Seymour and Patrick Rivers tried to double-down on this, making clear that their publishing and broadcasting activities were essential in bringing in the cash — but still people didn't listen and came horribly unstuck. The Nearings, if one is being uncharitable, were simply not honest. When I spoke to Eliot Coleman and Barbara Damrosch, Damrosch volunteered that "I remember being absolutely shocked and destroyed when Eliot told me that they had investments." Coleman, evidently also disappointed, was philosophical: "I'd defend them by saying, well, they came from upper-middle-class families, and they were now in their seventies and eighties, but you can't help coming from that background inheriting money."

Hay Bright herself says, "The little inconsistencies I could ignore." These included allegedly vegan Scott's taste for ice cream; animal rights advocate Helen owning a cat, "Puss-O";

the fact that, while they drank no alcohol, their apple juice had a little fizz and "a good kick to it"; as well as Scott's frustrations with raccoons, which led him to put claw traps in their blueberry patch and ask Hay Bright's husband Keith to stake it out with a shotgun. With their Maple syrup enterprise, they were, as she puts it, not buying candy, but selling it. But more than these trifles, over the years as the background information piled up, she concluded, "I didn't know then that — farm animals and kids notwithstanding — there was no way in hell Keith and I could have homesteaded the way the Nearings actually did it." There is perhaps a tragedy of her own behind this: as she documents in the book, her marriage to Keith broke up in bitter circumstances during these years.

Front and centre of the case against them is that in the twenty-eight months between December 1932 and April 1935, the Nearings had gone on a land-buying binge, acquiring 930 acres of land in three towns. This was presumably funded by a legacy from a J.J. "Koos" Van Der Leeuw, a Theosophist whom Helen had worked for briefly as a secretary and who had asked her to marry him, in the region of $30,000–$40,000. In her defence, Helen does mention this inheritance, but a veil is drawn over it.

Hay Bright digs into their finances. They let one Floyd Hurd work the maple sugar, gave him two thirds of the syrup, and kept a third themselves, thereby breaking their principle not to exploit labour. She uncovers evidence that rather than not "butchering the trees" at their large tract of land in Vermont, they did in fact sell the wood before eventually deeding over 550 acres (60% of their original 930 acres) to the town of Winhall for a municipal forest. Their accounts between 1952 and 1971 showed a net loss of $6,829.75 on their berry income. The bottom line on the berry venture is that the Nearings had no blueberry income until 1960. And two decades after planting the bushes, they still had not recovered start-up and maintenance costs.

Scott himself went on the record, of his own volition, to declare that he had what he described as a "modest annuity from paid-up insurance policies", and a like amount from a trust fund left by his sister Mary — this possibly coming from Scott's father Lewis, who had made his fortune in the wholesale liquor business during Prohibition. Hay Bright also suggests that, as Helen's family owned a successful clothing store in New Jersey and her father was well-known enough to warrant a *New York Times* obituary, she presumably also had an inheritance. She discloses that in the waning days of the popularity of *Living the Good Life*, the book was still bringing in an income of around $18,000 a year. None of these figures are adjusted for inflation.

Hay Bright concludes:

> Although they budgeted carefully, did grow a lot of their food, worked hard and didn't spend much money, it was banks, stocks, annuities, monetary gifts, inheritances, and unearned income from other people's labor that kept Scott and Helen going for most of their frugal homesteading lives, as far back as the early sugaring days in Vermont.

In her later years, Helen admitted to Hay Bright, somewhat of a friend, that "of course" both she and Scott "had money" from sources other than their cash crops and books.

Scott's death

Other areas of the Nearings' lives are also more complicated than was publicly known. In her book *Loving and Leaving the Good Life*, Helen writes that "a month and a half before Scott went, a month before his hundredth birthday, while sitting with a group at the table one day, he said: 'I think I won't eat any more.' He never took solid food again." Reading this as I worked my way through the research, I remember thinking, "Wow! What a great way to go!" The problem is, it isn't true.

The bond between the Nearings was very strong. Twenty years older than Helen, Scott realised that their life together at Forest Farm had given him a truly meaningful retirement. He wrote to her:

> Tonight I know, for sure, that if we did not have the farm I would have to choose between (1) getting an old man's job, which would barely pay expenses; (2) living on an old age pension, which pays less, or (3) living on my relatives or friends and always feeling unwanted or semi-wanted. By comparison, the farm is paradise. And you can see that I fully and thankfully realize what a treasure I have in you.

In the booklet *Free Radical* (1997), it is pointed out that rather than deciding to stop eating and quietly fading away, as is told in Helen's account, Scott was checked into a nursing home, returning to Forest Farm with a schedule of nurses and hospice workers coming to the house on a daily basis. When he stopped eating it was because he was, finally, about to die. His decision came in acknowledgment of this, rather than bringing that death about. As LaConte points out, "To fast until death before the body is ready, is to invite suffering". Over the years, Helen had heard from people who hadn't heard the true account and had been painfully unsuccessful in following Scott's path to a deliberate suicide. In the course of researching the Nearings, I came across people who still believed that his death had been precipitated in the manner described by Helen. Helen herself died some years later in a car crash. Her station wagon failed to negotiate a sharp curve and struck a tree. She was not wearing a seatbelt.

How do I feel about all this? In our time, it's customary to want to publicly humiliate other people. It's the easiest thing in the world to "cast the first stone". But which of us is an exemplary human being? The Nearings were evidently keen on setting themselves up as paragons of virtue, which they weren't. However, it's likely that they thought it was important that they set a good example by their actions. At the same time, they were fantastically generous to a great many people, not just with their money but with their time! Their lifestyle didn't stack up economically, but it was nevertheless virtuous and progressive. More than all of this, I find them to be entirely fascinating, and so many of their ideas vital and exciting.

Self-sufficiency in the UK

John Seymour

It's supposed to be always raining there, but whenever I go to Wales, the weather is glorious. Whether in Anglesey as a child, at music festivals in the Breacon Beacons, surfing on the Gower peninsula, attending the Hay-on-Wye book festival, or visiting a friend in the Black Mountains, the sun has got his hat on. May 2023 was no exception when I stayed at Pantry Fields, home of the gifted potter, artist, and gardener Anne Sears, John and Sally Seymour's daughter. It is literally next-door to the Fachongle Isaf house where the Seymours moved in 1964, as I discovered by wandering haplessly into that home first. Before we got to the business in hand, I walked up through the ancient woodland of Coed Tŷ Canol to the Cairns, from where one can enjoy the breathtaking panorama, the Atlantic in the distance.

When John Seymour died in 2004, he was wrapped in homemade blankets and buried in a nearby field. Seymour is famous for *The Complete Book of Self-Sufficiency* (1976), the wildly popular book which was the making of the fledgling Dorling Kindersley publishers and saw a reissue in 2024. However, there is dramatically more to Seymour than that book reveals. I understand from Anne and her husband David that in the latest edition, DK have aimed to restore more of

Seymour's own voice to it. Certainly, he is appreciated still, but in my view he deserves more acclaim.

With Seymour, the delight in reading him is in appreciating his winning personality, an entrancing and improbable collision of bluster and unpretentious humility. With his self-sufficiency books, *The Fat of the Land* (1961), *Self-Sufficiency* (1973), and especially the high-water mark of *I'm a Stranger Here Myself* (1978), this voice comes to the fore. When Seymour writes of "cloches" (glass bells, the use of which was pioneered in French intensive market gardening as a form of "in-situ" greenhouse) and how half the consignment he paid handsomely for were broken in six months, and he says that "I have only to look at a cloche for it to dissolve with a merry tinkle," or that an assertion is "crankish clap-trap and fiddle-faddle", we bear witness to a *Seymourism*.

I asked Anne whether he had farming in his background.

> No, his childhood was as different as you can imagine. It was like, sort of 'nouveau-riche Roaring Twenties'. He hated it, and he was always trying to break out of it... his mother was a go-getting socialite. She went to school with Wallis Simpson in America, and she was always looking for a rich husband... He kicked that away as soon as he could...

Born in 1914, as a teenager, Seymour wanted to go to America and be a cowboy. This sounds very exotic before one is aware that his father, from who he was estranged, Albert Angus Turbayne, was an ex-pat American — albeit one who worked as a book designer and binder, not herding cattle. By way of a compromise, in 1933 his mother enrolled him to study agriculture at Wye College, where he was sent to a big farm in Norfolk. Normally, for that inter-war period, they still worked with horses and used no chemical fertilisers. Anne, who asked me to refer to her using her first name, explains, "It was graft... hoeing all day in a huge field full of beet and getting up really early to feed the bullocks." The experience revealed to him that he was an altogether different person than his background had dictated.

Aged twenty-one, he eventually persuaded his mother to send him to South Africa. This began a stretch of travelling through, living, and working in "underdeveloped" countries that took twenty years of his life from 1934 to 1956. Even though he does discuss it in the introduction to *The Complete Book of Self-Sufficiency*, the importance of Seymour's exposure to the practices of Indigenous cultures can't be emphasised enough. Just as with Sir Albert Howard's experience learning with the Indian agriculturalists in Madhya Pradesh, Seymour discovered techniques corrective of the unsustainable new wave of chemical agriculture in the "developing" countries.

John Seymour in Africa

In South Africa, Seymour arrived amid a revolution in sheep farming. With the extermination of the larger carnivores, lions, leopards, and cheetah, and the introduction of wire fences which kept the jackals at bay (too cunning to execute) and steel windmills which pumped water to the flocks, agriculture was freed from being centred on the homestead, and larger territories could be cultivated. This was of similar significance to the sector as the introduction of turnip and ley farming was in England at the end of the sixteenth century. Seymour's first job was riding around these camps, satellites of the main farm, and checking whether the sheep there had been affected by parasitical flies — in which case they would need to be disinfected. He comments of this wandering through exquisite countryside, under blue skies, on a good horse, "I can scarcely think of a pleasanter way of passing one's time."

Time and again, Seymour reveals how much he detests the racist colonial attitudes he encounters. Of the Black farm workers, he comments, "As I got to know them better, and to know better the manner in which they lived, I reached the conclusion that their condition was, in fact, quite intolerable. They could not be said to be living at all." He constantly argues with the White South Africans about what he sees as the disgusting injustices inflicted upon the locals:

> The 'kaffirs' shouldn't be allowed so much freedom. 'They only get cheeky!' 'Give them an inch and they take a mile!' Such remarks pass entirely without notice in any South African white society... They are just something that everybody says. But they annoyed me, and I said so, and thus started my career as a kaffirboetjie, or Negrophile — 'pro-native.'

Seymour lived in South Africa for six years, and then spent the war serving with African troops in Africa and the Far East, and during this time he never stopped arguing, "because I differed from everybody else that I ever met on the subject of the treatment of Africans". Such principle and backbone from a White Englishman in Africa in 1934 are surely notable.

In Southwest Africa, what is now Namibia, he joins his pioneer friend Clinton Andrews at the homestead he had built up through back-breaking work in the desert. Andrews's setup feels like some kind of prototype for his later forays into self-sufficiency:

> Below a large catchment dam is a kitchen garden with a score of grapefruit trees, and there are chickens, ducks and a family of pigs. There is a large store-room full of preserved meat: meat in jars, meat in tins, and preserved fruit and vegetables. Asta makes bacon and ham, sausages, biltong and salt meat.

Seymour describes the store-room using an expression which he later recycles for his landmark 1961 book on self-sufficiency: it is "crammed with the fat of the land".

Working for a month on a typical cattle and maize farm in North Rhodesia, Seymour considered the native bush practice of shifting cultivation — growing crops on land till its yields drop and then moving on, leaving the fields to be reclaimed by nature. He defends this practice as being perfectly effective. The detestable, oafish, White farmer Biscoe who he is employed by, on the other hand, has farmed with modern methods. The land has been ploughed with three-furrow disc ploughs drawn by oxen. These turn up soil from a much greater depth than the manual hoeing of the Africans, and while his yields of maize have been maintained for longer, the soil is now completely exhausted. "He has taken everything out of them, and put nothing back."

At Almara in Ethiopia he sees

> the husbandman walking behind his little wooden plough drawn by a pair of oxen looks, but for the colour of his fine beard and noble black face, exactly like an English husbandman depicted in pictures of the fourteenth century. The very wheat that he harvests is an ancient type of bearded wheat, such as was grown in England at that time.

Seymour concludes *One Man's Africa* (1955) by saying that Westerners are forgetting entirely how to enjoy life, something he believes that the tribal African (presumably when not shackled by colonialism) is still aware of. In another glimpse into his unfolding manifesto, he continues,

> I do not think that we of 'the West' can find our way to a proper enjoyment of life by copying the African. We have got to work out our own way back to sanity. But I do think that there is a terrible danger of our leading the African into our own sour and bitter pastures.

John Seymour in the developing world

Published before he wrote up his experiences in Africa in *One Man's Africa*, Seymour's *The Hard Way to India* (1951) actually presents his thinking about agriculture in an earlier stage of its incarnation. A young man, on the one hand he plays devil's advocate to his recent farming education, and on the other he is caught up in the general post-war enthusiasm about "development" that characterised the Green Revolution. This combined the ideas that petrol-fuelled machinery, irrigation systems, as well as seeds tailored to respond to chemical fertiliser were the way forward for farming in the developing world.

Passing through Yugoslavia he notes:

> That is the problem which faces the peasant country which wants to mechanize its agriculture. The land must be farmed in larger units, and this can only be done by annoying the peasants. Fortunately, we annoyed ours several centuries ago, with the 'Enclosures'. The Yugoslavs are annoying theirs now.

In Turkey, he remarks, "The ploughing is apparently done by oxen... I saw one tractor from the train, although most of the country we passed through was perfect tractor country; but I afterwards found that Marshall Aid was to a certain extent remedying this deficiency". However, he notices that "a number of combine-harvesters that had been off-loaded at various stations along the line on the Turkish side". Comparing Turkey to Syria, in terms that are in opposition to the view he would eventually take, he thoroughly approves of the former:

> There is no doubt that the Turks are far ahead in agricultural development, at least. The barley, which was ripe, was being cut with binders or combines; and the wheat — not yet ready — looked as though it had been done well with fertilisers... On the Syrian side everything was done by hand; or by primitive ploughs drawn by oxen or donkeys.

Seymour describes the Sindh region as being desert or semi-desert where with great care a "miserable" crop of wheat can be grown by dry-farming. With enthusiasm he portrays the construction of the Lloyd Barrage, designed to raise the level of the Indus so as to irrigate the land. The Barrage, a low-head dam, was built of concrete and fitted with steel gates made in Ipswich, England. Of these irrigation engineers he blusters, "They are interfering with the balance of nature? It is man's destiny and his privilege to interfere with the balance of nature. That's what he's here for." Man is in the ascendant, he announces; he is "putting the wilderness into retreat" — "If we don't push back the jungle, the jungle will push us back."

In his next book, *Round About India* (1953), perhaps influenced by witnessing floods in Karachi two years before, Seymour's view of the city slums, and by extension of the drift from the country to city at the heart of the modernisation he has been celebrating, has shifted. "Give a man his fair share of the Earth's surface, and, if he survive one good harvest, and is not a fool, he never need fear being hungry again. But take him and dump him down in a city like Madras and he immediately becomes dependent on factors outside his control." Likewise, when discussing the huge estates, owned in many cases by the English, Seymour considers that, were he a local coolie, he would favour the estates being cut up into smallholdings and that he should be given one of them. "If this happened, 'efficiency' would no doubt fall off alarmingly. Efficiency at producing tea and rubber. As for efficiency at making people happy, well that is a horse of another colour. But nobody pays much attention to that kind of efficiency nowadays."

John Seymour on drugs

Seymour's *The Hard Way to India* and *Round About India*, describing his overland journey to India, represent him as being ahead of both the beat generation and the hippies in his preoccupations, as though he is working out the same evolutionary thinking at a faster pace. He is a proto-beatnik.

Anne Sears thinks that one difference was that "those people went there in search of enlightenment and... self-growth... When *he* travelled, he went there to be with the people and to observe..." What is perhaps surprising at this time in the early 1950s, and which again places him in the countercultural camp, is his willingness, as described in *The Hard Way to India*, to experiment with drugs.

In Pakistan he notes, "There were fields of good, bearded wheat, and potatoes, and others of poppies. Later on I found what the poppies were for." In Persia, where it is illegal to smoke opium, he stumbles across a policeman smoking opium with two fellows. He first tries smoking opium in a den in Tehran, and then with his friend "the old soldier", he gives it his unreserved attention: "I had my initiation as an opium smoker... It is a pleasant, restful occupation; but I found that it had little effect on me, although later I tried it in quite a determined manner."

During another session with the soldier, who "never left his opium pipe", he remarks, "I must have got through an ounce or two of the stuff. But — beyond giving me a rather pleasant hazy feeling of not caring very much — it had no spectacular effect." Later on, with his friend the scoundrel Mohesh, he visits a hashish den and each smoked a pipe, Seymour not liking it very much either. It's amusing to compare the hippies' fixation on these substances with Seymour's gentle disinterest.

John Seymour in India

Although the narcotics of the East didn't appeal to Seymour, like Gary Snyder and Allen Ginsberg, who travelled in India years later, in 1962, Hindu philosophy made a huge impression on him. Anne said he told her that his experience of it led him "to throw away all his preconceived ideas about religion". It had such a lasting effect that "throughout his life he didn't really value possessions. He wanted to rid himself of possessions all the time, which was a little bit nerve-racking for us obviously... He wanted us to have the same philosophy, I think." In his earliest self-sufficiency book, *The Fat of the Land* (1961), he writes, "I envy the sadhu whose sole possessions are a begging bowl, a rosary, and a rag around his middle. How unlike a sadhu we are at the Broom." Seymour, who frequently quotes the Bhagavad-Gita, would discuss these ideas with his friends like Satish Kumar, the renowned British ecologist, the economist E.F. Schumacher, and the political scientist Leopold Kohr. Together with Seymour, this group were the founders of the activist John Papworth's *Resurgence* magazine, which is described as the artistic and spiritual voice of the green movement in Great Britain.

Seymour's book *Round about India* is neither as amusing nor as scurrilous as *The Hard Way to India*. Seymour takes pains for it to have value as a cultural travel guide. His exposition is impressive, but in the high seriousness, some of the joy in his writing gets lost. Throughout it, he praises the subtlety and beauty of the Hindu religion, the profundity of its philosophy, and its limitless tolerance of other faiths. It's fascinating to see him encountering the Krishna sect long before it is introduced to the West and appreciating it in its native context. He writes of the loved-up psychology of *bhakti*: "The Krishna cult is the expression of personal love in Hinduism. Many of the god's followers feel the intense, almost passionate, love for him that some Catholics feel for the Virgin." Seymour goes on:

> The most delightful of the Krishna stories are about his doings as a boy among the cow-herds. They are tales of mischief. Of how he used to steal the milk and the butter, of how he played the flute, and of how he used to tease the gopis, or milkmaids, and incidentally make love to them!

In an exquisite passage which demonstrates how lucidly Seymour understands the Vedic philosophy, he renders an overheard conversation on a train between an oil man and a commercial traveller:

> We are like drops of water... which have been torn from their mother, the Ocean. The Ocean is God. The drops of water must strive to return to the Ocean... to reunite with God. That is what we call meditation. The attempt to reunite ourselves with God. We are each a fragment of God, torn away from the main body. We must strive to reunite.

While visiting the town of Ongole, his acquaintance Bawaj asks Seymour whether he would like to meet his mother. She had lived alone for six years at the top of a hill, a very craggy and secluded spot, in the tomb (the size of which not much larger than a dinner table) of her father's guru. She survives on coffee and oranges that the children take her. Bawaj's mother banished his father from seeing her, and rarely accepted male guests, but had expressed a wish to see Seymour. She marked his forehead with saffron and gave him an orange. Seymour, evidently moved, remarks, "She is sane. One glance into that old woman's eyes is enough to let you know that if she isn't mentally healthy, then all the rest of us are as crazy as foxes."

At the temple at Bhadrachalam, a key town of pilgrimage, Seymour takes *puja* — a ceremonial blessing. One senses that the religion really gets under his skin. His observations of Hinduism are woven with views on India's agriculture. As a sign of his perspective becoming more organic, he approves of the Jammulapalem village council's encouragement of compost pits. Later on, in the village, he witnesses the wife of a rich farmer, an elderly though still "extremely beautiful" woman, walking with a basket on her head half-full of cow dung. The woman paused whenever she came to where a cow had "eased herself", and stooped down to pick up the manure and put it in her basket, either for her compost-pit or to burn.

Seymour's guide notices him looking and remarks, "She is rich, but she's still a village woman."

At Ongole, Seymour discusses why the local cattle are in such fine fettle. Usually in India the cattle, he observes, were allowed to overbreed and the population exhausted the food. The answer lay in the fact that the cattle dealers in Madras — supplying Muslim, Christian, and Harijan communities — having no qualms about eating beef, bought the cows and their calves and "mysteriously disappeared them". An expert friend of Seymour's, whose name he withholds, insists that his countrymen must overcome their reluctance to kill cattle, but that the subject is strictly taboo in the society in which the cow is venerated, sharing the family living-quarters in the Indian village home.

Seymour ends up living in a village in the Punjab, Baswasni, where he goes native. Towards the end of his stay, living a vegetarian life, the community offer him thirty acres of land, canal irrigation, and a house to come and settle permanently. "And they even said that they would throw in a wife!" Like Albert Howard before him, Seymour concludes *Round About India* proclaiming, "India, one often hears, has many lessons to learn from the West. It will be a good day when the West realizes that it has lessons of much greater importance to learn from India."

Sally Seymour

In 1954, Seymour married the Australian potter and artist Sally Medworth. After a period travelling through the waterways and rivers of England on a Dutch sailing barge, the couple decided that they would be better bringing up their first daughter on the land. Still maintaining their respective careers as a journalist and a potter, they sold their barge and rented a run-down five-acre estate near Orford in Suffolk with two cottages, outhouses, and a field for ten pounds a year, in 1954. Needs must, and with their irregular incomes, they decided to make their own food. They knew nothing at all about gardening but bought a book on it. Of these early pioneering days, Seymour says they worked ridiculously hard.

As much as it's tempting to entirely ascribe the Seymours' choice of self-sufficiency to John's developing-world experiences, without question Sally was equally, perhaps even more, responsible. In *The Fat of the Land*, Seymour describes her as having led a Bohemian existence, so I asked their daughter Anne about it. Growing up, both of Sally's parents were artists. Her father, Frank Medworth, was Head of Art at what became the National Art School in Australia in Sydney. He had suffered a head wound in the war and had had his skull repaired with a metal plate. Sent on a flight to Mexico as a delegate for UNESCO, the air pressure on the flight disturbed the cranioplasty and Medworth took his own life as a result. Anne observes of his death when Sally was fourteen:

> After that, I think Sally and her family were really hard up in Australia, and the whole of their life was changed because they didn't have this breadwinner. It was difficult, and Sally's mother was very resourceful. In fact, the whole family are pretty resourceful. If you can't buy it or you don't have the money, you make it. And she brought that to the marriage.

Of her mother she says, "She was unstoppable... she would tackle anything." Because of his work as a journalist — and in fact his increasing success in that capacity — because of her role as a mother and because of the necessity in that role of being rooted to one spot, she ended up taking on more of the homesteading duties. But she loved it, and was brilliant at it, as is evident in one of his rare compliments to her,:"Sally uses no 'chemicals' in her Round Garden because there is absolutely no need. She has achieved such a high humus status there — the general fertility of the soil is so high — that to shove in 'chemicals' would be like taking coals to Newcastle." But Anne remembers of her father how "when he came back, because of his personality and the sort of person he was, he would barge in and try to take over. With no sensitivity..."

When she left him, apparently Seymour suddenly realised how much Sally held the place together, as he worked "front-of-house" with his books and broadcasting. Of his later ventures after their marriage, most saliently the school of self-sufficiency and community he organised, Anne remarks that "I don't think he ever found his second in command." For a period, Sally was still living at Fachongle Isaf, but then sold up. "She bought a smallholding up on the Preselis [local hills] and she lived there for quite some time. She made a beautiful job of it... it was just a wonderful place when she'd finished with it."

When I had arranged to stay at Pantry Fields I had no idea that Sally was still alive and living with the Sears. Now in her nineties, she had a stroke twenty years ago which left her unable to speak, but she understands everything. After supper, we went to say hello, and I got to see her exquisite recent drawings, of which I am a serious fan. She has an amazing glow about her.

John Seymour and animals

The model of what John Seymour calls "the one cow economy" delivers the responsibilities of animal husbandry to the smallholder. Henry Thoreau has the first word here: "I am wont to think that men are not so much the keepers of herds as herds are the keepers of men, the former are so much the freer." Of which comment, Wendell Berry remarks:

> Thoreau may have been the first to assert that people should not belong to farm animals, but the idea is now well-established doctrine with many farmers — and it has received amendments to the effect that people should not belong to children. But we all have to belong to something, if only to the idea that we should not belong to anything.

Animals, products derived from them, and their manure are often seen as entirely necessary to the healthy mixed farm's ecosystem. As Sir Albert Howard insisted, "No one has yet succeeded in establishing an efficient and permanent system of agriculture without livestock." The Seymours started their journey into animal husbandry with fowl. They bought geese and ducks and nervously let them out in the morning, the birds all somewhat magically returning for dinner in the evening. When a duck, Henrietta, returned back from the wood one day with a dozen yellow chicks at her heel, the Seymours concluded, "We had discovered the secret of rearing poultry. Simply leave them absolutely and entirely alone."

Looking after animals is one thing, but only having yourself to rely upon for their slaughter is an issue of far greater magnitude. So many of us eat meat, but self-sufficiency forces the smallholder to confront the ethical questions which most of us are happy to sweep under the doormat. As beat poet Gary Snyder puts it, "A subsistence economy is a sacramental economy because it has faced up to one of the critical problems of life and death: the taking of life for food." Anne Sears remembered that her father was

> really, really, sentimental about animals, but he managed to very effectively compartmentalise it. There's a natural order of life, and he was very firmly understanding of that. But he wouldn't eat battery hens. He wouldn't eat animals which were not reared outside naturally, because he hated the idea. Obviously, it's wrong.

Seymour, having lived among vegetarian Hindus for a long time, decided after "a great deal of thought" that it is right to kill animals. However, it is a decision he took with solemnity, "To connive at the killing of animals while being too lily-livered to kill them yourself is despicable." Seymour believed that vegetarians who eat dairy products or eggs were not seeing the full picture, pointing out that "the man who takes a high moral attitude about not eating meat, and eats eggs, drinks milk or eats butter and cheese, wears leather or wool, just does not have to be taken seriously at all". Apart from the ingenious system of the Hare Krishna farms, which we explore in the final chapter, to keep a cow or goat continually producing milk it is necessary to impregnate them. The female calf, the heifer, is useful of course as a future producer of dairy. But what about the male bull calf? English self-sufficiency guru Patrick Rivers clarifies, "The answer is to kill him, either at birth or as soon as possible afterwards..." Seymour gives the example of eggs: "You can't hatch eggs to provide yourself with hens to lay more without hatching out as many cocks as hens." Here Gary Snyder would take a wide view of the dilemma: "Other beings (the instructors from the old ways tell us) do not mind being killed and eaten as food, but they expect us to say please, and thank you, and they hate to see themselves wasted."

Of their cow, Brownie, Seymour writes very much like a Hindu householder would, stating that it was surprising what an affection that they felt for the old creature. "She is the cornerstone of the arch of our economy. Everything we eat is enriched either by her dung or her milk." Such a cow would need at least a ton of hay every winter. However, her addition meant scaling up their household with the addition of pigs to consume some of the huge four gallons of milk a day she produced. They also had to prepare more land to absorb her prodigious manure. This manure entirely obviated the need for chemical fertilisers. Not only did their food taste better, but they were also saving money which otherwise would go to the directors and shareholders of Fisons and ICI. However, although he was open to the possibility of soil fertility being maintained by vegetable composting and green manuring, and while he reflected that it might require less land to feed a family of vegetarians, that's an experiment he didn't fancy trying himself.

Seymour explains that it is necessary to keep pigs moving from plot to plot so they don't pick up parasites. Because the parasites of one animal do not attack another it is therefore possible (for instance) to follow pigs with cows, cows with sheep, sheep with geese, and return back to pigs again. All the while these animals are manuring the land and building up fertility for crops. It's quite easy to see the arguments for what is called "mixed farming", whereby the small farm's economy is assembled from these mutually beneficial relationships. Scaling a farm can break these virtuous cycles unless the large farm is carefully managed in a holistic manner. From this small-farm perspective, we can appreciate the problems of massive monocultures, where, for instance, only wheat is grown on a large farm. No doubt there's a sweet spot between the two positions. Notwithstanding this, keeping animals necessitates feeding them, and a smallholding can struggle to keep up with this demand. The constant killing required that one reads about in Seymour's books, necessary to sustain his more traditional diet, is occasionally overwhelming no matter how bracing and authentic.

Just as those practicing self-sufficiency can be confronted with all kinds of practical situations which make the choice even harder. Jean Hay Bright, no self-styled guru, describes her rocky road with the lifestyle with admirable frankness. In the first instance they had goats. Their goat Nicky gave birth to three kids. The first nanny goat was very weak and struggled to stand, so they planned to sell her, keeping her in a pen in the house and feeding her the mother's colostrum out of a pan. But both the other two kids had died; the second had been dead for a week or so and had begun to mould. Bright's partner concluded, "If we had to go through this trauma every time a goat kidded, the milk wasn't worth the trouble". Later on in their journey, the local slaughterhouse sent one customer back two left halves of a pig — insisting they were from the same animal. "After a few stories like that, people stopped growing pigs. Why spend all that time and energy if you couldn't be sure you would get your own pig back?" In

1977, they got rid of their cow, realising that they could buy raw milk from a neighbour who was milking three Jerseys.

John Seymour's philosophy

Behind Seymour's self-sufficiency writing are a set of very specific ideas. It's worth running through a few of them here. The first could be described as *the primacy of subsistence*. Although there is, no doubt, something honourable about feeding other people through farming, Seymour thought it wasn't worth bothering with. Obviously, because he had another stream of income, it was never essential for him to make money that way, but the antipathy ran deeper. He himself found this out from bitter experience. When he moved from Suffolk to Wales, he took a government subsidy so as to farm "properly". He got into debt and triggered a chain reaction of problems trying to drain land and turn food production into a business. He certainly wished that he had heeded his earlier views as expressed in *The Fat of the Land*: "The farming press nowadays runs an unending holy crusade to persuade people against being self-supporting — they want to turn every farmer into a money-grubber pure and simple..."

The next idea is his defence of the *intensive productivity of smallholdings*. Seymour would argue that small farms have higher yield volumes per acre than the massive monocultures of chemical agriculture. "Intensive" is used as a term to refer to chemical agriculture, even by people who should know better, whereas it can be more applicable to organic production. As we've seen "intensive" agriculture's classical incarnation is the wholly organic market gardens around Paris of the 1500s.

Innately connected with the intense productivity of smallholdings is the need for more rural labour to work the land. Seymour believed in the need for *more hands on the land*. He says, "If there were enough people on it — enough hands — I believe that our seventy acres could produce a dozen times as much food as it did before."

Key to this is the *reevaluation of farming* and the work it involves: being outdoors in nature and working hard with your body all day. It was Seymour's view that in the UK, a socio-historical reason for this is that British *industry* is subsidised, but British *agriculture* is not to the same extent. Since Peel's abolition of the Corn Laws in 1846, imported food had been subject to free trade, meaning that, without protection available to its own agriculture, the UK could feed its industrialised cities with cheaper food from abroad. In Seymour's view, this so-called "cheap food policy", and its prioritisation of the needs of the modern industrial workforce, meant that the UK's farm workers had been historically paid so little, demoralised, stigmatised, and driven from the countryside. When the Seymours moved to Wales, the farms around them were largely "winding down". Seymour would chuckle with his elderly neighbours at their jokes about their sons with their biros. There is much less money to be made, but of his own preferences for avoiding white-collar work, he said, "If I were to work in an advertising agency, I would want my labour to be assessed not at ten shillings or a pound an hour, but at a million pounds an hour."

A central plank of Seymour's self-sufficiency ethos might be called *the cow economy*. This was an idea he would have come across in India. It was practiced differently there. The male calves were not killed. As well as being used as manure, dung was burnt as fuel or smeared on the inside of houses. The cow was venerated. However, the idea of that animal being the foundation of the small homestead was the same. In fact, over time, and after the self-sufficiency books, Seymour arrived at the position that communities should divide up the performace of certain roles. Not everyone wants to look after a cow, and a cow can easily produce more milk than one family can use.

Seymour was not infatuated with the organic standard. Rather, he disapproved of chemicals from a practical point of view, a sentiment which would have been greeted with approval by farmers universally:

> I don't find myself that you can really taste the difference between a cabbage that has had a pinch of sulphate of ammonia shoved on it and one that has not. If my land lacks phosphate I put some slag on it, if I can afford it, and find it very good stuff. But I have to admit I don't like paying for slag — or any other artificials.

However, care for the soil was close to his heart. "When you die you will leave something valuable behind you: land in good heart. There's an immortality worth having." One of my favourite Seymourisms relates to this concern for good soil. While he acknowledges the value of composting, far better than piling up and turning that organic matter, he advises, is to take it and "put it through an animal". Like for instance one of his pigs, Sodom or Gomorrah.

On Instagram, I was bored to see people judging Seymour by his supposedly posh accent. In England, across the board, speech from the 1950s and '60s will sound that way. The actual upper-class speech of that era, of which class Seymour was certainly not, sounds practically unintelligible. The inference was that Seymour, perhaps like the Nearings turned out to be, was merely a rich man at play. The truth is that where the family lived was on the peripheries, before holiday cottages took off, and it was dirt cheap. Their family lived a precarious existence, hand-to-mouth, with a mortgage to feed. Seymour was a friend to both rich and poor, the least snobbish man imaginable. His daughter puts it nicely, "He was at home with any kind of person from any sort of position in society. He could dine with the highest lords and stay in the Hilton and just be at home there... and also stay in a tent by the side of the road with a load of gypsies and have a great time." In his wonderful book *I'm a Stranger Here Myself*, one of the gypsies,

Perce, comments, "'He aint no gen'lman… He's a kushti mush same as what we are.'"

John Seymour the futurist

We've argued that Seymour was, certainly with regards to the beats and hippies, years ahead of his time. It's not surprising, therefore, that he himself put a lot of thought into what the future should look like. As hard as it might be to square with the stereotypical idea of the future, with its fantasy of limitless energy and computers to brush your teeth, he was a futurist.

At the start of *Self-Sufficiency*, the prose book which predated the picture-book guide of *The Complete Guide to Self-Sufficiency*, Seymour discusses his experiences of self-sufficient peoples in India and Africa, and of how in these societies, when the children are educated, they grow up no longer satisfied with the village's self-sufficiency. Just like the West, he argues, for better or worse, they have evolved past the old models. What he is interested in, he claims, is post-industrial self-sufficiency, "that of the person who has gone through the big-city-industrial way of life and who has advanced beyond it and wants to go onto something better". This post-industrial self-sufficiency is very similar to the ideas at the cutting edge of permaculture, which we look at in Chapter 9.

To drill down into a specific scenario, we can give Seymour's example of growing wheat:

> I am not suggesting that this world go forward (you can never 'go back' — time moves forward and so nobody can ever go back) to threshing wheat and winnowing it in the wind. But I do think that all of us who live in areas in which wheat can be grown should go forward to growing wheat on farms in our areas…

Sometimes his projections are positive. "One day", he dreams, "the huge empty farms will be broken up again, and homesteads will grow up on them." On other occasions he foresees panic: "At the present rate of exploitation, though, the main fishing grounds will be sterile in ten or twenty years and the supply of fish meal will begin to dry up. Then we will be searching around frantically for a source of protein that we can grow ourselves, and beans will probably have to be the answer." His final words in *Self-Sufficiency* are pitched between the two poles: "It's all going to collapse. Either the oil will run out, or the grub, or the uranium-235, or the power of mankind to withstand the unutterable boredom of it all... He will go forward to something much sounder and better than has ever been before."

In a passage at the end of *I'm a Stranger Here Myself*, discussing the overwhelming edifice he is striving to dismantle, sadly his marriage to Sally now in tatters, a casualty of his working more and more away from home, Seymour reflects:

> How can one man — one man's will — fight a whole nation — a nation whom the gods, apparently wishing to destroy, make mad? But I have read my *Bhagavad-Gita*, and anyway was familiar with what was in it before I read it, and I knew that it is not the achievement that is important, but the attempt; not the victory but the fight, not the goal but the journey.

At Pantry Fields, the homestead where I visited Seymour's daughter Anne and her husband David, they and their community are quietly getting on with it.

> David makes sourdough bread and sells it... he makes about twenty-four loaves a week. We buy eggs off the neighbours, and we used to buy milk from them. And money does change hands but it's all here. Everybody has a surplus of vegetables and seedlings and seeds, and we all swap them.

She also gently points to progress in their thinking. Seymour definitely ate a lot of meat where maybe it wasn't necessary or even sustainable:

> Although he said you can do anything in his books, and it seems comprehensive the way he grows all these vegetables, we never actually used to grow that many varieties. But there's so much more information now... we do eat a lot more vegetables. And beans and nuts which we buy, but I am experimenting more and more with growing... I've got a whole row of butter beans out there.

Perhaps, then, beans are the answer?

John Seymour and the hippies

Writing thirteen years after *The Fat of the Land*, in its second edition in 1973, Seymour points out that they are no longer alone. "When we found ourselves becoming self-sufficient in food at the Broom we were probably the only family in England living this way." Later there were hundreds, he said, and tens of thousands more who wanted to. In America, he observed the communes, the self-supporters with their own magazines and newspapers, and even a school [he's likely to be referring to Ralph Borsodi and Mildred Loomis's School of Living]. And then there's the counterculture: "Of course nearly all hippies have as part of their philosophy the ideal of becoming self-sufficient. Few of them have achieved it as yet because they cannot tear themselves away from their guitars long enough."

Seymour could be militant when it came to commenting upon members of the counterculture who claimed, as Timothy Leary suggested, to "drop out":

> The so-called drop-out, or freak, or hippy, whether he lives in a pad in London or a broken-down cottage in the country, who depends on The Thing for his food, hasn't even started

> to drop out of anything. In any case, now that there are more and more of us self-sufficiency addicts, I think it is time we stopped using the term 'drop out' and substituted for it the term 'drop in'... A man living on national assistance, or 'the Health', or "the Unemployment', or a man working for some huge organization which is itself part of The Thing, or living on money that Daddy supplies him with and which Daddy has earned from The Thing, is as much a part of it as the Prime Minister or the chairman of I.C.I.... He can grow the scruffiest beard in the world, wear his hair like a Comanche brave, puff pot until it makes him dizzy — but he is still right there slap in the middle of The Thing that he purports to hate and to be trying to get away from. When he gets round to producing at least most of his food — then at least he has started along the road that frees him from [The] Thing.

Perhaps Seymour's first meeting point with the counterculture was around the ideas of communities, which is a defining characteristic of the back-to-the-land movement. Sally couldn't stand the idea. Whenever Seymour mentioned getting someone on the farm to help them, his wife would say, "Oh no — we don't want to start some bloody community!" But he saw the logic, possibly rooted in his experience of local households taking it in turns to kill a pig and sharing, the better than each killing a pig at the same time and the meat spoiling. He schemed of a way in which A can keep cows and keep everyone in dairy, while B grows corn and provides flour and animal fodder, with C concentrating on pig and poultry.

Seymour scoffs, in 1973: "I don't think personally that the hugger-mugger community in which everybody loves each other and nobody tells anybody else what to do because it's not democratic will ever work, anywhere." Rather, he favours small self-sufficient groupings living nearby one another, each with their own smallholding and home, as potentially working very well. He points to the "many great houses, mansions and the like, for sale and they sometimes sell at ridiculously low prices". Lots of hippie communities were inspired by Seymour, most notably the still-surviving Laurieston Hall community, founded in 1972 and housed in one such mansion outside Dumfries in the Scottish Lowlands. Even today they maintain a large, organic, walled garden in which they grow as much fruit and vegetables as they can, keep cows, pigs, hens, and bees, and do most of their own maintenance. Patrick Upton, who joined Laurieston in 1973, told the BBC, "We built our first goat pens using Seymour's books... We soon learned goats were cunning and agile. One time they got out and ate the rhododendrons, which are poisonous. I had to make them ill with warm oil and stay up with them all night."

I asked Anne Sears about his attitude to the counterculture. "He wasn't very forgiving of people, you know. He wouldn't suffer fools or people who didn't work hard, and he formed an opinion quite quickly, but he also surprised us and himself by then getting on with them. Horse-drawn was one of them."

The family was cheered up immensely by the appearance of a "splendid person" they called Horse-drawn, the son of an eminent surgeon, who arrived one day in a gypsy caravan. Planning originally on heading from London to Scotland in the manner of the folk singer Vashti Bunyan, he wound up by some accident of fate at the Seymours' farm in Wales and stayed with them for two years. Seymour, who as we have seen was critical of hippies at a distance, describes him:

> He was the first, perhaps, of a new wave of settlers that was to come to our countryside. He wore a beard, long hair, many of the appurtenances that we have come to know as marks of the Hip generation. He was the first of this movement to impinge on us, and we never found him anything else but delightful; he introduced our children to all sorts of disturbing ideas, which I confess, I feared somewhat when I first began to be aware of them, but find perfectly acceptable now.

Seemingly, at this point of actual encounter, Seymour qualified his opinion of hippies. Sure, there was one wing who were parasites on the straight world, smoking "pot" grown by and transported by the "squarest of squares" and playing guitars put together by "sweated labour" in huge Japanese factories. But now, meeting Horse-drawn, who by all evidence was a hardcore member of the movement in earnest, he was willing to concede that there existed another wing of the counterculture, "people who are determined to build a world of their own — to free themselves from the square capitalist world — to till the soil and grow their food and create their workshops and artifacts and live by their own honest efforts." Horse-drawn — who married the Seymours' "Handymaiden" (their affectionate term for their home-help), with whom he had a son — at the time of writing of *I'm a Stranger Here Myself*, in 1978, had moved to a little farm further inland. Very touchingly Seymour says, "It delights me to visit them".

Horse-drawn's real name was Richard Plewes, and perhaps through the influence of Seymour on his friend Satish Kumar, he contributed a couple of articles to a copy of the influential ecological magazine *Resurgence*, which still runs to this day. In one essay, Horse-drawn discusses an impromptu stone circle erected by participants of a Welsh festival in 1977 as if it were an authentic neolithic structure. The other is autobiographical. After an itinerant adolescence — being shuffled between boarding schools, walking alone through Wales and France, travelling to Malaya as an English teacher, and coming back — he tried farming, before discovering that "the agribusiness chemicals and poisons propaganda just wouldn't settle down in my head." Back wandering again through Europe, he discovered hashish in Greece and returned to England and farming again. He recounts how "during that year occasionally, without any artificial aids, the doors of perception opened quite by themselves. Once when bottling milk on a sunny Sunday morning the concrete floor of the dairy became as glass and lived."

Horse-drawn is inspired, in what he calls a "think" to take to the road:

> Anyway, this particular think was to build a caravan and stick a horse in front of it and travel that way. As a way of life it ought to yield plenty of time for pure thought. (Is a human DNA's a way of creating more DNA?) So I did that, and my left-handed horse led me to Wales. I was aiming for the Pennines, but she always took off without me first thing and took the first few junctions without my guidance. My old dog and I walked mostly, and the mare looked after the caravan. She knew more about horses than I did. And eventually we ended up in West Wales having started out just north of London.
>
> We couldn't fail to meet Seymour under those circumstances, and of course we did meet him. A thinking man of action at last. Someone who actually talked about ideals that were tenable and also put them into practice. He actually had a system for beating the system. Caravanning had its limitations. A lot of hassle sometimes about where to park, and you could be welcome anywhere as a curiosity for a short while, but you had to keep moving. No time really to write.

For him, the Seymour method of self-sufficiency was the solution: "Having tried lots of ways to beat the system, I settled for John's."

Writing in *I'm a Stranger Here Myself* (1978), from Seymour's language, there's no doubt that he had decided the hippies were his people: "We 'freaks' believe quite seriously that we are building an alternative society, an alternative agriculture and industry and commerce, an alternative lifestyle... We freaks have no doubt whatever in our minds to whom the future belongs, if future there is going to be." To this day, the link between Seymour and the hippie communes is intact. Anne informs me of the nearby Lammas eco-village and its charismatic leader, Tao Wimbush. "He runs his smallholding on the model of my father's smallholding. He talks about John Seymour quite a lot, and you can see that he does it really well. You know, better than we did. A lot better."

That day, Anne had taken me on a guided tour of her garden, there were things that one might expect — strawberries, loganberries, asparagus, and, ambitiously, apple trees grown in the espalier method — but also a whole range of plants more unusual for a Welsh garden: edamame, chilli, dandelions being cultivated for their roots, and yacon. As a present, I had arrived with an oak seedling from London, grown on my roof garden, and I left early the next morning with a yacon seedling. I grew it to full height and roasted it for lunch in December.

The Good Life

In the UK, we grew up with a television show, a sitcom, called *The Good Life* — its title, as I now know, stems from the Nearings' book *Living the Good Life*. The show follows the story of "the Goods": Tom, a forty-something designer of plastic toys for breakfast cereal packets (played by Richard Briers), and his wife Barbara (heartthrob Felicity Kendal). They decide to pursue self-sufficiency, not in the Welsh countryside, but in a back garden in Surbiton, a suburban neighbourhood of Southwest London.

Richard Briers, in fact, wrote a foreword for John Seymour disciple Patrick River's book *Living Better on Less* (1977): "Patrick Rivers does not suggest that everyone should just 'chuck it in' and start a farm in the back garden — he does show ways that we can begin to get out of the rat-race, and be healthier and happier." (As a sidenote, it's worth mentioning that Rivers's first book, *Living on a Little Land*, secured a written introduction from John Seymour himself and illustrations by Sally. Seymour writes, "[The Rivers] really are producing a great deal of their own very good food." Seymour's admiration is focused in the observation that "to take land from which nobody else could make a living and — with no input of oil-derived chemicals and a very small input of power — produce good food, is very difficult indeed".)

The television show, which maintained a delightfully frothy tone for four series of seven episodes, had a shock ending which aired on 22 May 1977. The episode starts inauspiciously with the news that Geraldine, their goat, has stopped producing milk. Returning from a celebration of Tom's birthday and their second anniversary of self-sufficiency, they discover their house has been vandalised. Amidst other graffiti the words "Punk Rock" can be seen written in red spray paint on the living room wall. Tom's neighbour Jerry, who works at Good's old company, and who would now be his boss, tries to convince him to pack in all the self-sufficiency nonsense: "You can have your old job back tomorrow, I can promise you that!" The mood is very sombre, awkward even, for the spectator, until out of the blue Barbara figures out why the goat has stopped producing milk. "She needs to be maided again, that's why!" And with that, the Goods pick themselves up and raise a toast with glasses of Jerry's champagne.

The tenor of the times had changed suddenly and precipitously from a sharing, bucolic, freewheeling one to a climate of conniving, urban, uptight brutality. This was echoed in all quarters of society, from a political swing to the right, to a pronounced emphasis on material wealth, to the sudden sonic violence of punk rock. In the UK, Peter York, author of *Style Wars* (1980), remarked of this radical shift in temperament in the 1970s, "You only had to talk about a social worker or an ethnic print dress... to get a laugh." In America, the target of US punk group the Dead Kennedys' "California Über Alles" (1979) was the liberal governor of California, Jerry Brown. Brown had the likes of beat poet Gary Snyder and humanure pioneer Sim Van der Ryn in his administration. The "cruel" tone of punk carried within it the pre-echoes of the first administrations of Margaret Thatcher (1979–1990) and Ronald Reagan (1981–1989) that swept away a lot of compassionate and progressive infrastructure.

And yet, just as Barbara and Tom picked themselves up and adapted to the new reality, so did the organic hippies. Craig Sams, for instance, was alive to the possibilities of punk (it was, truthfully, just an evolution of the counterculture — even an attempt to get to the real heart of its impulse). Sams described to me attending an early show by the Damned and the events of that evening. This story was turned into the first punk novel, *The Punk* (1977), by his son Gideon Sams (1962–1988), which sold fifty thousand copies, and then later by the director Michael Sarne into a film script for the movie *The Punk and The Princess* (1993). Like his brother Gregory, who in 1982 invented the worldwide phenomenon that was the "VegeBurger", Sams found viable ways to bring organic food out of its hippie ghetto to the mass market. This he achieved with products like Whole Earth Foods pioneering organic peanut butter, organic wholegrain cornflakes, and perhaps most famously, Green & Black's organic chocolate.

In the US, while the grants which had supported New Alchemy dried up in the Reagan era, John Todd took the knowledge he had gained purifying water with "green machines" and put it into the company Ocean Arks International, subsequently working with Findhorn's Michael Shaw in Living Technologies Inc. Using plants, they restored rivers, canals, and lakes around the world running operations across the USA in Sugarbush (VT), South Burlington (VT), Harwich (MA), Las Vegas, Providence (RI), Berlin (MD), and also beyond in France; Amsterdam; the Baima Canal (in Fuzhou, China), and in Scotland, at Findhorn itself.

BACK-TO-THE-LAND

An article, "Communal Life: A Visit to The Hog Farm" (1971) in *Mother Earth News,* summarised the mass exodus of the counterculture from the cities the country in terms of escape. "The recent back-to-the-land movement began when the original 'flower children' saw Haight-Ashbury in San Francisco degenerate into a deadly gathering ground for dope pushers and the university campuses into bloody battlefields." This refers in part to the events at People's Park in San Francisco in April 1969 when, in a Digger-style event, a hundred people descended upon this university-owned land, shipping in soil and planting flowers, trees, and shrubs with a view to greening it up. This prompted a standoff with police and their fatal shooting of James Rector and blinding of Alan Blanchard. A total of 128 local residents were admitted to hospital, and, eventually, governor Ronald Reagan sent in 2,700 National Guard troops. After being fenced off for a number of years, in the end, to paraphrase Joni Mitchell in "Big Yellow Taxi", this paradise was "paved over" — turned into a parking lot and soccer field by the university.

Writing in the book *Total Loss Farm* (1970), jaded peace movement activist Raymond Mungo also picked up this thread of their generation's escape from unpleasantness:

> It was the farm that had allowed me the luxury of this vision, for the farm had given me the insulation from America which the peace movement promised but cruelly denied... I woke up in the spring of 1968 and said, 'This is not what I had in mind,' because the movement had become my enemy; the

> movement was not flowers and doves and spontaneity, but another vicious system, the seed of a heartless bureaucracy, a minority Party vying for power not peace. It was then that we put away the schedule for the revolution, gathered together our dear ones and all our resources, and set off to Vermont in search of the New Age.

Academic Dona Brown thinks the movement had less to do with the 1960s, and that it's more accurate to associate the rebirth of the back-to-the-land movement with "the *end* of that era or with the beginning of the next: the 1970 massacre at Kent State, the Watergate crisis, the 1973 oil embargo." In her view, the defining year was 1970. By way of a barometer, that year, the magazine *Mother Earth News* was born, and within a few years it had half a million subscribers. In a flourish, Brown notes that "in fact, in her September 1969 performance of 'Woodstock' at Big Sur, Joni Mitchell did not sing 'got to get back to the land', but rather 'got to camp out on the land.'" It was only when a cover of the song appeared on Crosby, Stills, Nash & Young's *Déjà Vu* album in 1970 that the line was changed, perhaps signalling the new commitment.

But their motives weren't just negative. Timothy Leary's injunction to "drop out" implied heading to the hills. In a 1967 *San Francisco Oracle* interview, after his tour of communes in the US south, Leary was even more explicit about the offer of "the Simple Life": "If you understand how to do it, you understand that poverty is sensual, poverty is turned on, poverty is thrilling." In her excellent and moving book which recounts her parents' own back-to-the-land adventure in the context of the generation, *We Are as Gods* (2016), Kate Daloz tells the story of one Eliot: "Then one weekend in 1969, Eliot and some friends went hiking in the wilderness of California. On a remote mountaintop, they dropped acid. During his trip, Eliot had a profound epiphany that seemed to identify the nagging dissatisfaction that had plagued him since childhood:

what was missing from his life was a connection to Mother Earth, to the land."

The influence of LSD can't be underestimated. In an interview with documentary film-maker David Hoffman on the subject of the 1960s, Joni Mitchell says of psychedelics, "I think that that afforded people a view of nature, those who survived it (and there were some casualties)... Certainly, I would be surprised that people [who] took it, even if they were urban born, did not come away from it with some kind of ecological feeling." A large component of this was the fact that, under the influence of the instructions of "set and setting", people often took LSD in rural settings. Alan Watts's book on LSD, *The Joyous Cosmology* (1962), where Watts dips in and out of a garden, is an excellent example: "Oranges — transformations of the sun into its own image..." As the artist Tomi Ungerer put it neatly in the title of his book describing his and his family's move to a farmstead on the wild Atlantic coast of Nova Scotia in the early 1970s, *Far Out Isn't Far Enough*.

Books for the back-to-the-landers

Riding on the back of this ferment were books. Sure, there were a raft of reissues: Helen and Scott Nearing's *Living the Good Life* (1970), Ralph Borsodi's *Flight from the City* (1970), and B.F. Skinner's *Walden Two* (1976). This last, written by the pioneer of behavioural psychology, was originally published in 1948 and fictionalised a strictly organised rural community. In his new introduction, Skinner wrote of its rediscovery:

> But there was, I think, a better reason why more and more people began to read the book. The world was beginning to face problems of an entirely new order of magnitude — the exhaustion of resources, the pollution of the environment, overpopulation, and the possibility of a nuclear holocaust, to mention only four...

But there were brand new books too. Richard W. Langer's practical self-sufficiency guide, *Grow It!* (1972), was one such volume:

> Perhaps not since the fall of Babylon have so many city dwellers wanted to 'return' to the country without ever having been there in the first place. For the first time, the new generation reverses youth's traditional flow towards the city in search of opportunity. A cry of 'back to the soil, to real life!' leads the exodus. But just as the mechanically unskilled peasant floundered when tossed into the technocratic mechanism of the city, so today's new urban peasant, unskilled in agrarian survival, flounders when released in the meadow. What is lacking is a roadmap, a handbook for survival on the farm.

The international bestseller *The Secret Life of Plants* (1973), by Peter Tompkins and Christopher Bird, aimed to take the generation's yearning for the natural and connect it to the burgeoning spirituality of the day. The chapter "Soil: The Staff of Life" provides an excellent summary of the organic food movement, taking us from the archetypal chemical agriculture baddie Justus Von Liebig, through McCarrison and Wrench's studies of the miraculously healthy Hunza people (sadly refuted), via Albert Howard's composting discoveries in the subcontinent, Eve Balfour's foundation of the Soil Association, to the American J.I. Rodale's picking up of the baton of the British.

In the chapter "Plant Life Magnifies 100 Million Times", we meet Jagadish Chandra Bose (1858–1937), who invented the phenomenally sensitive crescograph device for measuring the growth of plants in the early twentieth century. Bose was an adherent of his nation's religious philosophy. Presenting his discoveries to the Royal Society in London in 1901, at the conclusion of a stunning lecture, Bose declared of his experimental findings that he

> perceived in them the one phase of a pervading unity that bears with in it all things… I understood for the first time a little of that message proclaimed by ancestors on the banks of the Ganges thirty centuries ago: 'They who see but one, in all the changing manifoldness of this universe, unto them belongs Eternal Truth — unto none else, unto none else!'

After one of Bose's lectures at the Sorbonne in Paris in 1923, the vitalist French Philosopher Henri Bergson (1859–1941) remarked, "The dumb plants had by Bose's marvelous inventions been rendered the most eloquent witnesses of their hitherto unexpressed life story. Nature has at last been forced to yield her most jealously guarded secrets." In the chapter, "Plants Will Grow to Please You", we are introduced to Luther Burbank (1849–1926), a legendary plant breeder who introduced a thousand new plants such as the Burbank potato (later hybridised into the russet), the plumcot (half plum, half apricot), and the Shasta daisy. Burbank confessed to the famous Indian yogi Paramahansa Yogananda (1893–1952) that he would talk to his plants to create a loving vibration: "'You have nothing to fear,' I would tell them. 'You don't need your defensive thorns. I will protect you.'" The counterculture lapped up this plant-based mysticism.

The book jack-knifes between some chapters which are well researched and full of intriguing historical information to others which strain one's credulity. Plant ESP, plants' supposed ability to count, and their receptivity to prayer are enchanting ideas but were a field day for sceptics. Clinging to these pseudo-scientific spiritual "tokens" also obstructs one's ability to see how more philosophically cogent ideas from the field of spirituality can help us contextualise growing and farming in a constructive way.

Farming and back-to-the-land

A very large component of the back-to-the-land movement was its urge to live communally. This distinguishes it from self-sufficiency, whereby people like the Nearings and John Seymour were, for all their awareness of the benefits of cooperative living, running single-unit homesteads. *The Modern Utopian* magazine lists a dizzying array of types of communes, the Nature Commune, the Craft Commune, the Spiritual Mystic Commune, the Denominational Commune, the Church-sponsored Commune, the Political Commune, the Political Action Commune, the Service Commune, the Art Commune, the Teaching Commune, the Group Marriage Commune, the Homosexual Commune, the Growth-centred Commune, the Mobile Gypsy Commune, and the Street or Neighbourhood Commune. There is a sense here of the culture creating spectacular variety which could no longer be contained within the boundaries of society. The sixteenth class of commune type given is "the Agricultural Subsistence Commune" where

> the main thrust is to farm or till the soil (mostly organic farming) so that the land will provide most, if not all, needs and make the commune independent and self-supporting. Many of these communes cultivate such specialized crops as organically grown grain, vegetables, and other produce, which are then sold to health food stores, health food wholesalers, or supermarkets.

For all the avalanche of popular and academic literature about the back-to-the-land movement and the communes, practically none of the writing and theorising in what are otherwise often wonderful books deal with this generation-wide "will-to-grow". I think there are several reasons. In the first case, today, right across society, people are oblivious of farming. Very few people know or even care where their food comes from, let alone how it's produced. They don't get why it's an important subject. That is reflected, not just in this specific literature, but everywhere. Secondly, intellectuals and academics, the kind of people who write about back-to-the-land and communes, are even more alienated from these matters, inhabiting as we do "ivory towers" and being preoccupied with questions of sociology, politics, and history. But farming? Fuhgeddaboudit. For instance, Jonathan A. Bowdler's monumental doctoral thesis, *The Countercultural Back-to-the-Land Movement*, says *nothing at all* about growing, only this about the Twin Oaks Commune: "They may have gotten back to basics with organic gardening, but they wanted their social structures to be modern and cutting-edge." Gardening organically is *not* going "back to basics".

Stewart Brand

For a time in the 1960s and early '70s, Stewart Brand's (1938–) thinking was always a year or two ahead of his generation. In John Markoff's strong biography of Brand, *Whole Earth* (2022), which we follow here, his "elite" background is repeatedly emphasised. Like Michael Murphy of the Esalen Institute, at Stanford University Brand was turned on to Eastern philosophy by the Zelig-like professor Frederic Spiegelberg (1897–1994). In the extended personal biography that he was required to write at the Menlo Park debriefing before he took LSD, Brand explained that he was interested in taking the drug as a learning experience in the hope that it would enhance his judgement and appreciation of beauty, especially as the latter related to his photography. Recently having discovered Zen Buddhism and its purported influence on art; this interest in Zen was another reason he wanted to try psychedelics. Initially, acid did not have a strong effect upon him.

Brand's interests in libertarianism, mysticism, and human ecology led him to be fascinated by the Indigenous Indian people of North America. He wanted to replace the stereotype of the Indian "problem" with a vision of their contribution. Central to this was an admiration of that people's ability to live in harmony sustainably on the land. A member of the council that represented the three tribes on the reservoir at the Warm Springs Indian Reservation in Oregon gave Brand the task of making a brochure. This would present the idea of "wise" development of the tribal land, which this particular member had envisioned as a site for recreation. In sharp contrast, the Indian Cowboys Brand spoke to confided in him that they were, in fact, uncomfortable with this scheme as it would necessitate the White man's involvement. It would be, rather, a first step in the land being stolen from them: "If white men had this land, there wouldn't be any wild horses."

This research formed the seed for Brand's "America Needs Indians!" presentation. Described by his biographer Markoff as "one of the first true multimedia slideshows", it comprised up to seven hundred slides and utilised a movie projector. It was shown at the third Acid Test. Phil Lesh of the Grateful Dead recalls its impact on him "To many of us — white kids who had grown up watching Westerns in the fifties — these revelations struck like lightning bolts."

On the road trip collecting photos from reservations, prompted by a message from the I Ching, Brand took the "medicine" — LSD. Navajo Mountain, to the north of where he was staying in a traditional Indian hogan dwelling, transformed itself into a giant deity with outstretched arms. Finally, this was the transformational experience he sought with psychedelics.

The three-night-long Trips Festival (1966) organised by composer Ramón Sender Barayón, author Ken Kesey, LSD chemist Owsley Stanley, and Brand himself, was the last time Brand showed "America Needs Indians!" On Thursday, the audience were not interested in Brand's avant-garde installation of teepee and slideshow. On the Friday night, the audience melted away before the end of the evening. On the Saturday, the Grateful Dead were in full swing, and afterwards Brand commented, "It was the beginning of the Grateful Dead and the end of everybody else."

Tripping on LSD on his rooftop on North Beach, noticing the buildings downtown were not parallel to one another, he came down with the thought of making public his question as to why NASA had not publicised a photograph of the whole Earth? Amazingly NASA ended up obliging. "The image of the whole Earth forced all who saw it to think holistically," wrote Andrew G. Kirk, the author of *Counterculture Green: The Whole Earth Catalog and American Environmentalism* (2007).

In July 1966, Brand and his partner — an Ottawa Native American, Lois Jennings — whilst attending a seminar at Esalen, lived off the land along the Big Sur coastline for three weeks. Once Brand shot a deer it became a lot easier. They continued with the experience at the Lama commune, which Richard Alpert, Ram Dass, had played a part in setting up. Although, with *The Whole Earth Catalog*, he would play a guiding role in the back-to-the-land movement, Brand got easily bored in the countryside. He and Jennings only stayed at the Lama commune for a couple of weeks. Talking later to Lou Gottlieb (1923–1996), who had played double bass in comedic folk troupe the Limeliters since the end of the 1950s, Brand proposed that, rather than going back-to-the-land permanently, having a "back forty" (a remote retreat) to escape the city occasionally, would be better.

The Whole Earth Catalog

In the summer of 1967 as his friends were still heading back to the land, Brand was heading in the other direction, engaged with the Portola Institute, Silicon Valley's first incubator. There was a sense that Brand's interests were drifting away from those of his peers as they set about building rural communities. He had already been involved at the peripheries of three such communes, the Garnerville Church, Lama, and Drop City. On a plane flying back from his father's funeral, he daydreamed about what he could do to help them. He remembered the L.L. Bean catalogue — in which you could buy things like blankets, boots, sweaters, and binoculars — and realised that the problems his friends were facing were to do with "access". What they needed was a means to acquire a certain tool or service. This was the insight which led to the creation of first the "Whole Earth Truck Store", a Dodge truck which served as library and shop, and then *The Whole Earth Catalog*, first published in 1968.

Brand's partner, Jennings, played a crucial role as both the driving force and as an effective general manager of *The Whole Earth Catalog*. Its categories were "Understanding Whole Systems", "Land Use", "Shelter", "Industry", "Craft", "Communications", "Community", "Nomadics", and "Learning". The first edition, which contained 135 micro-reviews, set its template as a kind of proto-internet. But *TWEC* was also an astonishingly erudite curator. By way of an example, I spent four years studying the currents of nutrition, psychoanalysis, and spirituality that swirled around the counterculture; reading hundreds and hundreds of books on the matter. I had never seen *The Last Whole Earth Catalog*, but within its "Learning" section, an impressive number of the key texts to which I referred are picked off. In some respects, here *TWEC* was writing history, because a mention in the *Catalog* for books like Jeannie Darlington's *Grow Your Own* or Alicia Bay Laurel's *Living on the Earth* was instrumental in their becoming bestsellers, and thus significantly shaping the zeitgeist. Its acuity is the same with regards to growing and farming in the "Land Use" section.

This acuity was because Brand, as well as having insights of his own (as we've seen with his reviews of books on biodynamics and more), picked *amazing* contributors. Now-legendary agricultural theorist Wendell Berry was given a free hand, as was esteemed geographical historian Gurney Norman, and the likes of geodesic-dome guru Lloyd Kahn, author of the classic book *Shelter* (1973). Kahn had built his own house in the Big Sur with a terraced organic garden and wrote to Brand in January 1969 in a letter they published:

> I'm writing from the perspective of having gone out in the semi-country, built a house, put in a water system, a garden,

> and I'm now building a shop and going to farm in the spring... We started with a bare hillside and had to do everything alone, and because of this, whatever pertinent information I could get ahold of was vital, because there was no one to ask.

The Whole Earth Catalog was fantastically successful. The last edition, a veritable bible which clocks in at 446 pages, sold over a million copies.

As a result of their being a non-profit, this success gave Brand the headache of having to figure out how to give away $1.5 million. But Markoff describes how, even right at the beginning with the first *The Whole Earth Catalog* in 1968, Brand was struggling. High on nitrous oxide from a canister they kept in the office, "he was listening to the Beatles' *Sgt. Pepper's Lonely Hearts Club Band* when suddenly the world went away, and then he found himself on the other side of a large room with Jennings shaking him saying, 'You're laughing hysterically.'" Brand had been pushed over the edge by nitrous oxide, so he abruptly stopped using it. The combination of these drugs, the explosive growth of the *Catalog*, and his failing marriage pushed him into a depression. It would be a significant factor in his decision to place an end date on the *Catalog*, which he set two years later as 1971, just as in the autumn of 1969 it began its exponential growth.

Lou Gottlieb's Morning Star Ranch

As Lou Gottlieb, the forty-three-year-old double-bass player of the Limeliters told the story, "Stewart [Brand] was talking about having a 'back-forty' in the country and I told him, 'Well I have one. Let's go take a look at it.'" Gottlieb, frustrated with his musical career, had installed a grand piano there and was training himself to become a concert pianist by the age of fifty. Gottlieb's property was perhaps the first satellite of the early psychedelic community that grew up in the Haight-Ashbury district of San Francisco. Some lived there permanently, but many hippies would travel back and forth from that district and Gottlieb's rural commune, an hour or so north, outside Occidental in Sonoma County. Writing in the invaluable compendium of interviews and information pulled together by Ramón Sender Barayón, *Home Free Home* (1977), former communard John Coate describes Morning Star Ranch as embodying the most far-out principles of the time: "At the farthest outer edges of the countercultural zeitgeist of the 1960s, you had Morning Star Ranch". Its very early genesis, starting in 1967, meant that a number of the people involved went on to be key founders of the mega-commune of the era, the Farm, in Tennessee. Gottlieb wanted Morning Star to be an example of what he called the "Open Land" principle: the land itself should select those people who wanted to live on it. Gottlieb went as far as deeding the property to God, which didn't stop its eventual mandated closure in contravention of zoning regulations.

Richard Fairfield describes the property in *The Modern Utopian*: it "consisted of approximately 32 acres of land. Forest, meadow, and orchard made up about half of the area; banks and inclines too steep for use composed the rest. The topsoil was not fertile, being generally a clay mixture that possessed only marginal potential for crop-growing purposes." In San Francisco in 1967, the Digger organisation, that fed hippies on the Haight for free, mostly with discarded food, had been scheming on ways to feed the anticipated hordes of young people. Gottlieb recounts:

> On March 14th a delegation of Diggers, including Digger Ed and Calvino DeFillippis, the talking organic gardener — a great theoretician who could never be caught doing any work — came to visit. They said two hundred and fifty thousand teenagers were expected to arrive for the Summer of Love and somebody had to feed these kids. They heard that Morning Star Ranch had an organic apple orchard, and wanted to know if they could have some of the harvest in return for work on the orchard. I agreed, even though the

> earliest apples would not be edible until around August. As a result, hippies started to arrive in quantity because, as I learned later, the Diggers put a sign in their Free Store encouraging people to visit the 'Digger Farm', giving our address. One older man arrived who claimed to be a veteran of the Abraham Lincoln Brigade; he really knew how to create a garden. The hen houses were disassembled to make shelters, and the place where they stood was cultivated as a huge garden that produced an amazing amount of vegetables.

The same garden, and the experienced elderly gardener, is described by communard Pam Read Hanna:

> As the weather got warmer, we started a garden by the chicken coop. That soil was miraculous — old chicken shit. Nothing like it. I planted radishes and Swiss chard and turnips and mustard greens, then corn and beans and tomatoes and squash. Everything grew from day to day like those time-exposure nature videos you see on PBS. Later, an older dude who always wore clothes and a straw hat came and took over the garden. That was a relief to me because it was huge by then.

Victoria remembers that "the fruit flowed as if from a cornucopia, apples from the orchard, six different varieties, walnuts, plums, pears, and quinces. It was a mind-blowing experience for everyone. That summer was paradise."

A *TIME* magazine article, of 7 June 1967, captures the bucolic scene before it curdled:

> The ranch is owned by Lou Gottlieb, 43... who has his hippie followers hard at work — rarest of all hippie trips — growing vegetables for the San Francisco diggers... That hippies can actually work becomes evident on a tour of the commune's vegetable gardens. Cabbages and turnips,

> lettuce and onions march in glossy green rows, neatly mulched with redwood sawdust. Hippie girls lounge in the buffalo grass, sewing colorful dresses or studying Navajo sand painting, clad in nothing but beads, bells and feather headdresses. (Not everyone is a nudist — only when they feel like it.)

The article in *TIME* was in some respects a high-water mark for the counterculture. Bill Wheeler, Gottlieb's friend, comments, "*LIFE* magazine had their beautiful article, all those pretty, you know, apple-pie photographs. And I mean, it's just yummy! It looked like: 'Oh my God, we made it. They've accepted us. Wonderful!' Two weeks later what happened? Manson. And the honeymoon was over."

The story of the old organic gardener is triangulated by Fairfield in *The Modern Utopian*: "One man who joined the commune in the spring was particularly influential in developing an organic garden and teaching all who were interested. Overpopulation drove him off the land before the end of the summer." Of the massive influx of hangers-on precipitated by the Diggers, and presumably also by the attractive publicity provided by *TIME*, Gottlieb writes, "As a result of that visit, Morning Star has had not eight but closer to one hundred and eight visitors, not one tree in the orchard has been touched [not a stroke of work done], the food bill has gone up by about three times from what it was, and we had a number of cases of stomach illness." Nevertheless — although augmented by Gottlieb — according to Hanna, the garden fed the commune. "In 1967 you could buy 100 pounds of good brown rice for $10, Lou often did, because nobody else had any money. With the brown rice and cooked greens and baked squash and green salads, we fed a lot of people that summer — often more than two hundred at a meal."

LSD and Eastern philosophy at Morning Star

Lou had met Timothy Leary at one of the love-ins earlier in the year, and in mid-July 1967, Tim arrived to visit the growing community. Lou gave him a tour, proudly showing off the alternative architecture, sitting in the orchard meadow for a while as Tim rapped to a circle of devoted listeners. Gottlieb recounted:

> Tim Leary is a great American, and one of the bravest men I have ever known. I have never come away from his presence without feeling inspired and instructed. He is one of the great teachers of our time, a Gnana Yogi. I would say that he has only one tiny defect, and that is that he loves to freak people out. And he does so with so much power and virtuosity that he has scared some people very badly.

The use of acid at Morning Star and its successor Ahimsa Ranch was extensive. However, its unmistakably chemical nature (in comparison with "natural" drugs like marijuana, peyote, and magic mushrooms) began to sit at odds with the back-to-the-land generation. Bill Wheeler, owner of Morning Star's successor, Ahimsa Ranch, wrote in terms we can understand within our context of growing:

> My own feelings about LSD are that it should be taken sparingly and only in a supportive environment. If the conditions are right, LSD can be enjoyable and educational, but if they are wrong, expect a bum trip. Acid is inorganic. Artificial fertilizer will produce big fruit, but the food value and the goodness are nothing compared to something organically grown. Most people, after a certain amount of LSD-taking, find they have gotten as much out of it as they can and turn to spiritual and yogic disciplines for a more lasting attainment of expanded consciousness.

As sure as day follows night, Gottlieb's experiences with psychedelics and the complimentary "grounding" aspect of growing plants were accompanied by a fascination with Eastern philosophy. Gottlieb entered into correspondence with Sri Aurobindo's lead disciple and heir, "the Mother", in Pune. He writes to her saying, "Morning Star IS THE WORK OF THE MOTHER! She MUST be apprised of EVERYTHING that goes on here..." Once Morning Star was established, Gottlieb set off to India "with the specific intent of seeing my guru, Mother Meera, at the Sri Aurobindo Ashram". He returned with the guru Chiranjiva in tow. Sender Barayón remembers:

> Lou had great hopes for 'Father', as his disciples called Chiranjiva. He expected him to settle at Morning Star and zap the county officials [who were trying to shut the ranch down] with high vibrations. Instead Chiranjiva spent more and more time in the city, and made it clear he didn't like life at the ranch. Its primitive earthiness reminded him too much of the poverty of India, just what he wanted to forget.

Chiranjiva was furious when Gottlieb's young partner Rena spiked him with a tab of LSD. He finally settled into the quadraplex on the northwest corner of Scott and Lloyd Streets in San Francisco, where he lived until his death. The guru acquired many American wives, in Gottlieb's words "marrying eight of the most unique and difficult women I have ever encountered". Gottlieb remembered:

> Chiranjiva has hurt me many times for my own benefit. I would say that the wound from which I have yet to recover is when he took me aside one day and said, 'Your whole Open Land thing is nothing but a re-run of Vinova Bhave.' Vinova Bhave is the disciple of Gandhi who originated of the Bhu-Dan (land gift) movement in India. I have never recovered from that blow... But Open Land in the United States is no re-run of anything.

Bill Wheeler's Ahimsa Ranch

Morning Star Ranch became increasingly mired in a legal battle with Sonoma County police and building code and sanitation inspectors, who eventually shut it down comprehensively in 1973, but not before bulldozing all the structures there three times. In response to these troubles, Gottlieb's friend Bill Wheeler opened up Sheep Ridge, his wooded 320-acres of land off the remote Coleman Valley Road. At its peak, Sheep Ridge — or as it came to be known, Ahimsa Ranch ("Ahimsa" meaning "nonviolence" in Sanskrit) — was home to around one hundred people at any given time. Morning Star's energy and key founders like Ramón Sender Barayón moved there.

Wheeler comments of the transition, "One day the land was peaceful and serene, the next it was swamped with hordes of people, kids, cars, noise, trash, and insecurity. Almost the same day Ronald Reagan proclaimed, 'There will be no more Morning Stars,' Sheep Ridge opened its gates." Discussing his motives, Wheeler reflected, "What I would like to say essentially about opening the Ridge is that it was a real leap of faith, a real leap into the darkness, or the light — or whatever you want to call it. And it was an incredible, very revolutionary thing. One of the reasons why I opened the Ridge was because I wanted a place in history."

Gwen Wheeler and the garden at Ahimsa Ranch

Gardening was a part of the history of Morning Star Ranch, but was more so at Ahimsa Ranch. The first gardener there was Bill Wheeler's wife, Gwen:

> Although it was the middle of winter, I found our vegetable garden at Irish Hill still growing. With that exciting discovery, I became increasingly interested in gardening. As the rains poured down, I sat by the fire and read books on growing things. I dreamed of living the simple self-sufficient

> life in the country. My first weeks of living close to nature made me feel so loving and gentle that I couldn't imagine raising animals to kill as food. I had met many vegetarians who were convinced eating meat was unnecessary, so that January it seemed right to become a vegetarian myself. Bill joined me in my decision.

Gwen describes the evolution of the adjacent community garden at the commune:

> A half-acre was fenced off in the middle of the ranch for a community garden where anyone could work or pick at any time. Due to a devout belief in abstention from organization, the garden went through alternating periods of abundance and scarcity. It was not uncommon for one tomato plant to get weeded, watered, mulched, pruned, and staked by as many as three people in one day and then be totally ignored for two months. But there was never a time when vegetables for dinner could not be found by a serious seeker. The garden also served as a social gathering spot. Mostly naked people could be seen lying in the sun, one hand gently weeding the radish patch, smoking dope, and rapping with friends.

Their own garden was close by:

> Across the road from the community garden was Bill's and my personal garden, which was half its size. It was my life. I lived in it and shit in it and worked in it about three hours a day. I knew every plant and every inch of soil as well as I knew the stitches in a sweater I had knitted. Bill did the heavy work, and I did the lighter tasks, the supervising, and the daily responsibilities. I was possessive of the work and the harvest of the garden and wanted everything to be done just the right way. It provided the main part of our vegetarian menus, and there was plenty left over to be shared.

In time, Gwen took to living outdoors in the vegetable garden. The first night, she awoke to find a gourd growing beside her head and never slept in the studio again. She and Bill slept under a tarpaulin, ate their own vegetables, and went naked all day long. Pregnant, she would spend the morning weeding, watering, hauling compost and mulch and digging up new plots, with occasional breaks to lie in the sun beneath the leaves of her plants to admire their colours and patterns against the sun and blue sky. Gwen had her baby, named Raspberry after their delicious raspberries, right there in the garden.

Alicia Bay Laurel

Bay Laurel is not her family name. Fittingly for this book about plants, at the sweat lodge at the Wheeler's Ranch commune, she scrubbed herself with fresh California bay laurel leaves, inhaled the essential oils rising, and started to sing songs she'd never sung before. She thought, "This is my herbal ally — so that's how I chose my name." Alicia Bay Laurel became a household name with her book, *Living on The Earth* (1970), a handwritten, illustrated guide to a kind of avant-garde, far-out type of self-sufficiency that sold a staggering number of copies in the early 1970s. Its review in the fall 1970 edition of *The Whole Earth Catalog* sums up its universal appeal: "This may well be the best book in this catalog. This is a book for people so, if you are a person, it is for you."

Alicia, who asked me to refer to her using her first name, had an unhappy childhood growing up in affluence in Los Angeles with uptight parents. The only person who was happy was their Mexican housekeeper, Maria Martinez, a *curandera* — a healer — who grew and concocted her own herbal remedies, growing medicinal herbs in the garden and drying them in her room. At San Francisco State College, in 1966, she signed up for a course in Gestalt Therapy, took purple Owsley acid on a houseboat, and "realised that every single thing in the entire universe that ever was and ever will be was connected and it was intelligent, and it was all communicating, and I was just part of it — and that changed me FOREVER". Thereafter she concluded that she wanted to live "outside of the city, living on a piece of land with some friendly bohemians". By way of (a) being checked into a psychiatric hospital by her mother (where Alicia set about cheering up all the other inmates), and being released by the doctors (who thought there was nothing wrong with her), (b) witnessing Timothy Leary's "Turn On, Tune In, Drop Out" speech at the University of Michigan, (c) catching and recovering from Hepatitis, and (d) learning about Wheeler Ranch through Stephen Gaskin's Monday Night Class seminars, and hitchhiking there — she eventually realised this ambition.

Alicia, still fizzing with pixie energy all these years later, told me about her life at what was even then a notorious commune. "I just was overwhelmed by how much I loved being there in the woods, and no cement, no clocks, no traffic, no jobs, no nothing." A grassroots entrepreneur, with an entirely uncynical gift for creative opportunities, straight away she started figuring out how to grow food:

> I was just like, how do you make food without going to the grocery store?... I had never grown vegetables before and I wasn't even very fond of vegetables because my mother bought many of them frozen or canned, and routinely overcooked the fresh ones... [at the commune] we had freshly picked garden vegetables, something I hadn't experienced before arriving at Wheeler Ranch. And they were unexpectedly delicious.

I asked Alicia how she learned how to grow food: "The Rodale books were popular because they were basically what was around in those days... This was 1969 when I got up there, and so there wasn't like a huge shelf of organic gardening books." In *Home Free Home*, Ramón Sender Barayón describes how Alicia's *Living on The Earth* book came together by way of offering a service to her fellow communards:

> Alicia began working on an intercommunal newsletter, describing in an unpretentious script and with simple line drawings the basic skills needed by newcomers to live primitively in an isolated rural community. She demonstrated with childlike fluidity how to build a shelter, shit in the ground, chop wood, have a baby, etc.

Sender Barayón suggested that Alicia show his friend Stewart Brand, the founder/editor of *The Whole Earth Catalog*, her handwritten and ink-line illustrated book layout. Brand directed her to his distributor, Book People, and promised that if anyone agreed to publish it, he would publicise it in *The Whole Earth Catalog*.

The instructions in the book with regards to growing are remarkably thorough, covering the full range of the process: planning, equipment, starting seeds, preparing, planting, compost, thinning, mulch, stakes, daily care, and harvesting. On composting, she writes:

> Compost: build a sandbox-like structure two feet high and cover it with a heavy black plastic sheet (to accelerate rotting and to keep flies from breeding in it — keep it covered at all times!) Place in it all organic waste (keep a bucket in the kitchen and collect it) (except meat scraps, which attract skunks). manure, leaf mold (rotting leaves from forest floor) and mineral supplements like granite dust (find out what your soil lacks). Chopped sea vegetation is rich in minerals. Stir well, shred by machine if possible. age 6 months before using.

Alicia described her way of thinking at the time to me.

> Did you see a book from that era called *The Secret Life of Plants*?... So, people who've taken psychedelics believe that everything is connected and everything is sentient and that it's all one. Okay? So that's the place from which most of us were coming from into gardening. We and the plants were part of the same family and we were taking care of them.

This ethos is expressed in Alicia's song "Planting Day Ceremony" from her enchanting album with Ramón Sender Barayón, *Songs From Being of the Sun* (1973):

> (To the Earth) Let the elements be harmonious, / welcome these children of the sun / and bring them to fruition, / (To the plants) You are collecting sunlight for us, / we will bring you water, we will bring you compost, mulch and posts to lean on. / We will sing your praises and protect you from blights, frost, / and passing deer herds. / Will you give us your sunlight when the earth collects your bodies?

The landowner Bill Wheeler, who made the 360 acres available to the hundred or so people living on it for free, describes the scene.

> When most folks were still in heavy sweaters. Alicia could be seen wandering around in the fog without a stitch of clothes, a book or some sewing under her arm. When the sun began to warm the air that spring, she was in the garden almost every day, doing yoga and tending the vegetables. She was the only community member who gardened regularly that second summer. Without her care the community garden would have never started. In those days she was also the only person on the Ridge who was neither 'without income' nor on welfare. She generated income from various creative projects that she sold, an activity then unique among Openlanders.

The rampant success of *Living on the Earth* catapulted Alicia into a different world. For instance, she was a featured guest for five consecutive days on *For Women Only* — aka *The Sonya Hamlin Show*, in Boston. "It was on that show that I met Helen and Scott Nearing..." Nevertheless, it seems like she could hardly be accused of letting the mainstream world mess with her mojo. She blew a generous chunk of the book's very large advance on a three-day party at Wheeler's Ranch, inviting over all of the communes in the area. Eight hundred people camped on the land, celebrating at night around a series of campfires, each with its chosen genre of music.

Women in the back-to-the-land movement

It's impossible to imagine the back-to-the-land movement getting past the suburbs without women. The men of this period were often idle and spoilt. Richard Fairfield puts it bluntly, "Women retain their subordinate roles as homemakers, child bearers, cooks, and bottle washers. Men roam the land in search of food, dope, and occasionally other women." Women with children also provided what was most communes' only reliable source of income in the form of government welfare.

When I spoke to her, Alicia was more generous when recalling these feckless men. "There were some guys at the commune that all they wanted to do was to get high." However, she feels that was understandable. Men who had been socialised from childhood to defend the tribe, once they had embraced non-violence and elected to oppose the war in Vietnam, needed to make some inner adjustment:

> But that translated into other things, you know, and it was like there was more consciousness available in the guys... And that was one thing that psychedelics did... It was like we were wearing very tight shoes, and the psychedelics would loosen all of the laces and you could take the shoe off and feel your barefoot on the ground and say, 'Who am I really?'

> And as the person came down from the trip, maybe they'd put the shoe back on because they wanted to be able to drive a car or write and read. But maybe they put the shoe on a lot more loosely and they began to look at things in a much more open-minded way. And that to me was excusable. The feminist movement came right on the tail of the commune thing... Women like me were saying, well, why can't I use power tools? Why can't I drive the tractor? And if we could drive the tractor, why couldn't men cook?

Alicia's exquisite and delightful children's book, *Sylvie Sunflower* (1973), which *Ms. Magazine* distributed nationally as an insert, grew out of these thoughts.

> What happened was this woman looked at *Living on The Earth* and she wrote me a letter and she said, 'The women in *Living on the Earth* are [performing] gender stereotypes.' You know, they're doing most of the cooking! Not all the cooking, I mean, there was a guy who was smoking fish. But I looked through the book again, through her eyes and I said, 'My god, it's true! I grew up with gender stereotypes and I am guilty of making gender stereotypes in my book.' So immediately I made this book, *Sylvie Sunflower*... So, you see one man who's grinding the wheat into flour and making loaves of bread. There's a woman who is a beekeeper and she's also a potter who has a kick wheel. And there's another woman who tends to the goats. I forgot to say that she made goat's cheese! And everybody plays musical instruments and there's a picture of a guy washing dishes and the little girl is helping him by drying the dishes. And so, it's an egalitarian cooperation between the sexes.

This question of the communes perpetuating gender stereotypes was often remarked upon. In an article, "The Communal Alternative" in *The Modern Utopian*, Herbert A. Otto comments, "I noticed a tendency toward the maintenance of traditional sex roles, with the women doing the cooking and sewing, the men cutting lumber etc. Upon questioning this, I repeatedly received the same answer: 'Everybody does what they enjoy doing.'"

A letter written to the UK's *SEED* magazine in September 1975 rounds on the editors:

> As two women and a man living and working on an organic small-holding we feel very strongly that the attitudes you put forward in *SEED* are reinforcing an implicit and explicit sexism that is all too prevalent amongst so-called promoters of an alternative society. We have noticed, for example, that the illustrations always show women with long-flowing tresses and dresses or as the naked earth mother type, nursing children, cooking or sewing. When are we going to have a picture of a woman in her jeans leaning on her spade? Have you ever tried digging, scything, sawing wood or walking across a muddy farmyard in a long flowing dress? The only articles written by women focus on so-called restrictive feminine activities, whilst anything to do with gardening, technology, animal husbandry etc are inevitably written by and for men.

Country Women

The *Country Women* magazine arrived precisely to tackle this issue. It was put together under the stewardship of Jeanne Tetrault and Sherry Thomas, who together spent seven years homesteading, and who wrote the greater proportion of the articles. They tidied up and expanded these into the classic homesteading book *Country Women* (1976). It promises on its cover to teach women "how to negotiate a land purchase, dig a well, grow vegetables organically, build a fence and a shed, deliver a goat, skin a lamb, spin yarn and raise a flock of good egg-laying hens". Both magazines and books are a goldmine of information, especially on the topic of rearing goats, these animals being iconic of the back-to-the-land movement. To this day in print, whatever your gender, *Country Women* is one of the very best and most comprehensive guides to self-sufficiency available. Written in a way which gracefully assumes no knowledge on the reader's behalf, with lovely illustrations, it is of a piece with other fascinating proto-internet tomes of the hippie era like *The Last Whole Earth Catalog* and *Living on the Earth*.

Jeanne Tetrault writes in "The Next Step", "From the very beginning, the women who lived on the farm took a primary part in the building, fencing, animal care, gardening and so forth..." It becomes immediately obvious that the men in the commune were useless: "Most of the men we lived with were seriously into writing and this (pre)occupation often limited their interest in and energy for the farm." Tetrault says this balanced the commune differently to others, but to be honest it seems very typical. She goes on to say that, in spite of their "difference", "we managed to fall into some classic traps. For a time all of us — men and women — assumed that the women were the primary housekeepers. It took some struggling and rule-making to equalize the work — and it was never wholly equalized." You'd think that at the very least the men would be able to take on "usual" male tasks, but it seems not. "If the electric pump broke, the women automatically expected the men to be able to fix it — or the man acted on that assumption, and though we were all equally ignorant, the pump was their problem."

The importance of written guides for women is flagged up by Carmen Goodyear in the *Country Women* magazine article "Homesteading". "As we are isolated on separate homesteads, some of the most accessible teachers are farm journals, magazines, and books. But women beware! Most of this information is written by and for men." Other women emphasise the importance of "learning-by-doing". This issue about education is summed up in an article by Ruth and Jean of Mountain Grove, "Our tractor":

> Our tractor looks like a huge-imposing muddy, and when it's turned on, noisy machine. The men who drive it seem so strong, so macho, so it was with some astonishment that I heard my partner Jean saying one fine spring evening that she would be willing to learn to drive the tractor. Since we always do things together it's a lot more friendly and fun that way. I knew this meant I too would learn to drive the tractor. I made one request; she would learn from the man, but she would teach me.

Back-to-the-land women could also turn for advice to women on farms. Jean Hoth writes in an article, "Belonging to the Land":

> Contrary to what the *Farm Journal* and *Hoard's Dairyman* might lead one to believe, the women on farms in this country are doing a good deal more than baking cherry pies and tending the chickens. Most farm wives as well as independent farming women are proving themselves to be capable farmers. They are running big equipment, pulling calves and cleaning barns, in addition to keeping books, gardening and canning.

Katherine C. George had run away from home in 1932 at the age of twenty-two and had married a woodsman in an isolated mountain village in Northern California. "In the late '60s many young people escaped from the city and came here just as ignorant as I had been. It has been fun teaching them all the ways of the woods that I learned from the old timers. I hope their farming and living in the woods makes them as happy and as contented as I have been."

There were situations in which women felt at a disadvantage. In "Breaching the Barrier", Jan Schutzman writes:

> The experience of feeling out of place recurs frequently as I deal in the world of agriculture. I shrug it off with difficulty,

> find it far harder to cope with than with the heavy physical work of country life. The agricultural industry is as male centered as any there is, and because much of the work is heavy and hard, derision is a major element in the various uncomplimentary looks most agricultural workers aim at a woman who is trespassing into their domain...

She comments elsewhere, "Occasionally, though, as I struggle to load the stove with a 35 pound log, or feel the rough contrast of the jagged hardness of split rounds pressing against the softness of my breasts, I am made wryly aware of the vulnerability of a woman's body in the arena of heavy physical work."

Sexist male attitudes didn't help. Carmen Goodyear pinpointed a particularly mean double-bind:

> This peculiar disbelief of women's authenticity as a productive animal farmer has been shown to me many times in my four years as a goat raiser and breeder. I would guess that almost all goat and cow dairies in this country remove the kids and calves at birth and pan or bottle feed them. The object, after all, is to get the milk from the mother for yourself. However, when we two women follow this procedure, we are accused of baby-snatching and substituting these poor animals as our own denied infants.

Even so, there's sometimes a self-critical tone that women needed to step up. In "Women's Life at the Garden of Joy Blues", Catherine Yronwode writes:

> But on a subtle level we all have a lot to learn. The men need to learn to treat the women as self-determinant beings whose ideas are of value, especially in carpentry. The women need to learn to take the initiative in such activities as getting firewood and building instead of waiting for a man to come boss them or guide them. How do we learn? By practice, by

> reading books, by being taught a skill from one who knows it. I've learned to do elementary carpentry from my mate, but really in some ways that's the hardest road to follow. He is too often watching over me, and I am too often begging help I don't really need.

On many occasions, however, the articles in the *Country Women* magazine transcend gender. There's nothing remotely "feminine" about Lucille Sadwith's writing on energy conservation in farms in an article titled "Food & Energy", or a column like "Watering your Garden" by Leona. This, as you'd expect, is just sound horticultural advice in no way addressing gender at all. The same applies to Jeanne Tetrault's extended essay on "Good Goatkeeping". In fact, farming offered interesting ways for women to step out of gender-based roles that weren't available in the city. Nancy Todd of the New Alchemists described a funny situation involving Hilde Maingay (whom we will meet again in the "New Alchemy" chapter of this book):

> A while ago, a group of us were turning the compost late one Saturday afternoon, an activity that has acquired the status of a near ritual. As we shoveled, someone commented on the smell, which was at that moment, as I remember, largely vintage cabbage. 'Smell,' said Hilde, who is our chief gardener and thinks well of compost. 'That's the new perfume.' To which one of the men, who has a voice which has been described accurately as stentorian tones, thundered, 'If this is the new perfume, then women's liberation has gone far enough.' And Hilde said, 'It's just beginning.'

Twin Oaks, Total Loss Farm, and Cold Mountain Farm

Back-to-the-land was a massive phenomenon in North America; for a while it was suggested that a million people took part in it during the 1970s. Dona Brown torpedoes this figure as "an estimate extrapolated up from the study of a small area in British Columbia, a hotbed of back-to-the-land activities". In the absence of any statistics, it's safer to be vague and say "a lot" of people were involved. Equally, it's impossible to offer up a comprehensive survey of growing and farming against the movement. We collect here these three communes, all of which had a degree of celebrity, by way of a sampling, to give a feel.

As much as rural communes could survive on the contributions of an occasional well-off member, or on food stamps — and confusingly, some, like Wavy Gravy's Hog Farm, were only *actual* farms for the blink of an eye — growing and animal husbandry were a major component of many. Legendary, and still running today, the Twin Oaks commune was set up in June 1967 by Kat Kinkade and run on the principles outlined in B.F. Skinner's *Walden Two* (1948). Located in Louisa County Virginia, they called it Twin Oaks, after a tree on the property, and not after Skinner's book, "because so many starry-eyed people would show up expecting us to be just like [Thoreau's or perhaps Skinner's] book". Richard Fairfield describes it:

> Visitors were required to work a specified number of hours and to pay a fee according to the length of their stay. As I discovered, it was fun to be a visitor picking and shelling peas, husking corn, and watching the tomatoes stew in a big outdoor vat. The members had already canned enough vegetables to last the winter, but were now worried about the lack of freezer space; they had no money to buy another freezer... A dairy cow and hay feed were kept in a small rundown barn. But at the time I was there the milk and butter were all being sold to the outside because the cash income was sorely needed.

Raymond Mungo paints a picture of his Total Loss Farm in Vermont, named thus because "not even one peach or a can of maple syrup makes it to market. And nobody who goes in there to stay has ever been seen alive again." There they "till the soil to atone for our fathers' destruction of it". Seen through a tripper's eyes,

> When the farm is there at all — as it is today — we can see it entire and miniature, like play-farm plastic toys you set up on the linoleum while mommy is busy at dishwashing. We can see the long shed with its stalls full of funny red Volkswagens, the big old barn, majestic and crimson, with hens and rooster enpenned, a chestnut mare named Janice, the doleful and true-blue cow Dolly, a very silly white goat... Beyond this barnyard setting, at once Norman Rockwell and Dalí, the long flat field where corn and potatoes, peas and melons, tomatoes and onions and love all grow, with the help of some well-chosen chants. And more stately apple trees, berries of every variety, herbs and spices cultivées, pears and flowers and hay and suddenly Mountains, one on another, stretching as far as tomorrow and yearning to play with the clouds like dragons.

At Cold Mountain Farm, in upstate New York, there were ups and downs. The communards told Fairfield that "starting a community farm is an incredibly difficult thing. We didn't fully realise this when we began. Setting up a new farm — or rather, rehabilitating, an old and neglected one — was at least a season's work." While they are freezing cold and their dirt road was nearly impassable, forcing them to walk through snow to reach their house, they were also trying to "find a tractor immediately to haul manure for compost heaps. They should have been started the year before as they require three months' time to rot properly, and we wanted to farm organically." Eventually they get their tractor fixed and begin planting at a furious pace a week behind everyone else in the area to get crops in before it was too late in a region with a short growing season. When it got warm, they took to wandering around naked. "The local people, who had originally just thought of us as 'strange' and had then begun to accept us as old-fashioned organic farmers, could now call us 'hippies' and forbid their kids to have anything to do with us." At the end of the summer, after a mass exodus common to all these communes which attracted fair-weather visitors from the city,

> the few of us who remained at the farm were doing fairly well, enjoying the fruits of our labours in gobbling up the zucchini, baby onions, carrots and parsnips; savoring the apples, pears and plums; gathering myriad blackberries, chokecherries and gooseberries for preserves; eating delicious brown fertile eggs.

As with the relationship of the Diggers to Morning Star Ranch, sometimes the aim was to provide food to the counterculture's stormtroopers at the frontline in the cities. At Cold Mountain Farm, the commune originally planned to provide free organically grown food to New York's Lower East Side hippie communities. Similarly, a commune in British Columbia aimed that "by next summer we hope to be able to ship free vegetables to Vancouver to be distributed by YIPPIE! or the VLF. Good spuds are not as spectacular as Molotov cocktails perhaps, but one does what one can."

The Farm, Tennessee

In the pantheon of America's great back-to-the-land communes, Morning Star Ranch and its spin off Wheeler's Ranch are the equivalent of Frank Zappa's the Mothers of Invention: foundational and exploding with possibilities. The Hog Farm might be something like Blue Cheer: short-lived but conceptually influential. Total Loss Farm: a one-album-wonder like Kak. Twin Oaks might be Jefferson Airplane: durable and popular. To extend the musical metaphor, Tennessee's the Farm could be compared to the Grateful Dead: a massive formation of staggering longevity which drew thousands of people away from mainstream life into its orbit.

There are some very good books written on the Farm: Douglas Stevenson's elegant and incisive *Out to Change the World* (2014), and Melvyn Stiriss's massive and highly personal five-volume *Voluntary Peasants* (2018). The Farm published their own books, so there's also the fascinating *Hey Beatnik!* (1974), which is billed as the original handbook for the community. The curious will be able to find PDFs of it available to download online. In addition to the interviews I did with two legends of the community, Michael O'Gorman and Albert Bates, there was no shortage of material.

Stephen Gaskin

Any account of the Farm must start with Stephen Gaskin (1935–2014). Gaskin belongs in the small company of Americans who, in the context of the LSD experience, set themselves up as gurus: the likes of Father Yod, Mel Lyman, Charles Manson, and Carlos Castaneda. Gaskin differed from the rest of this camp in that he was, basically, a very decent individual. Pitching themselves as the conduits of higher knowledge, these gurus differed from American *interpreters* of Eastern philosophy like Bhagavan Das, Ram Das, Allen Ginsberg, or Jack Kornfield.

Gaskin was a 6'5" former Marine turned university lecturer. Born in 1935, he was a little older than the baby boomers. By 1966 he had served with the marines in Korea, had already been married and divorced, and was teaching creative writing at San Francisco State University. He was politely informed by one of his students that, while he was fun and a bit cool, he didn't know what was really going on. The students told him to go and see the film *A Hard Day's Night* by the Beatles. Gaskin commented, "Well, just as they planned, I fell in love with John Lennon, recognized the power of youth as represented by the hippies, and started out on my own hippy path." Gaskin visited Haight Street and commented of it later, "There was an undeniable buzz happening that you could feel to the center of your bones." Picking up the sartorial trappings of the day, he grew his hair long and acquired a wispy goatee. Returning to campus in autumn 1967 after having been immersed in the Summer of Love, he had even trimmed his hair and donned a suit, but still couldn't keep his teaching contract from being cancelled. He recalled in the *Monday Night Class* book, "It wasn't that I got fired for being a hippy; it was just that I'd gotten too weird to be rehired by the time my contract expired."

Monday Night Class

Cut loose from the institution, Gaskin ended up *not* moving off campus, but instead discovered a free slot in the extracurricular timetable. This was being run as an experiment by the college in the manner of a free university. "He said there was an opening Monday nights. I said I'll take it. The first meeting had a dozen people. The next only six. It took me a year to get up to a hundred." Gaskin remarks, "The idea was to compare notes with other trippers about tripping and the whole psychic and psychedelic world." In the words of Farm historian Douglas Stevenson, "He offered a forum to the thousands of young people in the Bay Area who were eager to gain a greater understanding of the mysteries they'd glimpsed through the magic of the psychedelic experience." Classes had titles like "North American White Witchcraft" and "Metaphysical Education".

Recordings of Gaskin's transcribed raps were turned into a book, *Monday Night Class* (1970). It sold over one hundred thousand copies. Gaskin wrote that "hundreds, maybe thousands of people wrote me or have told me in person that this book helped them with their head when they were tripping". Its tiny *Whole Earth Catalog* review expresses this same appeal: "It's simple and straight; it helps me stay loose."

I *love* the book. It captures both an amazing moment in time and a cosmic lucidity. Gaskin's insights into the *etheric* state of consciousness are precious, and a little bit funny as well. "The higher you go up in the astral plane — the higher the vibration — the clearer the transmission gets, and the more strength of character and intelligence and will and love are required to get into the higher and clearer places. When you get really high and clear, you're telepathing in very good company." He also has a good handle on what's referred to as *integration*. "If you feel uptight, and you feel like you're on a high level, what you have to do is take care of the homework on the material plane… If you get loose from the bottom, you know, you're just flappin' in the breeze."

Gaskin, a voracious reader, digested the full spectrum of books on Eastern philosophy, and came to definite conclusions: "Mahayana (Buddhism) is the school that says, 'There is no final and perfect enlightenment for anyone until there is for everyone.'… It's the one that has room for everybody in it… That's why I decided that of the Buddhism strain, Mahayana Buddhism is the kind I like the most." The figure of the Bodhisattva, differing as it does from the Theravadan Buddhist concept of the *arhat* (who only seeks his own enlightenment) was crucial for Gaskin:

> What I mean by 'become planetary' is reaching the point where you know that you're also partly responsible ***sometimes*** for the welfare of mankind, and that in itself is heavy enough for you that it makes you want to straighten up… but getting planetary means that you'll buy in at the level of the vow of the Bodhisattva, which is taking responsibility for ***this*** universe — at least.

He writes in *Hey Beatnik!*, "I believe in the vow of the Bodhisattva. And that says that sentient beings are numberless, I vow to save them all."

Just like the beat poet Gary Snyder, who followed Mahayana Buddhism to ecology, Gaskin arrived back from the heavens with a similar perception. In an interview with Swedish TV in summer 1973 he said, “A spiritual revolution has got to be something that you do rather than you just think. And that’s what the Farm is. We’re doing our revolution. We’re not just thinking it.” Thinking ecologically, in *Monday Night Class*, he advises, “You should probably be careful that you don’t eat more brown rice, drink more water, and breathe more air than is absolutely necessary for your survival”. The connection between the environment and the individual was total: “You take care of your ecology because it’s your own flesh.” The Farm’s institution was therefore a realisation of this philosophy. At one of their gatherings, Melvyn Stiriss recalls, “Stephen waited silently for a while then he spoke about attention, energy, being here and now, and about ‘the urgency of the situation.’ He told the crowd to distance themselves from the military-industrial complex, get self-reliant, get back to the land with friends, grow food and be vegan.”

For all this, Gaskin didn’t seem to know very much about actual farming. Alicia Bay Laurel, who attended the Monday Night Class in San Francisco, quotes Gaskin in her book *Living on the Earth* — his koan is enchanting, but betrays an impracticality: “Find a little bit of land somewhere and plant a carrot seed. Now sit down and watch it grow. When it is fully grown pull it up and eat it.” Gaskin was aware of this gap in his knowledge, he writes, “Like, a lot of the farming stuff I don’t originate. It originates from other folks on The Farm, and sometimes I don’t even know what’s happening and I have to come and ask. But I dig it that it can happen without me knowing what’s going on.”

The Caravan

Gaskin answered the call to address a national convention of Christian ministers held in San Francisco in 1970. Waning congregations meant that the church was looking for ways to connect to a younger audience and Gaskin fitted the bill. He found himself being invited by church representatives to go on a speaking tour of the USA which, fortuitously, would coincide with the release of a book of his lectures being released as *Monday Night Class*. Realising that this could prove an excellent way of promoting the book, Gaskin agreed. The class requested to come along for the ride, and so in August 1970, sixty buses, and a motley gaggle of delivery trucks, converted bread vans, a station wagon, and a number of cars set off on the road. This was the Caravan. On returning to San Francisco, Stephen commented, "When we got back to the city, it had gone bad decadent. There were speed freaks sleeping in the doorways, skinny guys in black coats from New York selling heroin. It was awful! It was obvious that the nest had been fouled too much to build a fresh thing in."

The Caravan was back for only a week before all the drivers assembled for a last time in San Francisco. The plan was to set up a commune to serve as a good example of a utopian society — but local authorities in California had had their fill of communes; celebrated ones like Morning Star Ranch and Wheeler's Ahimsa Ranch had been decisively shut down. Land in California was expensive, and water, vital for self-sufficiency, was scarce.

The Caravan had received an unexpectedly warm welcome in Nashville and so departed for Tennessee hoping to find suitable land for farming. The going was slow. Then one of the Caravanners, who was part of Gaskin's newly assembled rock group, got talking to a young female employee at Gruhn Guitars in downtown Nashville. Her parents owned an abandoned farm in Lewis County about seventy miles south of Nashville. Martin Farm proved a good place to inhabit until a more permanent site could be found. This came in the form of the property of one Carlos Smith, who was getting out of farming. The Caravanners bought his Black Swan Ranch at the price of a thousand acres for seventy dollars an acre. Most of this money came from a few members of the Caravan who had small inheritances. Although, at a thousand acres, the Farm was likely to be the largest hippie commune in the world, in 1973 another opportunity came up to buy an adjoining property of 750 acres, of which a hundred acres had been cleared and was ready to cultivate.

Stephen Gaskin installed himself in what had been Carlos Smith's 1950s-style ranch home, which was the only house on the property which had running water, electricity, toilets, and a phone line. Gaskin used the building as a centre of operations and, as guru, held court there. In due course, Gaskin was built a large home by the community, moved in, then moved out again saying he appreciated the gesture but never really felt right about it, and that it made him feel like he was being put on a pedestal. He chose to have a tent home built for him and his family to the same standards as the others on the Farm.

Douglas Stevenson explains that "new arrivals wishing to join the community were required to make a personal connection with Stephen and make an agreement to accept him as their spiritual teacher, asking permission to stay." Thereupon new members were expected to surrender money and significant possessions like cars — but were allowed to keep their personal items like musical instruments. Everything was purchased collectively in the way of food, medicine, and necessities from these resources. The Farm became a mecca, and up to ten thousand people a year would come and visit. Stevenson describes it as the "most visible example of the counterculture alternative to the capitalist status quo".

Changeover at the Farm

As the 1970s progressed, the Farm began to become unstuck. Run almost like a franchise, as the Farm in Tennessee began to struggle, Gaskin and the central committee decided to bring its satellites elsewhere back into the fold. Even though its population had more than quadrupled, and at its height there were over a thousand residents, this hadn't been matched with an increase in housing or infrastructure. Every facet of life on the Farm was affected by dwindling resources. In the middle of this troubling situation, Gaskin elected to arrange a tour for himself in Europe. Seeing the kind of spiritual power wielded by the likes of Bob Dylan and Mick Jagger, Gaskin, like Father Yod or Allen Ginsberg, began to see music as a vehicle to draw in a larger audience and was putting his energy behind the Farm's band. Cash desperately needed in Tennessee went on travelling expenses for the band and Gaskin's sizeable entourage. This strained patience.

A task force was set up to try to understand what was going on with the Farm's finances. It discovered that each of the many different entities — like the Farming Crew, the Farm Clinic, and the Farm Store — working within the Farm had opened individual accounts at local banks. Some had taken out loans and racked up bills without any supervising centralised Farm accountant being aware of this. It was discovered that the community was in debt to the tune of at least half a million dollars, with some reporting that the sum was closer to a million dollars.

In October 1983, the Changeover took place. It marked the formal dissolution of Gaskin's authority. From thenceforth, every individual and family were responsible for their own personal expenses as well as contributing weekly or monthly towards the community's operating expenses. Stevenson remarks:

> We who had been so sure of ourselves, the hippie visionaries who were going to change the world, had failed. It was a crushing blow to our egos and the air was thick with sadness and depression... Stephen no longer had the power or energy to rally our vision, and as the symbol of and channel for our faith and trust in the universe, his role as a spiritual teacher disappeared like smoke floating through the air.

In 1982, it became apparent that the population was for the first time declining — first slowly, then at pace — so that by the autumn of 1983, it was down to seven hundred. Melvyn Stiriss was one of the people who left:

> We hung in four months after the Changeover, watching the Farm turn into — not exactly a ghost town, but a shadow of its former self. I worked at a plant nursery in Nashville to pay our dues, clinic membership, buy propane, and put food on the table. During this transitional period, there was a string of going-away parties — bittersweet farewells. Looking around a room at everyone dancing, seemingly flashing in and out of existence under a pulsing strobe light — I became acutely aware of the fleeting, transient nature of the universe and the knowledge that all this would soon be nothing but fond memories. March 10, 1984 — Having sold our trailer and said our good-byes, my family arranged itself and whatever we could fit into the little Datsun and drove slowly up the road towards the Gate — wistfully taking in last looks at what had been our home sweet home, our life work and our beloved community.

Albert Bates, who remained after the Changeover and is still there to this day, described to me the end of the old ways as marking a collapse in confidence:

> Loss of confidence is a good way to put it. Confidence in many different parts of the system. Loss of confidence in Stephen as a teacher, loss of confidence in governance of the Farm and unwise decisions that got us into deep debt. The other ways that we had had lots of confidence in the early years had eroded.

Although Gaskin had enjoyed some privileges with his leadership, he was by no measure corrupt. He hadn't been siphoning off money, and he and his wife, natural birth pioneer

Ina May, still lived in a converted, but dilapidated, army tent like the rest of the commune. After the Changeover and being the centre of everyone's attention for so long, people speculated that he must have been shocked to have been pushed to one side and now ignored. He would occasionally refer to the board members who instigated the Changeover as "closet Republicans". Stiriss visited him in later years:

> I found Stephen a sad shadow of his former self — low-juice, not exactly friendly, seemingly depressed. He had become partially blind in one eye after botched cataract surgery and could no longer drive, one of his favourite things to do. At my request, he and I retired to his bedroom and, like in the good old days, smoked strong pot and I got wrecked... Getting in my car, I was seized with the urge to thank Stephen and shouted to him as he walked towards the woods, 'Thank you, Stephen, for all you ever did for me.' He shouted back, 'You're welcome.'

In July 2014, aged seventy-nine, Gaskin died at home of natural causes and was buried in an unmarked grave somewhere on the Farm.

Michael O'Gorman

The Farm took farming as seriously, if not more so, than any other commune. But as they explained in a full-page newspaper advert addressed to their neighbours (neighbours who came to regard them as "Technicolor Amish"), "Although we'd been saying for a long time, 'As you sow so shall you reap,' we found out when we got our piece of dirt that none of us had really farmed before." It had become vital, very quickly, to appoint someone who *did* know what they were doing. If Stephen Gaskin, the Farm's de facto guru, was the Dead's Jerry Garcia — then Michael O'Gorman might have been its Bob Weir. But perhaps it's the other way around?

Michael O'Gorman has made significant contributions to America's cultural life. After his time at the Farm, he helped build three of the USA's largest and most influential organic vegetable farming companies. In 2008, O'Gorman founded the USA's Farmer Veteran Coalition (FVC), which he describes to me as the seventh farm he has run, from "the back of a pickup truck". The programme ingeniously cuts across political lines and has, according to many testimonials, saved the lives of numerous veterans. The organisation has exploded in size and now has close to fifty thousand veteran members; many now farm full-time, others farm part-time or have found work in agriculture, and still others were interested for a while but moved on to other things. Of these, 72% are post-9/11 service members, 20% are ethnic minorities, 16% are women, and an astonishing 59% have service-connected disabilities. O'Gorman himself has a background in anti-war activism (notably around the Vietnam War), but his son answered the military's call after 9/11, and he saw the scheme as a practical way to respond without recourse to judgement; as he puts it, to "beat your swords to plough shares".

I ask him why soldiers make such excellent farmers, and his first response was, regardless of opinions on the value of war, to point to the dynamic commitment that signing up represented: "There's somebody sitting in their armchair saying, 'We need to do this.' And someone saying 'I'll do this'... I was attracted to the concept of the people that were willing to say, 'I will do this. I'll put myself at risk. I'll go through the hardship. I'll separate myself from my family.'" The inference is that these are necessary characteristics of a farmer. O'Gorman points to the research done by Marcy Carsey, through the University of New Hampshire, that revealed that the smaller the rural community, the greater was the percentage of its residents who joined the military. There's a natural symbiosis between the roles: "The whole voluntary military was very rural". The flip-side of the situation was that young people signing up were leaving rural communities for lack of employment and opportunity.

Beyond the purely practical considerations of providing employment for returning veterans, there are issues around ecopsychology: "There's a very therapeutic aspect of [working with] the plants and the animals... And then at the same time, there's a lot of challenge." This challenge is part and parcel of what the psychoanalyst Victor Frankl would regard as "Man's Search for Meaning". As an occupation, farming shares with warfare a symbolic importance that's rare in many fields. The good soldier defends his nation; the good farmer cares for the land and feeds its people. O'Gorman says that returning veterans ask themselves, "Am I going to find anything that has that same sense of purpose and mission?" The FVC answers that question for them. It is a truly remarkable project, and O'Gorman says that the most common response he gets when people hear about it is "How come no one's done that?" Stephen Gaskin would often tell his followers of the virtue of the Bodhisattva — the figure that forgoes transcendence to remain on Earth until every single person is saved from samsara. There's something about O'Gorman's work with the FVC, when he could be retired sipping cocktails on the beach, that has the whiff of the bodhisattva about it. He jokes, "I'm not retiring yet, Matthew!"

While he will always be associated with the Farm — where he ran the Farming Crew between 1971 and its termination in 1981 — and the hippies, O'Gorman sees himself as a child of the civil rights era. "I was, I don't know, a precocious kid and was really a follower of a number of people in the civil rights and early anti-war movements... particularly John Lewis, a gentleman named Bob Moses, Julian Bond... A gentleman named Ira Sandperl who was a kind of a mentor to Joan Baez." Scott Nearing, a notable figure of this era, had "a huge impact on my life... he and his book *Living the Good Life*... Stephen talked about it a lot." Even before all of the revelations around child abuse, he was disillusioned with the Roman Catholic church that he was brought up in because of "their focus on money and... their support for the war in Vietnam". Because of his wife's interests, very early on he wound up in Stephen Gaskin's retinue:

> My soon-to-be wife introduced me to Stephen and his wife, Ina May, who became the Farm's lead midwife. Our first baby was the second born to the community when we were on the Caravan. We became the first couple to have a second child, the first to have a third, and the first to have a fourth. My wife became an important part of the midwifery crew and delivered hundreds of the community's babies. We kind of didn't waste too much time on birthing our family! But she was definitely a follower of Stephen and interested in *Monday Night Class*. And I was a little lukewarm about it actually...

Personally, perhaps with the benefit of distance, I find Gaskin — or at least the Gaskin of the "Old" Farm, before the dissolution of its first incarnation — a fascinating character. Among other historians of the Farm, Douglas Stevenson, Melvyn Stiriss, and Albert Bates express varying degrees of embarrassment about him. O'Gorman, no one's follower, seems to like Gaskin the least. He admits to being in favour of what they were doing as a community: "You know, I was comfortable with the people. I liked everybody and I was very interested in farming and the whole idea of a community... I was fascinated with what we were doing." But as far as Gaskin himself was concerned, by way of illustration he recalls a meeting at which Gaskin remarked upon O'Gorman's evident discomfort with his role of guru:

> At the first group meeting, which involved people eating peyote and happened on the Farm, at what we call the Martin Farm, when people first landed on a piece of property... people sat in the circle on this evening, and Stephen looked across at me, and said, 'Michael, I can tell you like everything about this, *but me*!' And it was a little prescient...

Prescient, indeed, as we will discover.

The Farming Crew

In the biography on his website, O'Gorman describes how "despite my youth and relative inexperience, I ended up in charge of growing the community's food." In 1969, he took only *one class* in organic farming given by author of the book *Organic Method Primer* (1973), organic farming pioneer Dr Bargyla Rateaver. With ample justification, Rateaver described herself as "the one who started the organic movement in California". Remarkably, on the back of that one class, O'Gorman ran agriculture at the Farm for much of his eleven years there, providing, at its peak, 90% of the community's food for a population which reached 1,500 people on one thousand cultivated acres. Vegans, they grew soybeans, peanuts, kidney, black, pinto, and lima beans, and black-eyed peas. They raised white corn, yellow corn, wheat, oats, barley, rye, sorghum, and buckwheat. There were fresh summer vegetables like sweet corn, onions, tomatoes, peppers, aubergine, cucumbers, and green beans; regional varieties like okra, crookneck squash, and butter beans; and cool-weather crops like cabbage, collards, turnip greens, and kale for days. They also grew potatoes and sweet potatoes which were good enough to be certified seed-stock and were sold thus. Every available scrap of organic matter, manure from the horses' stables, the waste from local cotton manufacturing, and spent hay from the fields, was collected. And all the Farm's food waste was composted.

In his five-volume, Day-Glo study of The Farm, *Voluntary Peasants*, Melvyn Stiriss gives a picture of what life on the Farming Crew was like, describing how he

> attended daily meetings with them in the office in the nearby tractor barn. Each morning we met and turned on; listened to big-picture planting and harvesting strategy, and took pleasure in observing Michael O'Gorman's cool, relaxed, egoless managerial style. We called Michael 'Mojo' because he always had good mojo working… The core Farming Crew

> was made up of a score of dedicated at-it-long-hours-every-day men, but many more men, women, and children showed up in the fields. Getting organized, Mojo used a blackboard to assign crops to specific crew members and to list tractor-driving schedules.

In the Farm's book *Hey Beatnik!*, O'Gorman himself describes the scene:

> We've got two hundred tillable acres and six hundred folks and the intention of feeding ourselves. Being vegetarians in Tennessee you can really grow most of what you eat. And we've got about one-fifth of our men farming… So as a crew we're finding out how to have a stoned connection with the dirt and the plant force and at the same time have a sane enough use of the technology that we can feed ourselves.

However, the million-dollar question was "organic". Stiriss describes how "there was a lot of discussion, some emotional, about being organic. Everyone was in agreement — we all wanted to grow organic, but the sad reality was that it seemed we couldn't afford to." Even fifty years later, it seems like the topic has not been put to rest. One of O'Gorman's newsletters explains of the Farming Crew Reunion in November 2023 that when they assemble, they will "talk about what we did and what we may have done differently". At the time, O'Gorman, who has made his reputation as someone who has proved organic can work at scale, elected to temper the crew's purist impulses explaining that "it got a lot heavier when we started treated farming like a real adult vocation instead of some sort of mystical hobby." Learning from their neighbouring farms played a large part in this. He explains, "Pay attention to how your neighbours farm. Your neighbours will respect your honest questions a lot more than you coming on like you know how to do it when they know you don't really." The exclusive use of draft animals was something of a back-to-the-land tenet, but their "first change was to buy some tractors and cut loose of doing it all by horses and mules. That expanded what we could do tenfold..."

At the heart of the matter was compost:

> One of our biggest changes came when we found out that there was no way to haul manure and compost to supply enough acres with the plant food to grow our crops. Somewhere in there beatniks got cultish about organic gardening and didn't get serious about getting fed. Even when you plow in all that organic matter, as much as it rains in Tennessee, important elements get leached out of the soil. And every farmer around uses commercial nitrogen, phosphorous, and potassium. What we do is add as much organic matter as we can, test our soil, and fertilize each field with the mixture and amount it needs. We've been finding that there's some chemical fertilizers that don't upset the ground's microlife. And as our fields get richer we'll need less. We put a lot of juice into adding organic matter to the soil. We haul manure and cotton trash — the waste products of the cotton gin. And every spring we plow in cover crops of vetch and clover.

Probing this history, I'm very careful to let O'Gorman know that I'm in no way judging him, and he admits to having fielded the question in the past. Looking back at the challenges they faced feeding 1,500 people exclusively from their own fields, for three solid years, on poor "class three" soil, when there were no organic wholesalers with whom they might offload some cash crops or buy organic, he thinks "we did some pretty reasonable compromises". Ultimately, the alternative was either eating their own food grown with some chemicals, or having to buy food grown with much more. Indeed, he's proud of the innovations they established in the use of cover crops: "We pioneered large-scale cover cropping. Nobody was cover-cropping the amount of acreage we worked. Even the Rodale Institute. They were just a small experimental farm." O'Gorman describes a clever technique which I have heard discussed by the British self-sufficiency guru Patrick Rivers. Rivers had his back against the wall with a need to quickly generate biomass on a small steep hillside in danger of erosion in the winter:

> When you grow a cover crop in the south, and you grow it over winter. You tend to want to fertilise it in the spring, to get the growth... And you want to get your maximum growth in the spring. And in order to do that, you have to add nitrogen. So, my theory was, well, if we want to add organic matter, a couple hundred pounds of ammonium nitrate per acre can turn into several thousand pounds of organic matter.

Through this method, O'Gorman could use a relatively small amount of nitrogen to, rather than feed crops, feed the growth of green manures.

Occasionally they would use pesticides. At the time he explained:

> We haven't had a real insect problem, mostly because we aren't monocropping year after year. And we've let lady bugs loose now and then, which seems to help. A lot of times we've gotten insects like Colorado potato beetles and tomato hornworms that we were able to stay on top of by hand-picking them off. But every once in a while, it's been, say, the Mexican bean beetle on our crop of snap beans, so we've gone through and dusted with either rotenone or a chemical dust with a one-day half-life. We had to go through some changes here, but we chose to plug into the overall life force and let the garden grow. You don't want to spray too much and upset the balance of all those critters in there, but on the other hand planting a crop of cabbages and letting the cabbage worms eat them up and their moths multiply

> and multiply is upsetting it too, and it's going to affect everyone's cabbage patch for miles around.

But they would never use herbicides to kill back weeds. "We don't want to use herbicides because the vibes are too weird around them."

Today there exists a spectrum of organic pesticides and herbicides. In combination with the higher prices organic produce can command in a now extensive organic marketplace, this allows for a degree of financial mitigation in the event of a crop's failure. This might have provided grounds for encouraging veterans to go down the organic route. Even though, from his own experience, O'Gorman feels that there's no issue organic cannot address, claiming to have "found an organic way to do everything", he has followed what he calls an ecumenical approach:

> When I started the Farmer Veteran Coalition, I decided to put my organic history [to the side], not make it a requirement… not even, you know, like a trojan horse. Where we're at, we're not really trying to convert people into how they farm. We really supported a broad spectrum of farming to make the organisation work…

However, "the reality is most young farmers wanted that kind of organic growing, with all things sustainable, and local…"

The end of large-scale farming at the Farm

What worked so well for such a long time at the Farm, and which seemed to offer such a powerful model to the wider world, went pear-shaped at dramatic speed. O'Gorman, pithily summarising what is likely to remain a bitter memory, describes to me how "we got overextended in the Florida deal… And the farm unwisely cut back on the farming after that." The Farm's historian Douglas Stevenson describes how,

> in order to practice their newly gained skills year-round, The Farming Crew began leasing land south of Miami, in Homestead, Florida, growing vegetables in the winter months that could be shipped to Tennessee. The Florida Farm also became a place to earn money. Initially this was to help fund the operating expenses of The Farming Crew. Work at a green-bean-packing house was so lucrative that it became a revenue stream for the main Farm in Tennessee, and eventually more than one hundred people were dispatched to Florida to work all the plant's shifts.

Around 1977, at the height of the Florida farming operation, a freak blast of cold air sent freezing temperatures south of Miami all the way to Homestead. The Farming Crew's crop was destroyed, accruing a loss estimated at $100,000 in a single night. The Farming Crew and the community's financial managers were in shock. This signalled the end of commercial farming endeavours which continued on a strictly self-sufficient basis, but then wound down from scale to something approaching gardening in October 1983. Stevenson describes how

> soon enthusiasm for the work at the green-bean-packing plant began to fade as well. After a few years with farming no longer the central activity, the relevance of the Florida farm diminished. Its population shrank as people drifted back up to the main Farm in Tennessee, and eventually the Florida Farm shut down for good.

Stiriss describes O'Gorman's showdown with Gaskin:

> One rainy Sunday morning in March, The Farm went 'high tech' and had services on radio. Stephen spoke and took calls

from folks listening at home. Farming Crew chief Michael 'Mojo' O'Gorman called in... Michael called to express his concern over Stephen's decision to shut down the satellite farms, and he had the balls to tell Stephen that he was making a big mistake. That was when the shit hit the fan. Though Stephen preached and taught receptivity, Stephen himself was rarely receptive to critical feedback. He turned defensive and challenged Michael's understanding of 'the big picture.' Mojo did not back down. In his own strong humble way, Michael showed admirable courage and held his ground. I spoke with Michael years afterwards. He reports a hilarious scene was taking place at his end at the Adobe multiple-dwelling house. While speaking with Stephen on the phone, Michael's wife, a midwife on Ina May's Midwife Crew, was pouring a pitcher of cold water over her husband's head to cool him down. Early next morning, Stephen showed up at the Tractor Barn — clearly Mojo's turf. Stephen brought backup — his two loyal PR men, Shutter Bug and Captain Video. When the three arrived, Michael was meeting with his thirty-man crew, planning the day's work. Stephen came in hot. 'Michael! You don't know shit! You call me out in front of everybody yesterday, and you don't know what the fuck you're talking about. I don't think anyone around here agrees with you.' Stephen challenged the group — 'Does anyone here agree with Michael?!' Big mistake. The Farming Crew loved and respected Michael, and they stood solidly behind their boss. Michael held his ground unflinchingly, and Stephen left steaming. Within a week, Michael and his family were gone — leaving a hole in the community and in the hearts of many dear friends.

A stoned connection to the dirt

When I quiz O'Gorman about the spiritual rhetoric he uses in *Hey Beatnik!* about the "stoned connection to the dirt" and the "plant force", I was expecting him to be a little amused by his younger self. Even though he did have a chuckle, he still holds fast to some of those feelings about growing. He reflects, "Yeah, I mean, it's my church... I've a reverence..." Referring to the farm he works with his brother, he describes it as a garden of Eden. "Nature, you know in a kind of a Walt Whitman-esqe way, is my religion."

Although LSD was not endorsed at the Farm, the use of "natural" psychedelics — mushrooms, peyote, and marijuana — was. In the same vein, I couldn't resist asking O'Gorman about his use of them:

> I only took LSD a handful of times. Like five times, which was unlike most of the people on the Farm. I didn't care for it that much. And I felt like people gave it an undue importance... I had a discussion one time on one of the [online] groups and discussions... I said, if I wrote a 400-page book about my life, psychedelics might take half a page. The things that impacted my life came out of my personal journey, you know, the life and death and love and loss. And, you know, the things of nature.

The biggest lesson he says he got from the Farm was "community". "And I brought that sense of community to the other farms I built, and even to the Farmer Veteran Coalition... I think the key element in all their growth was understanding the kind of power, and the beautiful interplay, of people working together." O'Gorman has for many years made it a mission to improve pay and working conditions for migrant workers, and the same theme of community is important in those relations too. "That really translated to working with farm workers from Mexico on both sides of the country, because there's a very communal nature to that culture. And when people work [together] there's a real sense of people really understanding and seeing farming as a team sport." He's disappointed at the lack of people from the back-to-the-land movement who actually ended up in agriculture. "I think of all the dozens and dozens, if not hundreds, of people that I knew that were all going to be farmers, and at a time thought they'd be farmers for the rest of their life. The only two people I knew out of that period of my life that stayed with it were myself and my brother." The only other he can personally recall is Michael Sligh, a key member of the Farm's Farming Crew who went on, like Eliot Coleman, to be an important figure in the formation of the US's National Organic Standards and who remains an active figure in the movement, now working for the Rural Advancement Foundation. There are others besides the individuals covered in this book, such as Gene Kahn of Cascadian Farm, profiled in Michael Pollan's book *The Omnivore's Dilemma* (2006).

Related to questions of community, and the health of the farming community, the need for more people to get involved in the sector, for more hands on the land, is for him "the number one issue about agriculture". Listening to O'Gorman, one gets the sense people are missing out on something profound:

> There is something that even I remember on the Farm, being really conscious that being a farmer transcended culture and time... I'm a farmer, the same as a dairy farmer in Wisconsin or a cotton farmer in Georgia. But I'm also a farmer the same as a woman with her goat herd in Africa or somebody a hundred years ago behind some mules. There's a real sense of... being part of something a lot bigger... and a really bigger group of people... that's powerful.

Macrobiotics, veganism, and vegetarianism

At the time, the vegans of the counterculture would describe themselves as following the macrobiotic diet. Macrobiotics was an evolution of the Japanese Shoku-Yo-Kai diet that became, as *TIME* magazine put it, "the Kosher of the Counterculture".

This was down to the influence of the charismatic George Ohsawa and missionary to Boston, USA, Michio Kushi. The emphasis it placed on avoiding animal products (fish was sometimes allowed), but also upon locally grown and seasonal food, had an outsize influence on the countercultural lifestyle. Richard Fairfield describes how, at Morning Star, "the meal was macrobiotic, zucchini tempura, rice and greens, though there was milk as well as tea"; at Cold Mountain Farm, "living off the land, the Cold Mountain people are putting together macrobiotic meals from local roots and flowers"; and then, at Ahimsa Ranch, "most of the residents adhere with varying degrees of fanaticism to a macrobiotic or vegetarian diet." The Weavers of Maine commune ate macrobiotic food too. Jake Guest of the Wooden Shoe commune remembers:

> You could not buy whole grains in this area [the Northeast]. There was no such thing as 'organic.' There were some stores in Boston — the whole macrobiotic movement. So, we formed these coops — these were buyers' clubs — so we'd get together once a month — voluntarily people would drive down to Boston and drive down to New York and buy food. We started out buying a lot from the suppliers of the macrobiotic people, Erewhon in Boston.

John Seymour thought the macrobiotic fetish for brown rice was quite wrong. "It is ridiculous for a whole generation of freaks in Britain to grow up thinking that the only good food to eat is 'brown rice,' for example. We don't grow rice in Britain. We grow wheat, and we should eat that — it's a much better food than rice anyway." It is certainly rarely appreciated that wheat would be a perfectly acceptable substitute for rice in the diet.

Alicia Bay Laurel joked with me that, more than anything else, hippies argued about food and the nuances of different diets:

> One of the magazines that interviewed me was *East Wes*t journal, which is a macrobiotic magazine. And they were so happy to have me that they had a luncheon for me, right? So I go to this luncheon, it's in Boston, and because I'm the kind of person I am, I made a big, beautiful, green salad with tomatoes and avocados in it because I'm from California and that's my idea of a great meal. And so, I sent it to them, and they looked at it like it was going to bite them.

This was not food the macrobiotics people would eat — vegetables should be cooked!

The Farm were exemplary of this nutritional sectarianism:

> We don't cop to the macrobiotic or fructarian diets because they're inadequate nutritionally and will make you sick and weak. Macrobiotics doesn't provide hardly any protein except for a carp (large goldfish) now and then, which is very yang and not vegetarian... The macrobiotic and fruitarian diets can cause kwashiorkor, the protein deficiency disease.

At the Farm, like at many other communes, they were vegans. In *Hey Beatnik!*, the Farm state, "There are various things that we agree on — like that we're absolute vegetarians, and everybody on the farm does that, and nobody smokes cigarettes, nobody drinks alcohol or wears leather or eats meat or dairy products." Gaskin was strongly opposed to the practices of dairy farming. "So we learned how to make soy milk, and we make eighty gallons of soy milk a day five days a week for about $20.00 worth of soybeans a day. And soy milk is comparable in protein to cow's milk." The Farm grew their own soya and made a tidy profit marketing their own soya ice cream, tofu and tempeh — a process and business that Albert Bates and his family were closely involved in. They explained, "We have a spiritual agreement to keep peace with the animals, so we don't eat meat. A typical meal for us: black-eye peas and cornbread, collard greens, sweet potatoes, mint tea, and sorghum cookies." Sorghum, from the same family of grasses as maize and sugarcane, became, for a while, like soya, an important crop for the Farm because of their avowed veganism. "When we came to Tennessee, we were still using honey so we thought we'd be beekeepers, until we found out it was just too heavy on the bees. Then we heard about sorghum. It's a light sweet syrup, and has been a Southern tradition for generations."

This philosophy was also being informed by ideas coming from thinkers such as Frances Moore Lappé who, in *Diet for a Small Planet* (1971), highlighted the gross inefficiency of the meat industry, this gets summarised nicely by the Farm. "It's so grossly uneconomical and energy-expensive to run soy beans through a cow and then eat the cow instead of eating the soy beans that it's virtually criminal." Moore-Lappé herself, however, took a softer angle. She resisted the sometimes-prescriptive righteousness that attaches itself to vegetarian and vegan diets by pointing out that

> a change in diet is not an answer. A change in diet is a way of experiencing more of the real world, instead of living in the illusory world created by our current economic system... A change in diet is a way of simply saying: I have a choice. That is the first step. For how can we take responsibility for the future unless we can make choices now that take us, personally, off the destructive path that has been set for us by our forebears?

If the communes weren't exclusively vegan, the inclination was to eat more vegetables than meat. Herbert Otto says:

> Marked preferences for vegetarianism and for organically grown food are noticeable in the commune movement... Roughly 40 percent of the communes I visited were vegetarian; 20 percent served both vegetarian and non-

vegetarian meals. The remainder usually served meat when available — usually two to six times a week.

In an article in *Country Women*, "Feminism and Vegetarianism", Jenny Thierman expresses concern about eating animals: "Elizabeth Gould Davis [in the book *The First Sex*] finds that 'the killing and eating of animals by man is a recent phenomenon and is related in time to the patriarchal revolution.'" But Thierman posed further questions too:

> After reading *The Secret Life of Plants* and tuning in more to my garden I wondered how I could continue 'killing' plants. Is pulling up a carrot different from killing a chicken? Is dropping asparagus into boiling water different from dropping crabs in? I stumble over finding an answer just as I hesitate before I pull up a carrot.

As Raymond Mungo recounts, the commune children could be seemingly less bothered by these philosophical questions:

> They once had a pig, but they killed it. 'Kill the pig! Kill the pig!' They chanted, chasing fat Rhonda clear around the orchard and finally doing her in — cutting her and cleaning her, hanging her up to bleed. A terrible controversy then, one of the few I can remember, for some of them stubbornly chewed on lettuce and grains while others dismembered old Rhonda, shanks and breasts and all, and gleefully ate her up for protein.

Marijuana

No doubt about it, one of the most important crops to the hippies was marijuana. The landscape for its cultivation in the cooler climes of North America and Europe changed dramatically in 1978. The legend is lost in a cloud of smoke, but either an individual from Kansas, or someone named "Douglas

Fir", returned from Afghanistan with seeds of the indica strain sourced in the Hindu Kush. Stronger than previous strains and native to colder climates, unlike previously available varieties, it could grow to maturity in only a few months.

In *Living on the Earth*, Alicia Bay Laurel gives instructions on its growing, but covertly refers to the plant, not as marijuana but, as "homegrown" — however, its distinctive leaves in her illustration are a giveaway. She writes, "To start seeds before the last frost: place rich soil in a can or large paper cup and water twice a day... A mantra such as AUM, recited over the seedlings will enhance their growth; they respond to love." More brazenly, in the light of the punishments associated with its use, Stewart Brand writes a review for Bill Drake's pioneering *Marijuana — The Cultivator's Handbook* in *The Whole Earth Catalog*: "How to grow good pot. The best book on the subject." The 1969 edition of *The Cultivator's Handbook* is decoratively festooned throughout with Chinese lettering, in keeping with the counterculture's fascination with Taoism. These glyphs are not present in later editions.

In the Introduction, "Myths — Facts and Fiction", the author Bill Drake talks about the ancient Chinese traditional use of hemp dating back to 2,800 BC, but also of its medicinal use in Europe and its cultivation in Kashmir, Afghanistan, and India. Interestingly, one of the "downright destructive" myths relating to the herb relates to chemical fertilisers. "One of these is that the more nitrogen you throw in, the better; but the fact is that an overdose of nitrogen in early life will kill the plants, and too much nitrogen at maturity cuts potency way down by limiting resin secretion." Later on, we are told, "you can help your plants towards health and happiness by working an organic fertilizer into the soil at least a week before you plant."

Where LSD was no longer endorsed at the Farm, marijuana acquired tremendous importance. As recorded in *Hey Beatnik*, the fact that it was grown organically was significant:

> If you're going to have anything to do with a material sacrament, which is what a psychedelic is, it should be in such a way that there is nobody interspersed between you and where you're going. That is, don't take anything made in a laboratory. If you're going to take anything, there's grass and mushrooms and peyote, which are the classic organic psychedelics. We believe that if a vegetable and an animal want to get together and can be heavier together than either one of them alone, it shouldn't be anybody else's business. We believe in psychedelics and that they expand your mind, but all the rest of the stuff that beatniks take is mostly a social fad. Don't lose your head to a fad. The idea is that you want to get open so you can experience other folks, not close up and go on your own trip. So you shouldn't take speed or smack or coke. You shouldn't take barbiturates or tranquilizers. All that kind of dope really dumbs you out. Don't take anything that makes you dumb. It's hard enough to get smart.

As Melvyn Stiriss describes it, marijuana was crucial to Gaskin:

> No one ever called Stephen 'King Stephen,' though His Highness would have been appropriate, because Stephen smoked more marijuana than anyone I have ever known. Stephen was, in his own words, a 'hard charger,' meaning he was a tough Marine and could smoke anybody under the table. So everyone in that room smoked a lot of marijuana, trying to keep up with the Grass King. [Now in retrospect, I believe smoking all that cannabis made the man a walking contact high for all who entered his field, and much of the energy we attributed to Stephen's charisma, heaviness and holiness was actually cannabis energy we felt.] One day, so stoned I was seeing auras on everyone, I was sitting across

> the room from Stephen. He held up his large palm and I saw, or hallucinated, his palm turn bright shining gold, like we see on gold Buddha statues, and Stephen seemed indeed a 'living Buddha.' We looked into each other's eyes, and for a moment, we seemed to swap places and I thought I briefly experienced being Stephen.

In time Gaskin was convicted and sentenced to a three-year stretch in prison for pot after a huge police raid on the Farm's three-acre marijuana patch. It wasn't even Gaskin's weed, but he thought, as leader, that he should take the rap.

Marijuana, the plant, takes a star-turn in Richard Evans Schultes and Albert Hofmann's *The Botany and Chemistry of Hallucinogens* (1973), billed there as "the hallucinogen most widely disseminated around the world". They provide this vivid description of its effects:

> Time may frequently seem to stand still, not to exist. The familiar, daily environment appears in a new and often glorious light. Forms and colours are changed or acquire a new, sometimes far-off significance. Ordinary objects lose any symbolic character, are detached, and radiate their own intense entity. Colours usually become richer, transparent, radiating from the inside. Visual and auditory hypersensitivity are common and often, especially with high doses of the psychotomimetic agent, lead to hallucinations.

Economics

One reason why farming isn't talked about against the background of the hippies is that the enthusiasm the generation brought to the situation waned. However, it's important to point out at the outset that this wasn't *exactly* their fault. The economics were stacked against the whole enterprise of self-sufficiency. The wider context is that, in Western societies, cheap food would increasingly be used by governments as a tool to prop up industrialised society. Through the agency of this cheap food, wages could be kept low in the cities. This came via imported food, at the expense of the countryside, through government's rural subsidies, and because of the new techniques of mechanised and chemical agriculture. The academic Dona Brown carries some excellent statistics on how food became a lot less expensive. In 1910, food made up 40% of a person's expenditure, and the previous generation of American back-to-the-landers would find growing their own food would save them a lot of money. However, by 1970, the most back-to-the-landers could count on saving was 10% to 15%. Added to which, things which had not previously been a factor became costly: land prices, taxes, and medical costs.

Even with the best will in the world, communards were disheartened. Following instructions in Rodale's *Encyclopedia*, Kate Daloz describes the commune at Entropy Acres planting carrots. The absurdly tiny carrot seeds are almost impossible to sow sparingly and the results on the two-acre plot created months of back-breaking work. "As the summer went on, the enormity of the task they'd undertaken continued to sink in. Every few weeks, the entire crop had to be thinned by hand to allow the remaining carrots room to grow unimpeded." Selling the carrots turned out to be a disaster also, even though, because they were organic, they were able to get twice the wholesale rate and had, at 18,000 lbs, a sizeable amount. Daloz does the maths: "After five months with five adults often working dawn-to dark, seven days a week, they'd grossed $3,000."

It's extremely difficult to grow food effectively, let alone to make money from the process. To get government subsidies, which are the factor which makes it possible for most farmers to exist, farming needs to be done at scale and following the model of chemical agriculture. Bizarrely, from an ecological point of view, there are, if not none, then very few subsidies available for organic farmers. Although the rural hippie communards often elected to grow their own organic food, as we've seen with Michael O'Gorman's experience at the Farm, to make the whole process financially sustainable could make it harder. Plenty of communes didn't even bother with growing food for this reason. Richard Fairfield writes of one of the earliest communes, Drop City: "The members had a small garden, but it was not productive and no one thought of it much of a resource. Food stamps were better."

Jackson Browne's song "Before the Deluge", from his most highly rated album, *Late for the Sky* (1974), is often cited as some kind of anthem for the movement. The lyrics run as follow.

> Some of them were dreamers, / And some of them were fools, / Who were making plans and thinking of the future, / With the energy of the innocent, / They were gathering the tools, / They would need to make their journey back to nature, / While the sand slipped through the opening, / And their hands reached for the golden ring, / With their hearts they turned to each other's hearts for refuge, / In the troubled years that came before the deluge.

As the lyrics spell out, the generation was deeply troubled by a sense of an imminent apocalypse. But when it became apparent that the Armageddon wasn't at hand (immediately, at least!), thoughts turned to other, more prosaic matters.

Sloth

Whether it's a fair assessment of the hippies or not, generally their focus and application has been called into question, and so it is in the specific material I came across. Richard Fairfield speculated about the motives of people who joined communes:

> And I thought of some of the people I had known myself: the mothers who wanted someone else to take care of their children; the fathers who were tired of holding down dull jobs to support a wife and children; all those people intent upon flight from responsibility... After a brief summer of orgies and fun in the sun, the long winter sets in and darkness brings dissatisfaction and disillusionment.

None other than Ken Kesey — author of *One Flew Over the Cuckoo's Nest* and lead Merry Prankster, who later turned agriculturalist — complains in an article in *The Whole Earth Catalog*, "All Asshole Farm Expose", about the attitudes and behaviour of visitors to his farm:

> I hope that this week is the Farm's lowest point for the summer, because if it gets any lower I don't have a decent place to live... you may not feel as bad about this place as I do: you may have just arrived and found a slightly stroppy free summer camp, where you can fuck without your mother finding out, there are no annoying counsellors and no schedule. But I think of this as my (at-least) temporary home. And I like my home to be clear of broken glass and papers, my tools and supplies put away, I like to keep track of my guests, take care of my animals, keep my clothes hung up out of the way, and keep the equipment running. But this farm is far from that.

Tex, a resident at Ahimsa Ranch, complained, "Nobody was helping me. I had a hard time just gettin' people to lug water to put in a pot. I had a hard time gettin' anybody to chop some firewood 'cause all they wanted to do was sit there and eat, smoke up the tobacco or the dope. They were willin' to do that." At the Myrtle Hill commune, in *We Are as Gods*, the chores of gardening, animal husbandry, crop production, and firewood collection, "the 'real' work they'd imagined for themselves during so many nights around the campfire — felt, in practice, uncomfortably close to drudgery."

According to Richard Fairfield writing in *The Modern Utopian*, at Cold Mountain Farm, general hippie indolence caused untold problems:

> The communal garden was a monstrous failure. After the original enthusiasm of planting, hardly anyone cared enough to weed the rows. (Of course, the huge amount of rain this year retarded the growth of the crops and caused the weeds to grow like crazy! And six acres is a hell of a lot of land to weed by hand. If we try again next year, we'll certainly get a cultivator.)

Stewart Brand's criticism of the communes

Perhaps surprisingly, one of the greatest critics of the tenets of self-sufficiency and the whole back-to-the-land impulse was none other than Stewart Brand, the very guy whose *Whole Earth Catalog* inspired so many people to try it. Brand explained publicly in 1975, "Anyone who has tried to live in total self-sufficiency... knows the mind-numbing labor and loneliness and frustration and real marginless hazard that goes with the attempt." In his journal he wrote, "Self-sufficiency is not to be had on any terms, ever. It is a charming woodsy extension of the fatal American mania for privacy. 'I don't need you. I don't need anybody. I am self-sufficient!'" In *The Whole Earth Catalog*'s successor, *CoEvolution Quarterly*, he condemned it again as having "done more harm than good. On close conceptual examination it is flawed at the root. More importantly it works badly in practice." Brand's opposition to self-sufficiency was philosophical, rooted even in Eastern philosophy: "It is a damned lie... There is no dissectible self. Ever since there were two organisms, life has been a matter of coevolution."

Just as he came out hard to a scandalised ecological movement as an advocate of nuclear power, a position crystallised in his book *Whole Earth Discipline* (2009), Brand's vision of the future called for greater degrees of scientific intervention. Using the writer Charles C. Mann's model of "Wizards" (like Norman Borlaug — who seek technological solutions to the question of sustainability) and "Prophets" (like William Vogt — who advise curbing our use of resources), we can classify Brand as a wizard. For instance, like today's advocates of terraforming Mars, Brand wrote in the *Quarterly* about the possibilities of colonies in space as early as the mid-1970s. One of his most bitter critics on this subject was agricultural philosopher Wendell Berry, who described this idea of Brand's as a "warmed-over Marine Corps recruitment advertisement... As you represent it, a space colony will be nothing less than a magic machine that will transmute little problems into big solutions. Like utopians before, you envision a clean break with all human precedent: history, heredity, character."

The permaculturalists Bill Mollison and David Holmgren took a more forgiving and sophisticated view of the matter than Brand. They wrote in *Permaculture One* (1978):

> We do not subscribe to the isolated fortress mentality of a totally self-sufficient approach, but believe in designing for the whole society of man... Independence in areas other than food is extremely difficult for small groups. Further, overall self-sufficiency is a pointless goal, but reduction of dependence on the wider industrial system can be taken a long way, reducing the need for people to work in the industrial society and to consume its products. Thus, the available fossil fuel energy can be freed for essential, rather than profligate inessential uses... More relevant and realistic is community co-operation. When people have established themselves in an area, a complex network of resources, skills and needs, with some specialization, should evolve.

> This inter-independence within a locality and independence in relationship to outside areas will establish itself in time, within a permacultural framework.

Eventually this form of "joined-up" self-sufficiency was inscribed into Holmgren's idea of "descent", which we cover in the "Permaculture" chapter of this book.

Gordon Kennedy

But back-to-the-land didn't *automatically* need to be about communal life. One of my favourite correspondents I encountered during the research for my last book, *Retreat: How the Counterculture Invented Wellness*, is a case in point. We have stayed in touch, so I asked him about his experiences. The organic farmer Gordon Kennedy is author of the classic *Children of the Sun* (1998) study of the Nature Boys, of which he is a scholar.

> The memory of someone like Gypsy Boots was imprinted in all of our childhood brains from the *Steve Allen Show*, because Boots had appeared on there over twenty-five times in the pre-Beatles '60s... circa 1961. A total wild man with long hair and a beard. I discovered his book *Bare Feet and Good Things to Eat* in about September of 1976. On July 24th, 1977, the *Los Angeles Times* published the article about eden ahbez written by his sister in law, and that gave me more info on his life, though Boots had mentioned him a lot in his book too.

Prototypical hippies who evolved from the German *Lebensreform* movement, California's Nature Boys were discussed in *Retreat*. They practiced their own Native Indian-style food gathering and were proponents of organic food and farming. "Old Ray", one of the last Nature Boys of Tahquitz Canyon, wound up at Morning Star Ranch.

Kennedy went back to the land in the early 1970s. His passion for hiking in the southern California wilderness led him to the desert canyons of the San Jacinto Mountains, where there was a sizable population of young hippies living in caves. Aged nineteen, he decided against going to college or working a low-paid job, so he found a cave, turned "feral", and began his new life:

> Over the next fifteen months, my life focused on a lot of foraging for food in Palm Springs, where I discovered things like figs, carob, prickly pear, grapefruit, tangelo, dates, etc. I also bought a farmer's almanac and some seed packages from a supermarket, and then tapped a spring at about 4,200 feet at my mountain camp, which was an amphitheater of large boulders. I started my first farm as a teenager at this wilderness camp, sleeping under giant boulders and growing virtually everything from these seeds I bought.

At this time in his youth, he decided that getting a piece of land and growing food would be his life. In due course he wound up working, learning the ropes, on orchards and farms in Oregon, Canada, and New Mexico before purchasing seven acres in Ojai. Today, true to his original vision, Kennedy grows organic dates in the desert on this seven-acre farm, which has its own natural hot water. Many a communard found their domestic arrangements disrupted by the actions of others. But from his early experiences Kennedy knew that he needed a piece of land in his own name so as not to get kicked out:

> The other mountain dropouts were people like Vietnam veterans, end of the world Jesus freaks, surfers from the coast, and some random idlers. So, this early lesson in political science gave me all the evidence I needed to realize that yoking with other people can be risky, or a total dead end. So, I was very serious about looking to purchase my

own land, in my name only, so I could remove the people who can't work or live in harmony.

FINDHORN

The north of Scotland has an unusual atmosphere. Though it *looks* like England and the south of the UK (albeit completely unspoilt), it *feels* completely different. I arrived at the Findhorn Foundation in the middle of the night in a rainstorm and let myself into "Genesis", the home that founders Eileen and Peter Caddy moved into after their early life in the caravan. Even just the knowledge that the Caddys had lived there gave the large static caravan an eerie quality.

On the second day, Caroline Shaw, with her then husband Michael Shaw, one of the earliest members of the community, showed me around. Caroline was delightfully bossy, vivacious, and entirely practically minded. The couple had been involved in the work of rehabilitating young offenders ("Helping one person at a time didn't seem enough to us") before, in 1974, Eileen Caddy put her arms around the waists of the "well-to-do" couple and encouraged them to come and live permanently at the community. She remembers, "The atmosphere there was palpable... something very enlivening, very attractive." Caroline had studied books by the Theosophist Alice Bailey and had had psychic experiences as a four-year-old following the death of her father in which she was still able to feel his presence. Aged twenty-one, when a treasured family cocker spaniel died, she saw an archetypical canine form rise from its body. These experiences destined her to live a different life.

Caroline had been the project manager for Findhorn's remarkable Universal Hall, which Peter Caddy had tasked her to build. The resources to construct such a huge building simply weren't available, until one by one, in what felt like synchronicities, they suddenly were. Caroline showed me the Caddys' original caravan of legend, currently fenced off; also, what was once the lavatory block, now a visitor centre, where Eileen would sit for hours at night receiving guidance. We saw "The Nature Sanctuary" meditation chamber, like a Hobbit's underground house, and the outdoor community singing chamber. Thanks to her husband, who was instrumental in their construction and gave us the code to get into their greenhouse, we were able to look at the "living machines", a series of connected water tanks in which plants clean the community's grey water. Later in the day I got to see the community's CSA vegetable garden and the adjacent Cullerne Gardens.

Peter Caddy

Peter Caddy, an old Harrovian with growing spiritual inclinations, had, in 1940, been commissioned as an officer with the Catering Branch of the Royal Air Force. In this capacity he was responsible for feeding troops. This, it can easily be forgotten, is a task of great significance, and in a theatre of war, is difficult to accomplish. At the tail-end of the conflict in 1945, after the surrender of Japan, Caddy travelled twice into Tibet, where he was awed by both the mountainous Himalayan landscape, with its rhododendrons and azaleas in bloom, and the people who had a simplicity, joy, and vitality. "Of all the places that I have ever visited in my life Tibet had the greatest attraction to me."

However, in some respects Caddy was disappointed by the mystic culture there. He had looked upon it as "being central to the spiritual government of the world", a reference to Theosophist Madame Blavatsky's channelled communications with the likely fictional Tibetan Mahatmas Koot Hoomi and Morya. It was disillusioning to find that, just like anywhere else, "many of the people had become crystallised in their thinking and customs". Even a lucky visit to Gyantse Dzong, which the Tibetan authorities had forbidden his group to enter, did not convince him. This visit was the result of Caddy's mule, which, bolting at the sound of the temple horns, charged uncontrollably into the monastery courtyard. On the other hand, he observed that this meant that "the spiritual work of our times was not confined or concentrated in any particular creed or country, but must find its expression everywhere".

As far as Caddy was aware, his expedition, a military holiday he had secured authority to organise so as to keep men from carousing the "fleshpots" of Calcutta, was the last into Tibet before the Chinese Invasion. Caddy's own account of his Tibetan travels is told very matter-of-factly. Where he self-deprecatingly describes personally turning back on his route to find a pair of stragglers who had dropped behind the party, in his book *The Magic of Findhorn* (1975), Paul Hawken, evoking Lawrence of Arabia gives it the telling it deserves: "Against the advice of his exhausted Tibetan guide, Peter plowed back into the teeth of the storm and walked another 30 miles before finding the lost member. Peter had gained complete mastery over his body. To other members of his party, his strength and endurance appeared supernatural."

Leaving the RAF in 1955, he took a job as the manager of the Cluny Hill Hotel outside Forres, north-east of Inverness. When transferred by management to another of their properties, the Trossachs Hotel, in what must have been a brutal fall from a life of privilege, comfort, and relative security, at the age of forty-five Peter was suddenly made redundant. On a snowy day in November 1962, Peter, his wife Eileen and their three boys, moved into a caravan at the Findhorn Bay Caravan Park, "The one place we knew we could never stomach." At the edge of a rubbish dump, "it was a bleak, treeless and dreary place, with row after row of mobile homes lined up like shabby privates on parade along the concrete lanes that had served as dispersal bays for aircraft from the adjacent RAF base during the War." Their plot was "beside an old garage with broken windows, and surrounded by old tin cans and broken bottles, blackberry bushes and gorse".

However, showing great character, rather than feeling morose, they looked to the positive. "We could be grateful for the clear air, the beautiful countryside, the freedoms, the peace, the love between us all, and many other blessings." While Peter claimed unemployment benefit and looked unsuccessfully for work, every day he would run along the beach and take a dip in the icy waters of the Moray Firth. In the evenings and when the weather was bad, he would pore over garden books of every type, "organic and non-organic, traditional and progressive — looking forward to a time when I might start my own small garden."

The Findhorn Garden

Come the spring of 1963 — in spite of his strenuous efforts, still unemployed — Caddy decided to begin a small garden in an eleven-by-six-foot area he had fenced off. The plan was to grow a few radishes and lettuces to support their meagre income. The conditions could not have been less promising; removing the surface two inches of tangled couch grass (itself an implacable enemy to gardeners) revealed nothing but sand and gravel. They dug this out down to a foot's depth, everyone helping to remove the stones. The turf was put at the bottom and the sand was poured back on top. There was literally no humus in which to nurse seedlings. Caddy set out using every kind of ingenuity and physical effort to build a soil onto this sand.

Concluding from his studies that he needed a good supply of compost, that very day, he discovered a large pile of rotting matter which turned out to be decomposing grass from a lawn. This deliverance of what is necessary, through a chance event in the nick of time, is a central motif of the Findhorn Foundation story — a phenomenon described by the founders as "flow". From this point forward, useful organic matter came thick and fast. Collecting a bale of hay he had heard had fallen from a lorry, Caddy gave a lift to a man who offered him manure from his field of horses. Local shops gave them spoiled fruit and veg, and a nearby whisky distillery their waste barley germ. Caddy would scan the horizon with his binoculars for plumes of smoke and follow them to their source where he would scavenge the potash from bonfires. Seaweed from the rocks, dead fish and swans, everything was added to the compost pile. He and Eileen helped a neighbouring farmer who had switched to artificial fertiliser harvest his potatoes. In exchange for their labour, they made off with an entire pile of four-year-old cow manure, which they carted away in tin tubs, rubbish bins, and buckets. With his compost heap now "steaming away like an ocean liner" and Caddy's radishes, lettuce, peas, beans, carrots, and spring onions thriving, he set about extending the operation to a steep slope behind the caravan so he could add turnips, celery, leeks, swedes, and other vegetables to his arsenal.

Dorothy Maclean and Eileen Caddy

Dorothy Maclean was the Caddys' friend and spiritualist confrere. She had joined the couple as the hotel's secretary at Cluny Hill. They had built an annex so that she could be with the family in their caravan and participate in their ongoing spiritual work. Maclean wrote in her mystical autobiography *To Hear Angels Sing* (1980), "It was a strange situation for us all: three mature and active people more or less hanging around together for no known reason. We had no jobs, having tried to get them without success." Throughout the long, cold winter of 1962, Eileen and Maclean would meditate for long periods of time, one or other of them having the vision of a certain "light centre" from somewhere round the world created by an American friend of theirs through telepathy. They might establish a telepathic contact and relate the communication to the others. Peter himself couldn't pick up these sensitive messages, like the two cosmic switchboard operators were able to, but endearingly, wasn't in the least bit sceptical of their talents.

While huddled in their caravan, Maclean describes reading autobiographies and murder stories while Peter mainly consumed gardening books. In fact, the gardening books weren't often terribly useful; none were specific to growing vegetables in the sand dunes of Northern Scotland. But perhaps Maclean wasn't as unschooled as she contended. One "message" she claimed to receive follows, "As you read and try to understand that book (*Agriculture*, by Rudolf Steiner), you come across what are called cosmic influences on the Earth emanating from the various planets." Clearly, therefore — whether from Peter's library it is unclear — in spite of what she says, Maclean *was* versed in the lore of growing. Peter must have been reading Steiner too because they even obtained a biodynamic preparation for the compost. As she recounts, "All of us, including the children, went through the ritual of mixing it in a big vat, going round and round giving it the prescribed number of turns. It was fun and hard work." Maclean, or perhaps the spirits with which she was in contact, also seemed au fait with the French intensive practice of transplanting seedlings. On 29 May 1963, a lettuce deva informs Maclean, "We do not approve of transplanting, for it weakens the plant forces..." Maclean chose the Sanskrit term "deva" in preference to angel; it means "shining one".

In May 1963, Maclean received a message to "feel into the nature forces", taking it as an endorsement of her rambling and sunbathing in the dunes. Relaying the message to Peter, he concluded that she was being offered information to help him in the garden. After a lot of badgering from him — and against her instinct — using the mantra "I am Power" he had given her, a couple of weeks later she received the first message from a deva of the garden pea:

> I can speak to you, human. I am entirely directed by my work, which is set out and moulded and which I merely bring

> to fruition, yet you have come straight to my awareness. My work is clear before me: to bring the force fields into manifestation regardless of obstacles, of which there are many on this man-infested world. You think that slugs, for example, are a greater menace to me than man, but this is not so; slugs are part of the order of things and the vegetable kingdom holds no grudge against those it feeds, humans take what they can as a matter of course, giving no thanks, which makes us strangely hostile. What I would tell you as we forge ahead, never deviating from our course for one moment's thought, feeling or action, so could you. Humans generally seem to know not where they are going. If they did, what a powerhouse they would be! If they were on the straight course, we could cooperate with them! I have put across my meaning and bid you farewell.

Taking the message entirely without scepticism, it is a call for undeviating, intuitive action. The sentiment is close to what Masanobu Fukuoka called for with "natural farming" (his ideas were not translated until 1975). It's reminiscent, too, of permaculture co-originator Bill Mollison's famous maxim, "You don't have a slug problem, you have a duck deficiency." Later on, they came to see this dynamic in action when, after fastidiously removing their wasp nests, they were plagued by caterpillars, the wasp's natural quarry.

Caddy was thrilled, writing to a correspondent, "To be able to grow vegetables with the direct help of the Archetypal being in charge of the vegetables! Cooperation between man and the nature forces! I have not heard of this being done before but of course in days gone by when man was nearer to nature it was probably done instinctively..." He would compose a list of questions he wanted Maclean to ask specific vegetables: dwarf beans, spinach, etc. Caddy would ask her when to water each plant and which ones needed liquid manure. All this when, in his opinion, she knew less about gardening than him, but he almost always acted on her suggestions. For instance, he credits advice from the devas for sparing his cabbages and Brussels sprouts from cabbage root grubs. Maclean was tasked with pleading with the mole deva to beg the moles not to eat the earthworms and disrupt the garden with their tunnels. Slowly, they vanished, and after the first summer no more entered.

As Caddy's technique evolved, he adopted the tight and companion planting techniques of French intensive growing: "Parsnips, for example, would be sown eighteen inches apart, and between the parsnips two rows of lettuce, and between the lettuce and parsnips, a row of radishes." In the tiny garden, he was eventually growing sixty-five types of vegetables (including many varieties of each), forty-two kinds of herbs, and twenty-one sorts of fruit. White sprouting broccoli grew to such proportions that it fed them for months. When Caddy eventually pulled it up with Eileen's help, it was nearly too heavy to lift. It was delicious, Maclean said, "we had forgotten how delectable a taste came from vegetables grown without chemical fertilisers." The garden was providing 70% of their food. This is just as well because his unemployment benefit amounted to £8 a week. It was food of such vitality that it began to attract admirers: a professional nurseryman and the County Horticultural advisor marvelled at Caddy's forty-two-pound cabbages and the quality of his soil on what were dunes. Caddy itched to tell them the secret of his success, that he was receiving metaphysical instruction, but Eileen received a communication that he was to remain tight-lipped.

In 1966, they finally confided in a spiritualist visitor and early member of the Soil Association, Sir George Trevelyan, according to Paul Hawken "an avid student of Rudolf Steiner". His view was that more than good composting must have been involved. Writing in the foreword to a booklet they produced, Trevelyan said, "The possibility of cooperation with the devas should be investigated seriously. The time has come when this can be spoken of more openly." It was still early days, the community numbering no more than twenty-five. In consequence, more people came to visit — such as horticultural experts like Lady Mary Balfour, sister of Eve Balfour; and Professor Lindsay Robb, a consultant for the Soil Association — who joined the chorus of praise. And more came to stay.

Although Eileen Caddy did a lot of work in the garden and particularly enjoyed scrounging for compost materials (she describes driving home with dead seagulls and salmon in the car, holding her nose all the way), her coverage of the gardening is restricted to one page in her spiritual autobiography *Flight into Freedom and Beyond* (1988). More than any other founder, she was keen to emphasise the Findhorn Community as a spiritual one. In her view, it all started when, visiting Glastonbury praying in a "sanctuary" in a private house, she claimed to hear God's voice telling her "Be Still, and know that I am God." In Danny Miller's 1990 documentary *Opening Doors Within*, Eileen says,

> I think a lot of people thought that Findhorn was started with the garden, and it wasn't. It was started with 'the still, small voice'. And I think that's very important that people realise that was how it started — was that 'voice within'. Not just the garden — the garden came second.

Eileen Caddy's inclination was picked up by the author Paul Hawken, who described the community in the following terms: "Findhorn was not to be a garden of plants, it was to be a garden of people."

Hippies

First published in 1973, predating Paul Hawken's *The Magic of Findhorn* (1975) by two years, the bestselling *The Secret Life of Plants* will have played a huge role in turning the counterculture on to the miracles of growing your own vegetables. The climactic chapter of the book is titled "Findhorn and the Garden of Eden", and gives an excellent history of Findhorn's foundation. Its luminous account was only burnished by rumours, which came back to the founders from London, that their strawberries weighed a pound. What Caddy had actually said was that their plants were so prolific that they would produce a pound of strawberries a day. It was the influx of the counterculture that saw the community grow from under thirty to, by the end of the 1970s, over three hundred members.

In a vivid illustration of the coming culture-clash, of post-war spiritualists grappling with the counterculture with whom, ostensibly, they shared a mutual interest in a New Age, Caddy noted that in 1968, "We were scarcely prepared for the next strange and exotic appearance and growth in the garden, however: 'the flower people'." Caddy describes the phenomenon as the "hippie invasion". Neil Oram, a musician, and poet who was later responsible for the ten-play cycle, "The Warp", arrived with his wife and daughter. Caddy describes them as "dirty and dishevelled hippies", and he insisted the visitors all bathe and wash their hair. Caddy's wing-man, ROC, an elderly seer from Edinburgh who claimed to have encountered the Greek god Pan, and who had encouraged the creation of a wild area in the garden, had some months before enjoyed a long conversation with another young hippie who had visited Findhorn. The hippies, in rejecting anyone over the age of twenty-five who dressed normally and had short hair, had avoided contact with various existing spiritual movements. As a result, in dropping out, they had found themselves cut loose from all communities. After this meeting, ROC received guidance to the effect that it was important for both sides to reach for understanding and tolerance. Hippies must eventually merge with those older and seemingly more traditional groups. The Findhorn Community was exceptional in its embrace of the counterculture. Having this open-mindedness paid off in terms of the growth and vitality of the community.

Although the Caddys made a fist of it with Oram and his family, Oram fell foul of Peter. Eileen packed all their possessions in a pram and drove them to the outskirts of Forres, pointing them in the direction of Inverness. But more arrived, the next being a girl called Sabina in her early twenties who had tried and failed to run her grandmother's farm in Ireland with half a dozen hippie friends. She had hitchhiked to Findhorn with her three-and-a-half-year-old son and ended up living there for several years. John Mitchell, the old Etonian author of *The View Over Atlantis* (1969), the classic study of ley lines, visited. Caddy and ROC, wanting to connect Mitchell, who adopted the dress and style of a hippie, to some of the older leaders of the New Age movement, brought Mitchell to meet Major Bruce MacManaway. Meeting Mitchell at his front door, MacManaway looked him up and down and asked him whether he would like a bath. Shortly, however, they recognised in one another a "scholarly approach to spiritual truths", Mitchell accepting an invitation to speak at the Dowsers Association's annual conference.

Caddy recognised Sir George Trevelyan, another close associate of his, as being the perfect person to relate to the hippies at an upcoming course at Attingham, the National Trust House, which runs educational events to this day. Trevelyan gave a course, "The Allegorical Journey", covering "everything from Homer's *Odyssey* to Tolkien's *The Lord of the Rings* — the latter being especially popular with the hippies". Caddy relates how "a troupe of them, in full regalia, did appear and sit at the back. After the lecture, they approached Sir George and told him that his talk was just what they were looking for, and they hadn't known that anyone in the older generation spoke their language." Trevelyan ran the same course for their friends, with sixty-five people attending. Caddy notes that "more and more of those who dropped out of society were drawn to Findhorn". A stream of hippies hitchhiked from the south, word having gone around that they could find accommodation, and everything would be supplied.

Regrettably, many of those who'd dropped out were unskilled, not having undertaken any educational training, and as such not having expertise (whether it comprise office, garden, cooking, plumbing, or electrical skills) that they could contribute to the community. Caddy asked one young man if he could dig the garden. "He replied, 'Yeah, I can dig anything.' So I handed him a spade and pointed to the ground that needed digging — but that had not been his interpretation of the word 'dig', and he soon tired and left."

But Caddy was impressed by one young man who, when lying in bed, had heard a voice call out, "Come to Findhorn." Like the biblical Jonah, initially he resisted the calling, but eventually worked his way to this northern coast of Scotland. The man said he had come to acknowledge the value of these early foundations of the New Age, and appreciate the discipline in evidence in the Findhorn Community giving it the strength to confront the forces of straight society. Caddy recounts, "He went on to say that so many of his generation, after receiving a vision (through the use of LSD or other drugs) of what has to be done in the future, had merely sat back, viewing the surrounding chaos and upheaval, echoing the words 'impossible, impossible'." The man concluded the New Age needed hippies and drop-outs with their vision of a harmonious world, but it also needed those of every age and their various gifts. The straight world would have to discard its materialism and outworn traditions, and the hippies their drugs and all-night living.

David Spangler

By 1971, Eileen said that young people at the Findhorn community, many of them from the United States, outnumbered the older ones by about three to one. The American spiritualist David Spangler was not personally responsible for this growth to around 150 people. However, "his presence injected new energy into what had been growing steadily for eight years". David Spangler is a well-known

American spiritual philosopher who spent three years at Findhorn at the time when it was attracting international attention. Spangler explains he had had previous experience with communicating with nature spirits as a very young child and that the existence of realms of life and energy beyond the physical were a confirmed reality for him. However, "since others such as ROC and Maclean were the usual sources of specific information and were in many ways more attuned to the garden process than was I, the communications I received generally focused on a principle of relationship or on a vision of what could unfold".

Spangler's introduction to Findhorn had been through the garden. In January 1969, he had been working as a lecturer and educator in spirituality and esoteric themes for five years. This had taken him across a wide area of the Western United States. Hearing a lot of talk on the subject of spirituality, he was hungry for some kind of manifestation. He was fascinated when a colleague showed him an advance copy of the Findhorn Press's booklet *The Findhorn Garden, An Experiment in the Cooperation Between Three Kingdoms* (1975). Spangler said, "I was enthralled. Here was the very thing I had been looking for, a living demonstration of a trans-physical reality, anchored in tangible manifestation."

Indeed, his reaction might be considered typical of the appeal of the "massive vegetables" in that era. On the back of the counterculture's stratospheric ascent to the most etheric realms, with the aid of the full spectrum of techniques of ego dissolution (LSD use, meditation, psychoanalysis, and psychedelic music), young people were looking for a way to connect and ground spiritual currents to the material world. What better vehicle, at once familiar and exotic, than Findhorn's giant cabbages? Remarkably, Spangler saw in it a "practical demonstration of a spiritual solution to the developing world crisis in ecology and pollution, as well as food production" — believing that communication with the devas might increase global food yields.

Paul Hawken

Even before visiting Findhorn in the early 1970s, Paul Hawken (1946–), a man of acute integrity and later a committed Buddhist, had had a rich life experience. As a young man, Hawken had suffered from asthma, which he claimed was cured by the macrobiotic food diet. He had worked with Martin Luther King's staff in Selma, Alabama, preparing for the Selma to Montgomery marches, and studied with Paul Goodman at San Francisco State University.

In 1967, having moved to Boston to participate in one of the Kushis' macrobiotic study houses in the city, he had taken over the running of the Erewhon retail store there. Erewhon connected to a customer base of the 500,000 students in Boston, a substantial proportion of whom were looking for a natural diet. They also supplied staples like brown rice to the back-to-the-land communes in the Northeast. This was part of macrobiotic food guru Michio Kushi's North American Empire. The first incarnation of Hawken's book *The Magic of Findhorn*, a booklet called *Findhorn — a Center of Light* (1974), was published by Kushi's *East West* journal.

Taking on the role of a youthful American spokesperson for the macrobiotic movement (*Reader's Digest* had described it as "The Diet that's Killing Our Kids"), Hawken famously debated natural foods with the impressive institutional figure Dr Frederick Stare, Professor of Nutrition at Harvard University. Hawken rebuffed the claim that the counterculture were food faddists, saying, as he recently paraphrased it, "From our point of view, we're eating foods that have been here since pre-biblical times, and most of what you're eating are concoctions that were invented since World War Two, along with the chemicals that are in them, so from our point of view *you're* the food faddist, *we're* the conservatives, and we're going to see how it works out for you". Together with author Fred Rohe, Hawken also launched Organic Merchants (its snappy acronym "OM"), a countercultural trade association for organic food retailers. Given his background in the natural food and farming business, as he puts it, "all mention in the media of alternative methods of agriculture crossed my desk". He had seen extracts of *The Secret Life of Plants* by Peter Tompkins published in the usually conservative *Harper's Magazine*, and as he sat in his cluttered and shabby warehouse in the old industrial section of Boston, he was rendered "psychologically flatfooted and analytically agape".

Hawken set off on a pilgrimage to Findhorn — on the last stretch, hitchhiking from Inverness. The day after arriving, he wandered around the community and the garden:

> I stopped to talk with Leonard, one of the gardeners, who was watering a bed of flowers. We walked around the garden together, he answering questions while I took notes on the names and varieties of flowers. He spoke in a thick Lancashire accent and was conversant with every plant name, common and Latin, and demonstrated a profound knowledge of gardening.

The pair eventually met up with Mathew, the head gardener. Peter Caddy no longer worked in the garden, being now closely involved in his leadership role. "He has turned the job over to several gardeners from Blackpool known around the community as the 'gnomes'. All of them were formerly apprentice gardeners and have combined much of the orthodoxy they learned with the lessons that Peter absorbed in his eight years as gardener." Hawken noted that as the gnomes took over Caddy's work, the garden had expanded, but many of the phenomenal aspects disappeared when they took over. Cabbages were back to their usual weight of three or four pounds and foxgloves reached four rather than eight feet.

Mathew, "a quick and prankish self-described ex-motorcycle thug from Blackpool" who pranced about the Garden and community as the jester, also explained their absence to Hawken in Caddy's terms. "The growth here was fantastic to demonstrate to Peter Caddy and to the others that it was possible... Just because some of these plants were growing in the middle of the cold in the dry sand didn't mean that they were happy about it." Mathew was philosophical, though, and explains in the hippie slang of the day, "If you show somebody a forty-pound cabbage, they get hung up in the forty-pound cabbage-trip and think only in terms of size, form, and quantity". Hawken, rather crestfallen, confides to the reader, "I must admit, I had hoped to see one of those cabbages." But there was still plenty to celebrate:

> Nevertheless, the garden is still astonishing to my eyes. I have never seen anything like it in my life. There is richness of colour and variety everywhere you look. Each plant seems to be in perfect condition. Weeds are hardly to be seen, but then there is hardly any room for them, the garden being so thick and profuse.

Mathew and Leonard tell Hawken that they did not perceive the nature spirits directly, but felt that they were intuitively guided by them. Leonard was one of the gang that described itself as "the Gnomes". When Mathew, known as "the Focaliser", left for Toronto, where he still lives, Leonard took on his job. The Gnomes, as Leonard described to me in our correspondence "were part of the hippie culture, believing in alternative realities and a spiritual dimension to life (amongst other things)... my friends and I made plentiful use of psychedelics (Hee, Hee!) before coming to Findhorn, where use of illegal drugs was not permitted". They first became aware of the community when a travelling friend had chanced upon it and had badgered them to investigate. They arrived as a gang from Blackpool in 1971 and were among the earliest from the counterculture to settle at Findhorn, where at that point there were less than thirty people living in the community. In total there were eight of them, all friends, who brought two children in tow.

Hawken says he had been expecting to meet a "Scottish Luther Burbank with straw in his boots, and daisies in his hair, someone who tapped the secrets of nature and who was now so far gone that communication would be difficult at best". The reality of the brutally frank Caddy with his air of a corporate president was something of a shock to him. The young freaks, hippies, and ex-druggies who were drawn to Findhorn by books such as Eileen Caddy's *God Spoke to Me* (1968), according to Hawken, found Peter Caddy "almost intolerable". This New Age was serious business. Hawken describes how

> young freaks escaping burnt-out lives in London were verbally thrashed by Peter for the slightest deviation from the rigid order and structure of the community. Few could see through the military stance to the soul beneath. They left, but more replaced them, and despite all the odds, young people actually started to stay and integrate into the community.

The Balfours and Findhorn

Lady Mary Balfour, Eve Balfour's sister, was the first of the sisters to visit, describing how "I stooped to handle and examine the soil, a thickish layer of half-ripe compost lay mulching the rather grimy, too fine sand below. To my eye and touch it was indeed pure sand of the most unpromising quality." Feeling "not a little awestruck", she concluded that "even the most chemically minded growers will admit that some folks have 'green fingers' — folk that can break the rules and still make plants flourish. Why? How? Wouldn't we like to know! Could that be just what the gardeners at Findhorn are beginning to learn?"

Lady Eve Balfour herself finally visited in 1970, as she related to Hawken when he interviewed her:

> I agree completely with [the Soil Association's specialist] Lindsay Robb. I couldn't explain the garden there by compost... I have seen other gardens as good on big estates going for hundreds of years attended by teams of gardeners, but never one better... I always feel so refreshed there, it recharges me. Findhorn is my place!

Lady Eve Balfour wrote in suitably mysterious terms to Peter Caddy:

> Just as we have to learn to be aware that we occupy a physical form, so must we become aware that this is true of every life form. While we identify entities (plant, animal or man) with their forms, we will only be able to see God as divided against himself. But when we manage to reach communion with the reality behind the manifestation, we can, in cooperation, work out compromises for the forms, acceptable to all.

Paul Hawken today

From his background in macrobiotics and Findhorn, Paul Hawken has gone on to have a long and celebrated career. Hawken became a student of the Zen Buddhist Roshi Shunryū Suzuki, author of the excellent *Zen Mind, Beginner's Mind* (1970), and member of the Tassajara Zen Mountain Center (five minutes as the crow flies from the Esalen Institute on the Big Sur Coast). He lived at the group's Green Gulch Farm in Marin County, north across the Golden Gate Bridge from San Francisco. Inspired by the garden tools devised by John Jeavons, he went on to market them in the Smith & Hawken garden supply company that sold thousands of solid spades, trugs, and boots. Hawken wrote a series of extremely popular and influential books, business guides, at the axis of commerce and ecology, like *Growing a Business* (1987), *The Ecology of*

Commerce (1993), *Natural Capitalism* (1999), and *Blessed Unrest* (2007).

The world's sustainability guru, courted by corporations and politicians, Hawken's most recent blockbuster is *Drawdown: The Most Comprehensive Plan Ever Proposed to Reverse Global Warming* (2017). This features a funny and self-deprecating foreword from King Charles III, comparing his humble *Ladybird Expert Book on Climate Change* (2017), to the book, a "magisterial and detailed exposition, in detail, of one hundred of the best and most promising solutions to climate change… this book is resolutely focused on a positive response to our current predicament and therefore deserves the widest possible readership." *Drawdown* focuses on a series of issues which relate to farming: the importance of a plant-rich diet, reduced food waste, multistrata agroforestry, improved rice cultivation, silvopasture (grazing beneath trees), regenerative agriculture, conservation agriculture, composting, biochar, farmland irrigation, managed grazing, and coming attractions like pasture cropping, perennial crops (kernza wheat), and ocean farming.

To gauge whether he was still in touch with the ideas of spirituality which originally inspired him, and to discover whether he found them useful, I approached Hawken (who has limited bandwidth available) with two quotes, which, in a somewhat Zen manner, he appended with his own.

> My quote: (1) Lady Eve Balfour: "Land… is not merely soil; it is a fountain of energy flowing through a circuit of soils, plants and animals."
>
> Hawken: I quote Jill Clapperton: "When you stand on the soil you are on the roof of another world."
>
> My quote: (2) Zen Buddhist teacher Shunryū Suzuki: "So it is absolutely necessary for everyone to believe in nothing. But I do not mean voidness. There is something, but that

something is something which is always prepared for taking some particular form, and it has some rules, or theory, or truth in its activity. This is called Buddha nature, or Buddha himself."

Hawken: What Suzuki Sensei refers to is called drala: Drala is the elemental presence of the world that is available to us through sense perceptions. When we open to trees, flowers, a creek or clouds we encounter an actual wisdom, though one that is not separate from our own. Beholding a river is much more than merely looking at a river; potentially, we are meeting the dralas. In the drala teachings, each of the senses is considered an unlimited field of perception in which there are sights, sounds and feelings we have never experienced before — that no one has ever experienced! Each sense moment, if we are present for it, is a gate into the elemental wisdom of the world. For me, it is the song of the world.

Roger Doudna

I paid a visit to current Findhorn resident Roger Doudna. Doudna lives in one of the circular wooden houses made from huge recycled whisky barrels near the Bag End area of the community. Despite living here for the most part since he arrived in 1974, he has kept his American accent. Doudna looks back: "I was definitely in the counterculture. My claim to fame was that I and some friends did a piece on marijuana harvesting in Lawrence, Kansas, which is the home of the University of Kansas, where I was enrolled in a graduate program. And that piece was picked up by *60 Minutes*." The show ran as "The Kansas Marijuana Harvest" in the CBS News network *60 Minutes* report on the "River City Outlaws" which covered their illegal pot growing amid the turmoil of 1970s Lawrence. "Basically, it was a portrait of the counterculture in Lawrence, Kansas, and fueled largely by marijuana harvesting.

Marijuana grew wild and prolifically in Kansas... And that was the economic basis of the counterculture."

The son of a Methodist minister turned professor of religious philosophy, Doudna finished his philosophy PhD in 1973 and, leaving the Midwest, made a beeline to California. He alighted first on a programme run by the Esalen Institute in Berkeley. "It consisted of a parade of new-consciousness types coming through in one of the empty classrooms on the Berkeley campus... Just talking about whatever their works were... biofeedback, Feldenkrais, transpersonal psychology, human potential, the whole Esalen menu." The same year, with some other graduate students, Doudna went to a new-consciousness event at Sonoma State University, north of San Francisco, and heard a man called John White, who had written a book called *The Highest State of Consciousness* (1972), "talk about big veg at Findhorn as a physical sign of the presence of God".

His interest was piqued:

> I followed up from there a group from Findhorn... the real event was January 1974, when the comet Kohoutek was supposed to appear in the sky over California, heralding the arrival of a new era and new age... [The comet] never appeared visibly in the skies over California, but it was an excuse for all the new-consciousness types in the Bay Area to convene in the Civic Auditorium in San Francisco, which as you may know, is a city-block-sized four-storey building, which filled with all manner of weirdos from all over the Bay Area. In the midst of which was this group from Findhorn... And they spent their whole presentation... talking about their time at Findhorn.

It's remarkable to think of young Americans like Roger Doudna, David Spangler, and Paul Hawken flocking to a caravan site on the outskirts of a small village thirty miles outside Inverness. Doudna recalls that Hawken was "just finishing up *The Magic of Findhorn* when I arrived here in November '74". And, just as with Hawken, he had to adjust his perspective on arrival.

> So, I'm in California, looking at all this new human potential stuff, all this new-consciousness stuff, all this new drug awareness, you know, psychedelics type stuff. And, in that context, I hear a story about a place... connecting nature spirits, with Pan, with space brothers, with the 'God within', with masters of the wisdom. And in that context producing remarkable vegetables and gardens as a tangible sign of this new consciousness... And the fact that they were also doing this Western Mystery school programme. All of it brought that Theosophy stuff out of the big blue books, and into something that was dynamic and happening now. That's what I thought I was coming to. And when I got here, I realised that my preconceptions were pretty weird, and wild, and over the top. But it was still a remarkably energetic, dynamic, and loving place. So, from that point of view, the vibe was congruent with what I expected. But the manifestation of it was significantly below my expectations.

Listening to Doudna recount this, I was thinking, here we are, nearly fifty years later in the dunes, in a quarter whose name is inspired by J.R.R. Tolkien, in a house made of a giant recycled whisky barrel. And just then, a neighbour dropped by, sang us both a song, and gave Doudna a red pepper she'd picked up for him at the supermarket.

I ask Doudna whether this hippie influx was the making of the Findhorn Foundation:

> It certainly would never have happened... the explosion of the community, and the development wouldn't have happened without young people. And interestingly, a lot of those young people are now my vintage. And one of our primary challenges is attracting enough young people to have a sense of the place carrying on.

Not a gardener, grower, or a farmer himself, Doudna instead was instrumental in creating the Findhorn guests' programme, which formed the focal point of the community's growth. He dates the birth of his own ecological consciousness to 1984 and a talk given at the foundation by the environmentalist Jonathan Porritt. "I saw that the environment ecology movement perfectly complemented the spiritual perspective." He has made Findhorn his life's mission: "It was that sense of being able to turn things around that has kept me here. Because how do you change the world? Well, God knows how you change the world! But, here, the mantra is 'One heart at a time.'"

Cornelia Featherstone

With regards to the influx in the early 1970s, another current resident, Cornelia Featherstone, agrees with Doudna to a certain extent. "I think it was very much alive before then, but what it became was ferment in a much larger field. Before that, it was very specific and quite esoteric in the true sense of the word, 'Not seen'." There was, as she puts it, something very dynamic about the "tweed and hippie conjunction in the '70s". I was extremely grateful when Featherstone came forward and, when I visited, offered to talk to me and make introductions. As a young child, she suffered in pain with an undiagnosed condition for six years, and resolved to become a doctor so as to ensure young children were listened to. Against the odds of her working-class background, and contrary to her previous academic trajectory, she qualified as a medic in her native country, Germany. Passing over a golden opportunity to be a partner in a general practice in Germany, and finding what she was looking for at Findhorn, she joined the community in 1987 aged twenty-nine.

She has been involved in some of the foundation's most important health and ecological initiatives, as well as serving as a local GP. Most recently she has masterminded the *Celebrating One Incredible Family* website, which brought together a dazzling set of resources about the Findhorn community and its colourful history for the sixtieth anniversary. It was an invaluable resource when researching this chapter. Featherstone is a skilled gardener, and in 2021 showed YouTube star gardener Huw Richards around her amazing vegetable garden. Watching that video gave me the first hint that Findhorn residents who grow plants have, in a practical way, questioned the foundational myths about the gigantic vegetables, and at the same time reached beyond those myths to more profound questions.

Clearly suspecting something was happening biologically, Featherstone said to me, "Why did they have these big vegetables on the sandy soils? And now they don't have them anymore? You know people put it down that we're not 'aligned' [to the spiritual world] anymore... which of course could well be true..." But she deftly points out that they do now have a deep humus-rich topsoil:

> That's something which we still haven't done as an ecovillage; we haven't measured our carbon sequestration, in the layers of soil that we have laid down in those last sixty years. It's a huge amount with all the trees. And it was sand! It was really exactly the same as [pointing further into the dunes by the Moray Firth] two hundred metres out there.

Featherstone is a mine of information about the foundation. Important topics for her are Peter Caddy's mistake — described as betraying a colonialist mindset, that of the Englishman assuming rights in Scotland — of naming the foundation "Findhorn". This was the village's name, and its appropriation as the name of the foundation has long been a bone of contention among villagers not wishing to be seen as "tree-huggers". The argument runs that Caddy should have called the foundation something completely different and left them out of it. Against this background of sensitivity towards Scotland's status as a colony of England, she is also keen to emphasise the role of Lena Lamont, born on the Isle of Skye in a crofting context, and a "Fourth founder", written by her own request out of the community's history but now celebrated for her infusion of native Gaelic mysticism into their spiritual work.

I was enchanted by Featherstone's own magical ritual when picking vegetables in her garden. This revealed a playful but coherent logic. "I have a jungle of green beans... I go in there and I know I need to harvest the ones that I can reach. I can't stretch to the taller ones, so they will become seeds. It's better for the plants and better for me if I can't get them. But I don't see them! I walk past and then I say aloud, 'Okay, if you want to come in today, you have to show yourself.'" And then the vegetables volunteer by making themselves visible to her. "You know 'Bing!' There's another one!"

Why the massive vegetables?

Vegetable growers who specialise in massive vegetables rely on carefully cultivated strains to produce their huge cabbages, carrots, and onions. But Peter Caddy didn't use such seeds. Beyond this I've heard many explanations as to why he was able to grow such preposterously large vegetables. The resident WWOOFER, Veronica Caldwell — returning to Findhorn, where she grew up, from Australia, where she had brought up her family — was working in the community's current CSA. Caldwell, a highly skilled grower, explained to me that permaculture co-originator Bill Mollison had put the exuberant growth at Findhorn down to the extremely long daylight hours in the summer at their northern latitude. Indeed, Dorothy Maclean herself noted something similar. On a walk, I did come across some insanely large rosehips which back some aspect of this up. However, if that was entirely the case, why did the sizes shrink over time? The soil was not being exhausted — far from it, in fact: Caddy was building up a remarkable layer of humus. In the course of my research, in conversation with legendary farmer Eliot Coleman, I came across what must be the definitive explanation. When you lime (and thereby alkalise) a sandy and therefore acidic soil, you unleash an astonishing amount of bacterial activity which had been suppressed by the acidity.

Coleman explained to me:

> There was a book, Paul Hawken wrote it about a community up in the north of Scotland that was mystically growing all sorts of fantastic vegetables and was called Findhorn... The first year there on the soil, they grew forty-pound cabbages... The interesting thing about that was, my very first spring here [in Maine in the USA], like them, we started with a very acid podzol... When you lime an acid soil, you cut loose the bacteria which have not been able to be as active as they would be in a sweet soil because the soil was so acid. And there's all sorts of tied-up nutrition in the soil that the bacteria haven't been able to process for the plants. When you lime then, you raise the pH and you cut loose a pile of nitrogen that first year. And so, we also, as well as Findhorn, grew a forty-pound... *a bunch* of forty-pound cabbages.
>
> The first year... I sent soil samples off to the university. And I found that what I thought was happening is exactly what *was* happening. You take a very acid podzol, throw some lime in there and you're cutting loose nitrogen to the point that you will have a forty-pound cabbage... I found if I took another piece of land I hadn't farmed on out of the forest and limed it I could get more forty-pound cabbages. If I went and scraped up all the needles and botrytis under the trees and then put it on the land that I had used once before, I could get at least thirty-pound cabbages. I couldn't get the forty-pounders there, but this was all coming from breaking loose nutrition that had been tied up because the soil was too acid.

However, just like Featherstone, Coleman might agree that the real miracle is that the community has rebuilt its topsoil to such a dramatic extent, and that that soil has maintained its productivity, and is able to support such an impressive garden as Featherstone's, sixty years later. I also admire Featherstone's open-minded attitude to the whole question of the devas. She cited a recent summit at the foundation which featured a conversation with Zen teacher Doshin Roshi and the theorist Ken Wilbur. They were mulling over the question of what the role was of intentional communities in the 1960s. "And there were a lot of things in that conversation, that struck me. But what I really took away as an answer to that question was the importance of reenchanting the world." Describing that era's background of disillusionment and fear, of the Cuban Missile crisis, the Vietnam War, and Rachel Carson's book on DDT, *Silent Spring*, Featherstone could see, as Jung would have concurred, mankind's need of a spiritual life as a touchstone of optimism and magic. It's through this prism that she still sees the value in the founders' inventiveness.

NEW ALCHEMY

The Todds

As a child growing up in Hamilton on the shore of Lake Ontario, John Todd had been devastated by the post-Second World War industrial development that transformed the farmlands, woods, and marshes which he had once explored near his home. Responding to his visible unhappiness, his father introduced him to books written by Louis Bromfield, a hugely successful author of fiction who had returned to the Ohio of his childhood to restore the land. This process he documented in *Pleasant Valley* (1945) and *Malabar Farm* (1948). The story of how Bromfield, as John Todd put it, "re-created an agricultural community with the holistic knowledge he brought back [from inter-war France]" made a huge impression on the young Todd, offering him a "marvelous tale of hope".

John and Nancy Todd met each other in Canada when they were in high school. Subsequently, he went to agricultural college in Montreal, while she stayed at home to study liberal arts at the University of Western Ontario. When she graduated, they married and, in the late 1960s, moved together to Ann Arbor for John to study his doctorate in biology at the University of Michigan. Nancy raised the children, while he studied the social behaviour of fish. Both, apparently, "thought our pursuits were much more interesting and that the other had been a bit deluded".

At the time, questions of the ecology had forced themselves onto the national agenda. John was particularly influenced by both Rachel Carson's *Silent Spring* (1962), on the perils of pesticides like DDT and their ilk, and the Club of Rome's *Limits to Growth* (1972) report, which pointed out the impossibility of the environment, and its current means of management, being able to sustain human population growth. Nancy describes how "we listened to reports on the omni-presence of DDT and the nitrate contamination of groundwater from fertilizer run off, the dangers of radioactivity, the poisoning of the oceans, and threatened and extinct species of plants and animals... We began to examine the fundamental needs of people, the basics with which they sustain themselves, and to ask if there might be alternatives to the present energy-dependent methods." As a result of Nancy's protest against the Vietnam War, they discussed how critics of the war "questioned the neutrality of science and its role in inflicting suffering and death". Together with John's fish-research colleague Bill McLarney, the couple speculated on ways of redirecting science towards nurturing and restoring people and the ecology. It was an idea they claimed stayed with them.

Their first experimental settlement, the beginning of what would become the New Alchemy Institute in Cape Cod, was on the outskirts of the Californian city San Diego. They participated in field trips to a ranch just above the Mexican border. Nancy reflected of this early foray, "Unlike the long-vanished Native peoples, we academics did not know how to find food or water or where to plant crops. We did not know how to survive there." After a few visits to advise their friends, who had rented it and were homesteading, they got as far as discovering water and suitable soil. However, at this moment the landlady arrived and announced "to our gentle, long-haired friends that she was raising the rent". Nancy describes being drawn to a "quest for viable alternatives to the prevailing dynamic". They "felt somehow called upon by our time. Asian scholars might say we were following the Tao — the way of nature..." Undeterred, they crossed the continent and resettled on Cape Cod.

The New Alchemy Institute

A very pretty part of the state of Massachusetts, Cape Cod is an hour or so south of Boston, on a peninsula which curves out into the Atlantic, decked with lovely sandy beaches. The Cape Cod site was an old dairy farm seven miles from the Todd's home, which the owners rented to their organisation. It was situated in what they describe as a "woodsy suburbia". John Todd was a miracle-worker when it came to securing financial support, and the main sources of funding were grant agencies and the contributions of the association's members. A great deal of work was done by volunteers, and the staff's paid salaries were conservative. A "scientific commune" of a kind, it differed from other communes in that no one lived there on site. John and his colleague Bill McLarney got jobs at the Woods Hole Oceanographic Institute nearby, and the Todd family moved to an acre and a half of land they had bought at Cape Cod. Like many other families of that time, they planted fruit trees, raised chickens, and grew vegetables.

A magical film by The National Film Board of Canada, *The New Alchemists* (1974), with a gloriously dopey voiceover by a Virginia Stikeman, is still available to watch for free online. It gives a dreamy snapshot of what life would have been like at New Alchemy on a balmy summer's day. Children swim in the lake, John Todd rides around the lawn on a bicycle, and the *New York Times* food critic tries their tilapia fish. We meet the young Earle Barnhart — with long hair, beard, and no shirt — building compost and making windmills, and his partner, the gardener Hilde Maingay, blonde, clutching an enormous ledger to tabulate her findings. The voiceover weaves its spell: "Here, the energy of the wind, runs the windmill, which pumps the water, that waters the garden, that grows the carrots, that feed the rabbits, that fertilize the earthworms, that feed the fish along with the carrot tops. And carrots, rabbits, and fish all feed the people."

New Alchemy was a magnet for hippies, but its appeal broadened over time. Writing in 1977, Nancy remembers:

> In the main in previous years, most of our visitors could have been loosely described as counter-culture, usually youngish, longish hair, faded jeans etc. Recently it has become impossible to categorize, for, besides the more predictable types there are families; some with small children, some with teenagers, and some with grandparents. Gardening clubs of older people stop by. Classes of school kids, sometimes entire small schools, come. And there are homesteaders and architecture and every other kind of student, would-be dropouts from business or academe, tinkerers who just like windmills, and fellow travelers in search of a less mechanized approach to life than society at present usually affords.

As much as New Alchemy — with their long hair and bell-bottoms living organically in nature — registers as a hippie outfit, psychedelic drugs and Eastern religion, two of the main countercultural staples, were never major factors at New Alchemy. Hilde Maingay and Earle Barnhart remember a few joints being passed around at parties (but they didn't grow marijuana) and a couple of members with spiritual inclinations, a Jesuit priest and the designer of their journal's covers who disappeared into the Moonies. The common ground they shared with the counterculture, apart from their quasi-communal lifestyle, was that they were all radically set against the Vietnam War, anti-nuclear, and actively in favour of equality for women.

New Alchemist Theory

New Alchemy's motto was "To Restore the Lands, Protect the Seas, and Inform the Earth's Stewards". And this last meant that the institute was both at the intellectual cutting-edge of ecological-thinking and — through scheduled visits, conferences, and their publications — active in education. It was extremely robust on the subject of its underlying principles and philosophy. Betty Roszak, wife of Theodore Roszak, who coined the term "counterculture", wrote a foreword for their collection of articles, *The Book of the New Alchemists* (1977), and, expressing a Jungian perspective, connects their activities with the strong contemporary currents in spirituality:

> This belated scientific recognition of the interrelatedness of earthly patterns and cycles is in fact a reformulation for modern times of an ancient idea: that all things on Earth are organically connected in a vast pulsating network. Further, the Earth is an organic being, itself in turn reflecting the life of the cosmos. 'What is below is above; what is inside is outside.' So goes the Hermetic formula, the origin of which supposedly lies far back in Egyptian antiquity... Even the most lowly and, to us, profane task can have a spiritual meaning if one performs it with such awareness. Work which today has become so despised and meaningless for many, could be transformed as in the appealing Hasidic story of the holy shoemaker whose devotion in stitching the upper leather to the lower sole was so intense that his activity became a ritual of binding the upper and lower worlds... If there are those like the New Alchemists who can restore this forgotten sacred vision to our impoverished awareness, then there is hope for renewal of the earth. Without the vision and the love it brings, all such labors remain meaningless.

Ideas inherent in Eastern philosophy, not exactly "spiritual" ones, but tainted through association with them by "scientific" people, and dismissed as "New Age", are found at the heart of New Alchemy's thinking. John Todd writes, in the context of the need to create alternatives to uniformity, "The first step toward countering homogeneity would be to create a biotechnology based on an ecological ethic... It would not be founded upon profit or efficiency considerations but on the philosophical view that all things are interconnected and interdependent." Likewise, Todd might make a comment like the following: "We are increasingly paying the price for treating land as a commodity rather than as something sacred and alive." On the face of it, it's a whimsical statement, but not if you consider both the ecological preciousness of soil (sacred) and a healthy soil biome's biological vitality (alive).

Mainly, however, New Alchemy expressed their opinions and agenda in scientific and statistical terms. With regards to agriculture, John Todd criticised large-scale use of chemical fertilisers, emphasis on single cash crops, the increase in biocides to control pests and weeds, and also the move away from local varieties. "If the new varieties are attacked by pathogens the consequences could be world-wide rather than local, and plant breeders may not be able to create new strains before it is too late." He gives the example of the Irish Potato Famine of the 1840s.

New Alchemy and fossil fuels

Richard Merrill, New Alchemy's first tenured agriculturalist and a well-respected organic gardener, who earned some notoriety for having been thrown out of the garden in UC Santa Cruz by Alan Chadwick, writes:

> In fact, during the last few decades we have simply been exchanging finite reserves of fossil fuels for our supplies of food and fibre... In the very near future, we will have no choice but to adopt agricultural techniques that utilize renewable energy supplies. These include: the recycling of organic wastes to supplement synthetic fertilizers; the use of renewable forms of energy (solar, wind and organic fuels) to help supply rural power needs; the application of

> ecologically diverse cropping patterns and integrated pest control programs to reduce the use of pesticides.

Earle Barnhart remembers something that he says never shows up in history:

> When New Alchemy was doing all this work, we believed that we were going to run out of oil. And that's the reason to do all this because the oil is going to run out, you better be ready to come up with your basic needs some of the way without oil — because it's going to run out. In fact, it never ran out and it will never run out. It's always there. They will always be able to get it. Now, the problem is the damage from fossil fuel, that's the reason to not use it now.

John Todd imagined the same kind of low-energy future that permaculturalist David Holmgren, whom we meet in the "Permaculture" chapter, classes as "Descent". "It may be that well-fed, healthy people with small amounts of energy available to them will redirect their lives towards stewardship and artistic and philosophic goals."

People and New Alchemy

As much as New Alchemy was preoccupied with progressive techniques, what's really interesting is the importance that was placed upon the way people interacted with agriculture. For instance, Richard Merril writes:

> The fallacy here lies in the assumption that the only purpose of agriculture is to produce food. Over the years many kinds of propaganda have locked us into this dangerous illusion, and we tend to forget that agriculture is dynamic and that its historic role has been to maintain productive land in order to sustain its people. In addition,

> a thriving rural culture has been vital in providing food and fibre and in absorbing dispossessed people during wars and economic depressions.

John Todd also considered the human dimension of farming:

> Planting and tending of ecologically sophisticated agricultural plots will require far more training, knowledge, and labor than is needed on contemporary farms. Yet this fact should prove an asset by raising the status of those involved. Persons highly skilled in the creating of good soils and raising nourishing foods will be highly respected and emulated. To work toward restoring the landscapes should become a major intellectual and physical pursuit of the present generation.

Hilde Maingay and Earle Barnhart

It's the end of September when I visit New Alchemy in Cape Cod. When it was run by John Todd and functioning as an institute in the 1970s and '80s, no one lived at the site itself. After its closure in 1991, key New Alchemists Hilde Maingay and Earle Barnhart bought the site with ten member families as the Cape Cohousing Committee. So now, in fact, the site is lived on. In some respects, this has elevated what was an experiment into something richer and more committed. When I arrived, Earle Barnhart showed me around their copious vegetable gardens. In the fenced garden enclosures, chickens roam freely. Following Eliot Coleman's initiative, they grow some vegetables which prosper at the same latitude in Korea: Chinese spring onions, Chinese onions, and Chinese chestnut. Coleman remembered the couple fondly, as well as Maingay's skill as a gardener, when I mentioned them to him. The Chinese chestnut, pear, and walnut trees which the New Alchemists planted in the 1970s are now huge productive trees. This late in the season, I still see peppers and tomatoes growing outdoors. There are kiwi fruit, pumpkins, potatoes, squash, and grapes. Leeks are planted outside any fencing because the rabbits won't eat them. They take their kale out of the soil and replant it indoors in the winter. Everywhere, pretty marigolds grow, an excellent companion plant with a whole host of benefits.

Earle takes me into their house, which is attached to the back of and opens into New Alchemy's old main building, the Cape Cod Ark. This ingeniously ventilated greenhouse also houses fibreglass aquaculture tanks, with water hyacinths growing on them, purifying greywater, the last tank in the chain containing fish. We sit at a table in the Ark and have a lunch of Earl's homemade bread, some cheese, and a delicious juice made from their own apples, which Hilde points out is more like apple sauce. As we eat and chat, rain begins to fall, pattering on the glass above our heads. A frog starts up. They explain to me that he is an old friend; he moves into the Ark from the garden in the autumn.

The couple have made ecology their life, and it's exasperating to them to find the world finally cottoning on to what they've been harping on about for all these years. Cape Cod has critical problems, of which Hilde reflects in her lilting Dutch accent:

> Well, when we were working on New Alchemy, we were aware of all the ecological damage... But since it wasn't to this level, there was enough reason for people to ignore it. The scientists and whoever was talking about it... they could just ignore it because it wasn't affecting their life... You can keep polluting up to a point, and then suddenly things crash, right? Well, we saw it, coming thirty, forty years ago. And people talked about it among the academics and activists, but since you could still be here and the country was relatively the same, food was still cheap, so nobody cared. And now, it's basically too late. I mean, in our eyes, it's too late.

Maingay explains that they keep on with their work just to give themselves hope. Barnhart describes the critical problems in the Cape Cod area:

> We also have freshwater ponds on the Cape. Hundreds of them, and people live around these ponds and they are all becoming polluted with toxic algae. So toxic that if their dog drinks the water, the dog dies. They can't swim in the water. You can't touch the water. Toxins blow off the water and the value of the homes around the ponds have gone down, but no one wants to live next to such a thing.

The local government has drafted new regulations that may require people to put in their own miniature sewers costing $50,000. People may have to move because they can't afford this. Barnhart puts it succinctly. "And so that's alarming... that gets people's attention really fast." These issues happening on their doorstep is what has finally caused the penny to drop:

> It's getting worse so quickly that people finally are waking up. Because it's affecting them! People don't care really if there's a hunger in Africa, they really don't. They don't relate it to their own life. They might, if they have a little extra money just... put in a little donation and feel good. But other than that, most people cannot think much beyond their own family.

Winding back the clock, I ask Maingay how she became an ecologist. "I have to think really far back because there were hints of it in my household, that was a little bit more progressive than most people around me. Like, we were the first ones that I actually knew anywhere of my friends or the street that had double-pane glass." Because they were Dutch, her parents were put into concentration camps in Indonesia during the Second World War. Growing up in Holland, that experience of incarceration combined with years of enduring grinding post-war poverty caused her family to adopt frugal habits:

> But they kept that even when my Dad had enough money that we could buy a house or when we had a job... They were always like that, I don't think we ever threw away food... It was personal conservation... mostly probably because of money, I would think... It was constant though. You know, 'Turn off the water! Turn off the water!' And [my mother would] always say to me, 'That's long enough for the shower' or 'Don't use hot water for this!' And [there] was, like, that constant awareness. So, it wasn't very hard to then pick it up later on when you learn more. It was pretty well ingrained, right? I mean that's what we do here all the time... I think the Dutch are probably better about it... They're not as wasteful as the Americans.

Barnhart describes his ecological fascination as stemming from an astonishingly progressive college education. Growing up on a mixed farm in the middle of Ohio in the Midwest, he attended New College in Florida (Sarasota), where he had a very progressive biology professor called John Morrill. "It was an innovative school. Very high level of academics. Very progressive. No grades. You had to be chosen to go there. You made up your own courses. You made up your own major. We chose our own course of study." In 1972, at a remarkably early date, he took classes about climate change and the effects of rising CO2 levels, as well as classes on pesticides spreading through the ecosystem as poison. "We were educated about the energy costs in the society going up, pollution from fossil fuels, all that stuff. So, I got all my ecology in college. It was the only place doing practical scientific solutions to those things... And then when I left college I came directly to New Alchemy." The reason being that Barnhart, a conscientious objector, had chosen to work with the organisation for two years as a form of civilian service in the national interest, as an alternative to going to Vietnam. "So, I've been here ever since, and I learnt everything here."

The Garden at New Alchemy

The New Alchemists' first grower was one of California's foremost teachers and practitioners of organic agriculture, Richard Merrill. Merrill's involvement would have smoothed the way for John Todd to secure the grants which were the lifeblood of New Alchemy. From the get-go, however, he was closely assisted by Maingay. Merrill was only to stay on board at Cape Cod for the first year, and thereafter Maingay took sole responsibility for the growing for many years. In her book about the New Alchemists, *A Safe and Sustainable World* (2005), Nancy Jack Todd describes how Maingay took over. "In February of the second year she sat down with a stack of gardening manuals and seed catalogues and, bed by bed, planned the year's progression on a giant chart that ran the length of the kitchen wall." She describes how "Over the years, under Maingay's direction, the gardens kept getting progressively better." Perhaps the most powerful compliment she gives Maingay was this: "If New Alchemy could have been said to have a soul, it was unquestionably the garden." When I asked Maingay what her qualification was to have been set at the helm of the enterprise, she laughed, "None!" Barnhart endearingly stepped in to bolster his wife, "Our theory is that you are a smart person, and you can learn anything... you can innovate in any topic as well as anyone else."

She reflected:

> Well, thinking back again: So, when I grew up, my dad really loved gardening. But our garden was as big as this [room]... He had a big walnut tree. And then he put in an apple tree, whatever it was... And it was a tiny, tiny, little lawn and then there was a little canal. But he tried to spend basically his

whole weekend there, and that was his thing, and I think the love for gardening rubbed off somehow.

Maingay would help him at times. "He would pay for every weed we picked out by hand. And I would have one penny per weed, pick it out, and then I would have enough money to get an ice-cream cone or something." But it was so small that that was the extent of her involvement. Later, however, when she came to the USA, she gardened ornamentally as a student, and when she met the Todds and moved to Woodshole in Cape Cod at the same time New Alchemy started, she plunged into it at her own home there.

John Todd had his head turned by two books — *Limits to Growth* and *Silent Spring* — so much that, when New Alchemy started, it was his priority to grow without pesticides. Barnhart explains, "So they said, we need to do some experiments, scientific experiments and find vegetables that do not need pesticides. So, no one had any experience with agriculture at all. And they said, well Hilde, why don't you do that?" Maingay said she wanted to do it. Her work in the garden was couched in terms of scientific experiments. None other than Wendell Berry, interviewed in *Mother Earth News*, complimented the work she was instrumental in carrying out: "People like the New Alchemists are also contributing something very important by getting the farmers and gardeners to do the experimental work themselves. This is exactly where the agriculture colleges and extension services have failed the farmers." As Nancy Jack Todd explained, "Every system, biological or technical, is carefully monitored in order that we may have an accurate understanding of the efficacy of our experiments and so we can obtain some idea as to the conditions under which various ideas may be transplanted to other environments." In practical terms, this meant a lot of note-taking, organisation of timings, observation, and weighing. In the first instance, tests of their soil revealed it needed urgent care. The group accumulated enough material to make twenty tonnes of compost, eventually assigning Ty Cashman to exclusively oversee composting, seeing to it that the pile was properly fed and brewing at all times. They put up handmade signs redirecting autumnal leaf-bearing trucks and cars to the gardens which created vast deposits they would turn into compost. They laid their hands on as much of the leisure-oriented area's horse manure as they could.

Maingay's ideas included planting Marigolds (the smell of which repels bugs), cultivating a field of sunflowers fourteen feet high, and concentrating on intensive growing techniques. She introduced raised beds, more convenient than working at ground level, and sheet composting. Thinking along the same lines as John Jeavons in California, from French intensive methods she adapted the close spacing of plants so as to discourage weeds and spare water. On these procedures, Nancy Jack quotes Hilde herself:

> This type of horticulture also uses mulching and composting, techniques that have been established over thousands of years, in conjunction with the new understanding and knowledge gleaned from modern science... It uses simple low-cost equipment, does not rely on nonrenewable fossil fuels for fertilizers and pesticides, and uses the soil area and the sun's energy effectively. Over time the soil is improved, and the production and quality of the crop is increased, while labor and materials from the outside remains stable or declines.

She experimented with ways of extending the season, devising a hybrid of the cloche and a miniature greenhouse. These rectangular wooden frames would extend a metre, or two, over a bed. Their effectiveness was tested in controlled trials. Maingay reported:

> The difference in growth was striking. A month after setting out, the plants under the extended cloche were two to three times as big as the controls. Two months after the first plant

> date we harvested the broccoli. The plants kept producing until the second week of October. Eggplants, tomatoes, and Bibb lettuce as well as basil also matured a month earlier. We were still picking vegetables in mid-November.

The results were impressive: "On one plot of less than an acre we grew one serving each of a raw vegetable, a green cooked vegetable, and a root or other nongreen cooked vegetable for ten people for every day of the year with some surplus."

Hilde postulated:

> Gardening intensively on a small acreage, using such practices as extending the season with cloches and solar-heated greenhouses, selecting local plant varieties for pest and disease resistance and for suitability to soil and climate, improving soil fertility, establishing food-producing forests, and animal husbandry are all strategies within our reach to heal the Earth and to secure the existence of future generations. All that is needed is people willing to tend the land and nurture the plants that in turn sustain them.

She contacted the local land agent to ask about the historic yields in Cape Cod, and how her productivity compared to average yields of grains and vegetables. Parroting the same nonsense one encounters repeatedly about inherently infertile and unsuitable soils, they informed her that the Cape could not produce anything but cranberries and some strawberries. As for the land's historic productivity at the turn of the century, the answer was even more negative: "Lady… what they called high yields back then we call a poor yield now." By the late 1970s, New Alchemy's organic yields were consistently three times greater than the Department of Agriculture's estimates for average yields for a comparable acreage using agricultural fertilisers, herbicides, and pesticides. Barnhart remembers, "You could grow an enormous amount of vegetables in a very small space if you were really good at it. One person on a tenth of an acre will provide a years' worth of vegetables for ten people, which is a lot... That is really small, five hundred square feet. People didn't have any of those numbers."

At New Alchemy they grew and ate tomatoes, cucumbers, zucchinis, pumpkins, and squashes. They had good yields of beans, lima beans, corn, carrots, turnips, and beets. They were excited to grow peppers and eggplants successfully for the first time. One year, they even turned their hand to wheat. Although Cape Cod had once been referred to as Boston's breadbasket, it hadn't been grown for over a hundred years. Nancy Jack Todd remembered, how "there is somehow a jubilant quality about the days when we harvest wheat that is hard to account for". Maingay and Barnhart say that when the organic plants were harvested and laid out for the New Alchemy workers to take home, they were snapped up. However, when people were invited to pick the produce themselves it was a different story: "They wouldn't even go take two steps". Harvesting took up a lot of energy, as she worked out in another experiment looking at how much you could grow on a certain amount of space without pesticides or machinery:

> Fossil fuel was a big deal at that time. So, reducing fossil fuel was the main objective, and for that I had to keep track of all my time spent on everything from seeding to weeding to growing to watering to harvesting. That's how we found out harvesting is about a third of the time. Everything was done manually, and then I had to calculate how much energy everything took. The embodied energy of everything. So, for instance, we would go with a little truck to the beach to get seaweed to mulch the garden. Now, that's a lot of energy. And we found out that one trip with the truck was more energy than the rest of the year...

Maingay discussed other experiments of theirs, like watering the vegetable patch with fertile fishpond water. This was effective only with two varieties of lettuce. There was an experimental programme on companion planting and insect resistance. Barnhart remembers one of his wife's experiments which ended up being recorded for posterity in the wonderful Board of Canada documentary *The New Alchemists*:

> They said, okay, we're going to plant twenty kinds of cabbage in a special [configuration] in rows and patterns. And we're going to grow them. And we're going to look at the insects and we're going to measure the cabbages and see which ones were most insect resistant. That was the goal... So, we grew all these cabbages, and they measured all the bugs, and we measured the holes in the cabbage... But the important part was you have to be very careful what question you ask because, after they were done, they did a review. And this particular cabbage had the most insects and this one had less... So, you would think, 'Well, that's the best cabbage, the one with the least [bug damage].' Right? But she went and measured the edible portion of cabbage from each variety and the one that had the most bugs produced the most edible cabbage. Now, you know, you would have written that one off. So, it turns out bug damage isn't particularly a bad thing. It has to be so much that it damages the production, then you worry about it. Don't worry about just bugs per se, and she figured that out.

Homesteading and retirement

Although the couple are as passionately engaged in the issues that have motivated them their whole lives, society would consider them as being retired. There is a special synergy between gardening and growing old that deserves to be reframed. Currently, although undergoing a wider renaissance, the mainstream culture around it can feel moribund. When you age, you acquire an emotional maturity and equanimity that doesn't, per se, have anything to do with your advancing years. It's rather that over time, based upon observation and experience, you confront realities and come to logical conclusions about life that, were one to think carefully about it, one would reach sooner. My view is that the people I interviewed for this book are remarkable for working out these priorities so young in their lives. What is the point in acquiring endless material goods? Why use stimulants excessively? Who really cares about your status? As these scales fall from people's eyes, other things become enchanting. Planting seeds, tending them, and watching them grow becomes fun. Surveying a garden, no matter how tiny, not just in the summer, but in the spring when it is full of hope, or tidied away in the winter, fills one with a simple delight. This shift in priorities, rather than a diminishment, is an escalation. The process of growing plants couldn't be more important. The activity is vital in engaging and aligning one with the axis of existence. It is the crucible of our own life as humans. As for the soil itself, mycorrhizal educator and orchardist Michael Phillips neatly paraphrased Rudolf Steiner with the expression "Man is the soil walking". It's not just individuals that would benefit from this maturity. American astrobiologist David Grinspoon believes that as a species we need to grow up and acquire a mature perspective if we're going to survive our own cleverness.

Maingay gently chides the old people who attend the same dance class as her in Cape Cod:

> Those people do nothing. They only watch movies. They're retired and they just spend their time entertaining themselves... I just can't believe how affluent people are that they can afford to do nothing and only spend [money]. To sit and do absolutely nothing... They feel pretty good though when they go to church and have discussions about something in church.

The economics of growing food are, as Barnhart points out, very poor "if you figure out the costs and the time to grow a potato versus buying a potato." But as Maingay counters, "That's the same as asking whether there is any value to your time when you are playing games or watching a movie?" Growing itself, the argument runs, provides both entertainment and exercise. The self-sufficiency guru John Seymour works himself up into a delightful lather about precisely this, about the sheer stupidity of paying people to play sports for you. As for paying people to make music for you, he would rather pull out his squeezebox and have a jolly singalong with neighbours and family.

Humanure at New Alchemy today

Issues around human waste (pee and poo) and fresh water are, in terms of their life today as activists, the two most important parts of Maingay and Barnhart's work. As Maingay puts it, "Who in the heck is ever going to be so insane to flush clean drinking water into a toilet. It's really, like, beyond belief." The couple showed me their cutting-edge waste disposal technologies.

First there is the "Cubie", devised by the Rich Earth Institute, a urine-collecting funnel attached to a container tank. The funnel has a ball sitting within it, which is raised when you pee into it and otherwise sinks, creating a check-valve to suppress smells. Most of the emphasis of their work is on urine because 80% of the nitrogen we throw away is in pee, and a mere 10% in poo, and 10% in greywater. Once heated to sterilise it, urine is a fantastic thing with which to fertilise crops. Furthermore, urine only amounts to 1% of the volume of a household's human "waste" products.

Poo on the other hand creates other issues, especially because its conventional disposal is an absurd waste of drinking water. The couple separate the two bodily functions, collecting the pee (either in the Cubie or in a diverting toilet), and use a Swedish waterless "Separett" diverting toilet for poo. The poo drops down a vertical, ventilated chute and is collected in sealed wheelie bins in the basement below. There it is accumulated until the bin is full enough and is sealed. Sealed bins, of which there are three carefully dated and maturing in the basement, are, after two years, opened. Barnhart empties their contents into a freshly dug trench in the garden, and this is covered with soil, upon which they plant. When two years have elapsed, any pathogens have died off. Their system works flawlessly, but it's not the only method of turning urine and shit into useful agricultural products.

Humanure and the counterculture

From Robert Davidson's legendary "Zappa Krappa" photo of the Mother of Invention to Mary Barnes at Kingsley Hall smearing herself with her own shit, the counterculture had a fascination with the stuff. In keeping with its willingness to confront socially awkward topics head-on, there is a rich vein of discourse about human waste running through the era's agricultural literature.

In *Being of the Sun*, Alicia Bay Laurel writes:

> Shitting into a hole in the earth is good for you & for the trees. It should be buried at least one foot deep & never uphill from or near a water supply... a Swedish anaerobic unit converts shit & organic garbage into sterile odorless compost; flush toilets pollute waterways. while meditating on sunlight you can fulfill your deepest earthly role as a builder of the soil and gardener of galaxies.

At the back of the book, Alicia gives detail of the Clivus Composter toilet from Sweden. Larry Korn writes in his own follow-up to Masanobu Fukuoka's *The One-Straw Revolution*, titled *One-Straw Revolutionary*, "I consider human manure to be a gift from the Buddha." Gary Snyder notes in his Pulitzer Prize-winning *Turtle Island*, "Learn how to use your own manure as fertilizer if you're in the country — as the Far East has done for centuries." Alan Watts in his book *In My Own Way* comments, "The amount of shit we allow to flow out into the oceans is simply wasted manure — wasted, neglected, ignored because our eyes, noses and mouths go one way and our assholes go another." Wendell Berry states, "It is possible to quit putting our so-called bodily wastes where they don't belong (in the water) and start putting them where they do belong (on thc land)". The Findhorn Founders recycled through the compost all unused scraps from the kitchen, as well as the "night soil", their own shit, from the caravan. The Nearings explain, "The night soil will be used mainly under apple trees, as mulch, to stimulate their growth. As knowledge and practice of ecology grows, and water becomes a scarcer commodity, earth closets may take precedence of wasteful water closets."

At Sevagram in India, John Seymour visits Gandhi's house. It is exactly as Gandhi has left it, a three-roomed hut, walls and floors a mixture of cow dung, and practically no furniture. There's a tiny bookcase with perhaps a dozen books on it, including Gandhi's famous copy of the *Bhagavad-Gita* in English. Gandhi developed the "Wardha-type" toilet — a mobile hut which straddles a three-foot deep trench, and which is moved along as the trench fills up. Grass or leaves are thrown on top as it is used. Seymour describes how, after as little as six weeks, the trench is opened up and the contents, a sweetly fragrant fertiliser, are used as compost on the fields. He writes, "There must be a way, and we shouldn't rest until we find it, of putting this marvelous fertiliser back into the land." At Fachongle Isaf, Seymour sets up a Wardha Latrine, wondering if he can make it work in the climate of Wales.

The root of this knowledge in modern Western thought is the legacy of the agricultural scientist Franklin Hiram King (1948–1911). F.H. King, as he is known, was first a professor of agricultural physics at the University of Wisconsin-Madison before becoming chief of the Division of Soil Management in the USDA Bureau of Soils. However, the results of his research at the USDA didn't sit with the orthodox dogma and meant that he was forced into retirement. King, a figure in the field of agriculture comparable to that of Nikola Tesla in electrical engineering, spent the last seven years of his life researching and writing up his findings.

F.H. King has long been celebrated. Louise Howard, Sir Albert Howard's wife, wrote of her husband, "On this crucial question of returning wastes to the soil, he always acknowledged his debt to the great American missionary F.H. King, whose famous book, *Farmers of Forty Centuries*... was to him a kind of bible." Lord Northbourne described the book as one "no student of farming or social science can afford to ignore... a classic". Lady Eve Balfour was a fan, also describing *FOFC* as "a classic", and in *The Living Soil* (1943) she reproduces a Dr L.J. Picton's plan for organising housing developments in a diamond formation with humanure collection at the rear, "an investment productive of fresh vegetables to be had at his door, and in one way or another repaying him his outlay".

And the humanure *should* be considered valuable. King describes farmers vying with one another to create the most appealing roadside toilets to attract passing travellers. Permaculture co-originator David Holmgren, referring to King, writes, "In China in 1900 the farmers who bought nightsoil from the various European cantons in Shanghai paid the highest price for the German product because Germans ate more meat than other nationalities and therefore excreted more nitrogen and mineral nutrients." Sim Van der Ryn — of whom more shortly — describes how in Hiroshima, "if three persons occupied a room together the sewage paid the rent of one, and if five occupied the same room no rent was charged!" Larry Korn reveals that the waste of high-ranking samurai officials fetched the highest prices.

Travelling in the Far East, in China, Korea, and Japan in 1909, F.H. King chronicled what was — in contrast to the disgraceful condition of an America blighted with erosion, falling yields, and depleted soil — a truly sustainable agriculture, one which had persisted for forty centuries. The eye-popping part of King's descriptions was the use of human shit and piss. "The human waste must be disposed of. They return it to the soil. We return it to the sea." King writes in stinging criticism of the habits of Western man and this neglect of humanure:

> ... the most extravagant accelerator of waste the world has ever endured. His withering blight has fallen upon every living thing within his reach, himself not excepted; and his besom of destruction in the uncontrolled hands of a generation has swept into the sea soil fertility which only centuries of life could accumulate, and yet this fertility is the substratum of all that is living.

In contrast: "In the Far East, for more than thirty centuries, these enormous wastes have been religiously saved..."

Recent insights on humanure

There have been informed contemporary critiques of the Chinese use of humanure. Joseph Jenkins, the activist and author who coined the term "humanure", believes that the Chinese did not compost their human shit. Indeed, King clearly describes the following happening: "And in reality, recent bacterial work has shown that fecal matter and house refuse are best destroyed by returning them to clean soil, where the natural purification takes place." This process, dumping poo directly on the land, as described by King, was not hygienic.

Composting is a simple but incredibly important process in which "brown" carboniferous and "green" nitrogenous material are combined in the presence of oxygen and moisture. After a time, aerobic decomposition by fungi and bacteria produces... soil. In the context of humanure, composting is essential because the heat the process generates wipes out viruses, bad bacteria, protozoa, and parasitic worms. An essential part of the humanure composting process which, according to Jenkins, is neglected is that composting will not take place in the loo itself. Think about it! Even if you have plenty of carboniferous material like, say sawdust, to add to your "evacuation", there's no circulating air in there, and in the absence of oxygen, the process will turn anaerobic, produce a lot of smelly methane, and not break down into soil. Jenkins is consequently infuriated by the term "composting toilet", its bowl is merely a temporary holding pen for material that needs to be added to the top (and centre) of an actual compost heap. He prefers to use the terms "compost toilet" or "dry toilet". Without composting — as full of potential as the ancient Chinese system seems — the process is flawed. As Jenkins writes in footnotes to King's original text, "Americans who have traveled abroad and witnessed the use of raw human excrement in agricultural applications have largely been repulsed by the experience."

More broadly, in a minor deviation from our argument, the aerobic versus anaerobic debate is far from closed. Youngsang Cho, Korean pioneer of the more recent JADAM Organic Farming, is a staunch proponent of anaerobic decomposition. Contemptuous of worries about the smell it generates, he compares the resulting anaerobic compost to Korea's Kimchi and argues that such isolated composting keeps all the nutrients in one place. This means they are not lost to the wind or through effluent. Cho argues that, above all, compost should be understood as food for plants. Are we not now lectured on the probiotic vitality of fermented foods like yoghurt and miso? Other composting techniques, such as the domestic-scale Bokashi technique, use anaerobic processes.

Duncan Brown, professor emeritus in the department of biological sciences at the University of Wollongong in Australia, is quoted in the footnotes of the latest edition of *FOFC* with this to say of the methods King observed:

> Gastro-intestinal diseases were endemic throughout the region. In Korea and Japan, fluke diseases were common because of the practice of eating raw fish grown in ponds fertilized with human excrement. But those diseases could have been largely avoided with a better understanding of their nature and mode of transmission. If properly used, devices like the relatively modern septic tank, and the more modern oxidation tank or the so-called composting toilet can avoid the dangers of gastro-intestinal diseases previously associated with the use of human excrement in manure.

Earle Barnhart of New Alchemy, who follows a different method to Joseph Jenkins, points out that gastro-intestinal diseases which occurred in the China documented by F.H. King were a result of not enough time being allowed to elapse in the decomposition of humanure. Chinese growers were often too impatient to wait sufficiently long and wanted to get the biology working on their fields. Barnhart told me that Mao smashed all the old ceramic poo cisterns the peasants used, in the Cultural Revolution.

Sim Van der Ryn

Before Joseph Jenkins's intervention of *The Humanure Handbook* (1995) — now in its fourth edition and a world-famous modern classic, a thoroughly informative and enjoyable read — the counterculture's humanure bible was Sim Van der Ryn's *The Toilet Papers* (1978). Wendell Berry wrote the foreword. It has been described as one of the favourite books of the 1970s back-to-the-landers. Van der Ryn was Emeritus Professor of Architecture at the University of California, Berkeley and, under Governor Jerry Brown, was California State Architect in the 1970s. In the book he calculated that "each day L.A.'s waste provides the nutrients to grow 5,000 tons of vegetables, enough to provide everyone in Los Angeles with a pound or two of fresh produce daily".

Van der Ryn summarised the current folly:

> Mix one part excreta with one hundred parts clean water. Send the mixture through pipes to a central station where billions are spent in futile attempts to separate the two. Then dump the effluent, now poisoned with chemicals but still rich in nutrients, into the nearest body of water. The nutrients feed algae which soon use up all the oxygen in the water, eventually destroying all aquatic life that may have survived the chemical residues.

He breaks down the full range of compost toilets then available: the Pit Privy, the Maine Tank, the Farralones Compost Privy. The last, the Drum Privy, the type that is installed at the New Alchemy institute works in the following way: "The drum is vented, and sawdust or earth is added after each use. In an average family, it takes three to six months for the drum to fill up, at which time it is lowered, rolled out and sealed for composting..." Of the photos of elegant compost toilets in the book, many are from Zen Buddhist institutions: The Tassajara Zen Mountain Center; and another institution affiliated to the San Francisco Zen Center, Green Gulch Farm.

In keeping with his countercultural adoption, Van der Ryn is a rebel. Attending a meeting in a windowless office on the twelfth floor of the San Francisco Health Department, where bureaucrats had convened to argue the health risks of compost privies, during a coffee break, "I pull a gallon jar from its brown paper sack under my chair and gently sprinkle the sweet-smelling stuff aged in our privy on the plants in the room. I imagine the plants smiling and smile back." But ultimately, as Van der Ryn points out, lest we forget poor Henry Thoreau's brother John, "Composting organic material containing fecal matter requires extra care because feces may carry pathogenic or disease-carrying organisms."

The end of New Alchemy

Nancy Jack Todd, referring to the shift from the Democratic Carter years to the Republican Reagan administration, writes that "in the culture at large, the idealism that had fueled much of the work in the 1970s was losing ground to a focus on financial gain that was judged the criterion for legitimacy." Maingay passed the baton to gardener Steve Tracy and his successor Dave Marchant. In the 1980s, in the new economic climate, grants were harder to procure, and the garden became a useful source of revenue. Tracy raised $4,000 at local growers' markets in his first year, and Marchant eventually raised $10,000 from the sale of their annual produce.

Nevertheless, the 1980s ended up being their busiest years, with annual visitors averaging ten thousand. A fitting conclusion came in 1987, before Hilde and Earle and their cooperative bought the site from the struggling foundation in 1991. Buckminster Fuller, populariser of that icon of America's communes, the geodesic dome, visited their Pillow Dome. As Nancy Jack Todd describes in *A Safe and Sustainable World*, this was "a tropical island of moist fecundity, green and teeming with plant life. Fish swarmed in the clear-sided solar-algae ponds, and the sentinel fig tree was laden with fruit". The ninety-two-year-old Buckminster Fuller turned to John Todd. "It's magnificent! It's what I've always wanted to see. My architecture combined with your biology. I think it's an extraordinary job you have done." He described to them the kind of work New Alchemy were doing as "the hope of the world".

I'd had such a lively and fascinating afternoon that I was sad to leave the couple Earle Barnhart and Hilde Maingay. They have found some magic in life. I'm not alone in being affected. Maingay told me:

> And still, up to this day, since we give tours now and again… There are a lot of people that have said, 'Oh, I visited you

in the nineteen seventies!' and that they will never forget. With their parents, or with school or when they were young. Just the other day a woman came by and said, 'I drove by here... when I was 10... And it changed my life.'

NATURAL FARMING

The hero of radical agriculture is the fascinating Japanese Masanobu Fukuoka (pronounced MAH-SAH-NO-BOO FOO-KOO-OH-KAH). Historians say Fukuoka created a system called "natural farming"; however, it is likely that Fukuoka would say that he did nothing at all.

Without the intervention of an outside agent, it's not impossible that eventually Fukuoka and his work would have become globally famous, but it's more likely that he would have gotten lost in the sands of time, like Mokichi Okada. The barely known cult leader Okada even had his own, not dissimilar form of natural farming. It was one of the spokes of his "Wheel of Health", alongside "physical purification", the light therapy of "Johrei", and his "science of nutrition". Using only "natural" composts and no agricultural chemicals or animal manure, Okada's "nature farming", founded in 1936, actually predated Masanobu Fukuoka's by a couple of years. There was even some jostling between the two, in which Fukuoka dismissed Okada's natural farming as Theravadan, the "little vehicle" of Buddhist theology, while Fukuoka saw himself as representing Mahayana, the "great vehicle".

It took the intervention of a special person, an entirely unassuming hippie, Larry Korn, to bring Fukuoka to the world stage. Korn explains how: "*The One-Straw Revolution* was published in 1975 in Japan titled *Shizen Noho: Wara Ippon no Kakumei* (The Heart of the World) and had little immediate impact in Japan. However, when it was translated into English, it became a sensation."

Larry Korn

Born in Los Angeles in 1947, a "city boy" by his own description, Larry Korn went to the University of California, Berkeley, in 1967 when it was a hotbed of free speech, women's rights, and anti-war sentiment. He studied the history of China, and when he graduated, he decided to go to Asia to see what it was like, setting off aboard the *SS President Cleveland* in 1970. As a young person travelling in Japan, he soon came in touch with free-thinking young people who had dropped out of the mainstream. As Gary Snyder commented in an interview with the *Berkeley Barb*, "If you drop out for a couple of years after graduating from college and wander around leading a semi-bohemian way of life, you can't get back into that society and have a job."

In particular, Korn connected with a group calling themselves *buzoku*, "tribal people" or sometimes "The Bum Academy". Wanting to return to the land and live as Indigenous people had in ancient times, they were closely connected in spirit to the back-to-the-land movement in the United States. Korn visited the group's volcanic island, Suwanosejima, far south of the Japanese mainland, in 1971. There he found twelve others living in an ashram, practicing karma yoga, and tending small plots growing sweet potatoes, squash, melons, and a few vegetables.

As a relatively young man, at first Korn struggled with the work and discipline, wishing he was doing anything else but clearing the fields of bamboo, which will run riot like a weed. Then, one afternoon, as he describes his own transformative experience tending the soil:

> I was working alone that day. I remember noticing that the pick was swinging into the soil just as before, the roots were coming loose, but it was effortless, as if someone else was doing the work and I was standing by watching. I was actually enjoying the sensations of my back muscles

> stretching out with each stroke and reaching out to pull the roots free. In fact, I was loving it. I became one with the bamboo roots and felt like I knew them personally. Then I looked up and saw the island in all its beauty as if for the first time, the trees swaying in the wind, the birds, the open sky. At that moment there was no place I would have rather been than right there in the field digging those roots.

Thereafter, Korn's main interest and responsibility on the island was farming. One evening, looking out across the half-planted field of sweet potatoes, he listened to the sound of the bamboo in the wind. Standing there silently to take it all in, he describes how "Then the soil spoke to me. From then until now, everything I have done has involved plants and soil in one way or another, a gift I could never have expected or imagined."

In my last book, *Retreat*, I was eternally grateful to meet and interview Bhagavan Das, the countercultural guru and icon, and the man who coined the term "Be Here Now". Baba, as I know and love him, spent time on Suwanosejima Island.

> They were growing soybeans as their main food crop. They also practiced spearfishing. So, the combination of soybeans and fish was their main food supply. It was a completely primitive indigenous lifestyle, totally back to the earth, similar to how the earlier Japanese lived. The tribe members were all young Japanese people who embodied a very loving vibe. I heard about them from Gary Snyder, a poet who lived in Japan for many years. When Gary told me about The Tribe I went to the island to live with them. They did Zazen every morning and evening together and I participated in those practices with them. It was very wonderful to live in a peaceful isolated lifestyle with them away from the modern noise of the cities.

Fukuoka himself noted of this counterculture that

> if you look across the country you might notice that quite a few communes have been springing up recently. If they are called gatherings of hippies, well, they could be viewed that way too, I suppose. But in living and working together, finding the way back to nature, they are the model for the 'new farmer.' They understand that to become firmly rooted means to live from the yields of their own land. A community that cannot manage to produce its own food will not last long. Many of these young people travel to India, or to France's Gandhi Village, spend time on a kibbutz in Israel, or visit communes in the mountains and deserts of the American west. There are those like the group on Suwanosejima Island in the Tonkara Island chain of Southern Japan, who try new forms of family living and experience the closeness of tribal ways. I think that the movement of this handful of people is leading the way to a better time. It is among these people that natural farming is now rapidly taking hold and gaining momentum.

Returning to UC Berkeley after his extended trip, Korn enrolled in the soil science and plant nutrition programme. Not having been taken over by agribusiness, it was a progressive class. One of Korn's professors proceeded to tell the students what happens when the soil is ploughed: vegetation is eliminated; the layers of soil are mixed together; mycorrhizal fungi strands are broken; the organic matter in the topsoil combusts at a faster rate, reducing fertility and its water retention; and the exposed ground is left open to erosion. The class were extremely distressed, with Korn even describing himself as being close to tears. "If ploughing is so bad," asked a young woman, "why do we do it?" To which the professor replied, "Because we don't know any other way to grow food." Korn made a note of this and remembered it when he happened upon Fukuoka's farm.

Masanobu Fukuoka

The most recent edition of Fukuoka's famous book *The One-Straw Revolution* (1978) features an introduction by Frances Moore Lappé *and* a preface from Wendell Berry, who acted as editor for it. These two were among the pre-eminent agricultural theorists of their day. To compare this to the field of science, it would be like having Marie Curie and Linus Pauling endorsing your doctoral thesis. In his preface, Berry compares Fukuoka with Sir Albert Howard: both started out in the laboratory but quickly saw its limitations. Fukuoka would say, "Modern research divides nature into tiny pieces and conducts test that conform neither with natural law nor with practical experiences." Berry, a committed Christian, asks the reader when considering Fukuoka's "do-nothing" farming to remember the gospel of Matthew 6:26, "Behold the fowls of the air: for they sow not, neither do they reap, nor gather into barns; yet your heavenly father feedeth them."

As a young man aged twenty-five, Fukuoka's job was working for the Yokohama Customs Bureau in the Plant Inspection Division. His main task was to inspect imported and exported plants for disease-carrying insects. With his ample spare time in the laboratory, he would carry out intense investigations in plant pathology, which he had studied at high school and at the Okayama Prefecture Agricultural Testing Center. He would spend days in "amazement" at the world of nature he glimpsed through his microscope.

In and out of love — carousing, as he refers to it — and working obsessively to the point that he experienced fainting spells in the lab, Fukuoka contracted acute pneumonia. He found himself confined to a freezing room with a broken window on the top floor of the Police Hospital with snowflakes curling around the room. Even when he was finally released from hospital, he could not pull himself out of his depression. To students of psychoanalysis and spirituality, the sequence of events has all the hallmarks of a healing crisis, part of what is sometimes also referred to as a kundalini awakening. Fukuoka confides in the reader, "I was in an agony of doubt about the nature of life and death. I could not sleep, could not apply myself to my work. In nightly wanderings above the bluff and beside the harbour, I could find no relief."

On one of these nightly walks, exhausted, he rested against the trunk of a large tree on a hill overlooking the harbour, neither asleep nor awake. At dawn, he stirred, watching the sun rise and the breeze chase away the mist. At that moment, Fukuoka an instant of true sanity illuminating the correct relation of things, as momentary as it is momentous, an instance of what we might call satori:

> Just at that moment a night heron appeared, gave a sharp cry, and flew away into the distance. I could hear the flapping of its wings. In an instant all my doubts and the gloomy mist of my confusion vanished. Everything I had held in firm conviction upon which I had ordinarily relied was swept away with the wind. I felt that I understood just one thing. Without my thinking about them, words came from my mouth: 'In this world there is nothing at all...' I felt that I understood *nothing*.

Fukuoka was delighted:

> I could see that all the concepts to which I had been clinging, the very notion of existence itself, were empty fabrications. My spirit became light and clear. I was dancing wildly for joy. I could hear the small birds chirping in the trees and see the distant waves glistening in the rising sun... Everything that had possessed me, all the agonies, disappeared like dreams and illusions, and something one might call 'true nature' stood revealed.

It's fascinating that Fukuoka details how he struggles to unpack his message. He describes it taking a few years to integrate this new understanding into his way of life. "At that time I addressed everyone as follows, 'On this side is the wharf. On the other side is Pier 4. If you think there is life on this side, then death is on the other. If you want to get rid of the idea of death, then you should rid yourself of the notion that there is life on this side. Life and Death are one.'" The people he explained this to apparently became very concerned about him: "'What's he saying? He must be out of his mind...' they must have thought." Wherever he went, he was ignored as an eccentric. Returning to his father's farm, he reasoned, "I thought that if here, as a farmer of citrus and grain, I could actually demonstrate my realization, the world would recognize its truth. Instead of offering a hundred explanations, would not practicing this philosophy be the best way?" Fukuoka's method of "do-nothing" farming began with this thought. However, chastened by his father on his return home, he was to double back for eight years, taking a job as Head Researcher of Disease and Insect Control in Kochi Prefecture. As an old man looking back, he describes his behaviour at Kochi as being completely irresponsible: "I argued with my co-workers asking them to consider my ideas denying the validity of science. Or else, under the pretense of investigating plant diseases and insect pests, I rambled through the mountainous interior of Kochi doing my own research about nature."

Fukuoka and Eastern philosophy

The idea of *nothing*, and grasping it as a concept fundamental to understanding reality, has a storied and manifold presence in Buddhism. As with many tenets of Buddhist philosophy, there are many, sometimes even contradictory, explanations of it. The two most coherent are as follows: one perspective is to explain understanding *nothing* as a realisation that there are no *essences* — and that there only exists *interrelation*. By this we might understand that the sun, a rice plant, its roots, and the soil are not individualised forms but only have meaning in relation to one another. A second equally relevant perspective within Zen Buddhism is to understand *nothing* as that form of vitality which is entirely natural. This qualifies *nothing* as having some kind of distinguishing characteristic — albeit a characteristic which is, so to speak, transparent. For example, we might surmise that while it is simple for a rock to behave naturally, as though motivated by *nothing*, for people it is very hard to be natural, not to interfere with themselves. It is of paramount significance that Fukuoka, whose vision of *nothing* has qualities of both, experienced his satori in nature.

Fukuoka himself refers to the centrality of the *Heart Sutra*, in which "the Lord Buddha declared, 'Form is emptiness, emptiness is form. Matter and spirit are one, but all is void...'" He would also discuss the concept of "mu", "Sometimes it is expressed as 'emptiness', 'nothingness', 'no mind', and in a lot of other ways, but the fact is, the more you talk about it, the farther you get from its true meaning. It is a perception that only occurs when the mind is completely tranquil."

Fukuoka would refer to natural farming as mu agriculture. "[Taoist influence upon Zen] Lao Tzu spoke of non-active nature, and I think if he were a farmer he would certainly practice natural farming."

In the countercultural era, Zen was at the forefront of recent memory. This was in part thanks to the eminence bestowed upon it by D.T. Suzuki (who wrote "In Zen there must be satori...") and Westerners like Alan Watts and Jack Kerouac. George Ohsawa made one of the macrobiotic movement's smartest moves in titling a book *Zen Macrobiotics* (1965), which truthfully had very little to do with Zen. At the same time, as the countercultural currents critical of what Eisenhower called the military-industrial complex were a hot political ticket, Fukuoka's farming-manifested satori met with a receptive audience.

Korn believed that Fukuoka's philosophy differed from the nondualist motive of most Asian spirituality: the desire to become one with the whole. And there was no set of techniques like meditation or yoga, or texts to ponder, to achieve Fukuoka's aim. "Simply serving nature by living humbly and providing for your own daily needs is seen as the most direct path toward self-awareness." Fukuoka would repeat to his students over and over again that the philosophy was everything and the farming was merely an example of the philosophy. "If you do not understand the philosophy the rest becomes empty activity."

Fukuoka said, "Extravagance of desire is the fundamental cause which has led the world into its present predicament... A life of small-scale farming may appear to be primitive, but in living such a way of life, it becomes possible to contemplate the Great Way." In his view, "if 100% of the people were farming it would be ideal". Larry Korn said of his sensei, "His message shows the way to a brighter future for humanity, a future in which people return to their appropriate place in the world and in doing so find peace within themselves. He considered healing the land and the purification of the human spirit to be one process, and demonstrated a way of life and a way of farming in which that process can take place."

Fukuoka's natural farming

The idea for natural farming came to Fukuoka one day when, passing an old field, he noticed healthy rice seedlings sprouting through a mass of weeds and grass. There was, it seemed, no need to connive to leave a rice paddy field flooded as was customary. In the light of this, he developed his own system for farming rice on his one-and-a-quarter-acre field. Individual seeds of rice would be encased in clay pellets (to protect them from rot, birds, and mice) and these would be broadcast by hand into the fields among the ripe stands of winter barley just before its harvest. Thus, the two crops were constantly grown in rotation. The rice and barley straw (the straw of his book's title) is returned to the soil as a mulch where it adds to the constantly improving soil fertility. Straw mulches were used in traditional Chinese agriculture. F.H. King notes their use in tea orchards to protect and fertilise the soil.

The custom of flooding the rice is intended to suppress weeds, and Fukuoka would flood his fields, but only for a week or ten days to discourage, not eliminate, weeds. Clover and barley seed is broadcast three weeks before the rice is harvested. His neighbours would have roughly 125 rice grains per head; Fukuoka had 225–250. His yields were comparable in weight were to those of modern commercial agriculture. Fukuoka's harvest was done by hand. The narrator of the Rodale documentary *The Close to Nature Garden* (1982) says, "His students don't mind, they enjoy the silent harvest using traditional hand tools." As the rice is harvested, the barley seedlings are already sprouting. Although he used no fungicide or pesticide, his crops were completely unaffected by the plant diseases or insect infestations which invaded his valley. On his twelve and a half acres of orchard's slopes, Fukuoka would grow vegetables and leaves under the trees. Larry Korn describes how, "during the spring, seeds of burdock, cabbage, radish, soybeans, mustard, turnips, carrots and other vegetables are mixed together and tossed out to germinate in an open area among the trees..."

Fukuoka summarised natural farming in four principles: (1) no tilling of the soil; (2) no chemical fertiliser or even organic pre-prepared compost — he would use straw mulch or leguminous cover crops; (3) no weeding by tillage or herbicides; (4) no dependence on chemicals. Organic growers probably struggle the most with the injunction not to use compost, something of a holy cow. This is not to say that putting organic matter back to the soil, Albert Howard's so called "law of return", is wrong; only that, according to Fukuoka it is, just like digging, simply too much hard work. "To make compost by the usual method, the farmer works like crazy in the hot sun, chopping up the straw, adding water and lime, turning the pile, and hauling it out to the field." He would rather see people just scattering straw, husks, or woodchip directly onto their fields.

If this sounded like "no work", Fukuoka's pupils were in for a shock:

> I advocate 'do-nothing' farming, and so many people come, thinking they will find a utopia where one can live without ever having to get out of bed. These people are in for a big surprise. Hauling water from the spring in the early morning fog, splitting firewood until their hands are red and stinging with blisters, working ankle-deep in mud — there are many who quickly call it quits.

Fukuoka liked to distinguish between non-intervention (literally doing nothing) and what he calls "taking human responsibility".

Fukuoka believed that since natural food could be grown with the least expense and effort, it should be sold at the lowest price. Although his fruit was prized for its deliciousness, he made a point of shipping it out practically unsorted so that he might "get to bed early". On one occasion, he was asked to send honey from his orchard, and eggs from the hens on the mountain, to a natural food store in Tokyo. He was livid when he found out that the merchant had marked them up at extravagant prices. "If natural food is to become widely popular, it must be available locally at a reasonable price."

Meeting Fukuoka

Living in Japan and travelling between traditional farms and communes, Larry Korn had often heard people talking about Fukuoka-sensei, but no one he met had actually been to Fukuoka's farm or knew the details of his farming techniques.

Korn first met Fukuoka one summer afternoon on his return to Japan, in 1974, when he was twenty-six years old. Arriving at the nearest village, he knew from the fields which was Fukuoka's farm:

> The rice was shorter than average, the color was dark green, almost olive, and there were many more grains to each head. The surface was covered with straw, white clover, and weeds, and insects and spiders were everywhere. This was in stark contrast with the neighbouring fields, which consisted of neat rows of pale rice plants growing in a flooded field with no weeds or insects of any kind. Mr. Fukuoka saw me, came over, and introduced himself.

Korn worked for Fukuoka for a year and a half on the island of Shikoku in southern Japan, returning frequently to his own farm in Kyoto to implement what he had learnt. In due course, in spring 1976, Korn worked with Fukuoka and the other students to translate *The One-Straw Revolution*, which was published in translation in 1978. Returning to the USA with the rough translation for *The One-Straw Revolution*, Korn set about trying to find a publisher for it. His first call was the University of California Press. "The next person I showed the manuscript to was Gary Snyder, a poet and environmental activist who lived in the foothills of the Sierra Nevada. He had recently returned from several years in Japan, where he studied Zen Buddhism and was instrumental in founding the ashram on Suwanosejima Island."

Snyder cannot have been staying at Suwanosejima when Korn visited there, having moved to America more or less permanently in 1969, but it seems likely that the Sinophile Korn, seventeen years younger than Snyder, was following in his footsteps. Approaching Snyder after a poetry recital, Snyder said he was more of a mountain person than a farmer and suggested that Korn send the manuscript to agricultural philosopher Wendell Berry. Berry, whom we have now met many times through the course of this book, is crying out for introduction, but we're going to cover him properly in the "Sustainability".

Berry was keen that the book was not pigeonholed as a "New Age" work and suggested that together he and Korn approach the Rodale Press, who were publishing *Organic Gardening* magazine. Rodale's in-house book design was perfunctory, and Berry lobbied for and received permission for him and Korn to design the book themselves. Korn contributed a delightful drawing of Fukuoka's heron. After the painstaking two-year-long process of creating the book, Korn stayed with Berry on his farm in Kentucky for a time, before moving to, and helping on, one of Berry's neighbours' farms. Berry explained to him the problems American farmers faced, this topic being the meat of his classic *The Unsettling of America* (1977).

Fukuoka abroad

Fukuoka's first visit to the USA came in 1979 under the invitation of Herman and Cornelia Aihara —macrobiotic teachers, themselves students of George Ohsawa — who ran a summer camp in the Sierra Nevada Mountains in California. Fukuoka in fact expresses considerable ambivalence about the macrobiotic diet, referring to it as necessitating a "discriminating perception" (a bad thing!), but later in his career, he did seem to acquire more political tact. Nevertheless, Fukuoka shocked many Californians by pointing out that industrial agriculture, terrible water management, intensive logging, and grazing were turning the state into a desert. People who compared its climate to that of the Mediterranean "are in denial about the ecological disaster they have created here".

One place he visited was the San Francisco Zen Center's Green Gulch Farm, a 115-acre farm located fifteen miles north of San Francisco. Fukuoka visited the one-and-a-half-acre flower, fruit, and herb garden there — which was influenced by the ideas of biointensive pioneer Alan Chadwick, and created by Chadwick's disciples, including Wendy Johnson, who gave Fukuoka a tour. On his first visit there, Fukuoka established a profound connection with the Native Indian horticulturalist Harry Roberts, who also worked at Green Gulch Farm. In the intervening years after his first visit, Fukuoka sent Roberts some Japanese cedars, related to the native redwood trees, but which throw down deeper roots and are therefore less likely to topple over. By the time of Fukuoka's second visit, in 1986, Roberts had died and was buried just across the valley from where the young Zen students were carefully protecting Fukuoka's cedar seedlings. The students told the visiting Fukuoka that Roberts would be calling out to him saying, "Let's plant seeds in the desert together." He joked on his friend's resting place: "It looks like a comfortable place. It might not be bad to lie down there with him." But he writes, "As soon as I had said this, I burst into an uncontrollable flood of tears... When I thought how he might be the only person I would ever meet who understood me, who would live with me and die with me, I stood rooted to the spot, heedless of the tears pouring down my cheeks." Masanobu Fukuoka had not even cried when his parents had died, it was only the second time he had cried in fifty years.

Fukuoka and ecology

In Fukuoka's subsequent travels to Europe, Africa, India, China, and Southeast Asia, he saw first-hand how human activity was turning the world into a desert. The later Fukuoka is, one delights in discovering, less of a voluntary peasant than a globe-trotting superstar. He receives visits to his farm from people such as Fritjof Capra, professor at the University of California and author of *The Tao of Physics* (1976). He flies to Somalia to assist a private nongovernmental organisation and help them promote modern agricultural methods. His dream of regreening the deserts of India lead him to vist Thailand to collect seeds from its ancient forests. Speaking to the governor of West Bengal, he sows seeds from an airplane into mangrove swamps at the mouth of the Ganges before meeting the Indian prime minister. We find him dispersing daikon and clover seeds along the side of the parched Californian highway from Oregon to California from the window of a speeding car. His ideas are used in the Philippines. In these interactions, Fukuoka reveals a genius in dealing with complex political situations — in the Madras area, not letting rip with criticisms but praising the results achieved through the strenuous efforts of the state government — all the while sensitive to the difficulties of people's lives and feeling the utmost concern for the environment.

Fukuoka tried different experiments in crossbreeding, most notably with breeding nonglutinous rice from Burma with glutinous rice from Japan. Unhappy with the results, he concluded that the process of crossbreeding was best managed by nature. He did, however, continue his programme by crossbreeding rice with weeds such as deccan grass and foxtail — but this was really to just amuse himself "by going in the opposite direction of what was being recommended by agronomists at the time". Nonconformist to the last, an interesting aspect of his ecological views is that he believed that plant quarantine systems are redundant.

Tillage

As we have discussed earlier, the central plank to Fukuoka's natural farming is the principle of no-tillage. Sir Albert Howard gives us a good description of why farmers till the soil:

> What was the purpose of this tillage, which is still the prime agricultural process? The first effect is, of course, physical. The loosened soil makes room for the seed, which can thus grow in abundance, while to cover the sowing with scattered earth or to press it into the ground protects it

> from the ravages of birds and insects. Secondly, tillage gives access to the air — and the process of soil respiration starts up, followed by the nitrification of organic matter and the production of soluble nitrates. The rain too can penetrate better.

Another plausible argument for tillage, which we must append to this, includes the way it is used as a method to uproot weeds.

To answer Howard's prescription, point by point: Fukuoka covered his land with a mulch of straw and did not compact it with machinery, thereby decreasing the necessity for manufacturing the fine soil growers call a *tilth* — which is suitable for growing seeds, and which is the "loosened soil" to which Albert Howard refers. Gardeners know, on this topic, that it is difficult to get seeds to "take" in coarse-grained compost. Because Fukuoka protected his seeds in clay balls, they were not eaten by birds and insects. To address Howard's second point, because his soil acquired its own natural structure over time, was not compacted by machinery, and was always protected by a cover crop from its baking by the sun, with its porosity established by the tracks of earthworms and the cavities of decomposed roots, it was both well-aerated and able to absorb rainwater like a sponge. As for weeds, unlike the biointensive process, which with its closely spaced planting doesn't leave enough room for them to take hold, in natural farming they are discouraged by the straw mulch covering and crowded out by rice or barley. Practioners of no-till also argue that constantly disrupting the soil in the long run creates more weeds, as the seeds of the old and previously entombed are resurrected to the surface by the process of ploughing. The most skilful natural farmers find a use for plants that other less imaginative growers might try to eliminate.

Although we have squared them off against each other, interestingly, both Sir Albert Howard and Masanobu Fukuoka took the forest as the perfect model for agriculture. As Howard puts it, "What are the main principles underlying Nature's agriculture? These can most easily be seen in operation in our woods and forests." He elaborates that his Indore process "merely copies what goes on on the floor of every wood and forest. It has not been patented and will not be patented." This Howard reduces almost to a koan: "The forest manures itself."

Certainly, from a countercultural perspective, no-till was low-hanging fruit. Referring to Thoreau's wish to "make the soil say beans", Gary Snyder hints at *his* sympathy towards natural farming: "To cause land to be productive according to our own notion is not evil. But we must also ask: what does mother nature do best when left to her own long strategies?"

The mouldboard plough

No-till or "no-dig", with its emphasis on preserving the soil's structure — not for instance damaging the fine networks of mycorrhizal fungi — is today viewed as of ecological importance. Not without its dissenters, it is popular in today's ecologically minded gardening and farming, made famous in recent years by the legendary Charles Dowding, who has shown how well it can work at his experimental market garden Homeacres, in Somerset in the UK. Today, cutting-edge no-till at scale has been proven by farmers such as Rick Clark of Warren County, Indiana. Clark sows cover crops and flattens them with a crimp roller pulled behind a tractor. The resulting mat supresses weeds. He then sows seed through it using a no-till air-seed drill which does not disturb the soil. No-till has been around for a while — in the UK, at least as long as the renegade gardeners Arthur Guest, F.C. King, Shewell Cooper, and Gerard Smith, all active in the 1940s and '50s. My grandfather, David Summers, an early signatory of the Soil Association, who between the end of the Second World War and the 1970s farmed 1,400 acres in the North Cotswolds, grew vegetables no-till. However, tillage's history is complicated, and the more one speaks to people who farm, the harder it is to make definitive judgements about it.

After centuries of merely hoeing the land, in 4,000 BC Mesopotamia and in the Indus Valley, ploughing was done with the scratch-plough, essentially a wooden stick that was dragged through the topsoil by a draft animal. First devised by the Celts in Britain at the same time, the mouldboard plough added a curved cutting blade. In its final incarnation, a mouldboard plough will pulverise the soil and nearly completely bury weed and seed residue that was on the surface. Howard says that its evolution was due to soil requirements as settled agricultural life developed in the heavy, moist soils of North Europe after the forests had been cleared. And it proved to be very effective when it came to putting food on the table. A standard mouldboard plough will go eight inches deep, but some versions can plough three or even five feet deep. No doubt there are efficiencies to this — but its action leaves the soil surface exposed and vulnerable to erosion, and it damages healthy soil structure and biology.

Farming consultant and teacher Edward H. Faulkner, author of *Plowman's Folly*, is often mistakenly believed to be an advocate of no-till by, in farmer Eliot Coleman's words, "people who don't get past the cover". I found myself correcting Faulkner's appearance in the "no-till" entry on Wikipedia. *Plowman's Folly*, was a surprise nationwide bestseller, selling nearly a million copies by 1945, on the back of America's travails of the 1930s in the dust bowl. J.I. Rodale, not a fan, complained, "Practically every magazine and newspaper has discussed it, mostly in a favorable light, 'Down with the villainous plow — the curse of modern agriculture,' they say..." Louis Bromfield recounts the story of how "two Hollywood actresses... in a Chicago hotel asked me, 'What is all this business about *Plowman's Folly*?'"

The book takes aim at the ravages Faulkner ascribed to the mouldboard plough. Faulkner argues that in folding surface vegetation far under the ground, the plough's signature action, it could not decay aerobically like compost, but would do so unhealthily, anaerobically. Decomposing vegetation, he believed, was best on the surface, as it would be in the forest. But rather than advocate not disturbing the soil at all, Faulkner favoured a combination of growing leguminous nitrogen-fixing green manures in the normal course of crop rotations, and then chopping them down into the surface of the topsoil with the process of discing, or disc-harrowing. In discing, an array of metal plates are rolled across the field's surface by a tractor. This both creates a tilth suitable for welcoming seed and folds the green manure into the soil's surface where it composts, thereby fulfilling Sir Albert Howard's "Law of Return". This process, Faulkner asserted, also encouraged the side product of carbon dioxide to dissolve in moisture to create carbonic acid, which would etch out minerals from rock, making it bioavailable. In the US, this technique was called "trash farming" and was celebrated and brought to national awareness by the writer Louis Bromfield (more on whom in the "Sustainability" chapter), a supporter of Faulkner's, in his books describing his regenerative work on Malabar Farm in Ohio. Still in use, the practice is praised by Eliot Coleman for its ability to enrich and not destroy the soil. In *Plowman's Folly*'s sequel, *A Second Look* (1947), Faulkner clarified that the method worked best on sandy soils and was less effective with clay soils, and that he did use fertiliser (a phosphate potash mix, not nitrogen), but that the basic idea was "the necessity for plenty of decaying material in the soil surface... Everything else was subordinate."

As for the mouldboard plough, Albert Bates of The Farm commune thinks there are much better alternatives, like the Yeoman's keyline plough, which cuts a line through the soil and raises up the top few inches without turning the soil over or exposing it to parching. This is used in combination with a technique of ploughing against (rather than along) the land's contours, so as to channel the flow of water, thereby curtailing runoff, loosening up compacted soil for plants, and allowing soil to drain without disrupting its layered structure.

The use of the mouldboard plough is particularly controversial in drier climes. In *Round About India*, self-sufficiency guru John Seymour visits a government agricultural research station. There they were studying not chemical fertilisers but green manures, leguminous crops that are usually ploughed into the field. Seymour discusses ploughing. Contravening local habits and common sense, the centre had been trying to encourage local farmers to use this eighteenth-century European invention, the mouldboard plough. Local farmers were, quite rightly, doubtful of it and the advisability of deep ploughing in the dry subcontinental climate. The local scratch-plough, no more than an iron-shod pointed stick, merely scratched the surface four inches deep and did not turn the sod. Seymour at this juncture equivocates that the local farmers might be being too conservative, but on the other hand, he thinks, they *might* be right. With hindsight, in the glare of the spotlights of regenerative agriculture, we can appreciate that the local Indian farmers may have been correct. Back home in Blighty, Seymour was an ardent digger. Suffolk was easy to dig, and his method was to do so extremely quickly with a big fork. He comments, "In my experience at any rate, the more you dig the better, and it is better to dig badly than not at all."

With all the avant-garde seemingly arranged against it, it comes as a surprise to hear the permaculturalist David Holmgren pointing out issues with no-till methodology. Holmgren refers to the no-dig "sheet-mulching" technique which, mimicking the process in forests, avoids tilling the soil by spreading organic matter (like Fukuoka's straw) or compost on the surface of the soil:

> It is annoying that permaculture has become equated with the sheet-mulch gardening technique as if it were the pinnacle of sustainable land use. For me the technique has always been an easy way to convert lawn and pasture into productive food gardens without the hard work of digging

> and weeding and by making use of locally abundant and wasted organic materials. While vast quantities of organic materials are available (from urban landscapes and farms), sheet mulching is a good use of what others undervalue or waste; but in a lower-energy future such materials will not be available cheaply.

Holmgren refers to both Rudolf Steiner and soil fertility expert William Albrecht:

> There are doubts about the health and balance of garden soils continually covered by quantities of organic material at a density 10 to 100 times greater than that possible from litter in any natural ecosystem. From a biodynamic perspective, excessive and continuous mulching is said to smother the life in the soil; from an Albrechtian perspective, over time it typically results in excessively high levels of potassium.

Throw into this now seething cauldron the approach of John Jeavons and the biointensive lobby from the first chapter, and their double-digging method, and certainly my confusion on the rights and wrongs is total.

Ruth Stout

One notable icon of no-till was the gardener Ruth Stout (1884–1980). The counterculture loved her. Alicia Bay Laurel mentioned her to me, and Stout's book can be found in the bibliography of her *Living on the Earth*. Jeanie Darlington says of her in *Grow Your Own*,

> Ruth Stout, an 84 year old gardener, has been mulching year round with nothing but hay for 25 years. She never uses any fertilizer except what the rotten hay contributes, doesn't maintain a compost pile, and never tills or cultivates. Her

> soil has been analyzed several times and has always been found to be very high in every necessary element and of course [is] very rich in humus.

Stout even got a rave review in *The Whole Earth Catalog*:

> Ruth Stout is a master gardener who's been refining her procedures for decades now. She's sort of like an elderly Zen priest, an old roshi who after years of work and study has distilled a large burden of 'knowledge' into a single gem of wisdom which he renders in a single haiku. Just at the point that I felt like I was really catching on to making compost and feeling kind of proud, I found out that Mrs Stout doesn't fool with compost anymore. Too much trouble. Doesn't fool with tools much either. Doesn't fool with anything much, except mulch. Just spreads a lot of hay around, plants seeds by poking a hole in the ground with her finger, and when it is time, goes out and picks the produce and eats it.

Even Larry Korn, Fukuoka's disciple, loves Stout. His only criticism being that her mulch technique will only work on relatively small plots. He even dreams of her meeting Fukuoka, saying, "I think that they would have really enjoyed meeting each other." But most of all he thought that they shared a humanitarianism. "They could have been perfectly happy doing what they did privately at their own homes, but instead they chose to share their experiences because they thought they might improve the lives of other people."

Ruth Stout was born to Quaker parents in 1884. After a full adult life in which she had been an accountant, business manager, factory worker, lecturer, coffee-shop owner, part of a mind-reading act, and a Russian famine relief worker, she settled with her psychologist husband in Connecticut. In the course of this, perhaps owing to the connection with Russia, she befriended the "Red" Scott Nearing who she described with her brother as one of her foremost garden advisors (an inscribed copy of her most famous book, *How to Have a Green Thumb Without an Aching Back* (1955), can be found in the Nearing library at Harborside, Maine).

Her busy neighbour Arthur Burr would, reluctantly, usually plough her garden for her in the spring, but in April 1944, the tractor had broken. "So now on this perfect morning I stood there in the garden longing to put in some seeds. I wandered over to the asparagus bed and said to it affectionately: 'Bless your heart, you don't have to wait for anyone to plow you.'" This is because asparagus is a perennial vegetable; in this respect it doesn't need as much looking after. But then Stout "stopped short as a thought struck me like a blow. One never plows asparagus and it gets along fine. Except for new sod, why plow anything ever?" By "new sod", Stout inferred that she saw value in breaking up the soil a bit when first cultivating land to grow on, but not thereafter. "Why plow? Why turn the soil upside down? Why Plow? I AM NOT GOING TO. I AM GOING TO PLANT!"

Stout had already formed the habit, in spite of all the warnings against it, of leaving all the vegetable waste such as corn stalks right there in the garden. "Now when I raked this mass of stuff aside to make a new row for the spinach I found the ground so moist and soft that I made a tiny drill with my finger." Thus, came together her own no-dig formula. She felt a little crestfallen when someone gave her a copy of Edward H. Faulkner's *Plowman's Folly*, which railed against the mouldboard plough. To be fair to Stout, Faulkner's argument is different, advocating as he does sowing a green manure crop, and discing it in. Neither did his technique use a year-round mulch like Stout did to suppress weeds. This, and indeed her free-wheeling natural philosophy, were, as she puts it, "a simplification of living", which she shared alone with the true pioneer Fukuoka.

In substantial respects, however, Fukuoka is more radical than Stout. She did not give up chemical fertilisers till her fourth season. She used lime and cotton-seed meal for added nitrogen on her strawberries, lettuce, spinach, corn, and beets. She describes "conscientiously" spraying poison on her plants to protect them from insects, at first reacting towards organic agriculture, "Tut, tut! That is going a little far." In her chatty way, Stout even advocates the use of DDT:

> Then we heard that Japanese beetles breed in lawns and, if you had your lawn soaked with D.D.T. just once, the beetles would get progressively fewer and fewer through the years. It was important, however, for your neighbours to do it too. We persuaded all the valley people to treat their lawns and the beetles have dwindled to almost none.

PERMACULTURE

A term coined by Bill Mollison in 1975 to describe his and David Holmgren's design system, today permaculture is the de facto alternative approach for gardening, growing, and farming. There's space within its conceptual framework for a range of both rational and intuitive methods, as well as intensive and natural approaches to cultivation. It has come to function rather like the category of rock in the musical universe. The genre encompasses a myriad of different forms from the abrasive to the bucolic, from the avant-garde to the mainstream. If you ask a permaculture practitioner to define the term, expect to get a whole variety of responses. In itself that's understandable — try and unpack any elegantly "enfolded" concept, like for instance the simplest tenets of Buddhism, and you will likewise struggle to get simple answers.

Throughout my research, I came across approaches that predated permaculture's celebrity that would today be classed as examples of it. For instance, Masanobu Fukuoka's use of his own straw as a mulch on his fields, or the New Alchemists' idea of having a greenhouse with food plants in it as well as fish (New Alchemist Earle Barnhart wrote an introduction to the American edition of *Permaculture One*). John Seymour was intrigued by another permacultural idea — what would now be called silvopasture. He observed large areas of good land in Mallorca "sparsely planted with food-bearing trees with good grass underneath on which animals grazed".

All of these are permaculture-type ideas, by merit of their being carefully designed systems, which are organised around strategically harmonising efficiencies. Perhaps the classic example is Bill Mollison's. As his co-originator David Holmgren remembers, "Mollison was in the habit of replying that there was not an excess of snails but a deficiency of ducks." Ducks love to eat snails. The great underlying truth of this harmonising efficiency is that the best possible example of it is nature's own processes — systems that often look like forests. However, to get in alignment with nature's process requires what Gary Snyder might call some "hard yoga". It demands close observation and thoughtful management. Mollison expressed this sentiment, what we might generously describe as a faint pre-echo of the concept, when, awed by the Tasmanian Rain Forests, he jotted down in his diary in 1959: "I believe that we could build systems that would function as well as this one does."

Although it has applications that extend to topics as diverse as oil consumption, architecture, legal systems, and psychology, permaculture's central focus is agriculture. In their book *Permaculture One* (1978), Mollison and Holmgren defined it thus: "an integrated, evolving system of perennial or self-perpetuating plant and animal species useful to man. It is, in essence, a complete agricultural ecosystem, modelled on existing but simpler examples."

> We jointly evolved the system in the first place as an attempt to improve extant agricultural practices, both those of Western agribusiness, and the peasant grain culture of the third world. The former system is energy-expensive, mechanistic, and destructive of soil structure and quality. The latter makes drudges of men, and combined with itinerant herding, deserts of what once were forests. Perhaps we seek the Garden of Eden, and why not? We believe that a low-energy, high-yielding agriculture is a possible aim for the whole world, and that it needs only human energy and intellect to achieve this.

Holmgren, in his wonderful and eminently readable book *Permaculture: Principles & Pathways Beyond Sustainability* (2002), pulls no punches about the importance of their work:

> Changing the management of farmland to use organic and permaculture strategies and techniques can rebuild this storage of soil carbon, fertility, and water to be close to those of natural grasslands and forests. It is arguably the greatest single contribution we could make to ensure the future survival of humanity.

Bill Mollison

Bill Mollison (1928–2016) was a generation older than Holmgren. By the time they began working together in 1974, having left school aged fifteen to help in the family's bakery, he had filled a wide variety of roles: shark fisherman, forester, wildlife researcher, museum curator, political candidate, and employee for the fisheries. Taking a degree in the University of Tasmania as a mature student in bio-geography, he stayed on as a lecturer in the psychology department and developed a unit for environmental psychology. Mollison and Holmgren met when Mollison gave a seminar at the Department of Environmental Design in the Tasmanian College of Environmental Education, where Holmgren was a student. Holmgren's interests had gravitated to how landscape design and ecology could be applied to agriculture, and the content of Mollison's talk piqued his interest.

Mollison pointed out in that lecture how Australia's rabbit infestation problem could have been resolved by rabbit trappers, but that they had no incentive to solve it because they didn't benefit from the land being in better condition. Therefore, the ownership of the land itself had had a damaging effect on ecological sustainability. Holmgren saw that Mollison thought completely differently to the regular academic ecologists he had encountered, and unaware of Mollison's small local celebrity, approached him with the outlines of a manuscript which was eventually to become the book *Permaculture One*. They worked together on the first permaculture garden on the outskirts of the Tasmanian capital Hobart for three years. Their work on the concept was collaborative, but it was Mollison's experience and drive that were responsible for the movement's success and growth around the world.

While Mollison worked to turn permaculture into a movement, the younger man Holmgren set about refining the practice on a number of projects in Tasmania and New South Wales before developing his Melliodora property at Hepburn Springs, on Dja Dja Wurrung tribal country in Central Victoria:

> Building my own skills in gardening, forestry, reading landscape, earthworks and building construction, all informed by permaculture design principles. While shunning the limelight of media attention and the credibility of further academic qualifications, I never totally ignored the role of communicator and educator about permaculture.

Over the coming years, Holmgren acted as a practical consultant to others, many of whom were participants in Australia's back-to-the-land movement. A recent film on him, *Reading Landscape* (2024), documents his remarkable expertise in this capacity.

For many people, what is most impressive about permaculture is its very "sciencey" treatment of agriculture. This strand is largely Mollison's contribution. In Mollison's books, there are a great deal of technical instructions, measurements, diagrams, terminology, and rules. Everything looks at once fascinating, but also a bit opaque. The ideas laid out in a book like his solo flight *Introduction to Permaculture* (1991) are credible, but the sheer torrent of ingenuity can feel a little unhinged. Holmgren comments on his colleague's "tendency to add speculative ideas beyond the scope of evidence or practicality (part and parcel for a polymath capable of integrating knowledge across the disciplines)".

After a first foray into the topic, I decided that, beyond Mollison's affection for Masanobu Fukuoka, I couldn't see a connection between the counterculture and permaculture. Thank heavens I dug into the work and ideas of his co-originator Holmgren. I put this directly to Holmgren himself and he explained that Mollison came from a scientific research background. "So, having been a rabbit trapper was his pathway into scientific research... that idea of the scientific basis of things and trying to provide that as credibility for permaculture..."

Mollison expressed what amounts to hostility to any idea of spirituality, and this clearly marks him as differing from the hippie countercultural generation. In his autobiography, *Travels in Dreams* (1996), he writes:

> As I have often been accused of a lack of that set of credulity, mystification, modern myth and hogwash that passes today for New Age Spirituality, I cheerfully plead guilty... permaculture is not biodynamics, nor does it deal in fairies, divas [*sic*], elves, after-life apparitions or phenomena not verifiable by every person from their own experience, or making their own experiments...

However, scratch a little deeper, and one finds him making statements like the following, which comes right out of the Buddhist playbook: "We are not superior to other life-forms; all living things are an expression of life. If we could see that truth, we would see that everything we do to other lifeforms we also do to ourselves."

David Holmgren

Many of the individuals we encounter in this book have worked at what were the peripheries of society. Whether it is the Nearings moving to Maine, Peter Caddy growing his vegetables in Inverness, or John Seymour settling in the west of Wales, they are most often in what was considered a backwater. The counterculture in turn embraced these remote locations. Holmgren, an Australian (whose nation, in the early 1970s, might uncharitably have been described as a backwater itself) went even further out by moving to and working in Tasmania. He has a thoughtful perspective on it:

> People (generally from North America and Europe) sometimes ask me why I think permaculture emerged from somewhere like Tasmania... Hobart, capital of Australia's second-oldest and most decentralised state, is not set within some settled European landscape but clings to the foot of the wild slopes of Mount Wellington. For me it symbolises this interaction between civilisation and wilderness.

Researching and writing this book, I've been conscious that while every situation and person I've included relates to the central idea of farming and the counterculture, some are more closely related than others. The very closest conjunction, and one of the best examples as to why it's such a fruitful axis of exploration, is David Holmgren.

Born in 1955, Holmgren's background was unusual. His parents were nonconforming Jews, both atheists, and — before leaving, at around the time he was born in the 1950s — both were members of the Communist Party. His strange school lunchboxes of "wholemeal bread sandwiches, carrots, celery and dried fruit" were at once the object of wonder and derision. He told me, "I suppose that having such radical parents relative to my peers, there was less to rebel against in that generation... of sex drugs and rock and roll, [and] revolution." To this end, the ideas of the counterculture served as a way to distinguish himself from his parents and what he calls "the first generation alienated" of the 1930s and '40s, which might be epitomised by the "Reds" Scott and Helen Nearing.

Notwithstanding this, his parents were both opposed to the Vietnam War, and Holmgren got in trouble at school for refusing to stand up for the national anthem during the nationalist fervour of Australia's early involvement in Vietnam. Furthermore, after he and his friends read Leary, Metzner and Alpert's *The Psychedelic Experience* (1964), they took Aldous Huxley's *Doors of Perception* (1954) off his parents' bookshelves. While he doesn't suggest his parents took psychedelics, to Holmgren they were an important experience:

> That was a major change, not... just from my parents upbringing, but [from] the sort of super-rationalist mindset that I had as a kid... first marijuana and then a series of very seriously taken LSD experiences made it clear to me at seventeen, there was more in the human mind than could possibly be grasped by a simple sort of rationalist materialist view of the world.

Holmgren was asked to touch on these experiences at a recent Entheogenesis conference in Melbourne. He points out such matters have become, to an extent, respectable after the work of Michael Pollan. In the talk he explored the ethnobotanical connection "between understanding all sorts of different relationships between people and plants and culture, and obviously, especially plants that are psychoactive". But talking to me, he went deeper into the memory of it:

> Well, for me, and my peers, we took the whole process very seriously, within the limits of our teenage capacity, without actual mentors in that process. And whenever we took LSD, it was always in a natural environment and away from complex social interactions or difficulties. So that natural environment was a context and a background for those

> things. But it was also for me a fairly intensive experience. And the last of them was very intense, much more than I'd experienced before. And I went through a process that would be described as a sort of ego death experience, quite extreme. And that was about the same time that I was completing academic studies and exams. I'd been the academic 'dux' [the top pupil in his class] of the high school I went to. And my friends who regarded me as a very stable, centred, practical person were really worried about my state... And in that experience, I had a sort of amnesic end to the trip where I 'cut off', couldn't comprehend or face what I was dealing with. And I think that also coincided with [events] shortly after completing studies. I was mad keen on hitchhiking, and I headed off, left Western Australia, and hitchhiked round Australia, travelling for a year. And in that time, I encountered a lot of different aspects of the counterculture in Australia. 1973 was a very pivotal year that you could say was equivalent to, maybe '67 or '68 in the United States, or maybe '69 in Britain, the Isle of Wight Festival... because there was that little lag in that youth culture that doesn't exist now... and in that time, I socially met a lot of people...

From this point onwards, turning eighteen, however, he would steer clear of psychedelics:

> In a sense I came to see, not so much that I was playing with fire, but dealing with things so complex whereas I was still socially inexperienced, you know, 'not in the world'. I was still actually sexually a virgin, and I thought I needed much more experience of the world before I could go any further with that process.

Quite quickly his travels around Australia led him to become socially experienced in all of these different expressions. These included "actually arriving in Nimbin, what became the centre of the counterculture in Australia, in the weeks after the Aquarius Festival". The Aquarius Festival (1971) is acknowledged as being more radical than the big music festivals of America and Britain because, rather than like Woodstock or The Isle of Wight, rock festivals which split at the seams, it was a self-organised, anarchistic takeover of a small country town in northern New South Wales. The town of Nimbin

> still has that historic association with it to some extent of 'counterculture tourism'. I was there only for a few weeks in my travels, but there were experiences there that also exposed me to a lot of different ideas... So, those are all before I went to Tasmania to study environmental design and met Bill Mollison and his network.

Permaculture and the counterculture

You wouldn't know it if you only encountered Bill Mollison's work, but the counterculture, and the precious glimmer that it presented for the possibility of social behaviour change, is fundamental to at least Holmgren's vision of permaculture. In an article titled "The Counter Culture as Dynamic Margin" (2000), he writes:

> The counter cultural movement of the late 60's and early 70's was extraordinary in many ways. For a significant minority of the baby boomer generation, the counter culture was about a lot more than sex, drugs and rock and roll although those were the prime expressions of a rejection of materialism, a desire to reconnect with nature, the search for the correct place of love, peace and wisdom in the world, voluntary simplicity and other notions which have become themes in a continuing struggle to reinvent ourselves over the last thirty years.

He describes permaculture as "one of the more pragmatically focused concepts which emerged in the mid-'70s in response to the questions and possibilities raised by the counter culture".

Holmgren believes that the counterculture offered a viable model for behaviour change in society. He writes in *Permaculture: Principles & Pathways Beyond Sustainability*:

> Never in human history has there been such a great need and opportunity for cultural and intellectual renewal from the margin. The countercultural movement of the late 1960s and early 1970s is perhaps the most dynamic cultural example of the value of marginal systems in social transition. The counterculture, misunderstood and denigrated in the cultural mainstream as a failure characterised by naïve and silly ideas, has been a major source of innovation. I see permaculture and the counterculture within a longer tradition of alternative movements within modernity, which have the potential to spark the transformation of civilisation necessary for inevitable energy descent.

Holmgren has no truck with kneejerk criticism of the movement:

> The idea that the counter culture has no history and no future is simply an expression of ignorance... If I were a revolutionary zealot seeking to rouse the faithful, I would assert that 'the counter culture has a history of persistence and gathering strength in the face of adversity while the current establishment has no history or cultural vitality.'

Bottom-up action

Somewhere at the very centre of the permaculture concept is an idea that I came across repeatedly in studying ideas of health against the background of the counterculture in my last book, *Retreat*. George Harrison of the Beatles put it thus:

"Well, again I'll quote Maharishi, which is as good as quoting anybody else, and he says, 'For a forest to be green, each tree must be green,' and so if people want revolutions, and you want to change the world and you want to make it better, it's the same..." Holmgren writes, "The slogan 'change the world by changing yourself' is recognised as a spiritual or inward-focused approach to working for a better world. There is compelling evidence, though, that this idea is a principle for an externally focused concept such as permaculture with its roots in scientific objectivity." Holmgren calls the strategy "bottom-up action" and believes that it is the most suitable method of activism for the post-industrial culture of necessitated lower energy use, "descent".

A factor in this, for Holmgren, was seeing how little his politically active parents were able to accomplish in their attempts to make a better world. He told me,

> It was interesting because I met Mollison after he'd been at the front lines of environmental activism for five years where he was actually at the same place. Whereas I was at it from an overview of reviewing my parents' legacy. And I suppose what I saw with the individual action, is that there was so much autonomy potentially there for the people who are part of the global middle class that had never existed for masses of people in the past. So, we could, if we were brave, choose to do things in, really radically different ways and get away with it... and society wasn't gonna kill us or throw us in prison here. And so that meant we could experiment, we could be our own guinea pigs. Because, if you're trying to project completely different models for society, it's impossible for those to be projected from the top, when there's no models or examples or smaller scale [experiments showing] of what the hell this actually is. So, for the possibility of any larger scale change, you need innovation, experimentation, working models, failures, lots of different learnings. And the possibility of individuals,

> and small groups of individuals, being able to do that in the modern world, because of information, and because of affluence, was unprecedented.

There were unexpected upsides to this kind of life experiment:

> I saw that, at a number of levels, it also was different from the leftist political philosophy, the sort I'd seen around me, where you've got to sacrifice yourself for the cause... The idea that as an experimenter, as an innovator, you could gain a benefit from what you were doing was seen as very suspicious in the left, political sense. Whereas in the counterculture it was 'No, we're enjoying ourselves. This is actually good for us.'... And that is valid, and that is part of the positive feedback loop that actually draws others in. Because it's a model of success rather than struggle and defeat. So, it has that potential to draw in and replicate, and it also then has the possibility that, if it gets scale, it has a subversive effect of pulling the rug out from underneath the consumer economy, which depends on the participation of middle-class: workers, consumers, investors... Prior to the modern world, it was only a very few people who had that role. Whereas collectively the middle class, the system depended on them enormously, and so, if you are actually withdrawing your participation, that is a radical action. Now you could say, 'Okay, well unless a lot of people do it, it doesn't have any effect,' and I'm not saying that bottom-up, changing the world by changing yourself has had this huge powerful impact, but I think it's at least as powerful as all of the efforts to change the system.

Higher purpose

Where Mollison was keenly opposed to the culture around spirituality, Holmgren, an atheist, is more open-minded, as befits someone who has come through the counterculture.

"Parts of the construction of spiritual relationships are obviously part of every sustainable culture that has existed on the planet. So, that from a functional ecological cultural point of view, we should be very cautious about dismissing spirituality and religion as a useless thing that we no longer need." Equally, he thinks that modern spirituality, if it was going to evolve, would do so naturally. Therefore, Holmgren is sceptical that it's a process that could be effectively *designed*, but "Spiritual beliefs about a higher purpose in nature have been universal and defining features of all cultures before scientific rationalism."

He does still keep a space for it in his thinking. He expects that

> as an emergent property, especially in a world of 'energy descent', of less resources and power in the material world, the non-material realities actually come to the fore as somewhere where growth is possible. Whereas in the material world it ceases to be possible. And I suppose over the decades I've been more open to that and not critical of those efforts that people are making to create that spirituality.

Part of this openness relates to the way in which ideas have power to shape the world, "And those can be material and non-material. And in a lot of ways, that idea that those are completely separate realms, I think, seems to not be the case in most traditional cultures."

Descent

Although agriculture, ecology, and landscape design is, in practical terms at least, at the centre of his work, Holmgren's central idea as it runs through his recent work is "descent". Permaculture, like the work of the New Alchemy Institute, emerged against the background of the Club of Rome's *Limits to Growth* report that came out in 1972. *Limits to Growth* shone a light upon the collision of economic and population growth and speculations about finite natural resources. The oil shock of 1973 (triggered by OAPEC, a league of Arab nations targeting Western support of Israel) and that of 1979 (caused by a dip in production after the Iran-Iraq war), although they were not caused by a physical shortage of oil, simulated one.

Holmgren, like many ecologists, views the exploitation of fossil fuels as a historical aberration. Since the dawn of the Industrial Revolution, in energy terms, we've led a gluttonous existence. With what is argued to be the imminent arrival of "peak oil", that's about to change. As Holmgren put it, "Permaculture is a creative design response to a world of declining energy and resource availability..." This has everything to do with "conventional" agriculture, involving the use of energy-intensive inputs like fertiliser and machinery — which, in energy terms, are costly to make and run — and a system of distribution which arises from food being grown at great distances from its markets. Holmgren's colleague Mollison came up with a figure in the documentary, *In Grave Danger of Falling Food* (1989): "Ninety-five percent of the cost of that food is in carting it to [the city], in packaging the food, and in taking the wastes away". Holmgren himself uses an effective analogy: "While teaching permaculture in Israel, I suggested that a glass of milk in Australia was perhaps 20% oil, while in Europe the figure was perhaps 50%; and that from what I had seen of Israeli dairy farming, 80% of a glass of milk must be oil."

But, somewhat joyously, it's not necessarily cause for doom and gloom. Holmgren writes, pointing to the appeal of modes of life such as voluntary simplicity and personal frugality,

> We have trouble visualising decline as positive, but this simply reflects the dominance of our prior culture of growth. Permaculture is a whole-hearted adaptation to the ecological realities of decline, which are as natural and

> creative as those of growth. The proverb 'what goes up, must come down' reminds us that, in our hearts, we know this to be true. The real issue of our age is how we make a graceful and ethical descent.

Holmgren thinks that "Reductions in over-consumption of food, drugs, material goods, media, and entertainment all have the potential to improve quality of life," and it certainly feels like he is on to something. As we've discussed, ideas of spirituality are enmeshed in these graceful visions of "descent". "Energy descent is likely to lead to a natural reintegration of spirituality and materialism that has been the norm of most of human history"; elsewhere he says, "The change of direction from growth to contraction, from materialistic to more spiritual values, is so fundamental that it will turn the world on its head."

Speaking to me, he describes how the perception that the counterculture failed relates to the history around this concept of "descent": "There's a lot of discussion about the failure of the counterculture, just looking at its internal inadequacies or naiveties or failures without understanding the larger geopolitical context." This context was the new political landscape of the 1980s and its global post-colonial ambitions. "The demonisation of the counterculture in the 'greed is good' era of the '80s, with what I call the 'Thatcherite-Reaganite Revolution', was where neo-liberalism was part of a whole action, and the disabling of many challenges to the system, including environmentalism, focused on the [previously established arguments around] limits of energy that were so strong in the 1970s..." As a result of this he believes that

> the *Limits to Growth* work was just completely cast aside as a total failure. And in a sense, the counterculture just got caught in this huge geopolitical struggle that involved the control of the countries that had the resources that kept industrial modernity going... And if those countries

> had managed to assert power, as they were attempting to do in the energy crises, and succeeded, then the Western world would have gone into a major structural, permanent recession or depression. And the ability to project empire power would have failed. Now what would have happened in relation to the Soviet Union in that context it is hard to know. But culturally, what would have happened in Western countries, is the counterculture would have flourished...

"Descent" is a concept I embrace, but it is complicated by one of the more shocking ideas I came across in the research for this book. This is a conjecture, presented to me by Earle Barnhart at the New Alchemy Institute, and explored by the author Charles C. Mann in his epic book *The Wizard and The Prophet* (2018). It is borne out by a century of observation of supposed fossil fuel obsolescence, and is starkly apparent in the light of modern techniques to extract fossil fuels from old reservoirs and discover new reservoirs, as well as the invention of new techniques for extraction. Presaged by the caveat that Mann doesn't think anyone who is not an economist will believe that a finite resource will be infinitely available, he quotes MIT economist Morris Adelmen: "It is commonly asked, when will the world's supply of oil be exhausted. The best one-word answer: never." This idea, one we need to consider, might mean the geopolitical situation is not forced to evolve, but in ecological respects, it doesn't change a thing.

RetroSuburbia

Permaculture has always been fascinated with the things people living in or on the outskirts of cities can do to provide their own food. In the 1989 documentary *In Grave Danger of Falling Food*, Bill Mollison sets up a food garden on the tiny balcony of a tower block, assuring the viewer with an optimistic statistic, that "about a fifth of the food for a couple is being produced here". Holmgren himself has argued that we need to regard gardening as a serious form of agriculture. His 2018 book *RetroSuburbia: The Downshifter's Guide to a Resilient Future* is an engrossing tome, and comes on like a Day-Glo version of John Seymour's *The Complete Guide to Self-Sufficiency*. Growing food is only one of the many topics it covers.

Right back at the dawn of the organic movement, thought was given as to what positive contributions city dwellers, who weren't growers or farmers, might be able to make to the health of the soil, and by extension their own well-being and that of the ecology. Sir Albert Howard had these words of advice in 1947:

> The man in the street will have to do three things: 1. He must create in his own farm, garden, or allotment examples without end of what a fertile soil can do. 2. He must insist that the public meals in which he is directly interested, such as those served in boarding schools, in the canteens of day schools and of factories, in popular restaurants and tea shops, and at the seaside resorts at which he takes his holidays are composed of the fresh produce of fertile soil. 3. He must vote to compel his various representatives — municipal, county and parliamentary — to see to it: (a) that the soil of this island is made fertile and maintained in this condition; (b) that the public health system of the future is based on the fresh produce of land in good heart.

Holmgren's *RetroSuburbia* is dedicated to Wendell Berry, "agrarian, ecologist and author", and Berry has, over the years, made some choice remarks about the importance of gardening in the acknowledged presence of its big brother, agriculture. In his classic book *The Unsettling of America*, Berry points out, "For one thing, the town or city household was itself often a producer of food at one time town, and city lots routinely included garden space and often included pens and buildings to accommodate milk cows, fattening hogs, and flocks of poultry." Writing in the back-to-the-land bible, *The Last Whole Earth Catalog*, Berry says,

> Odd as I am sure it will appear to some, I can think of no better form of personal involvement in the cure of the environment than that of gardening. A person who is growing a garden, if he is growing it organically, is improving a piece of the world. He is producing something to eat, which makes him somewhat independent of the grocery business, but he is also enlarging, for himself, the meaning of food and the pleasure of eating. The food he grows will be fresher, more nutritious, less contaminated by poisons and preservatives and dyes, than what he can buy at a store. He is reducing the trash problem; a garden is not a disposable container, and it will digest and re-use its own wastes. If he enjoys working in his garden, then he is less dependent on an automobile or a merchant for his pleasure. He is involving himself directly in the work of feeding people.

And in what seems to be a premonition of *RetroSuburbia*, Berry says in the same article,

> If you think I'm wandering off the subject, let me remind you that most of the vegetables necessary for a family of four can be grown on a plot of forty by sixty feet. I think we see in this an economic potential of considerable importance, since we now appear to be facing the possibility of widespread famine. How much food could be grown in the dooryards of cities and suburbs?

In *The Gift of Good Land* (1981), Berry echoes permaculture's call for bottom-up action: "Some people will object at this point that it belittles the idea of gardening to think of it as an act of opposition or protest. I agree. That is exactly my point. Gardening — or the best kind of gardening — is a complete action. It is so effective a protest because it is so much more than a protest."

It's interesting to revise our conception of a number of rural self-sufficiency scenarios as, truthfully, being suburban. Nancy Jack Todd, the New Alchemist, writes of that institute, "For all the Cape's charm, it is far from rural. It was and is a woodsy suburbia." An obvious candidate is Thoreau, living not in the wilderness but beside the railroad tracks on the common land at the edge of the town of Concord, popping home for dinners and to get his laundry done. Very similar sentiments are expressed by Masanobu Fukuoka's collaborator Larry Korn. He believed in the importance of taking steps to align ourselves with the natural order both inside and out. "It is mainly a process of removing obstacles, letting go of misconceptions, and living a simple life that is close to the heart of nature." We should, Korn believed, reduce our material possessions, and make thoughtful and environmentally sound decisions with regards to transport, housing, food, and entertainment. We should uncouple ourselves from the belief that accomplishing "great things" will lead to a fulfilling life. Like David Holmgren, Korn believed this could be accomplished even whilst living in the city. "Living at a slower pace, tending a small garden, and living a simple existence centred around the hearth..." People who do this are putting the brakes on the senseless destruction of nature by working to heal the land and live responsibly.

Even Masanobu Fukuoka could be turned on by suburban vegetable gardens. Fukuoka and Korn stayed for a few days at a back-to-the-land commune in the San Francisco area. Their hosts Mino and Fusako were apprehensive upon being asked to show the sensei their backyard vegetable garden because they were embarrassed by its untidy condition. Soon, however, they were walking down the back steps of the house to the garden. Korn tells the story:

> It felt vibrant and the plants all had good color, but it was overgrown. Mino explained that he had hoped to have the

garden cleaned up before Sensei arrived, but he had been too busy at work. Sensei made his way through the weeds and clover, finding a few vegetables here and there. Then he got a big smile on his face and announced that this was the most magnificent vegetable garden he had visited since coming to America.

Permaculture and Fukuoka

If there's one figure that the permaculturalists have a crush on, it's Masanobu Fukuoka. Mollison and Holmgren's *Permaculture One* actually came out in 1978, the same year the translation of Fukuoka's first book was made available, so there's no sense of them appropriating his ideas. However, as Holmgren points out, "The translation into English of Fukuoka's *The One-Straw Revolution* had a profound influence on Bill Mollison... Put simply, Fukuoka had developed a system for grain cultivation which reflected the ecological design principles which we had outlined for perennial systems in *Permaculture One*."

By the time of Mollison's own *Introduction to Permaculture*, in 1991, Mollison was able to salute their fellow traveller:

> Fukuoka, in his book *The One-Straw Revolution*, has perhaps best stated the basic philosophy of permaculture. In brief, it is a philosophy of working with, rather than against nature; of protracted and thoughtful observation rather than protracted and thoughtless labour; and of looking at plants and animals in all their functions, rather than treating elements as a single-product system.

On Fukuoka's second visit to the USA, in 1986, he met Mollison at a permaculture conference.

However, the admiration between the two camps was not strictly mutual. Larry Korn remarks that Fukuoka's natural farming is often included in the permaculture syllabus because "it adds a spiritual dimension some feel is lacking in permaculture". Elsewhere his criticisms sharpen, and in fact echo Holmgren's own reservations about the movement:

> When it first came to America it came across like a decentralised, grassroots movement with an egalitarian feel... Today, however, the trend is toward a more structured organization with a central 'institute' and a panel of experts to regulate tighter standards for curricula and certification. This effort is largely promoted by those who think that working within universities, government agencies, and other mainstream organizations will allow them to reach a larger audience.

Holmgren traces natural farming further back than Fukuoka to the religious organisation — more-or-less a "cult" — Sekai Kyusei Kyo. This "Church of World Messianity" was founded by its leader, Mokichi Okada, in 1935. Given that Fukuoka's transformative spiritual experience occurred in 1937 and his first book was the self-published *Mu*, in 1947 — many years before the translation of *The One-Straw Revolution*, in 1979 — it might be fairer to see him and Okada as being neck and neck. While the religion's key concept is Johrei, a method of channelling divine light for healing, the other two pillars are the Art of Beauty (a form of Japanese flower arranging) and the Art of Nature (natural farming). If we accept that Sekai Kyusei Kyo's natural farming is a forebear of Fukuoka's, then it has the same antiquity as Steiner's biodynamic movement(1924–39) and the organic movement in the UK (1940–46) — all of them expressions of fear of, and distaste with, the new industrial agriculture. No doubt Fukuoka, sometimes described as an agricultural philosopher, raised the bar higher than Okada, not only with Kyo's innovations, but also with no-till, no weeding, and inventions like the clay balls with seeds within them.

Permaculture and Indigenous cultures

Cultural appropriation is something that we are all much more aware of today, and keen to avoid. In her book *So You Want To Talk About Race* (2019), the author Ijeoma Oluo gives us a set of tools for approaching the topic. Oluo says:

> We can broadly define the concept of cultural appropriation as the adoption or exploitation of another culture by a more dominant culture... Appreciation should benefit all cultures involved, and true appreciation does. But appropriation, more often than not, disproportionately benefits the dominant culture that is borrowing from marginalized cultures, and can even harm marginalized cultures... The problem of cultural appropriation is primarily linked to the power imbalance between the culture doing the appropriating and the culture being appropriated.

Permaculture shares with many of the fascinating strands of alternative agriculture the manner in which it has paid close attention to the techniques of Indigenous cultures, be they the Austrian peasant class which inspired Rudolf Steiner or the Indian farmers at Indore from whom Sir Albert Howard learnt. Those lessons have been used to substantiate a practical critique of conventional chemical agriculture. In this important sense, if there has been appropriation, to return to Oluo's outline, it has benefited all the cultures involved and it has not harmed the marginalised cultures in the equation. In every case of this cultural appropriation, the pioneers (if sadly not always the disciples) have given credit where it was due.

Holmgren is aware of these questions and is sensitive to them:

> That's both been part of the lineage of permaculture from the beginning, looking at indigenous and traditional methods of land use as potential models, and it's also been

> part of a critique of permaculture as an agriculture needing to be decolonized — that it was created by two old white guys in a university... Permaculture's actually part of the collective wisdom of indigenous peoples, and so there is elements of truth in that, but sometimes permaculture evangelism is projected as 'Here's this completely new idea that has no origins.' Whereas I think that would be hard for people making a proper critique of my work and in different ways, Mollison's work, to not see those references.

Both Mollison and Holmgren, as well as being frank about their debt to the innovative techniques of Indigenous people, have presented those peoples in the most favourable light. Writing in *Permaculture: Principles & Pathways Beyond Sustainability,* Holmgren explains that "many permaculture designers who have worked in development projects in the Two-Thirds World (Holmgren's term for territory outside the first world) admit that they learnt more than they were able to contribute." Together, they write in *Permaculture One* praising the often denigrated swidden, or "slash and burn", techniques of Indigenous agriculture:

> It is nonsense to say that aboriginal populations are not agriculturalists, as their cultures regulate the harvest and management of the land and its products, using controlled fire and clearing as a tool, and selection as a (conscious or unconscious) propagating strategy. Any group that does not regulate gathering or hunting selects for their own extinction.

As for Mollison's relation to Indigenous cultures, and the trouble he took for them, Holmgren also remembers his colleague's earlier work:

> The time I met him in '74, he'd just completed an academic study on the family lineages of the Cape Barron Islanders.

> And as a result of that, they became recognised by the Australian government as Aboriginal people. So, he actually knew personally all the Tasmanian Aboriginal people before they 'existed' in that sense. There was this idea that all the Tasmanians died out, they all became extinct; that there was this hybrid culture between the whalers and sealers who stole young women from Tasmania to set up on the Cape Baron Islands... As a fisherman and a bushman, he had the connection to the world that those people lived in. And he had the social connection because he knew all those people. At the same time as that, we were reading George Augustus Robinson's journals, describing Aboriginal gardens, effectively, and were aware of this idea of Rhys Jones, the anthropologist and ecologist who in 1969 coined the term 'fire-stick farming' to describe Aboriginal land use. So, all of those things were part of the mix that was influencing permaculture.

Holmgren, while he is occasionally critical of Mollison, is mainly keen to advocate for his work and often speaks affectionately of him. An anecdote that had us both laughing our heads off concerned how his old friend would describe permaculture as requiring very little work. But Mollison's own reference point for this differed from that of us snowflakes today. "Mollison grew up as part of the pioneering generation. Working clearing the forests, just mind-boggling levels of physical effort... Going away to work on the shark boats at fourteen and then, splitting timber and toiling in the dismal swamps."

SUSTAINABILITY

Countercultural ideology is characterised by its dissent. It drew its attitude from the spirit that led leather-clad biker Johnny, played by Marlon Brando, in *The Wild One* (1953) to reply to the question "What are you rebelling against?" — "Whaddya got?" As strong a set of principles as the organic movement offered, a number of growers, farmers, and agricultural thinkers weren't comfortable within its boundaries. In recent years, although, thankfully, not often critical of the organic standard, many have struck out on their own. Somewhere in the ideas of these sustainability gurus, never purists as such, there often lurks the idea, a nod to economic fundamentals, that a farm which goes bust, which can't make a profit, is not a sustainable one.

Louis Bromfield

Louis (pronounced Lewis) Bromfield (1896–1956) won the Pulitzer Prize for fiction in 1927 for his book *Early Autumn* and worked as a screenwriter in Hollywood. There he became friends with the likes of Humphrey Bogart and Lauren Bacall. He had always drawn on luminous childhood memories of helping his grandfather on his farm in Ohio, and in 1939, bought then ravaged farmland, "rich farm land ruined and scarred with gullies", in Pleasant Valley in Richland County, Ohio.

In the book *Pleasant Valley* (1945), he writes of his return as he opens the great barn door:

> Then I pushed open the door and walked into the smell of cattle and horses and hay and silage and knew that I had come home and that never again would I be long separated from that smell because it meant security and stability and because in the end, after years of excitement and wandering and adventure, it had reclaimed me.

Bromfield used his platform to educate Americans about the importance of sustainable soil practices. It's reckoned that, at one point, he may have been giving lectures two hundred days a year. Bromfield was the first president of the organisation Friends of the Land, which published a journal, *The Land*. Malabar Farm became a showcase in which he set out to prove that "worn-out farms could be restored again." The writer E.B. White captures the atmosphere of the farm in a witty poem, "Sailors, trumpeters, mystics, actors, / All of them wanting to drive the tractors..." Bromfield's farming books, which bring a rare glamour and poetry to agriculture, were extremely popular and influential. They convey a dreamy, endearingly sentimental farm of the imagination.

Bromfield had previously visited Sir Albert Howard at Indore in India, where he witnessed Howard's practices first-hand. He described Howard's *An Agricultural Testament* as "the best book I know on soil and the processes which take part in it," but Howard's Indore method as being prohibitive because "the expense of time and labor made it impractical and indeed impossible". Furthermore, Bromfield never farmed organically. There are numerous references within his books to his use of chemical fertilisers. He writes, though, that "chemical fertilizer was not the *whole* answer but only a small, though vital, part". More broadly, Bromfield accused bad farmers of not farming, but *mining* the soil.

Instead, he championed the ideas of Edward H. Faulkner described in the books *Plowman's Folly* and *A Second Look* — what is described as "trash farming". Bromfield relied heavily on leguminous green manures, cover crops like rye, alfalfa, and clover. He used crop rotations to rest and repair the soil, spread his own barnyard manure on the land, and to his neighbour's consternation, mulched it with the straw that they would have viewed as a relatively valuable asset elsewhere in the farm's ecology. He was an advocate of contour ploughing, which follows the land's topography and, in what are effectively tiny ditches, stops rainfall washing the topsoil away; and with strip-cropping, he arranged his crops in long contoured strips. He set up terraced ditches, which function like the swales of permaculture, to trap runoff and direct it down into the water table. He planted grassed waterways, green belts arranged along valleys, or watercourses that mitigate erosion. He took care to reforest areas and fenced cattle out of woods to protect the trees.

Bromfield's next farming book, *Malabar Farm* (1948), saw a shift which aligned Bromfield even closer to the dominant models of agriculture while at the same time seeing him trying to follow sustainable practices. Out went the "overly diversified" farming and dreams of self-sufficiency that he'd practiced before. These derived from his encounters with a homesteader named Bosquet he'd befriended in France. Bromfield shed his unprofitable farming of potatoes, apples, chickens, sheep, and pigs, and switched to "grass farming" for cattle for beef and dairy. His farm with its hilly terrain, he had concluded, was best suited to that. Purists would decry this and point to the importance of mixed farming, but Bromfield wanted the farm to be profitable. For a while he had coasted on the fortune his books brought in, but he began to run into major financial difficulties. Scale meant being large enough to afford the machinery which simplified those tasks. He describes how

> it was only after three or four years that the light struck us. We could go down the road to a neighbour whose business is potato growing on a scale of thousands of bushels and buy all the potatoes we wanted far more cheaply than we

were raising them in terms of seed, labour, and fertilizer, and they were much better potatoes.

In *Malabar Farm*, Bromfield also drifts away from his earlier position on ploughing. He elected to use the Graham-Hoeme chisel plough — a big curve or hook that sinks to depths of three feet, which he argued broke up "hard pan" soil, encouraged roots to go deeper, and allowed rainfall to penetrate, improving drainage. This was to evolve into Yeoman's keyline plough. However, although Bromfield professed to see this as an extension of Faulkner's "trash farming", truthfully, it's a departure. He stated, "We use every method from trash mulching to the deepest kind of moldboard plowing according to conditions, purpose, and need." Finally, in the chapter "The Organic-Chemical Fertilizer Feud", he comes out much harder in favour of chemical fertilisers, deciding that "their inability to cause actual damage, runs in direct ratio to the organic material present in the soil". He scoffs at the organic purists and their lamentable yields — twenty bushels of wheat compared to his own sixty, scarcely enough to pay the taxes and interest — mocking a letter sent to him by an "organic fanatic" and the "economic fallacy of the purely organic school".

Bromfield and Eastern philosophy

Bromfield wasn't religious by nature. He writes, "For me religion and faith have never come through churches and rarely through men". However, he was widely travelled in the subcontinent, which he journeyed to twice. Bromfield visited Malabar Hill, home of the Zoroastrian community in Bombay. This is where, at the Tower of Silence there, the Parsees leave their dead to be eaten by birds. For him this was a vivid depiction of the cycle of life and its relation to returning organic material to the soil. In honour of India being the inspiration for his novel *The Rains Came* (1937), which together with its movie adaptation bankrolled his interest in farming, it is suggested by Bromfield's biographer Stephen Heyman that *Malabar Farm* was named after this experience on Malabar Hill. Bromfield writes of the hill farm at the top of his property: "Up there against the sky looking across the thirty miles of Valley and stream and lakes and woods and hills, one comes close to God with that sense of remoteness and grace which the Hindu knows..."

At the end of *Pleasant Valley*, there comes what sounds like a call to the back-to-the-land movement. "What we need is a new courage and a new race of pioneers, as sturdy as the original pioneers but wiser than they..." *Malabar Farm* got a review by Pat Patterson in *The Whole Earth Catalog*. They write that Bromfield established "something which would probably be called a commune if it were being done today (it wasn't called that then, as Bromfield and the people associated with him were ultra-respectable)". Whether it would qualify as a commune seems arguable, but it is nevertheless revealing of his embrace by the counterculture.

J.R.R. Tolkien

Hippie fascination with the works of J.R.R. Tolkien is well-known. From Led Zeppelin's references to *The Lord of The Rings* in songs like "Ramble On", "Misty Mountain Hop", and "The Battle of Evermore" from *Led Zeppelin IV* (1971), to the wonderful *LOTR* poster crafted by former KLF member Jimmy Cauty in 1976 and published by Athena, and which adorned a generation's walls, Tolkien's books *The Hobbit* (1937) and *The Lord of the Rings* (1954–55) were commune staples and read aloud in the dim light of hurricane lanterns. The books were also an influence upon the doings at Findhorn. When Robert Ogilvie Crombie, an affiliate of Peter Caddy, claimed to meet the deity Pan in the Botanical Gardens in Edinburgh, ROC asked Pan, "'You read Tolkien?' 'My literary tastes are impeccable.' He smiled enigmatically at me."

In their book, *Ents, Elves, and Eriador: The Environmental Vision of J.R.R. Tolkien* (2006), Matthew Dickerson and Jonathan Evans say of the other famous fantasy novel of the era, C.S. Lewis's *Chronicles of Narnia*, that "when we finally do see preliminary signs of a dependence on what today might be called agribusiness — that is, Calormen's commercial growing of food for export to Narnia — this marks the end and destruction of Narnia... but there are no visible signs of any actual agricultural work." On the other hand, "In the prologue to the Second Edition of The Lord of the Rings, and in the portions of the narrative set in the Shire, Tolkien shows us working farmland and many signs and implements of agriculture and a small-farm economy." He shows mills, farms, vegetable gardens, turnip fields, cornfields, mushroom farms, ploughs, harvests, and markets. When, at the end of the trilogy, there is a battle in the Shire, Hobbits build their barricades from old farm carts and wagons. Dickerson and Evans describe the farming of the Shire as representative of "sustainable agriculture".

Although Tolkien's vision of the countryside is a romantic one, his biographer Humphrey Carpenter associates it with the death of his mother, which forced his removal from the country idyll of his childhood in Worcestershire in the Midlands of England where he had moved in 1896. Tolkein described it as "the longest-seeming and most formative part of my life". The nearby village of Sarehole was swallowed by the advancement of Birmingham not long after the Tolkiens left. He nevertheless did have some farming experience, being conscripted by his brother Hilary to sell the produce he grew at an orchard and garden in Evesham at a local market.

Unlike Farmer Cotton, who is described as having a sound grasp of the right principles of agriculture, the character Pimple "owns a sight more than was good for him; and he was always grabbing more, though where he got the money was a mystery", not just a farm, but "plantations". Furthermore, Pimple exports the crops he grows. The inference being that, as he does not work the land himself, he has no stake in its well-being. But this is nothing compared to Saruman. Of his destruction of the woods of Isengard, Tolkien writes, "Once it had been green and filled with avenues, and groves of fruitful trees, watered by streams that flowed from the mountains to a lake. But no green thing grew there in the latter days of Saruman."

In "The Scouring of the Shire", when the Hobbits return, a character called Hob complains to Merry that even though they had had a good harvest, there was not enough food owing to exports to Mordor. "We grows a lot of food, but we don't rightly know what becomes of it. It's all these 'gatherers' and 'sharers,' I reckon, going round counting and measuring and taking off to storage. They do more gathering than sharing, and we never see most of the stuff again."

Wendell Berry

The growth of industry, mechanisation of agriculture, and movement of people to cities and towns resulted in the practices of growing and farming becoming divorced from the wider culture. In the very recent past, they would have been connected. Is there another example of a whole activity hewn off in this manner? As much as we are increasingly accustomed to pay people to play sports for us, make music for us, cook for us, and clean up our mess — we're usually able to do these things ourselves from time to time. But such a seemingly fundamental thing as growing food we can eat? These philosophical questions which relate to the integration of people into their landscape in a sustainable way are the terrain of the writer, activist, and farmer Wendell Berry. Berry certainly shares a lot with the organic lobby, but he has not, as far as I've found, proselytised for that movement — for his own reasons, always taking a wider perspective. If I had to recommend only one writer's work which strove to connect together the broken continuum of what *ought* to be "a culture", it would be Berry's. A staunch critic of the vapidity of modern urban society, he writes, "From a cultural point of view, the movement from the farm to the city involves a radical simplification of mind and character."

Berry was born to a tobacco farmer in Kentucky, in 1934. He passed into academia after being awarded a Guggenheim fellowship which took him to Italy and France. He taught English at New York University. This led, in 1964, to him teaching creative writing back in his home state at the University of Kentucky. He continued this until he resigned there in 1977. In 1965, he bought Lane's Landing, a twelve-acre farm in Port Royal, in north central Kentucky. After a stint writing for Rodale Inc. from 1987 to 1993, he returned to the English Department at the University of Kentucky. No fan of agricultural academia, he writes, "The expert knowledge of agriculture developed in the universities... has no cultural depth or complexity whatever. It is concerned only with the most immediate practical (that is economic and sometimes political) results."

Berry still lives on his farm at Port Royal which now stretches to 117 acres. Strictly speaking, Berry does not believe per se in the idea of sustainability, but as he says in *The Gift of Good Land* (1981), "I have seen enough good farmers and good farms, and a sufficient variety of both, to convince me beyond doubt that an ecologically and culturally responsible agriculture is possible."

Wendell Berry on the counterculture

Berry, aged eighty-nine, is fresh from publishing *The Need to be Whole: Patriotism and the History of Prejudice* (2022), an epic reformulation of his thoughts on race, a topic he first discussed in the highly respected *The Hidden Wound* (1970). He doesn't own a computer and claims that he is now rather deaf, so we corresponded with one another via letters. Berry was very generous to take time to write to me about the counterculture of which he grudgingly admits he was, "to an extent, in it. I spoke and marched against the Vietnam War, tried to befriend radical students, etc." He says of his return to Kentucky in 1964, "My own direction was toward the authentic agrarian culture of my family and neighbors here, but that made me, if somewhat marginally, a part of the back-to-the-land movement."

Berry was a close friend of the countercultural icon Ken Kesey from when they met at a Stanford writing seminar in 1958 until the time of Kesey's death. He describes Kesey as "'far out', but absolutely unlike anybody else in or out of the 'counterculture'". Berry says he himself was never a Merry Prankster, one of Kesey's more conventionally unconventional cohort of trippers. Indeed, looks can be deceptive. One would mistake Berry for a regular guy if one was to judge him superficially from a video recorded in 1974, with his tidy, short hair, formally dressed in a suit and tie, and talking in his lilting southern accent at the Agriculture for a Small Planet Symposium in Washington State. Berry describes Kesey as being "capable of profound seriousness, insight, and kindness". He informs me that Kesey's farm in Oregon was Kesey's family's own dairy farm and advises me to "ponder very carefully the NO he finally issued to hangers-on!" (The "All Asshole Farm" piece we covered in "Back-to-the-land" chapter). Kesey clearly loved Berry too. He pens a review of Berry's book, *Long-Legged House* (1969) in *The Whole Earth Catalog*:

> Wendell Berry is the Sergeant York charging unnatural odds across our no-man's-land of ecology. Conveying the same limber innocence of a young Gary Cooper, Wendell advances on the current crop of Krauts armed with naught but his pen and his mythic ridgerunner righteousness. He boasts a formidable arsenal of novels, speeches, articles, stories and poems from his outpost in one of the world's most ravaged

battlefields where he writes the good fight and tends his family and his honeybees. Consider him an ally.

Berry's friendship with another icon of the counterculture, fellow poet Gary Snyder, is immortalised in *Distant Neighbours* (2014), which collects together their nearly 250 letters to one another between 1973 and 2013. Berry first read Snyder's work *Riprap* (1965) in the basement of San Francisco's City Lights bookstore, and was immediately attracted to Snyder's practicality, work ethic, and love of the landscape. Snyder had lived twelve years in Asia, and returned to America in 1969 and set up a homestead in the foothills of the Sierra Nevada Mountains. Snyder thought that he and Berry were both working along similar lines in prose, poetry, and homesteading. Berry's *The Unsettling of America* (1977) was, for Snyder, "an incredibly transformative book". Writing of Berry in *The Real Work* (1980), Snyder says, "Wendell Berry is a man who does very high-quality work and is also a working farmer and a working thinker, who draws on the best of American roots and traditional mindfulness, like his Kentucky farming forebears, to teach us something that we're not going to learn by studying Oriental texts."

As well as providing articles like his "Think Little" piece, which echoes the concepts of E.F. Schumacher's *Small is Beautiful* (1963), Berry contributed crucial extensive reviews to *The Whole Earth Catalog*. These reviews turned a generation of back-to-the-land hippies on to foundational texts such as F.H. King's *Farmers of Forty Centuries*. "This is a book that can suggest things for you to do, if you have a piece of ground to do them on. Whether or not you have a piece of ground, it is a book that can change your mind." Berry also reviewed Sir Albert Howard's *An Agricultural Testament*: "*An Agricultural Testament* can be read as a confirmation and elaboration of Jefferson's belief in the supreme importance of the small farmer — the man devoted in final terms to his own piece of his homeland, who makes of the life of the land a human way of life."

However, as much as the hippies loved Berry, Berry was sceptical of them. He wrote to me,

> When you consider the destructiveness of the 'culture', a culture of another kind looks necessary. But the 'counterculture' wasn't it. It was shallow and temporary, too much made up of spoiled young people wearing themselves out trying to arrive at 'consensus' in 'communes.' I know several. If they had lasted three generations, you could have begun to take them seriously.

Berry was as scalding of the hippies in an interview published in *Mother Earth News* in March 1976:

> I think the popular drug culture and certain aspects of the peace and environment movements have led people to believe there's a great deal you can do with enthusiasm. I have a lot of enthusiasm, but I know how far it will get me. It doesn't last until dark when you've got a full day's work, or three or four days' work, to do in a day. If you get all the way to dark and to the end of the job, then you're going to be operating on something else. A lot of people have assumed that the main work in changing over from an urban to a rural life is to get out of the city. That's hardly the start. Learning farming is like learning an art; it takes a long time, and a lot of careful work. And we've failed to teach the young people to expect that a worthy thing might be difficult to learn.

In general, Berry is as sceptical as the writer David Shi about the worth granted that generation:

> What I'm saying is that the young have had lots of praisers and lots of detractors but few critics, which is really a way of saying they've had few friends. A curious phenomenon of the youth culture thing — and it's full of curious

> phenomena — is these old sycophants who hang about its skirts and try to touch and kiss the hem of its garment... Charles Reich is one of the best examples I know of a teacher who's copped out completely by becoming a sycophant of his students. I mean I'm completely against this idiocy of his that says surfboarding is an acceptable way of life. That's utterly absurd. [Charles Reich's book] *The Greening of America* is full of false apologies and excuses for people's failure to be responsible. Surfboarding is not a way of life. People are free to think it is because the care and responsibility for society has been broken up and parceled out to the experts. People who make a life of surfboarding are living off other people. They're leeches of the affluent society. They're parasites of a parasite. As long as we have people making some kind of amusement a way of life, you'll find they're getting their support from something destructive, like strip-mining or needless 'development' or war-making.

No question about it, Charles Reich, Professor of Law at Yale University between 1960 and 1974, was a bit sycophantic to the hippies; although, to his credit, he saw the potential that the countercultural generation represented historically. Specifically discussing agriculture, Reich's only pronouncement in *The Greening of America* (1970) is as follows: "The hippie agricultural communes are not a rejection of technology, they are a choice, by people who have had too much plastic in their lives, to live close to the soil for a while."

However, at the end of our correspondence, Berry softened a little. He remembered a group of back-to-the-landers who settled upriver from him at Monterey, Kentucky, of which key members, such as Gray Zeitz who runs the Larkspur Press, are still there:

> They are such dear, and by now ordinary friends that they long-ago ceased to be back-to-the-landers and have become settled members of the local community.
>
> ...
>
> Some of the back-to-the-landers need to be taken seriously, as you seem to know. They are to be found still in the Northeast and Northwest. Why they held on and amounted to something in those two upper corners, I don't know. I have known good people in both corners, have spoken at their meetings, etc.

Berry addressed the first meeting of the (Northwestern) regenerative collective Tilth in 1974 and spoke too at their twenty-fifth anniversary. He wrote to me, "I take a lot of satisfaction in that."

Tilth, now working effectively in urban farms, community gardens, and the wider Washington State landscape as the Tilth Alliance, published a wonderful *Whole Earth*–style compendium, *The Future is Abundant*, in 1982. It remains a fascinating index of what would have been a very useful resource for sustainable agriculture at the time, listing books, academic papers, and company and institution's addresses. It is punctuated by articles by the central Tilth cadre (Shery Litwin, Michael Pilarski, Mark Musick, Mike Maki, and Sego Jackson) and features heavyweight guest contributions from the likes of Larry Korn on Masanobu Fukuoka, and Gary Snyder on "Reinhabitation", which refers to "the tiny number of persons who come out of the industrial societies (having collected or squandered the fruits of 8000 years of civilization) and then start to turn back to the land". Just as the term "counterculture" sits uneasily with Berry, Mark Musick of Tilth wrote to me, "I personally think a more appropriate term would be 'awakening.' [Berry] was one of the first to clearly see and articulate the collapse of traditional agrarian culture, the separation of people from the land, and the destruction of the natural world." Notwithstanding this reservation about the label of "counterculture", before he became further involved in growing in the Seattle area, Musick himself was influenced by the civil rights movement and campus protests against the Vietnam War. As a university graduate working at the Evergreen State College in Olympia, he curated a section at their library dubbed the "Whole Earth Access section", buying every book listed in the *Whole Earth Catalogue*.

Wendell Berry on industrial agriculture

Berry takes aim at the features which characterise industrial agriculture: soil erosion, soil compaction, soil and water pollution, and pests and diseases resulting from monocultures and ecological deterioration. However, what's really fascinating and unique about his writing is how he telescopes back from these strictly agricultural concerns to wider and wider contexts. So, for instance, Berry will lament the depopulation of rural communities and even the decivilisation of the city. He will provide solid answers as to why industrial agriculture is a failure even though it produces such an enormous volume of food, explaining how chemical fertiliser use has disguised the decline of natural fertility. But then he will highlight industrial agriculture's increasingly intricate, and therefore fragile, economic and industrial organisation, and the total dependence of the population on these systems, for which there is no backup.

This panoptic systems-thinking allows him to articulate concepts like the following: "The gist is nevertheless plain enough: the industrial economy grows and thrives by lengthening and complicating the essential connection between producer and consumer." He goes on:

> This old sun-based agriculture was fundamentally alien to the industrial economy; industrial corporations could make

> relatively little profit from it. In order to make agriculture fully exploitable by industry it was necessary (in Barry Commoner's terms) to weaken 'the farm's link to the sun' and to make the farmland a 'colony' of the industrial corporations.

His train of insights culminates in dazzling but frightening observations like the following: "We are in effect, exporting our topsoil in order to keep our tractors running."

Wendell Berry on Indigenous cultures

Berry travelled widely in the "developing" world visiting farms and surveying its agriculture. He writes about the Peruvian Uchucmarca people, pondering how Andean farmers allow new varieties to grow between cultivated, wild, and semi-domestic species that thrive in the hedgerows around fields as a way of strengthening their seed stock. If a strain is overcome by a fungal blight, often a working substitute can be found among these hybrids that have been given free reign. And the drive towards dominant single varieties which characterises our monocultures — so dangerous when it causes events like the Irish Potato Famine and a whole crop is wiped out — is absent in the culture. Modern, generic varieties of potatoes "may yield two or three times as much as the traditional varieties, [but] they do not taste as good, are less marketable, and are significantly less nutritious".

In stark contrast with the completely accepted wisdom of modern agriculture, and with society's assumption that the worst thing you could ever stoop to be is a farmer, Berry is a staunch supporter of what we might regard as self-sufficiency and the subsistence farming principle. Subsistence is the form of farming which has traditionally characterised the developing world and preindustrial agriculture whereby all the crops and livestock and their products are used to feed the farmer and his household. He writes, "Might it not be thought that subsistence farming is the very definition of good farming…" Elsewhere he puts it, "In some respects, the traditional subsistence agricultures are the best agricultures, the best assurances of a continuous food supply, simply because they are not — or were not — dependent on outside sources that must be purchased." Furthermore, he is more and more convinced that "the only guarantee of quality in practice lies in the subsistence principle".

Berry singles out traditional cultures like the Amish (who for him represent the true apogee of what a "culture" should look like), but also the American Indians, "for their relation to this part of the earth seems to me to have been exemplary". He elaborates, of the American Indians:

> Local cultures and agricultures such as those of the Hopi and Papago do not deserve to survive for their picturesque trappings or their interest as artifacts; they deserve to survive — and be emulated — because they embody the principles of thrift and care that are indispensable to the survival of human beings.

Wendell Berry on Western society

Berry turns these insights back upon the grossly wasteful, ignorant, and indolent consumer society:

> Both the foraging in fields and woods and the small husbandries of household and barn have now been almost entirely replaced by the 'consumer economy', which assumes it is better to buy whatever one needs than to find it or make it or grow it. Advertisements and other forms of propaganda suggest that people should congratulate themselves on the quantity and variety of their purchases. Shopping, in spite of traffic and crowds, is held to be 'easy' and 'convenient'. Spending money gives one status. And physical exertion for any useful purpose is looked

> down upon; it is permissible to work hard for 'sport' or 'recreation', but to make any practical use of the body is considered beneath dignity.

Urban attitudes to the country and farming draw some of his sharpest invective. He writes, "So far as I can see, farming is considered marginal or incidental to the economy of the country, and farmers, when they are thought of at all, are thought of as hicks and yokels, whose lives do not fit into the modern scene." He suggests that the agricultural habits of the previous generation, with its husbandry, thrift, and practicality might have been cultivated to the extent that it began to function more, like the Native American Indian culture, in a truly sustainable way:

> That they were not cultivated or built upon — that they were repudiated as the stuff of a hopelessly outmoded, unscientific way of life — is a tragic error on the part of the people themselves; and it is a work of monstrous ignorance and irresponsibility on the part of the experts and politicians, who have prescribed, encouraged, and applauded the disintegration of such farming communities all over the country.

These attitudes held by the city dwellers are parcelled with others: "The mentality that exploits and destroys the natural environment is the same that abuses racial and economic minorities, that imposes on young men the tyranny of the military draft, that makes war against peasants and women and children with the indifference of technology." And being oblivious is no excuse: "Most of us are not directly responsible for strip mining and extractive agriculture and other forms of environmental abuse. But we are guilty nevertheless, for we connive in them by our ignorance."

Berry the unconventional Christian

Just as Sir Albert Howard connects healthy soil with healthy animals and healthy people, Berry extends the paradigm upwards from society to its spiritual orientation:

> It is wrong to think that bodily health is compatible with spiritual confusion or cultural disorder, or with polluted air and water or impoverished soil... The body is damaged by the bewilderment of the spirit, and it conducts the influence of that bewilderment into the earth, the earth conducts it into the community and so on.

Just like the Ecopsychologists, whom we meet in the "Ecology" chapter, Berry argues for a form of grounding, a reconnection to nature as a mental health solution:

> The so-called identity crisis, for instance, is a disease that seems to have become prevalent after the disconnection of body and soul... Treatment, it might be thought, would logically consist in the restoration of these connections: the lost identity would find itself by recognizing physical landmarks, by connecting itself responsibly to practical circumstances; it would learn to stay put in the body to which it belongs and in the place which preference or history or accident has brought it; it would, in short, find itself in finding its work.

In attempting to establish a framework for agricultural and ecological responsibility to address these questions of health of the land and the body, Berry concludes that his own long held belief in Christianity, "as usually presented by its organizations, is not earthly enough — that a valid spiritual life, in this world, must have a practice and a practicality — it must have a material result". In conversation with the Buddhist Gary Snyder, he will have come across ideas in that Eastern system of thought which fulfilled this. "I want to see if there is not at least implicit in the Judeo-Christian heritage a doctrine such as that the Buddhists call 'right livelihood' or 'right occupation.'" He looks, pretty much in vain, for pronouncements on the connection of ethics to the environment, quoting the philosopher Arthur Lovejoy's critique of Christianity: "The greater number of the subtler speculative minds and of the great religious teachers have... been engaged in weaning man's thought or his affections, or both, from... Nature."

Patrick Holden

I'm being driven through the Welsh countryside by Patrick Holden (1950–). He is thin but muscular, and has short cropped white hair, great vigour in his movement, and intense eyes. He is wearing shorts and Wellington boots. The car, a mud-streaked hatchback, reminds me of the farm vehicles I was driven in as a child. It smells faintly, and pleasantly, like a barn. On arrival, first, we stop by the side of the road. Holden wants to check that none of his cattle have broken out of their field on a nearby holding in the Arron Valley called Hafod, which they have rented for over forty years. This gives its name to the delicious organically-certified Hafod cheddar that has been made at Bwlchwernen Fawr Farm since 2007 — 80% of the milk they produce goes towards it. The retail price of the cheese is more than double that of conventional supermarket cheddar, but although the Holdens wish it could be more affordable, farming in their manner, obeying the principles of the circular economy and avoiding the use of chemical fertilisers and pesticides, would be financially unsustainable otherwise; the margins are so fine.

Holden jumps out of the car and crosses the road, and as he does so, the lively Ayrshire cows and heifers run across the pasture to greet him. It's a very touching moment. Because of the size of their herd, a relatively small eighty-five, Holden and his wife Rebecca, who looks after the animals, know them well, and are acquainted with many of their individual characters. On a later visit, I meet some of these delightful animals: Oats and Peas, who is the leader and an invaluable assistant to Rebecca in moving the herd around; the eccentric Mrs. Jones, who makes her own way into the milking parlour through the back door to jump the queue; and the Eeyore-ish, poor, put-upon Nina, who is always trailing behind the others. The current average herd size in the UK is 148, a figure that gets higher every year. Needless to say, at this scale, and with cattle not allowed out onto pasture, establishing a relationship with the cows would be, if not impossible, then much harder.

For the last seven years, the farm has implemented some of the "mob grazing" techniques made well-known by figures like Alan Savory and Gabe Brown. They've noticed milk productivity going up by 20% in consequence. The idea behind this is that a high density of animals are allowed to graze longer grass intensively, but only for twenty-four hours before they are moved onto another plot. The plants grow back more quickly than if they are eaten right down, and by this method, fields are also given much longer to recover before animals graze them again. The Holden farm's herd are never kept in a field longer than forty-eight hours, and sometimes for as little as twelve hours. However, some practitioners of the method use even shorter periods of time, and automate the opening and shutting of gates to shuttle the cattle through.

Described by Holden as relatively marginal land, the farm consists of three hundred acres, roughly half of which is too steep or sensitive to plough (Holden does plough); the remainder is rotated with crops then sown with herbal leys. These leys are a mixture of clover, chicory, and ribgrass provided by Ian Wilkinson at Cotswold Seeds. The grasslands include legumes, which means they fix nitrogen in the soil, and also make delicious grazing for the herd. The fields look quite beautiful sown like this and are buzzing with insect life. Holden says rather wistfully, that "It breaks your heart to plough a fertile ley." The family also grow oats and peas, which they feed as a muesli to the cattle. In the winter, when, owing to the areas high rainfall, the cows are kept indoors so as to prevent the fields being trodden into a swamp, this feed, along with silage they prepare from their own forage and grain they buy in, sustains the herd.

The farm has joined a community of others in reviving Wales's black oats, which came close to extinction. While it's no longer the case, historically, grains were grown in Wales, with crops like black oats proving very suitable for the climate. However, government-led crop "improvement" after the Second World War, amid concerns over national self-sufficiency, dictated that farming should be intensified, and most farmers in Wales gave up growing traditional oats. Consequently, the nation lost both its grain and its apple orchards, which were torn out to concentrate on livestock.

There are also other facets to the farm's output, bringing them closer to what Rudolf Steiner celebrated in "mixed farming", with its harmonised efficiencies. Pigs are kept in a wood at the edge of the estate, and delight in rooting up the soil and consuming the farm's whey from the cheese. Holden used to grow carrots for supermarkets until 2006. This practice was made impossible by the centralisation of packing, which required small producers to transport their carrots to Peterborough, in the Holden's case two hundred miles to the east. They only started growing carrots again on an acre after reaching an agreement to provide them to local Carmarthenshire schools. Given it's a dairy farm, they rear the young male calves, bullocks, to the age of a year to produce ruby or rose veal. This is distinct from white veal, a product of anaemia from an insufficient diet. Their animals have a nice life and a compassionate death.

Patrick Holden's connection to the counterculture

After counting the cows in the Hafod field, Holden drew the car up before a small bridge in the lane and switched off the ignition. As I was sitting in the front seat beside him, I asked him to describe his background. Holden's father was a Freudian analyst, a consultant child psychiatrist at the Tavistock clinic. For a sabbatical in 1971, his father took a post at the medical centre at Stanford University in Palo Alto in California. He brought his family along, and so, aged twenty, Holden experienced "the atmosphere of this shifted consciousness… led by what was going on in the Bay Area". He was, as he puts it, "massively affected" by the experience, and read books which sought to capture the zeitgeist, like *The Greening of America* by Charles Reich. Music was key to the moment, and in the UK in 1970, Holden had attended the Isle of Wight Festival, but when I ask him if there was anything that was particularly important to him, he didn't hesitate: "The Incredible String Band… they were more in touch with what we're discussing."

Inspired, Holden came back from California thinking:

> 'I want to get back to the land and set up a rural community.' So, a group of six of us thought, 'We'll do this, but we better prepare for it.' So I got a job on a dairy farm in Hampshire for the best part of a year, that was in 1972, on a conventional dairy farm.

He then "looked around to see how I could train in organic farming, and there was only one course… I went to Emerson College and did the agriculture course. That was learning in the morning and practice in the afternoon, which I now realise was a very powerful way to learn things." Emerson College, the Steiner adult education centre, has three biodynamic farms affiliated with it: Tablehurst Farm, where Sue Coppard launched the WWOOF movement; Plaw Hatch; and Busses Farm in East Grinstead, where Holden trained.

As I've seen in the research for my previous book, *Retreat*, and as is documented in books like Theodore Roszak's *Unfinished Animal* (1975), at the tail-end of the 1960s, the counterculture passed, as though through a prism, and emerged as a rainbow spectrum of spiritual beliefs. The first wave of converts were following Eastern religions like Zen Buddhism, Tibetan Buddhism, Mahesh Maharishi Yogi's Transcendental Meditation, and the Hare Krishna sect. As though extending out from the psychedelic experience, these tended to extol what I've described as the very "etheric" values of ego dissolution and non-dualism. As the counterculture worked its way through the logic of these thought systems, more people began to question the wisdom of philosophies which, excepting anomalies like hatha yoga or Mahayana Buddhism, didn't place due importance upon actually living in the world: in our bodies, our relations to people and animals, and the ecology.

Either enlightened or frazzled by psychedelic drugs (usually leaving them behind in any case), fleeing curdling political movements, neighbourhoods increasingly infested with hard drugs, and conflict on university campuses, the counterculture went back to the land at the end of the 1960s. As part of the same process, Eastern spiritualities tended to decrease in importance and other modalities came to the fore. Experienced within the structure of a daily way of life, the Hare Krishna movement maintained its relative primacy on the menu in this new "grounded" context. But gaining currency were the ideas of two teachers who emerged from Madame Blavatsky's Theosophy movement — the Austrian Rudolf Steiner and Jiddu Krishnamurti (1895-1986) — and those of Armenian mystic philosopher George Ivanovich Gurdjieff (1866–1949). Where once people might have read *The Tibetan Book of the Dead*, now they were, like Holden's close friend Peter Segger in 1973, poring over Steiner's *Philosophy of Freedom* (1894). So began that generation's long struggle to reflect a heavenly order here on earth.

Holden himself was fascinated by Krishnamurti, whose teachings are often summarised by his maxim "Truth is a pathless land", and who was introduced to him through *The Penguin Krishnamurti Reader* (1970). From that book, we can discover a quote which may have struck a note with the young Holden: "Only the truly religious man is truly revolutionary; and it is the function of education to help each one of us to be religious in the true sense of the word, for in that direction lies our salvation." Holden went every year to Brockwood Park to hear Krishnamurti talk until his death in 1986:

> I thought something was very powerful about what he was saying. It was a religion-less spirituality, with no gurus. That was definitely a huge influence on me and especially being in his presence, because he had incredible presence. Two thousand people used to go to Brockwood Park... He was a tiny man and he could hold the whole marquee.

Unlike his engagement with Krishnamurti, Holden's introduction to Rudolf Steiner, as he studied organic farming at Emerson College, was something of an accident:

> He was obviously another kind of master who had intuitive knowledge, to quote one of his books, *Knowledge of Higher Worlds*, but I was never really smitten with anthroposophy. I found the atmosphere of the movement and its followers slightly claustrophobic, which I found off-putting.

Regardless, Holden is today Patron of the Steiner organisation's Biodynamic Association.

Patrick Holden and Gurdjieff

It was Holden's encounter with the ideas of Gurdjieff that was to provide him with the philosophical framework that has defined his work in farming and influenced his work with the Sustainable Food Trust. I get the feeling interviewing him that he's as happy talking about this relationship of the macrocosm (spirituality) to the microcosm (farming) as I am listening to him. He was first introduced to Gurdjieff's ideas by the aunt of one his childhood friends, Jenifer Donaldson (Jenifer Elton Wilson, as she is known today), the young wife of Trevor Donaldson, a fantastically successful estate agent. Jenifer, who asked to be referred to by her first name, had been recommended Gurdjieff's work by a mysterious stranger in London. When she followed up this suggestion some years later, she came across P.D. Ouspensky's book *In Search of the Miraculous* (1947). This book by Gurdjieff's primary disciple elucidates Gurdjieff's system. Holden had met Jenifer in London even before his trip to California, when she was attending meetings of Ouspensky's circle, and he was sceptical. "I thought 'God! What Kool-Aid has she swallowed now?'" However, he notes that

> it wasn't until 1978 that I read that book, which was already in my possession because I bought it, but I didn't see it on my shelf. I read it in a blizzard when we were snowed in at the farm. And as soon as I read it, I thought this is something I wanted to follow up. So that's how I got involved with the teaching. I've been involved ever since.

There are some interesting examples of Gurdjieff's followers in the American back-to-the-land movement. In his book collecting then contemporary articles, *The Modern Utopian*, Richard Fairfield describes a group, not to be confused with Charles Manson's: "The Family, as they called themselves, got its start in Berkely, California, in early 1968, when five men and women from an encounter group decided to live together. In the encounter group they had learned to utilize various techniques, including ideas from the writings of Gurdjieff and Ouspensky." Bill Wheeler describes the arrival of a man they called "Gurdjieff Ray" and his group at the famous Wheeler's Ranch commune:

> Bill gently suggested they might find another campsite farther from any immediate neighbours. Moving behind the goat pen, they built a large plastic dome with a tiny entrance to crawl through. The walls, covered with photographs and religious decorations, were dominated by a large photo of Gurdjieff, whom they considered their guru... Once settled into their 'monastery,' as they called it, the 'Gurdjieff Boys' proved extremely energetic and a fine addition to the community.

Shedding some light on how the Gurdjieff philosophy differed from other spiritual disciplines, and had worldly applications, Pam Read Hanna, another communard at Wheeler's Ranch described an individual, Marty: "Marty was into Gurdjieff... Later, because Gurdjieff taught that if you were a success on the material plane then you could also be a success on the spiritual plane, Marty put on some street clothes and went to San Francisco and started a window-washing business."

Gurdjieff

It's an ambitious task to attempt to summarise Gurdjieff's thinking, but two principles in particular stand out. Both are explained by him to Ouspensky in Ouspensky's book, *In Search of the Miraculous*. The first is that a human being, straight "off the shelf" so to speak, is a mere automaton in need of awakening. Gurdjieff explains to Ouspensky, "'Look, all those people you see,' he pointed along the street, 'are simply machines — nothing more.'" The second, connected to the first, is that we are not born with a soul, and that only through strenuous work are we able to acquire one. "What may be called the 'astral body' is obtained by means of fusion; that is by means of terribly hard inner work and struggle.

Man is not born with it. And only very few men acquire an 'astral body.'" Gurdjieff himself describes this work as coming about "through voluntary and involuntary experiencings and information intentionally learned about real events which had taken place in the past".

The difference between Gurdjieff's ideas, which are posited as superior to the ideas of Eastern philosophy, and Eastern philosophy itself, are nicely illustrated by the following story recounted in Gurdjieff's own book *Meetings With Remarkable Men* (1963). Gurdjieff meets an old dervish. "I must remind you that at that time I was an ardent follower of the famous Indian yogis and carried out very exactly all the indications of what is called Hatha Yoga, and when eating I tried to masticate my food as thoroughly as possible." He is criticised by the dervish for this excessive chewing (a technique in fact favoured by a whole raft of Eastern disciplines, not least macrobiotics). "Now, in addition to the natural weaknesses of old age, you will have another brought on by yourself, because you are accustoming your stomach not to work... At your age it is better not to chew at all, but to swallow whole pieces, even bones if possible, to give work to your stomach." Gurdjieff has his mind blown by this common-sense interjection and asks the dervish for further advice on yogic breathing exercises. "Be so kind, Father, and also explain to me what you think of what is called artificial breathing. Believing it useful, I practice it according to the instructions of the yogis, namely, after breathing in the air, I hold it a certain time, and then slowly exhale it. Perhaps this should not be done?" The dervish spelled it out for him:

> If you harm yourself with your way of chewing food, you harm yourself a thousand times more by the practice of this breathing... When you breathe in the ordinary way, you breathe mechanically. The organism, without you, takes from the air the quantity of substances that it needs... artificial breathing, that is to say, a forced modification

> of natural breathing, facilitates the penetration into the organism of these numerous substances in the air which are harmful to life, and at the same time upsets the quantitative and qualitative balance of the useful substances.

He concludes, "Therefore — since you have asked me for it — my advice to you is: stop your breathing exercises."

Precious few of the Eastern philosophies approved of the use of drugs. With the exception of mavericks like Chögyam Trungpa, the line taken is that the meditative practices are a superior and effective alternative. However, in what must have been manna to the counterculture — and especially to Timothy Leary, whose Castalia Foundation adopted Gurdjieffian techniques for some of their workshops — there is a place for them in Gurdjieff's system. He tells Ouspensky:

> There are schools which make use of narcotics in the right way. People in these schools take them for self-study; in order to look ahead, to know their possibilities better, to see beforehand, 'in advance' what can be attained later on as the result of prolonged work. When a man sees this and is convinced that what he has learned theoretically really exists, he then works consciously, he knows where he is going... In all those schools which make use of this method, experiments are carried out only when they are really necessary and only under the direction of experienced and competent men who can foresee all results and adopt measures against possible undesirable consequences. The substances used in these schools are not merely 'narcotics' as you call them, although many of them are prepared from such drugs as opium, hashish, and so on.

Holden was happy to talk about his experience with drugs:

> My drug history is as follows. I don't mind people knowing this. I smoked (not that much) cannabis and grass in the '60s until we were right at the farm [when he stopped]. And I had two experiences with psychedelic drugs, one with mescaline and the other one psilocybin. I never took LSD... My peak drug experience was definitely mescaline... I think Aldous Huxley was right... that drugs open a door, and you have a glimpse of another reality.

But, as far as Holden is concerned, they aren't the answer:

> You can't rely on drugs. You have to work. Spiritual work should be to find a way through that door. Without having this, drugs will fade... It might give you a glimpse of something, that then it'll become eventually its opposite. And the real spiritual work is to realise the possibility of being more present to the miracle of everything, which is always there, every second.

As for the application of Gurdjieff's ideas directly to farming, Holden remarks, "It's interesting to reflect on how much did Gurdjieff speak about earthly activity and specifically, farming, and getting back to nature? Which obviously Steiner did a lot. The answer is not very much." Certainly, his intensely practical philosophy makes a space for it, but there is, however, a wonderful passage, again recounted by Ouspensky, which relates to carpet-making (from wool, an agricultural product) but also, in its account of social rituals, to farming:

> [Gurdjieff] told me a great deal about carpets which, as he often said, represented one of the most ancient forms of art. He spoke of the ancient customs connected with carpet making in certain parts of Asia; of a whole village working together at one carpet; of winter evenings when all the villagers, young and old, gather together in one large building and, dividing into groups, sit or stand on the floor

> in an order previously known and determined by tradition. Each group then begins its own work. Some pick stones and splinters out of the wool. Others beat out the wool with sticks. A third group combs the wool. The fourth spins. The fifth dyes the wool. The sixth or maybe the twenty-sixth weaves the actual carpet. Men, women, and children, old men and old women, all have their traditional work. And all the work is done to the accompaniment of music and singing. The women spinners with spindles in their hands dance a special dance as they work, and all the movements of all the people engaged in different work are like one movement in one and the same rhythm. Moreover, each locality has its own special tune, its own special songs and dances, connected with carpet making from time immemorial.

It requires pointing out that Gurdjieff is, almost by his own admission, a kind of charlatan. We put ourselves at his mercy when we heed him, because it's sometimes unclear whether we too are the objects of his trickery. This famous story from *Meetings With Remarkable Men* gives us some insights into him when, penniless, he sought to raise money:

> At the house I asked the landlady for scissors, clipped my sparrow to the shape of a canary, and then coloured it fantastically with the aniline dyes. I took this sparrow to Old Samarkand, where I immediately sold it, claiming that it was a special 'American canary.' I charged two roubles for it. With the money I at once bought several simple painted cages and from then on began selling my sparrows in cages. In two weeks I sold about eighty of these American canaries.

Madame De Salzmann

Holden explained to me that where Gurdjieff himself doesn't obviously contribute much towards this agricultural context, his anointed successor, the Swiss-French Madame De Salzmann (1889-1990) does. In her writings, and in the presentation of her ideas by the scholar of religion Ravi Ravindra, we are provided with more. De Salzmann's great maxim, complementary to Gurdjieff's idea of the need for the process of "fusion" within the personality to create a soul, is "*Restez devant !*" or "Stay in front!" That's to say, remain open to your personal suffering — don't try to erase it with stimulation or "act out", "Stay in front of the lack." De Salzmann emphasised Gurdjieff's idea that man needs to work to create his soul, but the purpose of this is so as to connect the higher realms with life on Earth. She says:

> Man has a special function, which other creatures cannot fulfill. He can serve the earth by becoming a bridge for certain higher energies. Without this, the earth cannot live properly. But man, as he is by nature, is not complete. In order to fulfill his proper function he needs to develop. There is a part in him which is unsatisfied by his life. Through religious or spiritual traditions he may become aware of what this part needs.

In Holden's own words:

> So if you ask yourself the question... What's the higher purpose of humanity? Maybe it's a question that can't be asked, or even answered, but if one tries to address that question, one might say that maybe all organic life has a purpose. As Steiner said, it acts as a buffer between the cosmos and the mineral matter of the earth. It feels as if it's a refiner of energy in some extraordinary way.

This is precisely where Holden sees the role of sustainability as it pertains to agriculture. It is a heavenly "alignment", of which "alignment", as De Salzmann puts it, "we can receive more subtle, higher influences only if our centers are disposed in a certain way."

Holden says of his attempt to, as the Buddhists might term it, follow that dharma:

> One of my own strivings throughout my life, and I don't feel myself that I've achieved it in any way, is to find a bridge between spiritual work on myself, and work in the world. So, what's the relationship? Say, I'm involved with the practice of sustainable agriculture, and I want to be an influence to help more people do that. That's my day job, and my work on the farm, and with the Sustainable Food Trust. But what's the relationship between that and inner work, and the connection between the two? I've always felt there must be a bridge between the two, that they cannot be separate, and I'm feeling more as my life goes by that they are not separate.

It is getting these higher energies down to earth that is the trick. De Salzmann says, "Just as trees make it possible for a certain kind of energy from the Sun to get down to us, by our work we can assist some higher energies to descend to the Earth." De Salzmann is reported saying, "Everything in the Work is a preparation for that connection. That is the aim of the Work. The higher energy wishes to but cannot come down to the level of the body unless one works."

Key to "the Work" within the Gurdjieffian system are "the Movements", the mesmerising and minutely choregraphed dances which followers perform together as an integrated group:

> The Movements can show us how to be in life, how to experience Presence and at the same time have a freer movement in manifestation. Instead of endless reactions — the conditioned responses of our automatism — there is the possibility of action coming from vision, from a conscious

> force that is higher. The Movements are a way of living the idea of presence.

Holden talks of his experience training in them:

> I go to a class every week. It's not a performance. They're exercises in inner attention through the body. That's a line of the Work... In the movements class there is a pianist, and somebody who's leading it, and then there are rows, and the front row's the best. Obviously, the people who are not very accomplished are in the back row, which is where I am! So, I have sometimes been in the second row... What they sometimes do during the Movements class, is that you'll be doing a movement and then the teacher will say, 'Okay, the front row, go to the back, then the second row is in the front, and then you do it again.' The back row eventually is in the front of the class. It demands everything, because you are exposed to your own thoughts and your incapacity... It requires total attention, there's no room for dreaming. You can see the activation when you're really connected in the body and the present, not dreaming, not distracted by random thoughts, which all of us have the whole time.

The Sustainable Food Trust

Holden's current focus is the Sustainable Food Trust, an organisation he set up in 2010. It came about prompted by his perception that it was no longer appropriate for farmers like himself, those not farming conventionally, to set themselves in opposition to mainstream agriculture. That approach had implied their superiority, created a lot of bad feeling, and stymied a more widespread adoption of the more sustainable techniques they were using. With the Sustainable Food Trust their approach is different:

> To the person who is using [the chemical herbicide] Roundup on their garden, what we should not say is 'You are bad, you are excluded, you are not part of our movement.' Instead we might suggest to them is that there is evidence that glyphosate gets into the biosphere in various ways and may be connected with environmental and human health problems, so it is not advisable to use it. Here is a better way, so why don't you come on the journey?

The organisation's documents like *Feeding Britain from the Ground Up* lay this journey's path out, advocating farms halving grain production, increasing "mixed" farming, growing more beans, and feeding waste to livestock. This, they suggest, will strengthen self-sufficiency and free up six million acres in the UK for tree-planting and nature conservation.

Measurement is the idea at the centre of the Sustainable Food Trust. This might seem to contradict Sir Albert Howard's statement that

> many of the things that matter on the land, such as soil fertility, tilth, soil management, the quality of produce, the bloom and health of animals, the general management of livestock, the working relations between master and man, the esprit de corps of the farm as a whole, cannot be weighed or measured.

However, it is precisely these practices and outputs that the Sustainable Food Trust's Global Farm Metric sets about quantifying. Livestock, products, economics, climate, community, nature, crops and pasture, farmers and workers, inputs, resources, governance, and soil and water are all scored. This introduces a welcome objectivity to the discussion of regenerative agriculture, which as organisations like the Real Organic Project correctly point out, is currently unregulated.

Holden, who rubs shoulders with royalty and powerful business leaders — recently fielding a visit to the farm from the head of HSBC bank — has a more trusting attitude to government than the Americans, who have seen the dilution of the organic standard in the United States by the USDA. He names ministers such as John Gummer and Michael Gove as having been particularly constructive over the years. The UK's Soil Association, of which Holden was director between 1995 and 2010, has often worked collaboratively with government; for example, in 2002, DEFRA (the Department for Environment, Food & Rural Affairs) published an action plan to develop organic food and farming in England. As a result, he has seen how governments can swing behind pre-established nongovernmental standards. In something of a re-run of this positive relationship he was able to forge with the organic movement and government, the Global Farm Metric is, in this sense, a policy framework "in-waiting".

At the Soil Association, Holden, with his colleague Peter Segger, was instrumental in introducing certification of organic. He describes this as being a necessity for the organic marketplace's survival. Just as he thinks it's unwise for organic people to be dismissive of the regenerative phenomenon, even though he identifies greenwash in the market, he's cautious to avoid disparaging the organic standard and its policing audits. However, over time, he's come to view organic as being insufficient in tackling the pressing issues facing global agriculture. The Soil Association, which has launched its own regenerative update, the "Soil Association Exchange", has evidently come to the same conclusions, indeed they are now looking to align with the Sustainable Food Trust's Global Farm Metric.

Although he has been farming there "in harmony with nature" since the day he arrived, Holden is modest about his achievements at Bwlchwernen Fawr:

> So, our striving, and it's only a striving, it's not a dogma, is to produce as much food as we can from our hill without just becoming a platform for imported *everything*... And

> we haven't got there. Certainly, we haven't got there with energy, we haven't got there even with animal feed, but we're quite a long way down the road.

Just as with Dave Chapman and his important mission with America's Real Organic Project, I'm mindful of taking up more of Holden's time than I should. Holden starts the ignition and drives us back towards Bwlchwernen Fawr. He points out to me that my journey out to visit the farm here in Wales was a pilgrimage, the thought of which lingered for a long time.

ECOLOGY

Concerns about wildlife, pollution, and pesticides were brought to a symbolic apex with the first Earth Day, arranged on 22 April 1970. Organiser Dennis Hayes wanted to "tie them all together, to weave them into the fabric of environmentalism, and to convince all of these targeted groups that if we all came together and recognised we were operating from the same set of values, we'd be much more powerful working together on our issues..." It resulted in twenty million Americans taking part in rallies across the country — roughly 10% of the population. As effective as Hayes's tactic has been of bringing together all the strands of ecological concern, we're going to tease out only one from its cloth. In terms of its pollution "homely ol' industrial agriculture" can tend to be obscured behind fossil fuel, transport, and manufacture, but it comes close fourth in many statistical rankings. When we factor in industrial farming's wider impact, its rank as a destructive agent is only higher. Turning back the clock, concerns around agricultural practices were instrumental in bringing an awareness of the ecology to the table in the first place. Extending the idea of ecology further, commentators in the countercultural era sought to connect society's abandonment of the practices of working on the land, and the collapse of the associated integrated relationship with nature, with mental ill health.

The gulf which opened out between city and country as a result of industrial agriculture also damaged — if we can call it that — the social ecology. The separation between these now socially antagonistic worlds has only sharpened. Writing in 1962, when many people living in the city would have had some connection to the countryside, Murray Bookchin wrote, "The city man, to be sure, does not need to be reminded that good soil is important for successful farming. He recognizes the necessity for conservation and careful management of the land. But his knowledge of food cultivation — its techniques, problems, and prospects — is limited." Today it is hard to imagine any city dwellers having even this basic level of awareness.

DDT

Synthesised first in 1874, the organochlorine DDT found no practical application until 1939, when a chemist — Paul Müller, working for the J.R. Geigy company in Basel — discovered that it killed insects and appeared to be harmless to mammals. Müller went on to win the Nobel prize in 1948 for his discovery.

Long before Rachel Carson brought DDT to the wider public attention in 1962, many voices in the organic movement expressed alarm at its use. J.I. Rodale railed, "Twenty years before [Rachel Carson] and her *Silent Spring* appeared, I began lashing out continuously against the dangers to plants, animals, and people of these poisonous insecticides." Writing in *Living the Good Life* (1954), Helen and Scott Nearing described how "foods are being poisoned in a different way." They explain, "These poisons are produced precisely for their lasting qualities. Read the advertisements of 'the amazing residual effect of DDT...'" Chemist turned organic gardener Leonard Wickenden made it the subject of a whole book, *Our Daily Poison*, in 1955. Giving an account of her 1958 tour of America, Lady Eve Balfour mentions reservations she has about the spraying of DDT. Sustained criticism comes in the social theorist Bookchin's remarkable *Our Synthetic Environment* (1962) which pipped *Silent Spring* to publication. He gives a solid background, and just as the grower Eliot Coleman pointed out to me, explains that the immediate predecessors to DDT were hardly great themselves: "In the 1930s, one of the most widely used inorganic compounds, lead arsenate, combined a suspected carcinogen (arsenic) with a cumulative poison (lead)." After the Second World War, pesticide use exploded. Their sales increased sevenfold between 1940 and 1956, with the next generation, the chlorinated hydrocarbons, epitomised by DDT, phasing out earlier types.

Bookchin describes their action in morbid detail: "Farm animals poisoned by DDT and other chlorinated hydrocarbons first become restless and excitable; the next stage is characterized by twitching, spasms, and, finally, convulsions." He goes into the issue of how insects become resistant to DDT after two or three years. Also, he explores DDT's new cousins in the expanding research field of toxic chlorinated hydrocarbons: chlordane, dieldrin, and aldrin — all of them more lethal than DDT itself. More widely, he mentions the growth promoters like stilbestrol, a synthetic oestrogen hormone, inserted in the necks of fowl and behind the ears of cattle; and the use of antibiotics and the associated risks of culturing antibiotic-resistant bacteria.

DDT was a cause célèbre among the counterculture and Rachel Carson an icon. In her song "Big Yellow Taxi" (1970) Joni Mitchell sings, "Hey farmer, farmer, put away that DDT now, Give me spots on my apples, but leave me the birds and the bees, Please". Hippie gardener Jeannie Darlington writes in *Grow Your Own*:

> There are now over a billion pounds of DDT or its toxic derivative in our environment. DDT doesn't break down, so it's all there in our bodies, and in animals and fish. That thought is disgusting in itself, but when I think of the smell, the delight and the wonder of putting ladybugs and praying mantids into your environment, it's impossible for me to understand why people so often choose such sick solutions to their problems, ones that harm the planet we live on.

A significant component of the countercultural opposition to these chemicals came from outrage at the Vietnam War. Dow and Monsanto, agricultural herbicide manufacturers, acted under instruction from the US Government to produce Agent Orange. The herbicide, containing a chemical called dioxin, defoliated millions of acres of forests and farmland in Vietnam. The Vietnamese government says up to three million of its eighty-four million people have birth defects or other health problems related to dioxin.

Rachel Carson

Driving up from Vermont, I stopped off at Southport Island, Maine. Rachel Carson's old cottage is up a dirt track through a wood. Deep Cove at its foot, the foreshore bedecked in seaweed, it has views across the estuary of the Sheepscot River. At the south tip of the island, I visited the Newagen Inn, which was frequented by Rachel and her girlfriend Dorothy Freeman. There in the rocks, among the tidal pools, is a plaque commemorating Carson. On it is a quote from a letter, written on her last day in Maine to Freeman, pondering the intransigence of life and the migrating butterflies they had seen the previous morning: "But most of all I shall remember the Monarchs". At this spot, half of Carson's ashes were returned to the sea. Having read so much about Carson, and so much she had written, it was very moving to be sitting there alone in the sunshine. Reflecting on the terribly sad story of her life, it was a long time before I could tear myself away, as though from a friend I would never see again.

Rachel Carson (1907–1964) is the subject of a number of biographies, but for research I followed William Souder's excellent *On a Farther Shore* (2012). She became well-known as an author with three books about life in the oceans, the first penned while she was working as an aquatic biologist for the US Bureau of Fisheries, *Under the Sea Wind* (1941). It was followed by the classic *The Sea Around Us* (1951), and *The*

Edge of the Sea (1955). In 1956, after the more muted success of her third book (following the commercial triumph of *The Sea Around Us*) Carson, who was dismayed by the dramatic increase in the use of chemicals, turned her thoughts more to that subject. What was sprayed onto the land in turn affected the sea; pesticides harmed the reproductive cycle of fish and fertilisers' eutrophication, in which the excessive amounts of nitrogen and phosphorous caused algae blooms and deplete oxygen in the water for fish.

The following year, a group of residents on Long Island, New York, filed a suit seeking a permanent injunction against the government's spraying of DDT in the area to control the gypsy moth. Carson, who had been taking newspaper clippings of its progress, was contacted by one of the plaintiffs, Marjorie Spock, who had been delighted to hear that the celebrated author was interested in insecticides. They corresponded and met each other when Spock visited Carson at her seaside house in Southport Maine. Marjorie Spock was a committed follower of Rudolf Steiner. She had met and worked with Steiner barely out of her teens when she abandoned her formal education and started studying his dance discipline, Eurythmy, and the ideas of anthroposophy at the movement's HQ, the Goetheanum, at Dornbach in Switzerland. Moving to the US, she worked closely with Ehrenfried Pfeiffer on biodynamic agriculture. Spock and her partner, Mary Richards, who suffered from multiple chemical sensitivity and needed a diet of strictly organic produce, were outraged by the state and federal government's aerial spraying of DDT over their land, as they saw it, poisoning it and destroying their crops.

Over the course of three years, Spock managed to have the case elevated as high as the US Supreme Court but ultimately failed in her bid, only winning the right to force the government to undertake a full scientific review of the action. Not only did Spock's persistence help give rise to the environmental movement, but through her daily reports to Carson, she provided her with expert testimony that the author used throughout *Silent Spring* (1962). Carson wrote, "I feel guilty about the mass of your material I have here." Spock wrote to Carson of *Silent Spring* before its publication, "I believe it's going to make the biggest difference anything could possibly make in the spraying picture".

In early 1960, while Carson was writing the two chapters of *Silent Spring* which focused on the link between pesticides and cancer, she discovered two masses in her left breast. These were removed but, scandalously, although it was found that one of the masses was malignant, Carson was not advised or suggested to undergo any further treatment. Spock, who shared Carson's intimacy about her cancer, suggested she see Ehrenfried Pfeiffer, who was encouraging, as anthroposophy maintains, the use of mistletoe to cure herself. Carson avoided a direct response to this idea, though others such as the countercultural black feminist Audre Lorde, originator of the concept of self-care, did pursue the Steiner cure as a last resort for her own cancer. As an aside, it is fascinating to note that Spock's older brother, Benjamin Spock, was author of *The Common Sense Book of Baby and Child Care* (1946). This book was often blamed by commentators — due to its revolutionary emphasis on encouraging parents to meet the emotional needs of their children and showing affection — with establishing spoilt behaviour in the generation of young adults that formed the counterculture.

Carson died in 1964, having at least witnessed John F. Kennedy's Science Advisory Committee's report of 1963, which largely backed her claims. When she was cremated, her brother Robert reluctantly agreed to let Freeman, Carson's paramour, spread half her ashes on the ocean at Southport Island. Freeman drove down to the south tip of the Island on a clear calm day in May 1964 and, as the swell of the sea broke against the rocks, poured out Carson's ashes.

Silent Spring

Silent Spring is usually understood as a book about the ecology. Certainly, an equal part of its emphasis is on the public health administration of DDT — for the gypsy moth and fire ant — but agriculture, and the implicit threat that DDT and other pesticides were entering the food chain is perhaps its hardest-hitting message. Carson terrified her audience with fears of pesticide's role as a carcinogen. Reading the book sixty-two years later, its measured power is still astonishing.

In the book, she writes how, added to the pollution from a spectrum of industrial causes, there is "a new kind of fallout — the chemical sprays applied to croplands and gardens, forests and fields". Carson details the horrifying manner in which these pollutants enter streams and lakes, causing fish to be poisoned or killed, the chemicals accumulating in greater intensities higher up the food chain as birds that have fed on them perish. "In the summer of 1960 the refuge staff picked up hundreds of dead and dying birds at Tule Lake and Lower Klamath. Most of them were fish-eating species — herons, pelicans, grebes, gulls. Upon analysis, they were found to contain insecticide residues identified as toxaphene, DDD, and DDE."

Carson writes on the living soil, "born of a marvelous interaction of life and non-life long eons ago". She describes how in experiments, "BHC, aldrin, lindane, heptachlor, and DDD all prevented nitrogen-fixing bacteria from forming the necessary root nodules on leguminous plants. A curious but beneficial relation between fungi and the roots of higher plants is seriously disrupted." Peanuts grown in rotation with cotton upon which BHC was applied heavily pick up considerable amounts of the insecticide. "Actually only a trace is enough to incorporate the telltale musty odor and taste." She accused farmers using pesticides of frequently exceeding prescribed doses, using the chemicals too close to the time of harvest, using several insecticides where one would do, and in other ways failing to read the instructional fine print.

She emphasises the totally unnecessary and counter-productive use of these chemicals by agriculture:

> In southern Indiana, for example, a group of farmers went together in the summer of 1959 to engage a spray plane to treat an area of river bottomland with parathion. The area was a favoured roosting site for thousands of blackbirds that were feeding in nearby cornfields. The problem could have been solved easily by a slight change in agricultural practice — a shift to a variety of corn with deep-set ears not accessible to the birds — but the farmers had been persuaded of the merits of killing by poison, and so they sent in the planes on their mission of death.

Elsewhere,

> In the name of progress the land management agencies have set about to satisfy the insatiable demands of the cattlemen for more grazing land. By this they mean grassland — grass without sage... The newest addition to the weapons is the use of chemical sprays. Now millions of acres of sagebrush lands are sprayed each year... Men of long experience with the ways of the land say that in this country there is better growth of grass between and under the sage than can possibly be had in pure stands, once the moisture-holding sage is gone. But even if the program succeeds in its immediate objective, it is clear that the whole closely knit fabric of life has been ripped apart.

The criticisms of DDT were understood against the background of the birth defects which resulted from women taking the pregnancy-sickness suppressant Thalidomide. Thalidomide caused limbs to grow partially and in a deformed manner. Of the comparison, Carson said, “It’s all of a piece... Thalidomide and pesticides — they represent our willingness to rush ahead and use something new without knowing what the results will be." Effects were also understood relative to the concerns about nuclear radiation caused by nuclear weapons testing, especially in the atmosphere, outer space, and under the sea which resulted in the Partial Test Ban Treaty of 1963. Although her detractors imagined her in league with the "lunatic fringe" of food faddists, anti-fluoride campaigners, nature lovers, and organic farmers, Carson takes a surprisingly compromised position, never arguing for a ban on DDT, only for its sparing use. She also made concessions to its role in genuine public health situations such as in the suppression of typhus in Italy during the Second World War. But she held fast to the fact that insects quickly built up a resistance to it, in *Silent Spring* noting, for instance, that the codling moth was by then resistant to DDT in practically all of the world's apple-growing regions.

Carson and holism

Carson often expresses her ideas in terms which Buddhists understand as the principle of dependent origination — the idea that everything is connected — but in terms that didn't require a heavy garnish of spiritual overtones:

> For each of us, as for the robin in Michigan or the salmon in the Miramichi, this is a problem of ecology, or interrelationships, of interdependence. We poison the caddis flies in a stream and the salmon run dwindle and die. We poison the gnats in a lake and the poison travels from link to link of the food chain and soon the birds of the lake margins become its victims. We spray our elms and the following springs are silent of robin song, not because we sprayed the robins directly but because the poison traveled, step by step, through the now familiar elm leaf-earthworm-robin cycle. These are matters of record, observable, part of the visible world around us. They reflect the web of life — or death — that scientists know as ecology.

Just as the use of chemical fertilisers reflects a very limited, intensely localised, "adolescent" grasp of science, so Carson celebrated holistic approaches to land management:

> Only by taking account of such life forces and by cautiously seeking to guide them into channels favourable to ourselves can we hope to achieve a reasonable accommodation between the insect hordes and ourselves... The 'control of nature' is a phrase conceived in arrogance, born of the Neanderthal age of biology and philosophy, when it was supposed that nature exists for the convenience of man. The concepts and practices of applied entomology for the most part date from that Stone Age of science.

Criticism of Carson

When her book came out, US secretary of agriculture Orville Freeman marshalled all his resources, not in investigating Carson's claims, but into an education programme to explain to the general public the benefits of their ongoing use. As it became clear this mild suppression was not going to check fears, in time, the establishment's reaction reached fever pitch. Fearing a push-back against all agricultural chemicals in the wake of a ban on DDT, Norman Borlaug, architect of the Green Revolution, chose the prestigious McDougall Lecture — before representatives of 160 nations in Rome — to rail against the opponents of the chemical. He denounced them as "the shrill, demanding, disharmonious, tri-tonal voices of the privileged... social dropouts, social parasites in reality". Later, at hearings at the Environmental Protection agency and at a press conference organised by Montrose Chemical, the world's largest manufacturer of DDT, he stormed, "If most DDT uses are cancelled, I have wasted my life's work."

But DDT hasn't ever completely gone away or ceased being used globally. In 2006, the WHO finally announced its endorsement of DDT to combat malaria — it had never rescinded its approval of the chemical for that purpose anyway — but this was an affirmative commitment to its use in this context. It is surprising, therefore, especially given that Carson never called for its total ban, that her critics persist to this day. Vocal among them is Robert Zubrin — perhaps less surprisingly, the author of *The Case for Mars* (1996) and the driving force behind Mars Direct, a 1990 proposal for a human mission to Mars. Zubrin produces data which he says refutes the connection between DDT and cancer in humans, its harmfulness to birds, and the threat it poses to ocean life. The WHO's malarial eradication programme did have success in its early years using DDT. By 1960, malaria had been eradicated in eleven countries and strongly reduced in a dozen more. Defending the use of DDT to subdue malaria, Zubrin writes:

> But, as a result of the mendacity and actions of Carson, Ruckelshaus, Wurster, Ehrlich, and their allies, DDT has been banned, and hundreds of millions of people who might have lived to enjoy those oceans, to sail on them, fish in them, surf in them, or swim in them, to play on their beaches or write poems about their sunsets, are dead.

For all the accolades bestowed upon her, Carson was also an unpopular figure, labelled a subversive, commie, health-nut, and a "spinster", this last being a coded insult for her lesbianism.

The Sense of Wonder

Silent Spring is, essentially, a hard-headed book, but Carson was once referred to as "a nun of nature". To find expression of this sense of spirituality we have to reach for her book *The Sense of Wonder* (1956). Written after *The Edge of the Sea* and before *Silent Spring*, *The Sense of Wonder* was an essay first published in July 1956 in *Woman's Home Companion* under the title "Help Your Child to Wonder". Because it was so well received, Carson expanded it into a short book which was published posthumously in 1965. My own hardback copy features elegiac nature photography by Nick Kelsh (of the kind Carson imagined would illustrate it) and an introduction by Carson's biographer Linda Lear.

Carson had first explored the woods and pools in Maine with her grand-nephew Roger Christie, accompanied by his mother. As much as *Silent Spring* hints at overtones of spirituality, concerning itself with compassion for nature, a respect for "the sacred", and an understanding of the mutual connectivity of life, she always wrote from a very grounded and scientific position. This is what made her so implacable a foe to the mechanistic forces of industry and state. For this reason, *The Sense of Wonder* is such an important document because, through the device of speaking to a young person, she is able to explore the immeasurable instincts we experience in the natural world.

The book starts one stormy autumn with Carson wrapping twenty-month-old Roger in a blanket and carrying him down to the beach overlooking Deep Cove on the Sheepscot River in Maine. In the rainy darkness, in the near distance big waves were thundering in. "Together we laughed for pure joy — he a baby meeting for the first time the wild tumult of Oceanus, I with the salt of half a lifetime of sea love in me. But I think we felt the same spine-tingling response to the vast, roaring ocean and the wild night around us."

Throughout the book, Carson picks up sensations which she shares with the reader, of the ghost crabs scuttling in the dark: "these small living creatures, solitary and fragile against the brute force of the sea, had moving philosophic overtones..." She encourages parents to "take time to listen and talk about the voices of the earth and what they mean — the majestic voice of thunder, the winds, the sound of surf or flowing streams. And the voices of living things..." Promising Roger that in the autumn they will go and hunt for the insects that play little fiddles in the grass, she describes the sounds of the garden at night:

> Most haunting of all is one I call the fairy bell ringer. I have never found him. I'm not sure I want to. His voice — and surely he himself — are so ethereal, so delicate, so otherworldly, that he should remain invisible, as he has through all the nights I have searched for him. It is exactly the sound that should come from a bell held in the hand of the tiniest elf, inexpressibly clear and silvery, so faint, so barely-to-be-heard that you hold your breath as you bend closer to the green glades from which the fairy chiming comes.

And yet there is a purpose to the exploration of the cultivation of "a sense of wonder so indestructible that it would last throughout life". Carson wants it to serve as an "unfailing antidote against the boredom and disenchantment of later years, the sterile preoccupation with things that are artificial, the alienation from the sources of our strength". In 1957, Carson's niece died and she brought the orphaned five-year-old Roger into her care.

Gary Snyder

Born in 1930, beat poet Gary Snyder floats above these two books of mine, *Retreat* and *The Garden*, like the Bodhisattva Avalokiteśvara. Snyder read his "A Berry Feast" at the Six Gallery in San Francisco when Allen Ginsberg debuted his celebrated poem "Howl" in 1955. He was the model for Jack Kerouac's hero Japhy Ryder in *The Dharma Bums* (1958) and was as such one of the key conduits of meditation and Eastern philosophy into the counterculture. With Ginsberg, in 1962, he met the Dalai Lama at Dharamshala, and the two chanted mantras at the Human Be-In at Golden Gate Park in San Francisco in 1967. Nature was important to him: he mountain-climbed, and worked as a fire lookout in the North Cascades in Washington State, as a trail builder, and a logger. Lawrence Ferlinghetti later called him "the Thoreau of the Beat Generation".

In 1964, discussing his values, "the most archaic values on earth... the fertility of the soil, the magic of animals, the power-vision in solitude, the terrifying initiation and rebirth, the love and ecstasy of the dance, the common works of the tribe", we see close up how far ahead of his generation Snyder was; more than any other individual, he was shaping the countercultural preoccupations which crested at the end of the 1960s and spilled out across the '70s. He explains that these values "are very basic to me, and to my friends... I think these concerns are basic to everyone, but most don't think about them, aren't aware of them. They buy vegetables in the supermarket, but don't think about the soil these grow in..."

Snyder on Suwanosejima

Between 1956 and 1969 Snyder zigged and zagged between California and Japan. In the last stretch, he had moved away from institutional Japanese Buddhism, in which he had become a Rinzai Zen monk at the Shokoku-ji temple in Kyoto, and he was a summertime participant in the "wandering poet" Nanao Sakaki's "subcultural" commune, Banyan Ashram, mainly focused on the volcanic island of Suwanosejima. This back-to-the-land group was dubbed "the Tribe". This is where Bhagavan Das and Larry Korn had followed Snyder's path to.

Snyder describes it as an "island farm":

> Nanao got the word that one of the southern islands off Kyushu was underpopulated because it was too isolated, and the soil was too bad and that no one would object if some people moved in there and did some kind of homesteading. So, he and seven or eight people went down and spent the first summer doing nothing but cutting back the bamboo,

> tearing out the root runners and planting sweet potatoes. Sweet potatoes were cheaper and easier to raise on the windy isles than rice. They also subsisted on foraged plants...

A picture emerges of the island in the extended description of his time there in Snyder's *Earth House Hold* (1969). One of the most active volcanic islands in the world, at the far southern tip of Japan, it lies between the mainland and the Okinawa Islands, rising precipitously from rough seas strong with ocean currents. Today, it has a concrete dock (and an airstrip). In Snyder's day, answering an anchored boat's whistle, a rowing boat would weave through a path in the coral reef to meet arrivals — the islanders delivering watermelons and live goats for exchange.

There were twenty-three head of black beef cattle on the island, but, as he explains:

> most of us would be vegetarians by choice, but this was a real case of necessity and ecology. The volcanic soil of the island (and the volcanic ash fallout) makes it hard to raise many vegetables there; but the waters are rich in fish. [Spearing them themselves] We offered our respects and gratitude to the fish and the Sea Gods daily, and ate them with real love, admiring their extraordinarily beautiful, perfect little bodies.

Snyder and homesteading

Certainly, Snyder's main preoccupations are poetry and ecology. However, crucially for us, he had a background in homesteading. His parents had an orchard, chickens, and a little dairy farm. It consisted of two acres in pasture, surrounded by woods. At age nine or ten, Snyder was allowed to sleep in a little camp he made hidden in the woods. When he settled with wife and child in the Sierra Nevada foothills in North California in 1969, he was part of the back-to-the-land current. In the poem "The Call of the Wild" from his Pulitzer

Prize–winning collection *Turtle Island* (1974) he writes, perhaps cynically, of that movement:

> The ex acid-heads from the cities/Converted to Guru or Swami,/Do penance with shiny/Dopey eyes, and quit eating meat./ In the forests of North America,/The land of Coyote and Eagle,/They dream of India, of/forever blissful sexless highs./And sleep in oil-heated/Geodesic domes, that/Were stuck like warts/In the woods.

But psychedelics weren't always bad in this context, it seems. He writes, "Peyote and acid have a curious way of tuning some people in to the local soil."

Snyder also writes approvingly of the way in which the back-to-the-land movement interfaced with local culture:

> The whole back-to-the-land movement, at least in California, at first had the quality of people going off into little enclaves. But the enclaves broke down rapidly as people discovered not only that they would have to but that they would enjoy interacting with their backwoods neighbours. A wonderful exchange of information and pleasure came out of what originally was hostile; each side discovered that they had something to learn from the other.

In the collection of his writing *The Real Work* (1980), Snyder describes how the nature of the seasons, and the work homesteading required him to do, meant that he wrote in the winter. It gives a snapshot of how his time was spent:

> Well, the way I live right now, I guess I probably write more in the winter. Because in the spring I go out in the desert for a while, and I give a few readings, and then when I get back it's time to turn the ground over and start spring planting, and then right after that's done it's time to do the building that has to be done, and when that's done it's time

> to start cutting firewood, and when the firewood's done it's just about time to start picking apples and drying them, and that takes a couple of weeks to get as many apples as possible and dry them, and then at the end of the apple season I begin to harvest the garden, and a lot of canning and drying is done maybe, and then when that season passes, to chestnuts and picking up the wild grapes, and then I've got to put the firewood in, and as soon as I get the firewood in, hunting season starts — and that winds up about the end of October... So December, January and February is my time of total isolation, writing, and I don't see anybody in those months.

Elsewhere he portrays himself "farming all the time", and describes planting fruit trees, putting in fencing, and taking care of the chickens. He says of his homestead, in *The Practice of the Wild* (1990), "The land my family and I live on in the Sierra Nevada of California is 'barely good' from an economic standpoint. With soil amendments, much labor, and the development of ponds for holding water through the dry season, it is producing a few vegetables and some good apples."

In an interview in 1971 with writer Richard Grossinger, Snyder explained:

> It's only back-breaking if you're trying to maintain a standard of living that's out of proportion to who and where you are and is dictated by the tastes of the city rather than the tastes of the country, which is what nineteenth-century American farm tastes were dictated by... It takes a long time to get to know how to live in a region gently and easily and with a maximum of annual efficiency. That back-breaking farm work of Anglo settlers out on the Plains and Midwest was hard because they were ignorant and competitive, and pushed by a capitalist system from behind. They went into hock to do their farming, for tools and for seed. And a lot of them never got out of debt.

When asked what the appeal of rural life is, Snyder says,

> It wouldn't be going too far to say that human creativity and all of the arts begin to wither if they are pulled too far away from fundamentals of how people really should and have had to live, over millennia. We are, after all, an animal that was brought into being on this biosphere by these processes of sun and water and leaf. And if we depart too far from them, we're departing too far from the mother, from our own heritage.

Like his friend Wendell Berry, Snyder thinks hard about the future of agriculture. In "The Four Changes" tract at the end of *Turtle Island*, there is a list of practical suggestions for living. In the "Action" section, Snyder calls for "effective international legislation banning DDT and other poisons — with no fooling around. The collusion of certain scientists with the pesticide industry and agri-business in trying to block this legislation must be brought out in the open." He talks somewhat apocalyptically:

> Agrarian reform will literally take place when the agri-business food production system breaks down. When that system breaks down, then hungry people from the city will be taking, or arranging to give each other, workable farm-size parcels of land out of those huge agri-business holdings. And people will have to do labor-intensive agriculture.

Snyder on Eastern philosophy

In *Earth House Hold*, Snyder writes about one aspect of what drew his generation into studying the East, "The suspicion grew that perhaps the whole Western Tradition, of which Marxism is but a (Millennial Protestant) part, is off the track. This led many people to study other major civilizations — India and

China — to see what they could learn." In *The Practice of the Wild* he elaborates:

> It seems that a short way back in the history of occidental ideas there was a fork in the trail. The line of thought that is signified by the names of Descartes, Newton, and Hobbes (saying that life in a primary society is 'nasty, brutish, and short' — all of them city-dwellers) was a profound rejection of the organic world.

As he puts it, "There are tens of millions of people in North America who were physically born here but who are not actually living here intellectually, imaginatively, or morally." Early on, you get the sense that Snyder finds what he needs in Buddhism as it pertains to making sense of the connection to nature. In *The Real Work*, Snyder quotes from a sutra: "The Buddha once said, bhikshus, if you can understand this blade of rice, you can understand the laws of dependence and origination. If you can understand the laws of dependence and origination, you can understand the Dharma. If you understand the Dharma, you know the Buddha."

Snyder was also explicitly critical of those philosophies' coalescence into institutional religions from an early stage, writing in 1969, "It became clear that 'Hinduism' and 'Buddhism' as social institutions had long been accomplices of the State in burdening and binding people, rather than serving to liberate them. Just like the other Great Religions." These systems of thought alone did not hold all the answers either. The Buddhist and Hindu traditions, "lost something which the primitives did have, and that was a total integrated life style..." Elsewhere he explains:

> Certain primitive cultures that are functioning on a high level actually amount to what would be considered a spiritual training path in which everyone in the culture is involved and there are no separations between the priest

> and layman or between the men who become enlightened and those who can't. What we need to do now is to take the great intellectual achievement of the Mahayana Buddhists and bring it back to a community style of life...

Much later on, in 1990, he comments, "The Japanese Zen world of the last few centuries has become so expert and professional in the matter of strict training that it has lost to a great extent the capacity to surprise itself."

One of the appeals of Buddhism's Zen, Soto, or Rinzai branches, was that they sought to connect daily life and spiritual practice. *Work* being the vital component: tending the plants, carrying the water, doing the dishes. This practice can take many forms. Snyder says,

> Some people in the world don't have to do a hundred thousand protestations, because they do them day by day in work with their hands and bodies. All over the world there are people who are doing their sitting while they fix the machinery, while they plant the grain, or while they tend the horses. And they know it; it's not unconscious.

All manner of things might constitute *practice*. "It is as hard to get the children herded into the car pool and down the road to the bus as it is to chant sutras in the Buddha-hall on a cold morning."

However, although we have lost this connection, this embedding in nature that we once enjoyed, there is hope:

> As the American Indians, as the Pueblo assert, we are in a transition phase right now: between having lost our capacity to communicate directly, intuitively, and to understand the life force, and the return to that condition. We are doing hard practice, hard yoga on Earth for these thousands of years because of some errors we made. But our practice will win us back that skill, that capacity, that direct knowledge

of the forces and energies of the universe. Those cannot be won by scientific inquiry or fancier tools; those can only be won by the most complex and sophisticated tool there is, the mind.

Snyder on the wild

Snyder may be both ninety-three and a living legend, but he still answers emails. I had corresponded with him briefly at the end of my book *Retreat*, and going into my research for *The Garden*, I contacted him again. His ideas, those in his books and poems, are expressed in a way that can be dense, and really require one to wrap one's head around what he means.

I explained that with this book, *The Garden*, I was trying to establish a connection between growing, farming, and the broader continuum of culture. Snyder replied that "I think my real problem with your approach is that I never think of agriculture or gardens except in the light of wild [and] natural process." By this statement, Snyder refers to the idea he expresses in *The Practice of the Wild*, where he outlines his view that gardening and growing, when done properly, are not processes through which nature is civilised, but ones in which the gardener or grower participates in "the wild". So, for instance, in that book he writes, "It has been said that 'good soil is good because of the wildness in it.'" We know biologically that this is true! The healthy soil biome is one which is by definition natural and full of wild living organisms. In *The Practice of the Wild*, all the way back in 1990, he writes of this living soil. "In a way the web that holds it all together is the mycelia, the fungus-threads that mediate between root-tips of plants and chemistry of soils, bringing nutrients in. This association is as old as plants with roots. The whole of the forest is supported by this buried network."

Snyder's view of "culture" is similar. True artistic culture (poetry, prose, music, painting, and sculpture, etc.) he does not see as a process of civilisation. Rather, like gardening and growing, it is a *participation* in the wild outside of the staid boundaries of civilisation. This too, from our appreciation of art such as abstract expressionism, dada, and art brut, and the music of rock, jazz, reggae, hip-hop, and hardcore, we know to be true. Therefore, to speak of connecting gardening and growing to culture is to misunderstand the nature of both — because in their correct manifestation both are the same wild things. It makes more sense, I suppose, to talk about trying to point out the natural affinity that already exists between "organic" agriculture and "vital" culture.

In his email, Snyder continues, "Native California cultures, especially in the valley are a case in point. A large population is not a goal." They are not seeking to expand their population but to continue living in harmony.

"In some cases, the opposite of cultivation can be seen, as "to go back to the wild" is to become sour, astringent, crabbed, unfertilized, unpruned, resilient, and every spring shockingly beautiful in bloom." This observes the reversion of cultivated stock to the wild. Elsewhere, Snyder refers to Henry Thoreau writing about the crab apple, that native wild apple from which the apples we know are cultivated. Thoreau writes, "*Our* wild apple is wild only like myself, perchance, who belong not to the aboriginal race here, but have strayed into the woods from cultivated stock." It also relates to going "out there" as Snyder puts it, "Going out — fasting — singing alone — talking across the species boundaries — praying — giving thanks — coming back." It relates to both the process of "going crazy for a while" and what Joseph Campbell called "the Hero's journey". He writes on this process, "What we didn't perhaps see so clearly was that self-realization, even enlightenment, is another aspect of our wildness — a bonding of the wild in ourselves to the (wild) process of the universe". Thus some qualities of what is recognised by society as madness are recast instead as the subject becoming natural.

He continues in his email to me, "Kat Anderson (her big classical volume on Native food) says the food the California

Natives gathered was equal or more than what is produced by agriculture now. Via hunting, gathering, and storing. Acorn storage structures 8 feet high, good for 5 years, etc." Here Snyder refers to M. Kat Anderson's *Tending the Wild* (2013); this landmark classic in anthropology explored how over twelve thousand years the Native Californian Indians carefully cultivated and knit themselves within a landscape which appeared to the ignorant European settlers as though wild, like a garden of Eden. Kat Anderson writes, "Much of what we consider wilderness today was in fact shaped by Indian burning, harvesting, tilling, pruning, sowing, and tending."

At the end of this tiny, extremely dense email, Snyder offered very sweetly, "I wrote a book that's still around, *The Practice of the Wild* — if I had your address I'd send you one. I still have some." I assured him that I had a copy, one I had only just started, graciously thanked him, and took my leave. You never want to outstay your welcome.

Frances Moore Lappé

Frances Moore Lappé (1944–) grew up Frances Moore in Texas. After graduating from the private liberal arts college, Earlham College in Indiana, in 1966, she married the toxicologist and environmentalist Dr Marc Lappé in 1967. Moore Lappé briefly attended the hotbed of countercultural activity UC Berkeley. Her famous book *Diet for a Small Planet* (1971) has sold 2.5 million copies.

At first, she thought that humans were creating the experience of scarcity but, after research at the Berkeley University library with her father's slide rule, came to the conclusion that it was just poor management. "I wanted to tell people that it was in our power, that we were creating this needless suffering in the world, and we could change it." She turned her original one-page leaflet into a booklet that got into the hands of a founder of paperback publishing in America, Betty Valentine, who had the idea to add recipes. The first 162 pages of Moore Lappé's book work through the theoretical underpinnings of her idea that it makes no ecological sense to devote agricultural resources to feed livestock when it is more efficient to grow the protein necessary to our diet. This comes in the form of a data-driven argument backed up by charts, graphs, and tables. The recipes only come in the last 188 pages of the book.

In 1970, given the terrifying population projections outlined in her reading of Paul R. Ehrlich's *The Population Bomb* (1968), Moore Lappé had asked herself the question "How close are we to the limit of the earth's capacity to provide food for all humanity?" She began with the assumption that "our food problems were agricultural ones that only the food experts could solve but came to the conclusion that feeding the earth's people is more profoundly a political and economic problem which you and I must help to solve."

In 1975, in the book's second edition, Moore Lappé breaks down the US's main protein resources. The following percentages were fed directly to animals: corn/barley/oats — 90%; soybeans — >90%; wheat — 24%; milk products — 2%. She is unstinting in her disapproval of American habits of eating: "To feed everyone in the world, the way in America we do it, would take three times the current world grain production." What is fascinating is that Moore Lappé calculates that today people forget that we get protein from all foods in some proportion or other. The "average" American actually eats almost twice the protein that one's body can use.

Another of Moore Lappé's shifts in consciousness came when at a coffeehouse with friends she realised that the tasty cup of cappuccino she was drinking represented "millions of acres of agricultural land in the hungry world". In keeping with her eventual focus on global democracy, Moore Lappé explores the plantation system, the example of Columbia where the local population can grow carnation flowers (where a hectare would then produce a million pesos a year versus corn's 12,500 pesos), or the increased production of luxury items like strawberries and asparagus.

She reflects on the damage to the soil from the point of view of its erosion, but also its productivity, giving the example of Kansas wheat, which had previously contained 17% protein, (the amount of protein in wheat being an accepted benchmark of its quality) but which had sunk to 14% by 1951. Of soil lost, nearly a billion tons eroded away and washed down the rivers as sediment, she remarks:

> Do we accept this virtually irretrievable loss to our greatest natural resources as a necessary trade-off in the battle against starvation? No — not when almost half of that harvested acreage goes to feeding livestock. The great pressure on our agricultural land, leading to the over-use of fertilizers and under-use of sound conservation techniques, comes not from hungry people but from the demands of our inefficiently produced meat-centred diet, a diet that bears no relation to our real biological needs.

Moore Lappé takes up the use of DDT and other chlorinated pesticides that Rachel Carson had brought to the world's attention with *Silent Spring*. However, she contextualises these chemical's effects within her protein framework by encouraging people to eat low on the food chain from protein-rich crops like legumes and nuts, rather than at the top from livestock, where it is proven these pesticides accumulate. "My purpose is to show you a way to minimize the amount of ecologically concentrated pesticide and heavy metal you ingest: by eating low on the food chain, you are simply reducing the quantity of most if not all pesticide residues in your diet."

E.F. Schumacher

Ernst Friedrich Schumacher — the son of a university economics professor — was born in Bonn, Germany in 1911.

He was educated in Bonn and Berlin and, in 1930, became a Rhodes scholar to England's Oxford University. Schumacher also attended Columbia University in the United States. In 1937, during Hitler's rise to power in Germany, Schumacher emigrated to England and during the next few years worked at various jobs in the fields of journalism, business, and farming. He became a British citizen in 1946. It was also in 1946 that Schumacher began a four-year stint as economic advisor to the United Kingdom Control Commission in Germany, a group which played a major role in paving the way for the post-Second World War German economic recovery. Schumacher left the Control Commission in 1950 to become the chief economist for Britain's National Coal Board, a nationalised industry, and the largest business in the United Kingdom. He would serve on that board for the next twenty years — twenty years that would also see him develop his idea of "economics as if people mattered".

The economic theory for which Schumacher is famous started to form in his mind in 1955, when he began a series of visits to Burma, India, and other developing countries. He was dismayed to learn that most aid programmes offered variations of just one quick and easy "solution": Replace your primitive hoes with our tractors, fertilisers, pesticides, and computers. Interviewed in *Mother Earth News* in 1978, he said, "To make the high technology we give them work, they need to make a tremendous capital investment—which they do not have—in fuels and fertilizers and pesticides and spare parts and training programs and complicated machinery, there is only one place they can get such things: from us, and at our prices."

Schumacher and Eastern philosophy

While he was the chief economist for the Coal Board in the early 1950s, Schumacher was a follower of Gurdjieff and was involved with the London Gurdjieffians around

Gurdjieff's main disseminator, Ouspensky. Schumacher was a life-long associate of Lady Eve Balfour, cultivated his own garden organically, joined the Soil Association, and even had them present a film at the Coal Board offices. Interested in philosophy and these ideas in his forties, Schumacher told *Mother Earth News* that he

> spent many years studying the whole of what is called 'philosophy'. But neither my rationalist scientific upbringing nor my study of philosophy gave me the answers I wanted. Nor did my experiments with psychical research. And then I happened onto a book about Buddhism and that was what I was looking for. I dropped everything else and read all I could find on the subject.

He noticed that many of the texts he read had references to a school in Burma (by which he meant the Theravadan community in Rangoon). He was keen to visit there when, fortuitously, in 1955 he was invited by the Burmese government to advise their prime minister. When there, Schumacher visited "the school" and studied Vipassana meditation with U Ba Khin, formerly the accountant general of Burma, who had established an organisation called the International Meditation Centre. Not what could be called a renunciate, Buddhism nevertheless had a major impact upon his thought: "Well I don't claim to have attained vipassana, but I did come away from Burma with a different view of things. And in the beginning, as I saw my life in this new light, I was very unhappy. The things I had been doing had ceased to make sense."

Central to this reassessment was a recalibration of the idea that, as a rule, more money meant more happiness:

> My work with developing nations quickly showed me the fallacy of this line of thought. You simply cannot assume that raising a country's GNP will raise the standard of living of every individual in that country. In actual fact, the

> development programs that have been implemented in the emerging nations during the past few decades have almost universally produced quite a different result. They have substantially increased the incomes of a fortunate small minority and drastically lowered the incomes of the rest. And not only lowered their incomes, but destroyed their culture and plunged them from poverty into misery.

He told *Mother Earth News*:

> Oh there's no doubt that our neglect of the spiritual aspects of life in favor of the deification of material goods has eaten into our very substance. By so single-mindedly cultivating an ever-expanding greed and envy, we have debased ourselves. We have made our lives far less than they could be. We have destroyed our intelligence, happiness, and serenity.

Schumacher, whose ideas were a touchstone for the culture we are surveying, was a close friend of self-sufficiency guru John Seymour, and wrote the foreword for Seymour's *The Complete Book of Self-Sufficiency* (1976). In that, he wrote:

> In the modern world, during the last hundred years or so, there has been an enormous and historically unique shift: away from self-reliance and towards organization. As a result, people are becoming less self-reliant and more dependent than has ever been seen in history. They may claim to be more highly educated than any generation before them; but the fact remains that they cannot really do anything for themselves... At most of these trades I would be pretty incompetent and horribly inefficient. But to grow or make some things by myself, for myself: what fun, what exhilaration, what liberation from any feelings of utter dependence on organizations! What is perhaps even more: what an education of the real person! To be in touch with actual processes of creation.

Small is Beautiful

Written in 1973, Schumacher's *Small Is Beautiful: A Study of Economics as if People Mattered* is his most famous work. An economist, he described humanity as though it were a businessman rapidly consuming its own capital. How had we made this mistake?

> Even the great Dr Marx fell into this devastating error when he formulated the so-called 'labour theory of value'. Now, we have indeed laboured to make some of the capital which today helps us to produce... but... this is but a small part of the total capital we are using. Far larger is the capital provided by nature and not by man — and we do not even recognise it as such... We must thoroughly understand the problem and begin to see the possibility of evolving a new life-style, with new methods of production and new patterns of consumption: a lifestyle designed for permanence.

Schumacher delineates changes to be made in industry and one in agriculture: "In agriculture and horticulture, we can interest ourselves in the perfection of production methods which are biologically sound, build up soil fertility, and produce health, beauty, and permanence. Productivity will then look after itself."

In the chapter "Buddhist Economics", he refers to the principle outlined in the Eightfold Path of "Right Livelihood". Rather than viewing labour as a disutility in which one sacrifices one's leisure and comfort, Schumacher favours a Buddhist conception of work. "The Buddhist point of view takes the function of work to be at least threefold: to give a man a chance to utilise and develop his faculties; to enable him to overcome his egocentredness by joining with other people in a common task; and to bring forth the goods and services needed for a becoming existence." Where modern economics assumes that a man who consumes more is better off, a

Buddhist economist would see this focus on consumption as irrational; "The aim should be to obtain the maximum of well-being with the minimum of consumption". From the point of view of Buddhist economics, therefore, production from local resources for local needs is the most rational way of economic life, while dependence on imports from afar and the consequent need to produce for export to unknown and distant peoples is highly uneconomic and justifiable only in exceptional cases and on a small scale. He describes the "keynote" of Buddhist economics as being "simplicity and nonviolence".

In *The Proper Use of Land*, Schumacher examines the trend of history whereby civilised man

> overgrazed and denuded the grasslands that fed his livestock. He killed most of the wildlife and much of the fish and other water life. He permitted erosion to rob his farm land of its productive topsoil. He allowed eroded soil to clog the streams and fill his reservoirs, irrigation canals, and harbours with silt. In many cases, he used and wasted most of the easily mined metals or other needed minerals. Then his civilization declined amidst the despoilation of his own creation or he moved to new land.

There are, he pointed out, no new lands to move to. "In our time, the main danger to the soil, and therewith not only to agriculture but to civilization as a whole, stems from the townsman's determination to apply to agriculture the principles of industry."

Schumacher believed that farming needed to be seen in a wider context wherein it would be able to fulfil three tasks: "to keep man in touch with living nature, of which he is and remains a highly vulnerable part; — to humanise and ennoble man's wide habitat; and — to bring forth the foodstuffs and other materials which are needed for a becoming life". He believed that "we should be searching for policies to reconstruct rural culture, to open the land for gainful occupation to larger numbers of people, whether it be on a full-time or a part-time basis, and to orientate all our actions on the land towards the threefold ideal of health, beauty, and permanence". Agriculture needed to cling assiduously to three truths revealed by nature's living processes. "One of them is the law of return; another is diversification — as against any kind of monoculture; another is decentralisation, so that some use can be found for even quite inferior resources which it would never be rational to transport over long distances." Making an argument in 1963 which Mark Fisher echoed in *Capitalist Realism* (2009), he states that if society failed to look after its land, "it is due to the fact that, as a society, we have no firm basis of belief in any meta-economic values, and when there is no such belief the economic calculus takes over".

Gaia

Although neither James Lovelock nor his longtime collaborator Lynn Margulis (1938–2011), both scientists, could be described as being countercultural, their work is crying out to be considered in the context we have established of holism and spirituality. Frankly, people would wonder why they were not mentioned.

James Lovelock (1919–2022) was, as well as a scientist, an environmentalist and futurist. Embellishing A.J.P. Marti's chemical analytical technique of gas chromatography, he created the electron capture detector. This device of "exquisite sensitivity" was the first to detect chlorofluorocarbons in the atmosphere and, in his words, "helped Rachel Carson to write her immensely influential book *Silent Spring*". Lovelock's research led to him taking a role helping Shell consider the global consequences of fossil fuels in 1966, three years before the foundation of Friends of the Earth.

Lovelock, who was working for NASA at the time he came up with the Gaia hypothesis, said that this "view from space" enabled him to see the Earth from a different perspective than his colleagues. It was, in his words, a "holistic" view. The name was recommended to him by the author William Golding. "Without hesitation he recommended that this creature be called Gaia, after the Greek Earth goddess also known as Ge, from which root the sciences of geography and geology derive their names." In his book *Gaia: A New Look at Life on Earth* (1979), Lovelock elaborates: "The idea of Mother Earth or, as the Greeks called her, Gaia, has been widely held throughout history and has been the basis of a belief that coexists with the great religions."

The Gaia theory is nicely explained by Lynn Margulis.

> The Gaia theory is that the surface of the earth is regulated and modulated. The temperature and the acidity and the concentration of gases like oxygen and methane are not here by chance alone. They are here as products of interactions of the organisms. So, what we as people have generally considered the environment to which life is adapting, a passive life which is adapting to an environment that is changing, is the wrong way to look at it. The way you want to look at it is that life is actually changing its environment — and then it is responding to that, but after responding it's changing it more — that it's not a monologue — it's a dialogue.

Plants and bacteria made huge contributions to these changes. Lovelock ponders the nature of what life amounts to: "life is a member of the class of phenomena which are open or continuous systems able to decrease their internal entropy at the expense of substances or free energy taken in from the environment and subsequently rejected in a degraded form". He noted that Erwin Schrodinger saw entropy reduction as a common characteristic of any form of life.

The book was very controversial within the mainstream science which both Lovelock and Margulis essentially sat upon the fringes of. In the preface of the 2000 edition, Lovelock wrote:

> Now twenty-six years on, I know her better and see that in this first book I made mistakes. Some were serious, such as the idea that the Earth was kept comfortable by and for its inhabitants, the living organisms. I failed to make it clear that it was not the biosphere alone that did the regulating but the whole thing, life, the air, the oceans, and the rocks. The entire surface of the Earth including life is a self-regulating entity and this is what I mean by Gaia.

Agriculture does not escape Lovelock's consideration. He creates the story, the fable, of a Dr. Intensli Eeger, who plans by genetic manipulation to develop a greatly improved strain of nitrogen-fixing bacteria. "By this means nitrogen in the air could be transferred directly to the soil without the need for a complex chemical industry." The end result of such an intervention was cataclysmic; an alga called P. eegarii takes over the planet. "Within six months more than half of the ocean and most of the land surfaces were covered with a thick green slime which fed voraciously of the dead trees and animal life decaying beneath it."

The widespread popular appeal of the Gaia hypothesis, though, has everything to do with the way in which it *seems* to legitimise the New Age thinking which the counterculture had an affinity with. Evolutionary biologist Lynn Margulis, whose work was on the role of symbiosis in evolution, was even less sentimental than Lovelock. She prefers "the idea that Earth is a network of 'ecosystems' over any personification of Mother Gaia". Margulis famously scoffed at human attempts to care for the living Earth. "Our self-inflated moral imperative to guide a wayward Earth or heal our sick planet is evidence of our immense capacity for self-delusion." Momentarily conceding to Gaia's personification, she described her as "a tough bitch".

That appears to put her at odds with the idea of a sustainable agriculture.

On the face of it, Margulis refutes any religious intention when she criticises other scientists' hidden assumption:

> One widely held unstated assumption is the great chain of being. It defines the venerable position of humans as the exact centre of the universe in the middle of the chain of being below God and above rock. This anthropocentric idea dominates religious thought, even that of those who claim to reject religion and to replace it with a scientific worldview.

This is because, in her view, "all beings alive today are equally evolved. All have survived over three thousand million years of evolution from common bacterial ancestors. There are no 'higher' beings, no 'lower animals', no angels, and no gods." This position might be anathema to a Christian, but there's no incompatibility here from the perspective of Eastern philosophy. The monk Thich Nhat Hanh summarises Buddhist thought when he writes, "Know that the world is woven of interconnected threads."

Lovelock, a futurist, shared with Stewart Brand an insistence upon the need for nuclear power, advocating other "wizardly" solutions for climate change such as moving the entire population, not to the countryside, but into massive cities. To combat rising temperatures, he advocated mimicking volcanoes to put sulphur gas into the stratosphere to form a haze which blocks off sunshine.

Ecopsychology

When the countercultural generation took psychedelics, many found that the priorities they had been "programmed" with — for many commentators epitomised in the hierarchical nuclear family depicted in US Television sitcom *Leave it to Beaver* — were disassembled. The status-oriented and materialistic attitudes of their parents didn't seem as appealing. The blatantly unethical behaviour of the state in Vietnam compounded this impulse to reevaluate the lifestyle they had been handed. As soon as they started interrogating these machinic assumptions with which they were programmed, it led, inevitably, to an evaluation on a much wider scale. In going back to the drawing board, the context of consideration was infinitely wider — and that included the natural world around them. It seemed somehow that the neurosis and alienation of modern life might relate to a disconnection from that natural world. An early communard of Cold Mountain Farm, Joyce Gardiner writes:

> We had plowed and begun to plant the earth, but we had not pierced our own ego skins. Decay and stagnation had already set in. I went into the woods to meditate. The woods explained: it was high time we plowed the earth of this community. We must apply the blade to ourselves and cut back the outer skin to expose the pulsing flesh. And then we must harrow and pulverise the outer skin and use our egos for compost. Then, in the new flesh, we must plant the seeds of the people we wish to become.

In some respects, with these two books — *Retreat* and *The Garden* — we are doing nothing more than following theorist Theodore Roszak's (1933–2011) train of thought. Roszak was famous for coining the term "counterculture" with his book *The Making of a Counter Culture* (1969). The term "ecopsychology" was his next most famous coinage. Just like the generation he tracked, and the evolution of their thought, Roszak became increasingly preoccupied with ecology. In *Voice of the Earth* (1992) Roszak asks, "What is the source of the 'epistemological loneliness' that characterizes modern life? Can it be our ecological ignorance?" For Roszak, the best contemporary expression of the drive to connect both with the environment and our own bodies was Gestalt therapy. Gestalt therapy's pioneers, the psychoanalyst Fritz Perls (1893–1970) and intellectual Paul Goodman (1911–1972), drew this interest in the body from the pioneering psychoanalyst Wilhelm Reich (1897–1957). Roszak criticises both Freud and Jung for having very little nature in their formal theoretical work. Even the contemporary psychologist, the saintly Abraham Maslow (1908–1970) — who towards the end of his life *had* widened the purview of humanistic psychology from a focus upon the autonomous individual — is an article of Roszak's censure. He regarded Maslow as "a sad but instructive example of what befalls ambitious psychiatric theory when it lacks an environmental dimension". Roszak noted approvingly of Gestalt therapy that "only the Gestalt school has introduced a larger, more fully biological context for therapy that seeks to unite figure with ground, organism with environment; it is the only school that used the concept of ecology in its theories."

Gestalt therapy also had a huge debt to Eastern philosophy. Talking of Goodman, Roszak writes, "In the Tao, at least as he understood it, he found the principle of organic self-regulation whether of the body, the community, or the environment. The homely wisdom of Lao Tzu, the Chinese peasant sage, became the basis of Goodman's Gestalt Psychology." Roszak concluded that "the ecological ego matures toward a sense of ethical responsibility with the planet that is as vividly experienced as our ethical responsibility to other people."

Part of this connection to nature lies in a reevaluation of what society understands to be madness. Just like Gary Snyder, with his idea of "the wild", Roszak believed that "the bridge we need to find our way back to a significant sense of connectedness with nature may lie in that shadowed quarter of the mind we have for so long regarded as 'irrational', even 'crazy.'" Roszak expresses this in the formulation "What the id conserves from its long maturing process is our treasury of ecological intelligence".

One of the most interesting and astute voices in the field of ecopsychology was Ralph Metzner (1936–2019), colleague of

Timothy Leary and Richard Alpert (later Ram Dass), pioneer in psychedelic research, and psychotherapist. In the paper "The Psychopathology of the Human-Nature Relationship", in Roszak's collection *Ecopsychology* (1995), Metzner wrote:

> Elsewhere, I have argued that due to a complex variety of social and historical reasons, a core feature of the Euro-American psyche is a 'dissociative split between spirit and nature.' We have a deeply ingrained belief that our spiritual life, our spiritual practices, must tend in a direction opposite to our nature. Spirit, we imagine, rises upward, into transcendent realms, whereas nature, which includes bodily sensations and feelings, draws us downward.

Metzner says, "For most people in the West, their highest values, their noblest ideals, their image of themselves as spiritual beings striving to be good and come closer to God, have been deeply associated with a sense of having to overcome and separate from nature." However, "the idea that the spiritual and natural are opposed or that spirituality must always transcend nature is a culturally relative concept not shared by non-monotheistic religions or traditional societies".

Steven Harper

Ecopsychology can seem very fixated on the idea of wilderness, the experience of which, at its most superficial, can be rather like attending a museum. No emphasis is given to actions wherein one can participate with nature, rather than just spectate it. In an essay by Alan Thein Durning in Rozak's collection, "Are We Happy Yet?", the writer lists pastimes that are infinitely sustainable: "Religious practice, conversation, family and community gatherings, theater, music, dance, literature, sports, poetry, artistic and creative pursuits, education, and an appreciation of nature all fit readily into a culture of permanence." There is no mention of farming, growing, or gardening.

The connection is finally made in an essay by a Steven Harper:

> Over the years I have found myself, more often than not, recommending gardening to workshop participants who seek ways of staying connected outside of the wilderness environment. When practiced in a sustainable way, gardening and farming are activities in which people and wild nature intermesh and begin to coevolve. Gardening yields deep insights into how we can physically, mentally and spiritually find creative balance between wild nature and human nature. Gardening immerses us in a basic natural cycle that directly sustains our life. We get our hands dirty and our bodies sweaty. Gardening can be the physical embodiment of symbiosis and coevolution, the 'ground' in which we practice what we have learnt in the wilderness. We give to the Earth as well as receiving.

I was delighted to find Harper's lone voice. What seems to be the most obvious idea in the world, that gardening is good for your mental health, is bizarrely absent in the context of ecopsychology. I thought I needed to find out more about this person, so I looked him up. Alive and well, Harper's website describes him as "a wilderness guide, workshop leader, personal and organizational facilitator, and author". Harper, who lives on the Big Sur coast, leads wilderness expeditions informed by the therapeutic modality of Gestalt practice. To my astonishment, he was also the co-founder of the Esalen Institute's Hot Springs Farm, which I didn't even know existed! I had been fortunate to visit Esalen's vegetable garden in 2018 researching my book *Retreat*, but had failed to make the connection to this new research on farmers and growers. It felt like a moment of serendipity.

When I managed to interview Harper, he talked to me about Roszak's twin coinages of "counterculture" and "ecopsychology". The two concepts are mutually codependent, like yin (the heaven-bound *counterculture*) and yang (the earth-directed *ecopsychology*). Roszak was to write by equal measure books which looked at the "etheric" currents in society — *The Making of a Counter Culture* (1969), *Unfinished Animal: The Aquarian Frontier and the Evolution of Consciousness* (1975), *From Satori to Silicon Valley* (1986) — and those which reflected on nature and "integration": *Where the Wasteland Ends* (1972), *Person/Planet: The Creative Disintegration of Industrial Society* (1979), and *The Voice of the Earth* (1992). Harper knew Roszak and remembered two conferences they organised at Esalen in 1992 and 1993 "that had a 'who's who' in the room... it was quite remarkable. James Hillman was there and David Abram... some top people in the environmental movement... Together trying to define ecopsychology."

Gestalt practice

When I asked Harper about his inspiration in setting up Hot Springs Farm, although mentioning the oil shocks of the 1970s, he contextualised it in Gestalt practice, his mentor Dick Price's revision of Fritz Perls's Gestalt therapy. Harper was very close to Esalen's co-founder Price in the five years preceding his death, the two running together a workshop called "Gestalt and Hiking Practice", and with Harper being a trained mountain guide, often accompanying one another on wilderness expeditions around the area. One of Gestalt practice's tenets is "the capacity to be self-responsible", not in the sense of having responsibilities but of being able to be responsive. "And the difference would be that normally I'm in *reactivity*. As opposed to true here-and-now *responsiveness*... How can I be *responsive*, not just to myself at the *interpersonal* level, but also at the *intrapersonal* level?

Gestalt practice also interests itself with the natural self-regulation of systems:

> If there's *awareness* and *choices* and *possibilities* the organism is pretty wise, and we see this in ecology. Often if we leave a damaged ecosystem alone it repairs itself. If we come in and go, 'We've got to fix this!' and we know this from early fire ecology, 'Oh, there's been a fire! We got to reseed!' Well, it turns out the re-seeding does incredible damage and has all sorts of other ramifications: creating monocultures, pushing out diversity.

Fundamental to all of this is the idea of learning to grow *self-awareness*. "If you're not aware... how can you even be aware that you're in a rut?" Inspired by these philosophical ideas, in the 1970s Esalen sought to better contextualise itself ecologically and set about working on the issue. "How can we as *aware* human beings working on the interpersonal also be aware of the wider ecology that we're part of? The whole project was called the Energy Resource Project. Our sub-project was called the Food Resource Project". Harper gives as an example from that era an occassion when, rather than using electric heaters, they went out and cut cordwood for wood-burning stoves. Speaking in the Esalen Institute documentary *Growth!: An Evolution of the Farm & Garden*, he puts it succinctly:

> It felt like to me that there was an early renaissance in, not that we were going to grow all of our own food or produce all of our own energy, but it was like, how can we be partially engaged in all of the parts of our lives that make up our life. So that we know what it means to be alive and be connected to a place.

Hot Springs Farm

Harper was building on foundations laid previously. Pam Walatka, an Esalen Residential Fellow from 1967–69 who had just left the Peace Corps, planted an organic vegetable garden in at least half of the space north of the North Point House in 1968. She needed instant access to excellent lettuce where there were no local shops. This is because her boyfriend, well-known Esalen group leader Will Schutz, liked to throw spontaneous dinner parties. At that time, there was no Esalen garden; there was a big field of wild grass, and nobody was growing vegetables there. Growing several kinds of leaves, she remembers making chard soup for Abraham Maslow. Dick Horan, an early Esalen caretaker, talked to Pam, asking her about the patch, about the quality of the soil. She said, "It's fabulous! It's dark and crumbly — beautiful soil!" Horan asked whether she thought it was a good idea that they start growing there for the main lodge — and she said, "Sure, great idea!" Horan, who picked up the baton from Walatka's pioneering, describes how her garden was "a regular little homespun garden" with tomatoes, carrots, lettuce, beans, and squash — but that after a few years of his stewardship and the energy and commitment of Esalen's work scholars, it became this "garden of Eden... It was like a paradise for a gardener."

Still, beyond this garden, there was not a farm as such on the site where there is today. To its north was just a wilderness, except for a small plot of marijuana hidden in the bushes. In September 1979, Hot Springs Farm expanded the garden dramatically, with Steven Harper and Bruce Neeb clearing the land, taking out large boulders, and putting in the infrastructure and irrigation system. Harper picked up the baton passed from Walatka to Horan. He had come to Esalen as a work scholar, and part of the deal was that he worked in the garden — something he'd never done in the past.

> I had only done a little bit of gardening growing up... to me, it felt like, to have my assigned task at Esalen that I'm learning to garden, I had hit the jackpot. *And* I'm getting to go to these programs! Some people didn't like the work part

> of it. For me, it was, wow! And Esalen was bringing in, and I continued to later bring in, some of the top Biodynamic French intensive people that had been impacted by Alan Chadwick. Alan Chadwick was very influential and the style of the beds at Esalen were double-dug Biodynamic French intensive... We went and visited almost all of the Chadwick influenced gardens in the California area.

The Food Resource Project didn't just focus on the farm, but in a manner we are familiar with from permaculture and the New Alchemists, sought to integrate food production within the wider ecosystem:

> We were buying from fishermen that were fishing the kelp beds off of Esalen. And we thought we could do our own fishing. They're just using this small aluminium boat with a Johnson kick [an outboard engine] around the back, 20 horsepower, and they're going out in the kelp beds and coming back with 300 pounds of fish. Then we can get the fish guts from that, that's great compost. We can maybe gather some kelp, wash the salt water off the kelp, and create really good compost!

The idea too was to involve the wider Esalen community in the farm work:

> After Bruce and I did a lot of work on our own clearing, to make a border around there to create a little microclimate, we needed to plant different trees. So, to include the community in that, we had all the trees all set out around where we wanted them to go. Every department took off for two hours: office, the maintenance, laundry, cabins department, they all took off and came up to the farm. We dug holes and planted the trees where we had marked them to go.

The duo of Harper and Neeb also made a foray into humanure, deciding to

> build a composting toilet for the gazebo school teachers because they didn't have a toilet. We made this out of recycled materials. Bruce, Esalen's architect of the time, Leon Trice, and myself, we built the foundation and then recycled redwood from Santa Cruz from a house that had been torn down... We learnt pretty quickly, and that was inspired by Sim van der Ryn, who had written a book, *The Toilet Papers*. Van der Ryn had also created an institute called the Farallones Institute which had a lot of Alan Chadwick's core students in it who we invited down to Esalen to teach. I had also been up there to take workshops... But this book he called *The Toilet Papers* was how to build a composting toilet. And to give Sim Van der Ryn a place during Jerry Brown's first governorship, Brown made Van der Ryn the state architect. This is how forward-thinking California was in the '70s.

Grounding

One of the most important ideas to me that came out of the research around *Retreat* was — on the back of the disembodied and dematerialised culture of the era that went hand-in-hand with both LSD use and heavy meditation — the concept of "grounding". The Buddhist Teacher Jack Kornfield, author of *After the Ecstasy, the Laundry* (2000), has made the idea of grounding a central part of his teaching. In that book, he describes how a young karate student freaked out explosively after three months sitting in meditation. Part of the remedy? "We had him walk and work and later dig in the garden. In about three days he came down." Harper, whose website refers to his interest in Kornfield, sees grounding in relation to knowledge of the local ecology. Harper would lead wilderness groups into the environment around Esalen where they would live outdoors for five or six days. For the more receptive attendees he would weave in information about the natural history of the area. He says that

> At the end of that... they would often know more about Big Sur than staff that had lived in Esalen for fifteen years. Esalen could be very insular. And it could be very much on the intrapersonal end of things, maybe the interpersonal. But people had no idea about... the larger ecosystem: the meeting of the ocean, the ocean environment, even the redwoods... People were not able to identify a bay tree. Any seven-year-old in a culture would be able to tell you a hundred plants and what they were used for. And yet here, there's a disconnect. So, some of this, at least in my mind, was to help ground and connect all the wonderful, really deep inner work that was being done at the institute.

Talking to Harper, a scholar of the ways of the Indigenous Esalen peoples who once lived in the area, the very idea of what farming is, and can be, began to dissolve at its edges. This is the fecund interface which fascinates thinkers like Gary Snyder, David Holmgren, and Albert Bates:

> Even the hunter gatherers on this land, turns out, really weren't so much. They were *Hunter-Farmer-Gatherers*. They were clearly selecting and choosing which plants were in the ecosystem. Acorn was their primary food source — that was their staple. Every culture has a staple: corn, rice, beans. For the Native coastal people, that was acorns from the oak tree. So, they're collecting acorns; they're also pulling out the competitors to the acorns. They're planting, pushing acorns into the soil as they're going along. So, they're creating habitat.

Just like the Aboriginal peoples of Australia, they set fires for a number of reasons:

> For safety, if you burn fires frequently, you're not going to get one out of control which you can't outrun... It also puts a check on tick populations and rattlesnake populations. It increases low growth, which is better for rabbits and deer. So, if you're going to be hunting, it's actually creating more animal diversity that is possibly edible. You're selecting for plants that you can gather. So, if we take the model of 'pure wilderness', this wasn't it. Indigenous people were altering the landscape; they weren't just being 'benign', they were clearly engaged with the landscape, but with the knowledge of over thousands of years.

Harper has experimented sustaining himself on this kind of "farming":

> I did some experiments living for a whole week off Native foods. I was pre-harvesting acorns, because they were stored, they weren't available year-round... In a tidal pool, usually at new moon or full moon, when the tide is low, I could collect limpets and mussels, all these intertidal pool creatures that the Native people harvested. Right there is enough to make a living off of! Then I had acorn meal to crush and bleach out the tannins and cook. I then had the green leaves I could harvest of so many different annuals coming up... Any one of those three categories I could have made my way. Just from the inner tidal pool there's the brown algae, they're all edible... And of course, I could also fish... and *there's* an incredible protein source that for a week if I lived off it, and there was nothing else, that'd be fine.

Astonishingly, living like this in the high Rocky Mountains found Harper entering a different relational space:

> I would see more wild animals during that time than any other. And my belief is a couple of things. Firstly, for a whole month, I'd already been drinking the water

> of that mountain range... I'm just sweating out the smell of the water of the area. Secondly, I've eaten all my food that was brought in from outside and I'm no longer eating that. I'm only eating the food of the mountain: blueberries, wild onions, and the trout that I've caught fishing. Everything I'm sweating out is now the plants, animals, or fish of the area. I would walk up to animals, and they would just turn and look at me, where they would normally spring away.

His state of mind changed too, and he became "more sensitive, more relational... having a sensate feeling of threads of connection that were physiological".

Harper argues that these same threads of relation occur when growing vegetables in one's garden:

> I started to have a feeling inside myself, like I can tell this carrot screams when I pull it out. It's not without its own event of losing its life. Because I had been its companion, from putting in a seed, to weeding around it... and now I'm the one ending its life for my benefit. I had a harder time making an argument about vegan/vegetarian/carnivore. We can appreciate the taking of life from our human viewpoint more easily when we kill a rabbit, or we kill a chicken. We can see that it bleeds red, and it makes a noise... But I would make a case that all of the other ones, they also scream. It's just not in the same human way that they have the moment of their life coming to a close. And that's Gary Snyder's line.

In *The Practice of the Wild*, Snyder writes, "There is no death that is not somebody's food, no life that is not somebody's death." Harper reflects, "That idea is very humbling, and also for me it takes away a little of the judgement".

Albert Bates

On YouTube, in a seminar delivered for the Whole Village Ecovillage, Albert Bates starts his talk with the words "I'm Albert Bates, and you're not." It's a funny, offhand comment, but gives us some sense of Bates's confidence in his own status as a living legend. Bates is one of Tennessee commune the Farm's greatest figures. He is in the Farm's pantheon alongside Stephen Gaskin (the guru), Ina May Gaskin (Stephen's wife, who had a revolutionary role as a promotor and educator of natural childbirth), and Michael O'Gorman (the organic farmer and founder of the Farmer Veteran Coalition). Bates, who writes online for an audience of subscribers at *The Great Change* blog, is the author of many books and is well-known in ecological circles, where his thinking is frequently focused on the axis of agriculture. As he wrote in 2010, "Globally agriculture accounts for about 14 percent of the total greenhouse gas emission, including 47 percent of methane emissions and 84 percent of the nitrous oxides." Craig Sams was the first to draw my attention to Bates. The two share a passionate interest in biochar. Bates wrote one of the best books on the substance, *The Biochar Solution* (2010). He acknowledges a critique of biochar that has damaged its institutional acceptance, but carefully refutes it.

Bates and biochar

Biochar is simply charcoal. It's any material made from cellulose (straw, paper, cardboard, wood, hemp, etc.) that undergoes a process called pyrolysis, whereby it is burned in a low-oxygen environment and everything *apart* from the carbon is burnt away. Most typically, charcoal is burnt in normal oxygen-rich air for the purpose of cooking or heating. But with biochar, it can be either simply buried in soil as it is or treated with specially brewed compost teas to prime it and then buried. The best way of describing the resultant underground mass is that it's like a coral reef for microbes which collect safely in its pores. It also is an effective reservoir and conduit for water. Bates has become one of its most visible advocates and philosophers.

Bates's experiments with biochar began with a crude drum kiln. In it, he made charcoal at low temperatures (between 300 and 600 °C). He "left it to marinate in urine from a pissoir outside his own bedroom", then combined the result with compost and shovelled it into raised garden beds. He was delighted with the results, and so began his journey into the miracles of biochar. It is one of the most conspicuous fields wherein agricultural methods are at the forefront of the ecological dialogue. As a technology, it is incredibly potent. Speaking to renowned soil scientist Elaine Ingham, she confided to Bates that its potential to reverse climate change frightened her.

> "'Biochar is too powerful,' she told me. Once the industrial complex, with its credit markets, government incentives, and subsidies to farmers gets up and running, biochar could become a juggernaut, pushing the soil-atmosphere carbon balance into an overcorrection and ushering in a rapid-onset ice age. 'We don't need it,' she said. 'Just good soil-building practices could cancel out global CO2 emissions and balance the atmosphere of the whole planet.'"

The following gives us a glimpse of the potential strength of biochar. William Balée, professor of anthropology at Tulane University in New Orleans, a foremost expert on historical ecology, thinks that the Amazon Rainforest is a human artifact which occurred when, after the collapse of Amazonian civilisation following the disastrous colonisation from 1500, flora and fauna took advantage of the staggering soil fertility inherited from the now lost civilisation. A number of other theorists also believe this to be a prime factor in the "Little

Ice Age", as reforestation sequestered vast amounts of carbon dioxide.

Bates at the Farm

Bates involvement with the Farm commune in Tennessee, where he lives to this day, goes back to 1970. His mother bought him a copy of the *Monday Night Class* book when he was a law student. Standing outside in a queue for the all-night version of *War and Peace* at the Bleecker Street Cinema in the West Village, he saw twenty or thirty white buses round the corner. It was the Caravan. Bates ran over, and the hippies invited him to Sunday morning service the next day in Union Square Park. Falling asleep in the seven-hour movie during the Battle of Borodino, he awoke to an empty theatre and made his way over to the service. Missing it, as they were winding up, nevertheless, he got on board and chatted.

His next encounter came after reading in the *New York Post* of a Tennessee commune guru's arrest and imprisonment for growing marijuana. Connecting the dots to Stephen Gaskin (who had taken the rap for weed grown at the commune), he wrote to Gaskin in Lewis County Jail and volunteered his legal services. Bates told me:

> So next thing I knew, I had a loft in NoHo, which is a kind of bohemian area between Washington Square and Houston Street and Bowery. And so, I had this artist loft I was living in... it was a fifth floor walk-up. And I had a knock at the door, which is unusual, and I opened the door. And here's this guy with long hair and bib-top dungarees, and his wife who's got gingham on down to her ankles, and they're holding out a can of Old Beatnik pure Lewis County Sorghum Molasses — the first product of the Farm. And so, they said, 'Here. Here is your retainer.'

In 1972, his law degree complete, Bates decided to follow the Appalachian Trail, the 2,200-mile-long hiking trail that stretches from Maine in the north to Georgia in the south. Getting as far down as the Smoky Mountains in Tennessee, he decided it was a good moment to visit the Farm. It was 3 November and cold. Arriving, he saw a Scenicruiser twin-level coach being loaded up to take Gaskin and his rock band on tour. They were setting off on a three-month tour to promote the Farm Band's debut album. Gaskin appeared driving a Jeep, remembered Bates's letter to him in prison, told him to jump in, and gave him a fifteen-minute interview to ascertain whether it was going to be ok for him to stay for a while. They were gone till March. That winter, known as Wheatberry Winter, was rough. Accommodation and food at the Farm were very limited. Bates slept in a tent and drew on the experience of his hiking trail to hang in there. When Gaskin came back,

> I went up and spoke with him after a Sunday morning service. And I said, 'Well, I'm still here and I would actually like to stay. I'm kind of falling in love with the place. It's kind of what I've been dreaming of…' And he said, 'Sure!' And I said, 'Well is that all there is? Is there not, like, an initiation?' And he says, 'You thought that was easy?'

Bates was the first person I came across to give the maybe unfairly maligned Gaskin some props. He thinks it has something to do with his arriving and witnessing the Farm running on consensus for those initial three months:

> It was actually quite efficient and had nothing to do with Stephen, and then when Stephen came back, he didn't really assert any authority, he was just like, okay, I'm your preacher, I'm your poet, I'm the guy who stands up and speaks for you sometimes and when the press comes calling, but other than that, I'm just another guy living here. And so, it was

> kind of like going to live with Gary Snyder, right? You're not expecting to have him be your boss. That is, you're lucky to be in a community of several hundred people and he's a poet in residence.

I'm a fan of the *Monday Night Class* book, a transcription of Stephen's raps given to that congregation in the Haight-Ashbury. I think they capture some very "high" thinking quite magically. And Bates, a fearsome intellect and hugely erudite man, was grateful for Gaskin's presence as a poet-in-residence:

> As you mentioned, he has a certain kind of talent. And I would say it is that... he had a really excellent sense of the spoken word. I had the opportunity also to edit some of his writing and he's a really shitty writer for somebody who was an English teacher doing creative writing. I read his science fiction book in galleys, and it was awful! As a speaker, as a master of the spoken word, he was 'par excellence'. He was, you know, way up in the top level of the world class.

Bates and horses

When Bates arrived at the Farm, straight away he was assigned to Michael O'Gorman's farming crew.

> After seeing off the Scenicruiser to California, bye-bye. We all hopped into a truck and went out to the Sorghum fields to cut cane. And cutting sorghum was a lot like harvesting sugar cane with machetes. '*¡Venceremos!*' [meaning 'We shall overcome!' in Spanish, a reference to the Venceremos Brigade sent by Students for a Democratic Society to Cuba to cut ten million tons of sugar cane in 1970]. We're all out there, working side by side trying to cut the cane, and there was maybe fifty of us in this field, cutting with machetes. And I'd do that all day and load up these trucks. And so

> on, making sugar cane, which went back to the sorghum molasses.

Of their Sorghum experiment, O'Gorman writes, "We got together with the neighbours and planted a total of 140 acres of cane. We really didn't have any notion of how big 140 acres was, but when we'd tell old-timers how much we had growing, they'd usually either have a fit laughing or just shake their heads, amazed." The commune were always keen to find out what skills people had to offer. There was no call for Bates's legal skills, but

> it turns out my sport in high school was equestrian arts, dressage, three-day eventing, jumping, stadium jumping, high jumping, I went to the junior Olympics and competed... So, I was actually quite a good horseman and knew something about training horses. And I had been used to training horses on the lunge, but what they needed was draft horses. So, they had colts they were bringing up and were Belgian Colts, but they hadn't any training. So, I started working them on the long line. That was part of the farming crew — to work these draught workers into harness and so my skill as a horseman came into play.

In the book *Hey Beatnik!*, Dawn and the Horse Crew discuss their responsibilities charmingly in terms nobody should disagree with: "If you plan to keep horses, remember that you're getting involved with life and death karma." The animals are described thus: "Horses are intelligent, sensitive and telepathic..."

There were non-agricultural tasks that Bates undertook with the horses: collecting and delivering water and food. But, as was not uncommon with the rest of the back-to-the-land movement's shift away from petrol-powered machinery, they were also working the fields. "In season, we would be out. I would be behind on a riding cultivator, in the case of two horses, or walking behind a cultivator, in the case of one horse. And also, how I trained horses was that way." Bates elaborates:

> Not so much sowing seeds as weeding. You'd have this harrow that would go next to the plant down the row. And with the horse leading, you'd harrow as you go down the straight line. And then maybe you would plough a field later if you're clearing the field. If you were getting ready for seeding, usually, we would have a small tractor that would go through and straighten the rows, make it ready for seeding, and then the tractor would go through with a couple people sitting on the back, or seeders, shaking and dropping seed. But sometimes we would do that with horses. And the horses also did mowing. So, we had a big sickle bar mower where we'd cut hay, and we would do manure spreading. Particularly in the winter, we would take manure out of the barns, and we'd also muck out other people's barns for cow manure, horse manure, goat manure, or whatever we could get because our soils were very poor. We would bring back this manure from a twenty-mile radius of the farm. And then the horses, because they could get into the fields in winter where the tractors couldn't, they would haul this manure spreader through the fields spreading the manure. By spring, those fields were lush and ready for planting.

Bates and permaculture

We've already heard of the conflict surrounding Michael O'Gorman's decision not to exclusively follow organic principles at the Farm. It turns out Bates was a prime dissident. Bates describes himself as one of the early permaculturalists on the Farm, but it's fairer to him to describe him as using some of the permaculture techniques avant la lettre. As we have seen in our study of the discipline, that's not uncommon. He does however, as you would expect, express tremendous pride in having met and established a friendship with Bill Mollison.

The Farm (Gaskin and his organisation Plenty) had won the Right Livelihood award in Italy in 1980, and in 1981, Bill Mollison had won the award. Bates met Mollison at the tenth-anniversary gathering of Right Livelihood laureates in Italy in 1990. Mollison was in fact a fan of the Farm, which had had an influence on the design of the Tagari permaculture community which Mollison and others established in Stanley, Tasmania, in 1979.

> And so, Bill and I became friends at this ceremony and hung out a lot and sat together on bus rides around the Italian countryside... He was busy writing *Introduction to Permaculture* at that point in time and Reny [Mia Slay — Bill's wife] was doing some body illustration for that. So, that kind of embedded permaculture into me and I brought it back to the Farm and I think it was a vastly superior technique than anything we had practiced previously, which was very labour intensive... but not very smart.

Talking of O'Gorman's approach to the farming,

> I think that that inorganic side of Michael was also, in my view, kind of lazy. [Permaculture] was replacing a mechanistic, chemical, kind of technology. And taking the steps to design it well, from the get-go. And one of the things we did after I came back and started teaching permaculture on the farm, was we keylined everything. In early days, earlier than that, we had actually done some good work in terracing some of the more erosive fields. So, we had a road grader. And after that was done making most of our roads, we put it to work terracing the fields so that the runoff didn't go on to the Mississippi River eventually, so it would stay high in the landscape and become soil. And we get more of that with keylining using permaculture techniques.

Hand-in-hand with his exploration of biochar, the pores of which are most effective when primed with a microbial host, Bates worked up a knowledge of microbial teas. In *The Biochar Solution*, he describes how Elaine Ingham the soil scientist has been investigating how the Steiner soil preparations work. She discovered that the whirlpool whisked into the barrel was significant. If through the stirring process the microbial life from the buried cow's horn is mixed into oxygenated water, then the organisms ("the good guys", Ingham called them) and nutrients are transferred into the tea. The significance of this is that Bates promotes the idea that, contrary to what is commonly assumed, the Steiner preps do not function in the manner of homeopathic treatments. Homeopathy is a widely derided alternative medicine in which the potency of treatments is in inverse relation to the dilution of their active ingredient. Instead, the biodynamic preps are, he believes, what are known today as microbial teas, and work like probiotics do in the human body to promote healthy bacteria in plants and the soil. We are all familiar now with the idea that practically invisible bacteria can have significant effect — also the idea of faecal inoculations, whereby small samples can improve gut health in a host. Could the preps be working therefore as breeding source for healthy bacteria? He described to me how on the Farm they would

> [use] microbial teas like effective microorganisms, blending, and brewing our own compost teas after I brought Elaine Ingham to the Farm to teach. She gave a microscope course and taught us all about that. We created our own system where we owned a keyline plough and a thousand-gallon-batch compost tea brewer. We did all of the horse pastures, all the major fields were redone, and I think if we had known that, if we'd done that back in the '70s, we never would have needed to get into chemical salts and all of that. We didn't know what Elaine Ingham teaches. We didn't understand the microsphere. We didn't understand the complex biology

> of the soil food web. You know, there's a whole thing there. We were destroying biology by adding chemical fertiliser and we didn't need to be doing that. We didn't need to be creating a dependence of the plants on chemicals instead of on the biology of the system, and now we know better. So, we're not doing that anymore. Haven't done it for many years. And I think that everything we're doing is far more productive than what we did in the early years.

When I inquired at the Farm's reception, the word came back that all growing had stopped in 1983, when O'Gorman left. But Bates says there's plenty of activity:

> I think every household here gardens... When we started in the 1990s, we acquired the mushroom business, The Mushroompeople. And we started selling shiitake log kits and oysters. And maitake, and enokitake and matsutake and all the other Japanese forest mushrooms. And people on the farm, said, 'What's that?' And so, they all started getting kits and they all started their own oak log collections in some shady place out in the garden or next to the shed. And now everybody's got shiitake in season and dries it for the other seasons. And so, everybody's got mushrooms all the time... Everybody is still growing food. There are houses that are deep in the forest, and it's very difficult to grow well there, so their gardens are in a community garden, which is out in the open field. There's a fenced-in area, and just this year it doubled in size from the previous years. I think COVID was one impetus, where more people had more time to garden. But it's still expanding, and I think everybody gardens. Not everybody gardens in their own home, because they can't, but they do garden. Like, they'll have a shared space in some clearing that's a neighbourhood space.

The only deterrent is that they are, as he puts it, in a "food shed", the opposite of the urban "food deserts" with incredible fresh produce all around them. "There's 40,000 Amish in this state, and in any direction that you care to bicycle, you're going to run into an Amish farm, and they are horse-drawn entirely and spreading the manure on the fields rather than buying fertiliser and for all intents and purposes farming biodynamically..."

Bates on the future

Bates thinks a lot about the future. To quote him in full:

> We've got to the point now where we've over-stressed everything, we have to get back to something that's much more harmonious with nature. What does that look like on a planet of eight billion people? And can you actually sustain a population of ten or twelve billion people? On something resembling Indigenous methods? And that's, I think, a challenge and a frontier that we're working at. A lot of what I'm working on and studying and writing about these days is tackling that now from two directions. One is bringing population down in a graceful way, and I think that it's happening naturally, you can read it's happening, at least in the industrial world. It's not so much in the 'underdeveloping' world, but more in the 'overdeveloped' world, it is starting to come down now. And the other half of that is providing an adequate food supply. And I'm not averse to lab-grown meat analogue. I'm not averse to vertical farming in skyscrapers. These kinds of things, you know, *maybe* they'll provide something for all those people that we need to take care of while we bring the population down. On the other hand, it's like carbon training, it's not the end goal. It's a way to help bootstrap and get us through... The end goal is to switch over to a system that mainly involves trees and perennials. So, the planet as a whole had six trillion trees on it after the last ice age, maybe ten thousand years ago after the deglaciation. Now,

we're down to one to two trillion trees. There are a few initiatives out there... Maybe, we'll get to three trillion. Well, you need to put back all six trillion of those trees. So, how do you do that? And also feed a lot of people. Well, if as they've calculated it's available without disturbing farmland, without disturbing parks and recreation, and cities and so fine, there's that. But then also, let's think about food trees in the cities, putting food trees into the silvoculture and using tree crops, much more than we use now, because of the climate benefits, and the various other ecosystem recovery methods, biodiversity, and everything else.

So, nut trees, like acorns, a vast crop here in the Farm, we don't use it at all. And yet acorns were a major food source for the Native peoples here before the white people arrived. And there are lots of other plants we can point to that are indigenous here. Nut crops is one of them, water crops is another. There are lots of water plants that we don't use. We don't even know how to use them anymore, but they were Native food plants. Wild rice of various kinds and things like azolla. And so, we could actually be feeding ourselves much more through wildcrafting than we do today. And I think that's a whole frontier; as big a frontier, if not bigger, than fake meat.

New Age odour

As we are talking, I can't help but notice behind Bates a big picture of the Buddha. Bates points out another picture, its neighbour on the wall: "'Saint Greta', Greta Thunberg, and I got her in the picture that was taken with a silver nitrate camera in the Standing Rock Reservation when she was there with the water keepers." Next is a "Shipibo hand-woven tapestry, which is woven from the people in the Peruvian Amazon, near

Iquitos, where I did a ten-day ayahuasca retreat with Shipibo shamans." Of that trip, Bates told me:

> In that experience, my question, what I was asking the plant, was 'What is the remedy for our climate catastrophe? What could we be doing to remedy this situation that we find ourselves in?' I never got an answer. I got a lot of other interesting hallucinations, but did not get an answer to that question. But as the years went by following that, I would continuously have people come to me with pieces of the solution. And often as not, they had also had ayahuasca experiences. So, you can place that in any kind of context you want... but in actuality the plant was giving me the answer that I had wanted.

Bates tends to keep this stuff to himself.

> I find that there is a certain, I don't know, 'odour' to spirituality...[laughs]. That's a pity, but it happens. I've been to Findhorn many times, I'm a Findhorn fellow, and I was just on a call with them about their crisis and reorganisation. I totally appreciate it and listen to them but when a Findhorn person speaks for any length of time, they tend to go off into an airy-fairy vocabulary that is not my thing.

In recent years, his taste and his interests in this field has changed. He mentions books which draw on Indigenous wisdom: the teachings of the Native American Kondiaronk of Quebec that found their way into David Graeber and David Wengrow's *The Dawn of Everything* (2021); *Sand Talk: How Indigenous Thinking Can Save the World* (2019), by Tyson Yunkaporta; and *Braiding Sweetgrass: Indigenous Wisdom, Scientific Knowledge and the Teachings of Plants* (2013), by Robin Wall Kimmerer. "I think that kind of stuff appeals to me more now than the secret yogas of Tibet or any of the traditional texts."

Given that it absorbed so much of my energy researching it, I had hoped to visit the Farm in Tennessee. That way I would have been able to interview Bates in the house he's built there. However, in contact with Douglas Stevenson, the commune's historian, who also lives on site, I didn't get the encouraging vibes I had from everyone else I travelled to. In his book *Out to Change the World*, Stevenson wrote of the 1980s:

> Because of its reputation, The Farm still had a steady flow of visitors, but what had once been part of the fun, showing off our community, became a burden. Most who came to check us out were disappointed not to find the legendary commune brimming with hippies, and these visitors were often critical of the changes. They wanted to see endless rows of crops, not abandoned fields lost in weeds. Farm folks began to avoid interaction. These commune tourists had no clue about the struggles that all of us who stayed were going through just to keep the farm alive.

I would expect the same sentiment probably applies to a significant extent to visitors today. For my last book, *Retreat*, I made the effort to travel and conduct interviews as far afield as California, India, Switzerland, and Japan. The story demanded it. In writing a book on an ecological subject, it didn't seem right to burn up thousands of air miles. How appropriate would it have been to fly to Australia to talk to David Holmgren? I make no apologies for my West Coast US trip in which, in only a week, I conducted three interviews and visited seven significant sites. As Holmgren says, "Long-distance and overseas travel is for long-stay, multipurpose visits." But beyond that journey to New England, it was fortunate that, barring Australia, every other necessary interview and visit was within the British Isles.

The Unabomber

In *The Greening of America* Charles Reich described the back-to-the-landers as being at war "with the corporate state", they wished to free themselves from "the domination of technology". In almost every case it seems that war was waged peacefully. Ted Kaczynski (1942–2023), known as the Unabomber, was a notable exception. Between the years of 1978 and 1995, he was responsible for sixteen package bombs, seriously injuring twenty-three people and killing three.

Kaczynski was a maths prodigy with a difficult childhood. Under pressure from his parents, he attended Harvard University at the age of sixteen on a scholarship. Kaczynski did not, as far as the record shows, take LSD at Harvard *or ever*, but it has become a commonly repeated myth that he did. A "straight arrow", he didn't take *any* drugs or even drink. The idea that he did stems from the fact that, as a student at Harvard, he was the victim of cruel, pointless, and illegal psychological tests at the hands of the creepy and imperious Professor Henry Murray. Murray (1893–1988) — who is famous for the Thematic Apperception Test, used for many years in personality profiling — had, at the same time been turned on to acid by Timothy Leary. Murray only used LSD briefly, but he supervised Leary's Harvard trials with it.

Kaczynski rose within academia to become an acting assistant professor at the University of California, Berkeley. Alston Chase, his biographer, believes that the combination of his humiliation at Murray's hands at Harvard, his disastrous childhood dominated by his parent's ambitions for him, and the overwhelmingly nihilistic "Gen. Ed curriculum", an infamous requirement of the Ivy League Universities' education, made him drop out in 1969, head back to the land, and plan his revenge on industrial society.

In an interview with Anarchist paper *Blackfoot Valley Dispatch*, Kaczynski describes finding the land:

> Not knowing what else to do, I just took off toward the west on Highway 200, which at the time I think was called Highway 20, to see what I could see. As I passed through Lincoln I saw a little cabin, almost just a kiosk by the side of the road, with a sign advertising real estate. I stopped and asked the realtor, an old man named Ray Jensen, whether he could show me a secluded plot of land. He showed me a place up Stemple Pass Road. I liked it. I took my brother to see it and he liked it too, so we bought it. We paid $2,100 in cash — in twenty dollar bills — to the owner, Cliff Gehring, Senior.

Like other back-to-the-landers of the era, Kaczynski threw himself into rustic life. But unlike most, he pursued his primitivism scientifically, carrying it to extremes. He read books on woodcraft, botany, organic chemistry; on poison antidotes, nutrition, pesticides, Indian customs, rifle shooting, and first aid; on wilderness medicine, seeds, controlling weeds, and identifying trees, shrubs, animal tracks, mushrooms, and edible and poisonous plants, as well as both wildflowers and non-flowering plants.

Kaczynski would eat wild animals, mainly rabbit, but also deer, elk, hare, grouse and porcupines, and he would forage berries and wild roots. But he also had a vegetable garden. "In my garden I grew potatoes, parsnips, beets, onions, two kinds of carrots, spinach, radishes, broccoli, and on occasion orache, Jerusalem artichoke, and turnips. I would dry wild greens and garden vegetables, and sometimes berries, for use in the winter."

One of Kaczynski's only friends was an elderly lady, Irene Preston. He would drop by to see her and bring her turnips or carrots he had grown. Letters from Kaczynski to her related in a light-hearted way his struggle with "pesky rabbits" laying siege to his garden. Visiting Kaczynski's cabin, built as an "exact replica" of Henry Thoreau's, his biographer Alston Chase noticed a spacious root cellar, which FBI agents had found contained sacks of potatoes, carrots, and other vegetables, and where "woven wire around what had once been a vegetable garden lay badly trampled by night animals".

When asked by the *Blackfoot Valley Dispatch* whether he was self-sufficient, Kaczynski replied,

> By no means wholly self-sufficient. I needed store-bought staples such as flour, rice, rolled oats, and cooking oil. I bought most of my clothing, though I also made some. Originally, complete self-sufficiency was a goal that I wanted to attain eventually, but with the shrinking of the wild country and the crowding-in of people around me, I got to feeling that there wasn't any point in it anymore, and my interests turned in other directions.

However, he notes,

> My last winter in Montana, 1995–1996, I was hard up. But when you have to dispense with the things that the system provides, it's surprising how well you can do by improvising on your own. I had no commercial fruits or vegetables, whether fresh, dried, or canned, but I had plenty of my own dried vegetables. I had some dried black currants and rhubarb, and I had squirrels and rabbits for meat. The commercial stuff I had was just flour — whole wheat and white — cooking oil, sugar, and I think I had a scanty supply of rice.

The Unabomber Manifesto

Kaczynski proved to be extremely difficult for the FBI to catch. But in 1995, with the vague promise of suspending his activities if it was published, he submitted a 35,000-word manifesto to media outlets. UCLA Professor James Q. Wilson would praise the manifesto in the *New York Times*, saying that it was "subtle and carefully developed, lacking anything even faintly resembling the wild claims or irrational speculation that a lunatic might produce... If it is the work of a madman, then the writings of many political philosophers — Jean Jacques Rosseau, Tom Paine, Karl Marx — are scarcely more sane." *The Oregonian* newspaper observed of the *Washington Post*'s publication of the manifesto as a fifty-six-page supplement that "nobody actually read it".

For all his supposedly sanctified motivation, Kaczynski doesn't come across as either a compassionate person or someone who cares about the environment. He says in the manifesto, "Since there are well-developed environmental and wilderness movements, we have written very little about environmental degradation or the destruction of wild nature, even though we consider these to be wildly important". This squares with a note the FBI found at his cabin: "I don't even believe in the cult of nature-worshippers or wilderness-worshippers (I am perfectly ready to litter in parts of the woods that are of no use to me...)" His real target was industrial society:

> The degree of crowding that exists today and the isolation of man from nature are consequences of technological progress. All pre-industrial societies were predominantly rural. The Industrial Revolution vastly increased the size of cities and the proportion of the population that lives in them, and modern agricultural technology has made it possible for the Earth to support a far denser population than it ever did before.

This was not always the case: "Ancient cultures, that for hundreds or thousands of years gave people a satisfactory relationship with each other and with their environment, have been shattered by contact with industrial society, and the result has been a whole catalog of economic, environmental, social and psychological problems."

Kaczynski's ideas

Among the many books in Kaczynski's library, there are none on growing — prompting the thought that he must have read Rodale in the library. A fully itemised list can be found, but it includes such titles familiar to the counterculture as Louise Dickinson Rich's *We Took to the Woods* (1942), Edward Abbey's *The Monkey Wrench Gang* (1975), Herman Hesse's *Siddhartha* (1951), W. Somerset Maugham's *The Razor's Edge* (1944), Sigmund Freud's *Civilization and its Discontents* (1930), and Henry David Thoreau's *Walden* (1854). From among them, Chase points to the influence upon Kaczynski of Colin Wilson's *The Outsider* (1956), Paul Goodman's *Growing Up Absurd* (1956), Bill McKibben's bestselling *The End of Nature* (1989), E.F. Schumacher's *Small is Beautiful* (1973), and Leopold Kohr's *The Breakdown of Nations* (1957). The last, Kohr, an Austrian economist who had preached the values of smallness, was, like Schumacher, a close ally of John Seymour.

Kaczynski owned and had read Theodore Roszak's critique of industrial society, *Where the Wasteland Ends* (1972). At one point, when warning against science's reductionist methodology, Roszak names the behavioural psychologist Professor James V. McConnell of the University of Michigan, who claimed that "the day has come when we can combine sensory deprivation with drugs, hypnosis and astute manipulation of reward and punishment to gain absolute control over an individual's behaviour". As a result of this inclusion, thirteen years later in November 1985, Professor McConnell received one of Kaczynski's packages. The device injured McConnell and his teaching assistant, Nicklaus Suino.

BLACK FARMING

Soul Fire Farm

I set off from Eliot Coleman's farm at 1am. I loaded my bags into the car and drove through Maine in the darkness and mist. I ate pancakes and maple syrup in a diner in Vermont and arrived at Soul Fire Farm in upstate New York at 11am, where I slept in the car park till the afternoon. Named after the Lee Perry song "Soul Fire", the seventy-two acre farm is owned and was set up in 2010 by the charismatic young Black woman Leah Penniman. She grew up one of three Black Kreyol children in a conservative rural White town in the 1980s. Her initial interest in the ecology as a child channelled into a passion for vegetable farming that led her to study agriculture with Indigenous peasant farmers in Haiti and West Africa. However, the farm ask that the enterprise of the whole collective — not just Leah and her sister Naima — be celebrated and that their efforts be situated within the broader context of Black farming. This group spent four years building up a foot of topsoil on land which had been heavily logged and, before their intervention, had a failing grade. Penniman herself was on a sabbatical but did appear at one point, greeted us, and then cheerfully stomped across the top pasture hollering to her team. Our tour hosts were the patient and expert Maya and Danielle.

In one respect, this was an example of a well-managed organic CSA. However, there were a number of the farm's features that hinted at the collective's ancestral legacy: there is a Jaden Lakou, a creole-style home garden with a high level of plant diversity; raised beds are kept in the fashion of the Ovambo people of Namibia, and they keep Nubian goats. It has been convincingly argued that the CSA model itself in North America was pioneered by the Black Tuskegee University professor Booker T. Whatley. Whatley devised a "Clientele Membership Club" and pick-your-own system in his "Whatley Diversified Plan for Small Farms", which was widely adopted. From a strictly business perspective, Whatley was also an advocate of organic agriculture's low inputs. Soul Fire Farm used to provide one hundred boxes of produce to the local area, but this is now streamlined to twenty-three, as today, they organise themselves more as an educational centre providing workshops, and their focus pivots more towards ecology. Penniman has now written two notable books: *Farming While Black: Soul Fire Farm's Practical Guide to Decolonising Land, Food, and Agriculture* (2018) and *Black Earth Wisdom* (2023).

It's unlikely that Soul Fire Farm would see itself as belonging to the counterculture. Just as, in relation to wellness, the Black lesbian feminist socialist Audrey Lorde, creator of the idea of "self-care" and author of *The Cancer Journals* (1980) and *A Burst of Light* (1988), would not have understood *her* activity as countercultural. However, there are intersections which demand attention. Furthermore, the counterculture's relation to Black culture is worthy of examination.

White communes

The issue of racial diversity in the back-to-the-land movement was, owing to the overwhelming majority of participants being White, not something that was often commented on. There are Black people associated with the movement — Greg Watson of New Alchemy Institute, or Ira Wallace of the Twin Oaks commune — however, they are few and far between. In fact, historians of the movement have described it as relating, almost as an extension, to the phenomenon of "White flight", whereby White Americans migrated from the US's inner cities to the suburbs. The back-to-the-land counterculturalists, (goes the argument) travelled a little further, that's all… In his thesis *The Countercultural Back-to-the-Land Movement* the academic Jonathan A. Bowdler condemns the movement, as it "primarily served the racial and class interests of the participants", and elsewhere takes Scott Nearing to task: "Nearing believed urban degeneration was particularly detrimental to white Western-European families because wage labor undercut women's eugenic roles as mothers and homemakers."

In their book *Continuing The Good Life*, the Nearings themselves comment of the profile of their visitors. "We do not remember having one black youngster come…" One of the most interesting descriptions of the situation plays out in the pages of Ramón Sender Barayón's collection of material about Morning Star Ranch, *Home Free Home*. Victoria describes how

> Nina Simone came up to visit Lou [Gottlieb], a marvelous person with a great aura and dignity. She walked around the land with him before returning to his studio to play the piano and sing. 'Lou, there aren't any black people here,' she said. 'Well, what can I do?' he answered. 'I want them to come, but we don't invite people. They just show up.'

Sender picks up the thread later in the book: "Some black brothers finally started showing up including Junior, Jason, Mystery, and Jimmy Small, amongst others". There were, however, problems which Sender Barayón, rightly or wrongly, says were caused by the Black members of the community: "The racial tensions at Morning Star were reflections of a general problem: many blacks who took acid bummed out. They had been under the thumb of the white man for so long that LSD only released bitterness and negative feelings." While there's no reflection on the topic by Stephen Gaskin in the original edition of *Monday Night Class*, in the 2005 edition which features commentary by him, Gaskin remarks, "I have come to realize how fortunate I have been to be born in this country and in the 20th century and to middle-class parents, as a male, and tall, and with a deep voice, and white."

There are very few discussions around race on the record, but as with the lessons Sir Albert Howard or Bill Mollison learnt from native peoples, diversity could offer glimpses of other ways of life. Alicia Bay Laurel described to me how living at Shepherds Ranch forced her to adapt:

> And I didn't know how to clean because I came from a wealthy family who had a maid. So, I had to learn how to clean a house. But all of it just enchanted me, learning how to do these things, and being independent of that big, horrible reality that my parents were so beholden to. The whole idea that I should get a university degree and then get a job that would pay a lot of money. And then I could live the same lifestyle that my parents lived in the big house with the brown person doing all the things that they didn't want to do... I idolised that brown person. She was an older woman from Mexico, and she was a curandera. She was wise in the ways of herbs, and she grew her own herbs in our backyard and cured herself of whatever illnesses she had... She was an old woman by the time I was born, but I adored her. So, I wanted to plant things, I wanted to grow things... I wanted to learn about herbs. I was too young to learn about herbs by the time that she was sent back to Mexico, when I was about five or six, because they wanted to have somebody younger and more energetic, which they got.

Still, as dramatised in the TV series of Alex Haley's *Roots* (1977), Black culture sought to build bridges to the back-to-the-land counterculture. In the course of the American Civil War, we meet a destitute White couple who have migrated from South Carolina to its north. "Old" George Johnson (a young man with long hair) and his wife Martha (clad in a gingham floral dress) are instantly recognisable as representing hippies.

Adopted by the Black community, "Old" George is tasked with overseeing the slaves on the plantation but, in a nod to the counterculture's higher ethics, has no stomach for the cruelty that the job requires of him. In due course, the young White man is instrumental in saving the central character Tom's life from a whipping at the hands of Evan Brent, and finally the couple travel with the community to their new land in Tennessee.

Ultimately, it is easy to be too cynical about the validity of the predominantly White and middle-class counterculture. That this upheaval was happening to a relatively narrow section of society, one which lacked racial diversity, didn't necessarily detract from its positive impact on this issue. The Black Centre for Contemporary Culture Studies theorist Stuart Hall cosigned the essay "Subcultures, cultures and class", which argued of countercultural opposition's impact on the White middle classes that

> at the simplest level their emergence marked the failure of the dominant culture to win over the attachment of a sector of its 'brightest and best'. The disaffiliation from the goals, structures and institutions of 'straight society' was far-reaching. Here, the countercultures provided, at the very least, that social and cultural breathing-space — a hiatus in the reproduction of cultural relations — in which a deeper disaffiliation was hatched. It cracked the mould of the dominant culture.

Karen Washington

Karen Washington is an elder stateswoman to today's young Black farmers. Leah Penniman asked her to write an introduction to her book *Farming While Black*. Washington is a pioneer of the movement, setting up the "Garden of Happiness" on an abandoned lot in the Bronx in 1988. In 2010, she was one of the co-founders of the Black Urban

Growers organisation. Most recently, in 2014, as a grower, she co-founded the organic Rise and Root Farm in Chester, New York. It's a cultural faux pas to automatically connect Black people to urban music, basketball, or athletics — indeed that's one of the stereotypes that Black farming works against. However, I was intrigued, and it was important to my central thesis, whether Washington thought there was a connection to the counterculture. Debate rages about the start and end point of the "true" counterculture. In his book *Counterculture Through the Ages: From Abraham to Acid House* (2004), Ken Goffman frames it as an almost perennial current. This, I think, stretches its boundaries too far. However, the argument for its persistence from the mid-fifties is at least plausible until the total culture of early hip-hop. As Black writer Nelson George, author of *Hip Hop America* (2005) commented, "For those looking for manifestations of rebellion, for some last gasp of public defiance before the '60s spirit completely died, graffiti fit the bill."

The question, the last I asked, was whether graffiti related to what she was doing, taking over abandoned lots in the Bronx:

> They were considered rebellious. And back in the day we weren't considered gardeners. We were considered more 'guerrilla gardeners'. So, there was a parallel between both, because we were resisters. We're fighting, we were fighting against the establishment that was preventing us to say what we had to do. They wanted to silence us as we fought for the right to grow food. We fought for the right to show some sort of self-expression, and the status quo tried to drown us out. So, people with artistic talent did graffiti on walls on subway cars on buildings and people in the inner city, started taking abandoned lots and started growing flowers and food and started to take over. And in both cases during that time of the 1970s and '80s, the cities were going through financial crisis. They had a lot on their hands and

> there was a lot of turmoil going on, especially in New York City, where I'm from. And so, people just used ways to show their own disagreement, their own way of self-expression when people in government did not hear them. People, when people with power did not hear what we were trying to do, we took matters into our own hands. As a way of self-expression. So, the artists did graffiti and the gardeners commandeered lots and started planting stuff. We were both rebels in our own way.

Slavery

In some respects, it seems like Black farming in the US was a rising tide suppressed by perceptions of farming held by the Black community. Black Panther leader Eldridge Cleaver said that during slavery, "black people learned to hate the land", but also insisted that among Black people there lay "a deep land hunger". Washington puts it thus:

> I would say I came aware of it really as an adult, you know, growing up. Farming and just being part of nature was never talked about at home or at school. Farming was always considered slave work and I think as I got more involved in growing food and starting to peel away the falsehoods and listening to people speak and doing a lot of research to find out the truth of the matter of why, as African Americans, we were brought here. And the truth of the matter here was that we were brought here because of our knowledge of agriculture. The colonists could never survive, especially when they came along the [South Carolina] Lowcountry. They could never survive in the swampy climate and so, that sort of just changed my whole viewpoint of my ancestors and how I've learnt to appreciate the fact that they went through so much, they travelled so many miles. To an unknown territory in an unknown land so that I can live. I'm living my life because of the sacrifices that they made,

> but also understanding the rich history and legacy that they left behind. And what slavery did and what continues to be done today is to erase or minimise the impact of African Americans or African culture.

Howard Zinn, in his classic *A People's History of the United States* (1980), gives a background context:

> Everything in the experience of the first white settlers acted as a pressure for the enslavement of blacks. The Virginians of 1619 were desperate for labor, to grow enough food to stay alive. Among them were survivors from the winter of 1609–1610, the 'starving time,' when, crazed for want of food, they roamed the woods for nuts and berries, dug up graves to eat the corpses, and died in batches until five hundred colonists were reduced to sixty.

It's estimated that twelve million people were forcibly deported from Africa. Of that figure, at least ten million made it to the New World alive. Food provision for each stage of the triangle trade across the Atlantic was critically important. In their botanical history of the contributions made by Africans brought to the New World by the slave trade, *In The Shadow of Slavery* (2009), Judith Carney and Richard Rosomoff go into the tragic details. The success of the enterprise rested on keeping several hundred people alive for eighty days on the open ocean. As a result, slavers wanting to cut a corner would fill the boat with inedible rice still in its hull, its hard protective covering, then command the female slaves on the ship to remove these hulls by milling. This milled rice was then fed to the slaves. In an unforeseen twist of fate, rice that is suitable for planting must be still in its hull. There are many accounts of the Middle Passage wherein grains of unmilled rice are tucked into children's hair so that they might be able to grow it in the New World for sustenance, sometimes as parting endowments from mothers they would never see again.

Many African crops found their way to the New World. Like rice, taro was used as food on the slave ships, and the unused root stock, perhaps after a couple of months beginning to sprout, is likely to have been "brought" from the ships. The same was true of the kola nut, the peanut, the rootstock of plantain, millet, sorghum, the black-eyed pea, okra, sesame, guinea squash, etc. Other tubers like plantain and yam were ideally suited for the slaves to grow as their own food as they require little cultivation, enjoy high yields, and are not time-consuming to cook.

Not only did they bring their crops but also centuries of agricultural expertise in similar climates. This expertise was never appreciated. Washington points out:

> White settlers and colonists, whatever sort of invention, or whatever sort of application that my ancestors used, or indigenous people used, it was co-opted. You have to understand that, back in the day, we weren't considered human, we were considered more property. So, if we came here with skills, or ideas, no matter what, those skills and those ideas were taken away and then used for Whites to say they were the ones that invented it, or discovered it.

It is very striking that in what is now the Virgin Isles at St Croix, the soil was neither turned by a plough nor dug with a spade, but that the African farmers' own preference of light surface tillage with the hoe was the chosen technique. Carney and Rosomoff, whom we are following here, state that "the European preference for plow agriculture was not widely employed on plantations. The African method was instead predominant". Plantation owners themselves knew nothing about growing in the tropics but were quick to take credit for the slaves' ingenuity.

As Washington has pointed out of the South Carolina Lowcountry, White settlers tried and failed to grow regular European crops, before eventually succeeding in three commodities, cattle, rice, and cowpeas — the last two both brought there and cultivated by Africans. In the same manner, sesame graduated from the slaves' gardens to a main crop. Originally, to be given a plot of land for their own cultivation was a "privilege". But over time it became compulsory, as plantation owners wised up to its merciless efficiency, and slaves became responsible for growing all their food. These "yam grounds" eventually disappeared as the insatiable demand for sugar plantations ate up every inch of square space, and provision plantations grew up to feed the captive slaves.

Agricultural expertise was not just restricted to crops. African food animals and their bedding aboard the ships were seed vectors for the highly nutritive African Guinea grass so prized for grazing. The Senegambian Fula tribe's technique of penning all animals after dark and tethering animals at a stake so as to focus manure and prevent animals from wandering into cultivated areas were also noticed by Europeans. The cowboys of the mid-sixteenth-century Hispaniola estates were from the Wolof, Fula, and Manding tribes of West Africa.

Washington sees this same process of cultural appropriation alive in a lot of agriculture today:

> You know it went from organic agriculture, now to regenerative agriculture. At one time, it was biodynamic agriculture, it was permaculture. It was all these things that again have really short-changed the work of indigenous slaves, Africans, that brought their history and brought their knowledge of agriculture. So again, you have people with power and privilege that are undermining the whole construct of agriculture, what it was built on. And so, what we're trying to do is just making sure that the voices and the knowledge of people who have not been given that, are brought to the forefront. For years I've gone to conferences and workshops... you don't understand, to be able to go to an organic conference, a biodynamic conference, a

> permaculture conference, and you sit in a sea of Whiteness, and you sit there, and everything is related around the Whiteness concept, and never, never, does one stop to say, wait a second, what about Indigenous people? What about people of colour that have been here doing the work? Or for millions and millions of years and never giving that recognition. They don't even give recognition to George Washington Carver.

George Washington Carver

Black American farmers today give respect to figures like the CSA pioneer Booker T. Whatley; to Harriet Tubman, the abolitionist who worked land in Cayuga County; and to the civil rights icon Fannie Lou Hamer, who set up the Freedom Farm Cooperative. However, George Washington Carver is certainly the most widely known Black American agriculturalist. His cosmic leanings mean that he was familiar to the countercultural generation, as he appears in *The Secret Life of Plants*. Carver is approvingly covered in the chapter "The Wizard of Tuskegee". Tompkins and Bird quote him: "Through the flower, I talk to the infinite, which is only a silent force."

Carver was born into slavery around 1865. From a very young age, when he ran a plant hospital in the woods and local people delivered their suffering plants to him, he had a gift for horticulture. Abandoning a brilliant career as a faculty member at Iowa State College, he left to join the de facto US Black community's leader, Booker T. Washington, at the foundation of the Tuskegee Institute in Alabama. Here, understanding the leguminous value of the peanut and its ability to regenerate the soil, he was instrumental in encouraging its growth as a crop. Not just that, but, as a scientist, he worked in the laboratory to devise a dazzling array of uses for it, ranging from food and drinks to medicine and cosmetics, and from dyes to detergents.

From whence this knowledge? Carver describes how he asked the Almighty Lord what the universe was made for. He received the advice to ask for something "more your size, little man". Quickly, the question was whittled down to why the peanut was made, upon which "the Great creator taught me to take the peanut apart and put it together again. And out of the process have come forth all these products". He described himself as not being among the class of scientists "to whom the world is merely the result of chemical forces or material electrons".

Hugging trees

Unlike Carver, a Christian, Washington does not place any faith in organised religion:

> You know what, I grew up as a Catholic, [laughs] God help me! And for me, it's just being in a place where I can feel the essence of being with the universe... I don't know who God is, but I pray to God. I pray to the spirit. I pray to the ancestors. I listen to the wind. I hug trees. And so, for me, that's my interpretation of my own spiritual content. I sit, and I feel the wind and I can feel the spirit of the wind. I look at the mountains, and I can feel the energy that comes from the mountains. I sit, and I just talk to the universe. I talk to my ancestors, whose spirit I can feel around me. I can't name it, but I can feel it... You know, something has guided me to where I am now. It didn't happen overnight. I think through my life, I've been guided to find this sort of mission that I'm on — to be very outspoken and to be an example for others to follow.

Washington herself has a background in physical therapy and sees the therapeutic value of growing:

I had a conversation with a person the other day because I got a letter from a person that was incarcerated. I've been in prisons, and I see the prisons that have farming and gardening projects, it changes their way of relating to something, to plants, to something that's living. You are cooped up, and some of them are lifers, so you'll never get a chance to go out. You never have any other sort of contact besides the people that are already incarcerated. So how do you get close to something that's living? And so, a lot of them turn towards gardening and find ways of restitution by growing something. Maybe they were incarcerated because something very bad happened. So then how do you correct that? By offering and finding love and gentleness in growing plants or flowers. And so, I've seen how gardening has changed people, is therapeutic for a lot of people. It helps a lot of people when it comes to stress. It has a calming effect, decreases anxiety. For me, I remember being very, very frightened about growing on a larger scale and again, those negative voices enter my head about, 'Why am I doing this? Why am I farming? Is farming slave work?' And I said, the only way I am going to conquer my fear is to go to the soil and put my hands in it, and that's what I did. I went to the soil, and I stuck both my hands in that soil. Because I wanted to feel that instant connection of belonging, and I did. And so, I know the effects of gardening. And I know the effects that it has on human beings. Because you are connected with another living being, which is a plant or tree or a flower. So, there's definitely some sort of reciprocity that's there.

Land ownership

One of the unwritten aspects of our story is land ownership. Here are some figures from Professor Pete Daniel's *Dispossession: Discrimination Against African American Farmers in the Age of Civil Rights* (2013):

> In 1910, African Americans held title to some 16 million acres of farmland, and by 1920 there were 925,000 black farms... after peaking in these decades... the trajectory of black farmers plunged downward. In a larger sense there was an enormous decline among all farmers mid-century. Between 1940 and 1969, the rural transformation, fueled largely by machines and chemicals and directed by the USDA, pushed some 3.4 million farmers and their families off the land, including nearly 600,000 African Americans. From 1959 to 1969 alone, 185,000 black farmers left the land, and only 87,000 remained [by 1974]. Farm failures were endemic, and in the 1950s, about 169,000 farms [of all races] failed annually; between 1960 and 1965, some 124,000 failed each year; and 94,000 per year failed between 1966 and 1968.

It's something Washington is closely engaged in:

> Yesterday, Olive [Olivia Watkins, CEO of the Black Farmer Fund] and I were able to attend the James Baird Foundation Awards, the award ceremony. So, Olive and I both got the humanitarian award for The Black Farmer Fund. It definitely opened a lot of eyes as we took that stage. And we've told people exactly the work that we're trying to do, as Black farmers in the United States are slowly disappearing and it's based on land laws, limited resources, and debt. And you'd be surprised how so many people came out to me and said, 'I didn't know this that Black farmers only have 1% of agricultural land in the United States.' And so, you know, for us to really just go out and try to make a difference and try to make people see that whatever happens to Black farmers happens to all farmers. And what I try to get people to understand is that if farmers take care of land and grow food to feed people, and you care about diversity, when you look at your livestock, you care about diversity when you're growing your food, then why aren't you moved by the fact

> that you have a race of farmers that are disappearing when it comes to land ownership?

The laws of partition are a major factor in the separation of the Black community from its own property. Landowners without wills will have their property inherited by all their descendants, who thus together become legal owners. Laws of partition mean that corrupt lawyers and predatory developers only need to convince one heir to sell in order to force the sale of an entire property. But Washington has developed ways of dealing with the subject:

> I try to stay away from that word of land ownership because people get afraid. They hear the words 'land ownership' and it goes directly towards reparation, and people get afraid when you try to use that word 'reparation'. And so, what I try to tell people is that we want to be stewards of the land and caretakers of the land. Because you don't live long enough to own anything. So, let's take that fear out of people wanting to own something. So, you take that ownership away. And you say, look, let's be stewards or caretakers of the land, that way in the mindset of people it's like, 'Ok!' So that in fact that land is passed on to the next generation, and I think if we use those words in that context, then I think that it makes people feel more at ease in terms of turning over land or giving up land, instead of thinking that they've got to hold onto it.

Wendell Berry on race

In her book *Black Earth Wisdom* (2023), Leah Penniman quoted Wendell Berry from *The Hidden Wound* (1970), where he writes of White people, "Because he did not know the land it was inevitable that he would squander its natural bounty..." In the same book we can find Berry discussing White people's responsibility for this destruction: "The white race in America has marketed and destroyed more of the fertility of the earth in less time than any other race that ever lived".

Berry's work is regarded with the utmost respect even by the most recent race theorists. In that book, Berry makes some startling statements about the damage caused by racism: "If white people have suffered less obviously from racism than black people, they have nevertheless suffered greatly"; "If the white man has inflicted the wound of racism upon black men, the cost has been that he would receive the mirror image of that wound into himself." The root of this conjecture is that it was out of contempt for physical labour that Black people were used to relieve White people of their burden. This unwillingness to dirty one's own hands, Berry believes, is "a serious flaw of character".

In the *Hidden Wound*, writing in 1970 at the age of thirty-four, Berry describes himself as "a man whose life from the beginning has been conditioned by the lives of black people..." Berry's great-grandfather John Johnson Berry had owned a "mean" slave who was too defiant and rebellious to do anything with. He therefore sold the man to a brutish former Dixie captain cavalier called Bart Jenkins who "came in the night, and knocked the man on the head while he was asleep, and bound him, and led him away with a rope". Berry describes how within his native speech, one formed in and around small farms, where Whites and Blacks dealt with each other in close quarters, "there was a silence, an emptiness, of exactly the shape of the humanity of the black man; the language I spoke in my childhood and youth was in that way analogous to a mold in which a statue is to be cast". Berry reflects that "it seems to me for most of my life I have been involved in the filling out of this hollow, or this silence, both unconsciously and consciously, both unwillingly and willingly."

When he was three, Nick Watkins, a Black man, came to work for his grandfather on the farm where Berry also lived with his father. Nick stayed with the Berrys until his death eight years later, and Berry reflects that "during that time one of my two or three chief ambitions was to be with him." As an older man, he was alive to the potential politicking this friendship would have meant for Watkins. With a jolt one day, as Nick playfully warns a rumbunctious boy in his care that "John's going to get you!", he realised that John was in fact his father, and glimpses the power wielded over Watkins. On top of Watkins' tasks such as driving a team of mules pulling a mowing machine, at the same time keeping an eye of Berry's grandfather who had a tendency to nod off in the saddle, he was expected to also look after the White children: "When he had my brother and me, and maybe another boy or two, to look after as well, Nick must have been driven well-nigh out of his mind, but he never showed it." Their unlikely friendship had very unusual depths, none more poignantly manifested than when Berry asks Watkins to his birthday:

> I foresaw none of the social awkwardness that I had created... Nick, trying to compromise between his wish to be kind to me and his embarrassment at my social misconception, quit work at the time of the party and came and sat on the cellar wall behind the house... My grandmother, to her credit, allowed me to follow my instincts in dealing with the situation, and I did. I went out and spent the time of the party sitting on the cellar wall with Nick.

Berry tells us none of this to suggest, as the joke goes, that "some of my best friends are black", but rather to claim some insight into the situation brought about by "a prolonged intense contact with lives and minds radically unlike my own". He concludes, "I don't think the whites have dealt with their misery anything like so well as the blacks have." What is this misery that the Whites have disguised and pretended didn't exist? He lays down his thesis. The movement away from the land and the activity of farming, which was looked down upon as a miserable existence, drove people to the cities in a migration towards money. Society was conceived "as a pyramid on which the only desirable or honorable or happy position is the top. People not at the top envied those above them, despised those below them, and apologized for themselves. Happiness was conceived as success." Against this foolishness Berry sets the example of Nick Watkins:

> The image of a man who has labored all his life and will labor to the end, who has no wealth, who owns little, who has no hope of changing, who will never 'get somewhere' or 'be somebody,' and who is rich in pleasure, who takes pleasure in the use of his mind! Isn't this the very antithesis of the thing that is breaking us in pieces.

Berry counters an imaginary voice that lectures him, "You're a fine one to talk! You with your professor's wages..." Replying, "I have, I think, no way of dealing with this except to leave the question open."

Berry sets out his operative concept:

> As the white man has withheld from the black man the positions of responsibility toward the land, and consequently the sense of a legally permanent relationship to it, so he has assigned to him as his proper role the labor, the thousands of menial small acts by which the land is maintained, and by which men develop a closeness to the land and the wisdom of that closeness.

As Berry puts it, it is the White man's idea that certain work was only fit for Black people. A White man doing this work believing it was unworthy of his status would fail to come to philosophical terms with what he was doing:

> It seems to me that black people developed the emotional resilience and equilibrium and the culture necessary to endure and even enjoy hard manual labor wholly aside from

> the dynamics of ambition. And from this stemmed an ability more complex than that of the white man to know and to bear life. What we should have willingly learned ourselves we forced the blacks to learn, and so prevented ourselves from learning it.

While Berry credits Black people with producing an authentic culture based upon elemental experience, the Whites as a group "have produced here only a pernicious value system, based on greed and egotism and the lust for status and comfort..." What the Whites have produced of cultural value has come into being in the face of either indifference or opposition on the part of most Whites; it has been produced by exiles or renegades such as T.S. Eliot and Ezra Pound, or local eccentrics like Henry David Thoreau, Walt Whitman, William Faulkner, and William Carlos Williams.

In *The Hidden Wound*, Berry places White people's treatment of Black people as integral to their imbalance:

> As soon as we have fulfilled the hollow in our culture, the silence in our speech, with the fully realized humanity of the black man — and it follows, of the American Indian — then there will appear over the horizon of our consciousness another figure as well: that of the American white man, our own humanity, lost to us these three and a half centuries, the time of all our life on this continent.

In *The Need to be Whole* (2023), in which he goes over the same ground as *The Hidden Wound* in more detail, with more nuance, and erudition, Berry is able to conclude, "Our society's ignorance of farming lies at the root of systemic racism and mental illness."

INDIA

If I'd started this book with a chapter exploring India's philosophy and the soil, you the reader would likely to have been utterly baffled; perhaps the relevance of India to the subject is now more apparent? With international travel, and globalised book publishing, in the countercultural era the ideas of Eastern philosophy washed west like a wave. Beyond the influence of the ideas of Buddhism and the Vedas, the philosophies of Steiner and Gurdjieff are, to a great extent, adaptions of ideas which came from India. The *etheric* counterculture as I've documented it in *Retreat* uses these ideas of Eastern philosophy to cast off into inner space. However, the *integrated* counterculture we've explored here in *The Garden* took note of non-Western ideas such as the cycle of life and, through Eastern philosophy's focus upon interrelationships, explored our connection to the environment.

Everywhere we have encountered the peaceful and supremely logical influence of Eastern culture and philosophy: Henry Thoreau reading the Upanishads, Sir Albert Howard working with the farmers in Indore, John Seymour travelling and learning in the subcontinent, Lou Gottlieb at Morning Star Ranch communicating with the Mother at Auroville, Peter Caddy journeying up to Tibet, Masanobu Fukuoka refining Buddhism, Louis Bromfield's experiences in Bombay and with Sir Albert Howard, E.F. Schumacher's idea of Buddhist Economics, and ecopsychology's debt to Taoism. In her last book, *Loving and Leaving the Good Life* (1992), Helen Nearing, girlfriend to the young Krishnamurti, explains how she and

Scott Nearing would often invoke the following when asked about growing old:

> There are stages of youth, householder, philosopher, and hermit which are recognized in India. Youth is the period of learning how to live, studentship. Middle age includes the duties of the family man and social being, the worldly activist. The last stage is that of abstract thought and meditation, the hermit, the non-attached.

However, even today there's a lot of conventional suspicion towards "alternative religions" in the West. Especially when groups are accused of acting like cults. Having said that, people are as conflicted today about Christianity, which in my youth was "standard issue". Perhaps through a sustained examination of Buddhism, the Vedas, and Taoism, I've got pretty relaxed about it all. Certainly, in my view, the ideas, especially of Buddhism, are no more than the best sort of common sense.

The Green Revolution and Norman Borlaug

It is the great tragedy of this post-Second World War era that just as Eastern thinking rose like a tide in the West, the West sought increasingly to meddle in the East. Just as the Vietnam War was an exercise in the containment of communist influence in the Far East, so too was the policy of the Green Revolution a ham-fisted Western-backed modernisation of Asian, and notably Indian agriculture. Nick Cullather writes in *The Hungry World: America's Cold War Battle Against Poverty in Asia* (2010),

> To win over 'the submerged masses in the old imperial lands' the West needed a proxy, 'a very big and very poor country' in which to demonstrate a 'take-off from the ancient stagnant poverty of Asia toward a progressive, independent, modern

> economy.' India was not just an ally, but a surrogate in the Cold War's most decisive encounter.

The plan was as follows: "Mark off India as a developmental model that was both attractive and distinctly Western — inspire aid officials, economists, and the press to first create the 'problem' of hunger and then make solving it an international goal".

Norman Borlaug (1914–2009) is central in the question of the Green Revolution. Borlaug's family, Norwegian immigrants to the US, were subsistence farmers. He had been poor all his childhood but always well-fed and decently clad. Charles C. Mann writes that as a boy he "worked dutifully but without enjoyment. He particularly detested harvesting maize." But he had also witnessed the fickle nature of farming, his grandparents being driven out of the wheat business by a stem-rust outbreak in 1878. Borlaug witnessed a fight which broke out in Chicago in 1933 at the height of the Great Depression. Milk, of which there was no shortage, and which was being sold at a loss, was being ferried around in milk trucks guarded by the police and army. This was to prevent striking agricultural workers from overturning the trucks driven by "scabs" who were selling milk. Borlaug claimed later that seeing this crowd of famished people being bludgeoned was his primary motivation to improve crop yields. But this was not a scenario of want; it was a political situation. Borlaug's conclusion missed the point.

Borlaug studied plant pathology at the University of Minnesota, and his subsequent work was funded by the Rockefeller Foundation in Mexico. Searching for a universal grain, he was breeding the same strain of wheat in Mexico in two locations at different latitudes and climates. Never having taken any courses in plant breeding, he was violating a basic botanical dogma. But, with a one-in-a-million stroke of luck, he had stumbled across a strain of wheat, Ppd-D1, which was "photoperiod insensitive", which meant its internal growing clock was broken, and it wasn't choosy about what zone it was planted in. By crossbreeding varieties, he came up with a strain which was rust-resistant and highly productive when fed fertiliser. Further breeding produced a short, stubby stem which could carry the now swollen stalk's heavy load of grain. Five years more bred the wheat some flavour.

At the International Rice Research Institute in the Philippines, at that time funded by Ford, the rice equivalent of Borlaug's semi-dwarf, disease-resistant wheat varieties was called IR8. Just like Borlaug's wheat strain, it needed to be part of a "package" which included irrigation and chemical fertiliser. At this point, then, the scientific infrastructure for the Green Revolution in India was in place, all that was needed was a sufficiently serious moment to roll it out. Nick Cullather writes, "In green revolution lore, famine is the seminal event, the fulfillment of years of warning and the nadir from which India's agricultural resurgence is measured."

Famine in India?

Trying to push an aid bill through congress, President Johnson, hanging his hopes on the failure of the harvest caused by the 1965 November monsoon and the subsequent scorching of large areas of northern India, declared a "world war against hunger". The press took up the baton with support of chemical fertilisation and birth control. Inconveniently, however, Indian officials declared the 1966 famine a sham. "There is no famine," a ministry statement confirmed. Back and forth went the accusations and the flat Indian denials. Foreign correspondents could produce no photographic evidence of starving Indians — a *Times* (London) headline announced, "Food Ships Streaming into Famine-Free India".

Prime Minister Indira Gandhi had denied up till that point the existence of a famine. She reclassified it in a way sympathetic to America as not *exactly* being one "in the sense in which we knew these words before independence... There is an acute shortage of food in our country in specific scarcity areas. There are no people dying of starvation." Cullather describes her as allowing the food emergency to exert increasing authority over the provinces.

Despite lurid front-page news, the idea that millions faced starvation was at odds with official casualty and crop estimates. Bihar, the worst-affected state, reported yields at 96% of normal. Some commercial crops had been wiped out, but by flooding rather than drought. Certainly, there were anecdotal claims of starvation, but as one Indian legislator told an American researcher, "The landless and the poor suffer like this normally." President Johnson himself admitted that "they haven't had a goddam big failure. They've just produced 11 million more tons than they had last year. But... they want ten million free tons, and we want it for our farmers and so nobody here is stopping."

The natural disaster, a situation of some kind of magnitude however it is sliced, was the ticket for India to be encouraged by the US to adopt the supposedly more reliable model of chemical agriculture. The cost of adopting the new model was, soon enough, higher than the American aid budget, and therefore a net loss for India to support domestically. They were on the hook for dwarf wheat seeds, American irrigation expertise, and fertiliser imports. But the most important American gains were geopolitical. The USAID director explained to congress that the package was "an incentive to make sure these countries have their eye on the producer and rather than the consumer... to allocate more of their resources to agricultural development rather than industrial development", by that means neutralising them for American influence and inoculating them from the communist.

Problems with the Green Revolution

In terms of the international version of events, the Green Revolution averted famine and enabled India and Pakistan to overreach Malthusian limits. The tsunami of wheat that poured out of the Punjab in 1968 sold the story once and for all. This latter story has become the enduring consensus. High-yielding varieties put more calories in Asian diets, but they were less nutritious. Early on, they doubled productivity, but these amounts diminished. Good years showed huge harvests, but in poor ones, with blight or drought, they struggled in comparison to local varieties. The problems came in many forms: the rural ecology was permanently blighted by monocultures; incomes rose, but equally so did rural unemployment; farmers became dependent upon expensive imported inputs; nitrate pollution affected land and water; pesticides wreaked havoc on ecosystems; aquifers were drained dry; soils were waterlogged or caked in salts when irrigation water evaporated; small farms failed and were eaten up; and rural communities collapsed because of an exodus of farm workers to the city. Simultaneously, the oil and fertiliser costs associated with the techniques soared. In what is regarded as the most influential study on the Green Revolution by the Oxford University economist Keith Griffin, *The Political Economy of Agrarian Change* (1974), the conclusion was that "The story of the green revolution is a story of a revolution that failed." The historian Charles C. Mann, a reliably impartial commentator who takes pains to argue the positive sides of technological intervention, and who supports GMOs, summarises that "between 1970 and 1989, more than three hundred academic studies of the Green Revolution appeared. Four out of five were negative."

As it was transforming Western agriculture, sometimes in the image of Eastern ones, countercultural commentators were horrified by the Green Revolution. At the New Alchemy Institute John Todd said,

> The green revolution has not been shaped by an ecological ethic and its keenest enthusiasts are usually manufacturers of chemicals and agricultural implements backed by

> government officials rather than farmers and agricultural researchers, many of whom are aware of the immense complexity of stable agricultural systems.

Describing it, Richard Merrill said, "There is a disquieting feeling that we are witnessing the agricultural equivalent of the launching of the Titanic, only this time there are several billion passengers". Decentralist Mildred Loomis scorned:

> Borlaug and the persons heading this 'Green Revolution' were hardly decentralists. The new wheat and rice would be grown in thousand-acre fields; they required lots of water for irrigation. With these new grains were exported huge harvesting machines, tons of chemical fertilizers and sprays to fend off fungi and insects. This was a 'Green Revolution'?

Vandana Shiva

The most implacable enemy of the Green Revolution is the author and activist Vandana Shiva (1952–). Shiva's criticism of the reductionist science which supports industrial agriculture is burnished by her impressive accomplishments in physics at the doctorate level. Shiva runs the organisation Navdanya, which is devoted to keeping seeds "open-source", ensuring growers' rights to save seed, and running seed banks. Working with other groups, she has successfully fought off attempts by conglomerates to patent the seeds of both neem and basmati rice.

The Green Revolution and its disastrous consequences are central themes in Shiva's books *The Violence of the Green Revolution* (1989), *Monocultures of the Mind* (1993), and *Stolen Harvest* (2000). Through her writing, we can trace the chain of issues created by Western influence and the principles of industrial agriculture. Although her commentary is wide-ranging, she is particularly hard-hitting on the subject of monocultures, often discussed against the backdrop of the Punjab, a region once known as the breadbasket of India, but increasingly beset by ecological and social troubles.

India's staggering production of wheat and rice at the dawn of the Green Revolution is given by its supporters as evidence of its success; however, Shiva presents statistics from Jatinder Baja that show that aggregate crop production was higher in the years before the Green Revolution than after it. She points out that,

> as in the rest of India, indigenous agriculture in Punjab was based on diversity. Among the non-food crops indigo, sugarcane, cotton, hemp, assafoetida, and oilseeds were grown. The horticultural crops included guavas, dates, mangoes, limes, lemons, peaches, apricots, figs, pomegranates, plums, oranges, mulberries, grapes, almonds, melons, apples, beans, cucumbers, carrots, and turnips. The uncultivated areas were covered by date-palm, wild palm, willows, acacias, sissoo, by apple etc.

She lists a panoply of different millets, pulses, and oilseeds. Furthermore, this reduction in diversity ignored the role of plants cultivated to provide fodder for animals, and fertiliser for soils. The massive productivity of this wild diversity was replaced mostly by wheat and rice.

Shiva gives as an example of the clumsiness of the industrial agricultural approach the case of the green leafy vegetable bathua. Declared a weed because it competes with wheat, and choked back with expensive and ecologically ruinous pesticides, bathua is a useful crop in itself and a good source of vitamin A. An absence of vitamin A will cause blindness, which the "omniscient" industrial agriculture sets out to address with the growth of genetically engineered "Golden Rice" with vitamin A. Elsewhere, she writes of other traditional crops which have been disparaged: "Only a biased agricultural science rooted in capitalist patriarchy could declare nutritious crops like ragi and jowar as inferior."

Monocultures not only dramatically weakened the diversity of useful local agricultural production, which did not show up on conventional agriculture's radar, they were also built

> on the displacement of genetic diversity at two levels. Firstly, mixtures and rotation of diverse crops like wheat, maize, millets, pulses, and oil seeds were replaced by monocultures of wheat and rice. Secondly, the introduced wheat and rice varieties reproduced over large-scale as monocultures came from a very narrow genetic base, compared to the high genetic variability in the populations of traditional wheat or rice plants.

These genetically uniform plants don't have the natural resistance to disease that engineered varieties do, and therefore require fungicides. There were other options, and "the inevitability of the Green Revolution was built on neglecting the other avenues for increasing food production that are more ecological, such as improving mixed cropping systems, improving indigenous seeds, and improving the efficiency of the use of local resources."

Shiva is, perhaps unusually for the developing world, an ardent supporter of organic agriculture, pointing out that, "in India, the poorest peasants are organic farmers because they could never afford chemicals." She attacks the common assumptions about it:

> While organic agriculture is a low-input, low-cost option, and hence an option for the poor, it is often presented as a 'luxury of the rich'. This is not true. The cheapness of industrially produced food and expensiveness of organic foods does not reflect their cost of production but the heavy subsidies given to industrial agriculture.

Although she was not involved in any kind of counterculture, I was very keen to talk to Shiva against the background of Hinduism and organic agriculture. I was, for instance, interested in how the idea of something being sacred related to its environmental importance. She writes, "At the social level, the values of biodiversity in different cultural contexts need to be recognised. Sacred groves, sacred seeds, sacred species have been cultural means for treating biodiversity as inviolable and present us with the best examples of conservation." I couldn't establish a connection to her through her website or Navdanya. I was sure I would succeed in asking a her a question when attending a meeting when she delivered an address at the Schumacher Center, "Regenerating Local Food Economies: Feeding Eight Billion". They were celebrating fifty years since the publication of *Small is Beautiful*. But even there I failed to speak to her.

As it stands, then, the best representation of this, not *exactly* mystical aspect of her thinking, is represented in an interview she gave to Russell Brand on YouTube in 2022:

> If we realise that we live in a powerful world full of energy... and that energy is a creative energy of the universe... and our power is the spiritual power of aligning ourselves... which we [Hindus] call 'rta' and the right action... that's what [Buddhist] dharma is... aligning yourself with that power... then we are very powerful... and these people who think they are beyond all accountability can be brought to account.

International Society for Krishna Consciousness

The Hare Krishnas, known formally as ISKCON, equalled by the followers of Maharishi Mahesh Yogi's Transcendental Meditation, have an umbilical connection to the counterculture. In that era they set up in the Haight-Ashbury in San Francisco, in New York, and in London. The group's leader was the guru A.C. Bhaktivedanta Swami Prabhupada (1896–1977), or Prabhupada for short. After retirement from running a chemist's, Prabhupada became a sannyasi. In 1965, he was the first Hindu preacher to take advantage of the removal of national quotas by the Hart-Celler Act that year, as he travelled alone to the United States. Prabhupada established himself first in New York, then in 1967 in San Francisco.

Because of its close connection to the Haight-Ashbury scene, there are amazing accounts of Prabhupada visiting Morning Star Commune. Lou Gottlieb describes the scene in *Home Free Home* (2017):

> On April 8th, 1967, my daughter Judith and I went along to San Francisco and drove Swami A.C. Bhaktivedanta along with two of his devotees to Morning Star. I had been to some kirtans and met Prabhupada, as he was called by his disciples, earlier in the year at the little storefront on Frederick Street in San Francisco where he had established his first West Coast center of the International Society for Krishna Consciousness. On the way up Highway 101, I asked the Swami to fasten his seatbelt. He said that there was no need for him to do so, because he was protected by Sri Krishna at all times. Then I made some observation about Ramakrishna, the famous 19th-century Bengali holy man... Swami Bhaktivedanta placed his hand on my arm and said gently, 'Once you have discovered your true path, all further investigation of comparative religion is mere sense enjoyment.'

Victoria, in the same collection, describes the day:

> For the Swami's visit, we set up a temple in the orchard and made him a flowery throne. It was an exquisite spring day, the air soft and clear, blossoms still on the apple trees, the birds singing like something out of a fairy tale. A large crowd greeted him. He spoke and began chanting 'Hare Krishna' while everybody danced and sang. We absolutely floated in

> bliss. He was a really great teacher because he just became one of us. It was a great experience of springtime and love of God.

Followers of the religion, which worships Shiva, the cow-herder, hold the cow in especially high esteem. Ramón Sender Barayón describes the Krishna's fascination with the milking of the cow at Ahimsa Ranch: "Several devotees gingerly took a teat and squeezed, giggling all the while. They returned to the city with a container of fresh whole milk and placed it as an offering on their temple's altar."

The sacred nature of India's cows and their dung is often remarked upon by Vandana Shiva: "Cow dung is worshipped as Lakshmi, the goddess of wealth. The cow is sacred because it is at the heart of the sustainability of agrarian civilisation. The cow as goddess and cosmos symbolizes care, compassion, sustainability, and equity." Shiva emphasises this with statistics:

> It should be noted that two-thirds and more of the power requirements of Indian villages are met by some 80 million work animals of which 70 million are the male progeny of what the Western perspective sees as 'useless' low milk-yielding cows. It has been calculated that to replace animal power in agriculture, India would have to spend about US $1,000 million annually on petrol. Indian cattle excrete 700 million tonnes a year of recoverable manure: half of this is used as fuel, liberating the thermal equivalent of 27 million tonnes of kerosene, 35 million tonnes of coal or 68 million tonnes of wood, all of which are scarce resources in India; the remaining half is used as fertilizer. As for other livestock produce, it may be sufficient to mention that the export of hides, skins, etc. brings in $150 million annually into the national coffers. With limited resources, indigenous cattle produce a multiplicity of uses.

New Vrindiban ISKCON community

In the United States, the ISKCON set up the very successful New Vrindaban commune in the West Virginia countryside in 1968. It is still running today. The commune was the focus of an article in *Mother Earth News* in July 1972. Paramananda says:

> In 1968 Kirtanananda and I purchased the original property, and our Spiritual Master, His Divine Grace A.C. Bhaktivedanta Swami Prabhupada, began giving instructions on how to develop it into New Vrindaban... We chanted Hare Krishna every morning and evening, then in the spring of '69 — as though in response to our chanting — came women, children, three cows, two workhorses, a pony for the children, a pickup truck for running into town and an old power wagon which made it up and down the road until it finally exploded after four months.

Hayagriva Das, the community's co-founder and president, explains their cattle herd:

> We do keep cows for religious reasons. The big commercial milk farms, you know, slaughter their stock when the animals are five to seven years old. Since a cow will normally live to an age of 19 or 20, that means that they're not even allowed to live out half their years. Here, on the other hand, our cattle are kept throughout their natural lives.

The interviewer, Howard Wheeler, asks them whether they believe self-sufficiency is possible:

> We do ascribe to the underlying WALDEN idea of self-sufficiency and minimization, for the basic 'I-am-not-this-body' philosophy of Krishna consciousness aims toward

this. Simplify. Simplify. At the same time, we have to run a community. Thoreau didn't have to contend with sixty people, or a hundred, or — in the future — maybe a village of several hundred. He was simply setting down the ideal as it applied to the individual, and no doubt on an individual basis it can still be realized. In fact, it can be realized more rapidly on an individual basis, for on a communal basis the type of self-sufficiency that you find in WALDEN takes a good deal of time. For example, we feel that land and cows are essential for self-sufficiency, but we have to acquire the land first and then the cows and maintain and fence in pastures and feed the animals in the winter. If you recall, in WALDEN Thoreau often chastised the farmer for working so hard keeping up his farm. We could be similarly criticized if we weren't working for Krishna. In other words, Thoreau said that man didn't have time to cultivate his transcendental consciousness because he worked too much. But working for Krishna is the same as cultivating transcendental consciousness.

Bhaktivedanta Manor in the UK

Shyamasundar Das (born Samuel Speerstra in Oregon in 1942) was one of the group's earliest members. Das organised the famous Mantra-Rock Dance at the Avalon Ballroom in 1966, where Prabhupada headlined alongside Allen Ginsberg and rock groups the Grateful Dead, Moby Grape, and Big Brother & the Holding Company. In 1968, Das then set off in a group of five followers to establish ISKCON in the UK and seek out Beatle George Harrison.

I wrote to Shyamasundar Das, who has published a three-volume biography detailing his time working with ISKCON leader Prabhupada. He replied, "All glories to Srila Prabhupada! Many thanks for your letter. Any farming at Bhaktivedanta Manor was undertaken after I left there in late 1973, so no memories there. We did buy one cow in August 1973, and there were plans for farming at Prabhupada's request..." Das suggested I read Volume 3 of his *Chasing Rhinos with the Swami* (2021) book and signed off, "May Krishna bless your bold literatures!"

George Harrison had offered to buy the fledgling ISKCON movement a headquarters, an ashram just like his own house at Friar Park, but whenever he showed up to view properties, the price would suddenly skyrocket. Consequently, he told the Krishnas to find their own place and told them that he trusted them completely. So, on a cold and drizzling day, Shyamasundar Das drove forty-five minutes up from London to Letchmore Heath to what was then called Piggot's Manor. Entering the village itself with its quaint houses, some still thatched, was like travelling back five hundred years. Writing in *Chasing Rhinos with the Swami*, Das describes how "the manor itself was three stories high, with about thirteen thousand square feet of floor space. It was built in a mock-Tudor style, with over-hanging gables and a half-timber, half-stucco exterior. We could have been in Shakespearean times." Shown the grounds, they saw six acres of lush green pasture. "Whose cows are those?" they asked. "Oh, they belong to Tom over at Battlers Green Farm — he's got a grandfathered grazing lease on this pasture." Das notes to himself, "Hm — we'll see about that."

The purchase eventually went through, and in 1973 the globe-trotting leader of the movement, Prabhupada, called the payphone in the manor's main hall. "On my way to India I wish to stop for one week at London to visit the manor house that George has given." Das chartered a helicopter to bring the leader, who was suffering from a heavy cold, from Heathrow directly to the manor. A sea of devotees filled the lawn, preventing the chopper from landing, Das frantically waving them back. The Hare Krishnas were overcome with emotion; there wasn't a dry eye in sight. "We led Prabhupada up wide oak stairs to his big suite of rooms, and when he entered he said in a loud voice, 'All glories to George Harrison!'"

In the summer of 1973, Prabhupada was joined in his suite by John Papworth, the Church of England clergyman who founded *Resurgence* magazine, and the progressive economist E.F. Schumacher. The men are attacked by three of Prabhupada's senior clergymen in a diatribe against Christian priests and animal slaughter. Schumacher held his ground:

> Well, I happen to be a vegetarian. But I would hesitate a long, long time before I would make meat-eating the touchstone on which I would judge a Jesuit. And the evils that are going on that have to be fought are, by comparison with meat-eating, gigantic. And therefore, refuse to accept that even a meat-eating Jesuit may be a far better man than a vegetarian who is engaged in all sorts of nefarious practices...

As they settled in, the subject of cows moved to the top of the agenda:

> Some devotees were out looking for cows and peacocks. Prabhupada wanted cows, and we had advertised cows in our press release. We should have cows. Bhaja Hari found a milk cow for sale in Letchmore Heath, and Partha went to some Indian supporters and raised the cash. A few days before the festival, an Ayrshire cow with brown and white patches was herded through the village and settled into our horse stables... Her name was Pradyumni.

The Hare Krishna method of producing dairy drew comment from among the people we have met. In *Self-Sufficiency* (1973), John Seymour goes into the sad drama of how to wean a calf from its mother and the various techniques of immediate separation ("If you do this, you don't have my blessing..."), through to separation after a week, to, as the Hare Krishna farm and other Hindu communities propose, sectioning off various of the mother's teats to the calf — and milking the others. Then there's the methods of forcing one cow to rear four calves, of which Seymour concludes, "Ain't it a beggar, said the Queen of Spain. We've done it once but we'll never do it again." Elsewhere, in *I'm a Stranger Here Myself* (1978), Seymour explains, explicitly referencing the Krishna method:

> There is no reason why one should not have as much milk as one needs and leave enough for the calf. This is, in fact, what we do at Fachongle Isaf now and it works perfectly well. But unrestricted commercial competition rather than straight human greed has forced dairy farmers into wanting every drop of milk they can get...

In *Permaculture*, Permaculture co-originator David Holmgren writes approvingly, "This outcome of a system designed to maximise milk output per kilo of fodder can be contrasted to the slow, steady approach required on dairy farms run by Hare Krishna communities, where every calf born, female and male, must be cared for over its natural life."

Stuart Coyle

Sitting down to research this book one morning towards the end of April 2023, I discovered the existence of the cow-protection farm at the Hare Krishna HQ, Bhaktivedanta Manor, in Watford. In one of the swiftest interview-come-visits I've ever arranged, I hopped on the train, and at 4pm that same day greeted Stuart Coyle in the farm's car park. Coyle, who also goes by the name Shyamasundar Das, is a big gentle man with an Irish background. Describing his younger self to me as "a searcher", he became a disciple of the Hare Krishna movement in 1978 and has been part of the manor since 1986. Feeling out of his depth as head priest at the altar at the manor, and inspired by his visits to the community's farm, he applied to manage it when the post became vacant. He was delighted and relieved to be accepted for the role and managed the farm between 1992 and 2014. In that period, he was responsible for both the redesign of its buildings and the restructuring of its farming practices in line with the teachings of the Vedic texts. Coyle, who has now retired, feels that cow protection is his calling and in recent years wrote the fascinating book, now in its second edition, *Protecting Cows: A Handbook of the Principles and Practices of Vegetarian Cow Husbandry* (2022). The book offers a working solution as to how cows can be cared for and produce milk without killing them. The whole topic is held to be one of deadly seriousness; in the Bhagavata Purana it says, "The Supreme Personality of Godhead said... the brahmanas, the cows and the defenseless creatures are my own body." Elsewhere in that text it points to the cosmic consequences of their slaughter: "To kill cows means to end human civilization." Prabhupada, the Hare Krishna leader says:

> In the kali yuga [our godforsaken era], the calves are separated from the cows as early as possible... the cow stands with tears in her eyes, the sudra milkman draws milk from the cow artificially. And when there is no milk the cow is sent to be slaughtered. These greatly sinful acts are responsible for all the troubles in present society.

As outlined in his book, the principles of cow protection are as follows:

1. Cows should not be killed.
2. Milk is for humans as well as for the calf. When it is looked after, the cow gives more milk than the calf needs. She likes being milked and will often line up eager for her turn where she gets some food, a brush down, and human interaction.
3. Bulls are kept for breeding or neutered and trained as working oxen, and suitable work is developed for them.
4. Hand milking is the principal method. The milker nestles up beside the cow and can feel her breathing and motion.

The need for milkers draws more people into the farm's employment. When they are being milked, Coyle explains to me, "They get into some nice vegetables and some grains for their satisfaction and also their nutrients."

5. Calves are given their fair share of the milk, and the surplus is for humans. As a rule of thumb, for Western dairy cows, the calf can be with its mother exclusively for two weeks, after that the milker can take three quarters and leave a quarter for the calf. At six months the calf is weaned. Coyle tells me, "They'll bond together. They'll be together. The calf drinks directly from its mother... And you can see the calves are completely chilled out. The mothers are chilled out. They're fully satisfied. And then after these six months, they are like teenagers, so we wean them fully then."
6. Calves suckle until they are about six months old. Even details like this Coyle gleaned from the scriptures, [from Krishna Book Chapter 13, paragraphs 11 & 12]:

> These cows had their own calves, and the calves that were grazing beneath Govardhan Hill were large; they were not expected to drink milk directly from the milk bag but were satisfied with grass... Elderly cows are taken care of by the men, and the calves are taken care of by the boys; and as far as possible, the calves are kept separate from the cows, so the calves do not drink all the available milk.

7. Cows' lactation periods are extended, after weaning, for as long as practical without annual impregnation. Coyle notes that the extended lactation can go on as long as ten years, although on average it is four years. The phenomenon of extended lactation is not described in the Sanskrit texts or in Prabhupada's writings but has evolved through the practice of numerous ISKCON farms. It must have been noted over the centuries, but somehow its significance has

not been promoted. Draupadi, a Meuse-Rhine-Issel cow at Bhaktivedanta Manor, gave milk for ten years and was still giving fifteen litres per day in her last year of lactation.

8. Dry cows are encouraged to give milk even without having a calf.
9. Only suitable natural foods are given to the cows, such as grasses, vegetation, and grains. Coyle writes, "Grasses are seen as the main and best food for cows. If you can arrange a variety of grasses for your cows to graze they will be happy and healthy. Different grasses have different healing and nutritional properties, so variety is essential."
10. Downer cows, those who no longer stand, are properly cared for until their natural departure. Coyle shows me their sick pen where they care for dying animals. "We have a crane which can lift between 3,000 to 2,000 kilograms. And sometimes if you need to, you can lift the cows up. You can turn them over. You got a beautifully padded floor." This care extends beyond their natural life. "So when a cow dies, we have a little ceremony; we invite the community together. Which we would if they were like any person."
11. For those who want to use the body of a cow, just wait until it dies naturally. Coyle explains that the soul within the cow's body has moved on to its next bodily residence, and so it no longer needs the body. He cites the following quote from Prabhupada, in conversation in Paris on 11 June 1974, which sheds an interesting light on the idea that the movement is inherently vegetarian: "We don't say that you stop eating meat. You eat meat but don't take it from the slaughterhouse. Or don't by killing. Simply wait."

The whole system works. As he puts it to me,

> What you see in their faces, for us it's evidence that this is right, because they're happy; they are peaceful. The calves are happy and peaceful. It's just a wonderful, natural system. There's milk for the calf, milk for the people, the calves are happy, the cows are happy, the milkers are happy, the drinkers of the milk are happy... this is a natural life. People feel they derive benefit from every stage of this.

Cow-protection farm

I feel very honoured to have Coyle lead me on a tour of the farm. The current employees, out of respect to him, stop to tell me what a foundational contribution he has made. At the outset, he sets the scene:

> Obviously, with the barn, the whole farm building, it's built around our ethos of cow protection, the Sanskrit word is '*gorakshya*' — the word found in the Bhagavad-Gita — and that dictates our ethics. Our ethic says that ultimately there's a spiritual energy overseen by God, Krishna, and we are sparks of God, we're souls. And thus we're animating these bodies. There's also a soul animating a cow's body. So, our relationship with the cow is not just on the physical level, but understanding they have a subtle energy, and also a transcendent identity. So, we interface with the animals, we're interfacing with them on the fact that they're animals and they have unique abilities that they share with humans, and we share our abilities with them. And it's kind of orchestrated with a divine arrangement.

The farm has been carefully thought out to, as much as possible, make sense as an ecosystem. They keep Meuse-Rhine-Issel cattle, not Indian breeds, because the former are more productive. Coyle explains, "So on average, we'd expect 10,000 litres per cow. Whereas the Zebu Type in India, you only get about 2,000 litres. So, it's 1/5 of the milk." The manor has seventy-seven acres, on top of which they rent fifteen acres. That does for grazing, but there's no surplus therein for making hay for the winter, so that needs to be bought in. As with any properly run farm, the animal's dung and urine is carefully mixed with straw and returned to the fields for their fertility. Coyle shows me their immaculate dairy facilities which provide most of the dairy needs for the manor and its many residents and visitors. Some dairy is bought in, but they are on a trajectory to have it fully supported.

The one key respect in which they differ from conventional dairy farms, that they don't kill the bull calf, has called for careful management. However, Krishna farms do neuter most of the bulls at a year old, whereupon they are called steers, bullocks, or oxen. In itself, the process of sterilisation is not without its own moral dilemmas, as I know from spaying our family's cats. It feels like the cow-protection movement views it as the "least worst" manner of managing the situation. In the same spirit of management that "protecting a cow doesn't mean you let the calf drink all the milk". Coyle writes, "In the practical application of the symbiotic relationship between cows and men, one is required to castrate most of the bulls... Looking at history, one will find ample evidence showing that the castration of bulls has always been an aspect of bovine husbandry." Neutered bulls, oxen, are docile. The bull which is not neutered is a much more difficult animal to handle. Potentially aggressive, he has to be kept separate from the heifers (young females) and cows. Coyle introduced me to Hari (all the cattle have Indian names), a very big bull whose job it is to impregnate certain cows; so intense, the guy was almost smoking. I recall the dairy farm I lived beside as a child, the field with the bull in it, and instructions to at no point ever go in. With the oxen, the issue becomes what to do with them. Historically, and in India where they are held as sacred, they would be valued as draft animals. In terms of agricultural history, the use of horses as draft animals occupies a relatively small window. Of course, their dung and urine are still useful, but that's short-changing them.

At Bhaktivedanta Manor, the oxen are used to pull worshippers from the manor to the farm in a cart; they are also yoked up to till the soil in the fields in which grain is growing. Coyle shows me their homemade yokes and describes to me the atmosphere of working the land with the animals: "Hear the yoke creaking. The steam coming off the back of the oxen." Still, Coyle wasn't satisfied they were being put to enough use. To this end, incorporated upon the farm's redesign, there is Coyle's own invention, the ox mill. His inspiration for the ox mill came when he saw a magazine feature on Gita-Nagari farm in North America, where they use teams of oxen for sawing wood. Coyle made a mill using recycled parts from trucks. They bought a Ford cargo truck axle and modified it. Four arms stick out north, south, east, and west from a vertical mast, and the yoked oxen walk in a circle, driving. The system is fitted with a gearbox with a clutch and can be used to roll oats, grind beans, or make flour. Coyle says that "the novelty of turning in a circle for three-hour stretches wears off pretty quickly. To adjust for this, we alternated between operating the mills to walking the oxen." He remarks charmingly, "I suppose you could have suitable music playing to enliven the heart and mind of the oxen driver and oxen." He explains to me that "we'll be pressing oil for the kitchens; we'll be doing flour for our own use and for visitors, and also grain crushing, grass chopping." Coyle is understandably annoyed, in the light of his efforts to get the draft animals working, that the current management saw fit to buy a tractor, their "material handler", which saves shovelling up the dung from the stables — something he can see the rationalisation for — but the tractor is "competition".

Making money is perhaps not a priority for such an enterprise. But Coyle explained to me how the farm is in the black. "No, it's not loss-making, otherwise it wouldn't exist. In fact, it makes huge profit. Right? Because people are giving money because [they're protecting cows]. They're just giving you money because of that." The farm is a focal point for charity in the Hindu community. But even if that were not the case, it would remain a very effective business model. Coyle gives the example of the Ahimsa Dairy Foundation in Rutland, described by him as "spawned from the inspiration [director Sanjay Tanna] got from here". It is a smaller operation than the farm at Bhaktivedanta Manor, which is the largest cow-protection farm in Europe. "Some years ago, they had two thousand people waiting for the milk. And they were selling their milk at £4.50 a litre. So, there's a market out there." At the time of writing, the Ahimsa Dairy waiting list is still closed. To even be considered for a place on it, you have to become a member and pay at least £9 per month, with membership bands going up to £90 per month. Honestly, it's a wonder more farmers haven't thought to tap into this slaughter-free milk market. I bought a copy of Coyle's book for myself, and a hardback edition which I gave to Patrick Holden when I visited him in Wales. Coyle explained to me that Holden had once visited the farm and inscribed the book to his fellow dairyman, "From the cathedral to cows."

Krishna McKenzie

It's a measure of the elasticity of Hindu culture, India's drive to export its way of thinking, and its confident ease with its appropriation that, like Stuart Coyle farming cattle the Vedic way at Bhaktivedanta Manor, Krishna McKenzie is another White man adopted and brought into the Vedic traditions. McKenzie's migration to India is a remarkable story. His first conduit was Jiddu Krishnamurti's school at Brockwood Park. Aged fifteen, he was at a conventional school on the Isle of Wight and desperately unhappy.

McKenzie's mother had been a disciple of Osho's and was fascinated by the culture around spirituality. McKenzie remembers, "There were so many gurus' faces on the walls and there were so many books about anything from crystals to Sufism". Trying to find somewhere else to send her son to school, she remembered Brockwood Park, having attended a talk there, but couldn't remember where it was (life before the internet...). Luckily, someone from the school posted a flyer for events showing Krishnamurti videos on the message board in the Holistic Healing Centre where they lived, and the connection was made. McKenzie switched to the school and very quickly found his feet, flourishing in the climate. "It's such a beautiful place. It's an old Edwardian Mansion. And it's in beautiful grounds with giant redwoods and an organic garden. They grow food and it's all vegetarian. It's like a family."

McKenzie arrived at Brockwood Park in 1988, two years after Krishnamurti's death in 1986. Krishnamurti's teachings were still felt as a "very sincere and strong energy at the school". Krishnamurti's associates, the physicist David Bohm, Mary Lutyens (architect Edwin Lutyens's daughter), and Krishnamurti's assistant Mary Zimbalist were still in circulation. In his second year at the school, the multimillionaire Friedrich Grohe of the Grohe bathroom fittings company, a close friend of Krishnamurti's, paid for the students of Brockwood Park and the Oak Grove Krishnamurti School in California to visit India and the Krishnamurti schools there. McKenzie thinks he might have been the only student who troubled to pick up the local language of the south, Kannada. Coming against the background of his own parents' divorce and his previous discouragement in education, his popularity at school, and feeling so at home in India were a welcome surprise.

Back in the UK, he formed a close connection with the school's gardener, Friedrich Kharar. A quirk of Brockwood Park was that all the staff were paid the same wage — scrambling any ideas of their relative status. Rather than peddling the usual fare of wisdom lectures, the German gardener intrigued McKenzie:

> I found him much more 'authentic' in his approach. It wasn't so much talking; he was always working. His whole thing was Mother and Sri Aurobindo from Auroville [where he had lived], and Karma yoga and giving yourself without too much talking. He was always working with the plants in the garden, and you could feel like he was almost talking to the plants.

Working on a relatively complex experiment in the school biology lab one day, McKenzie had something of a moment of satori:

> We were using micro-pipettes of RNAs in aqueous gels, and it was quite serious stuff. And I remember looking outside the window and seeing the immensity of nature. You know, it's the autumn and these copper beeches are losing their leaves, and just thinking 'Wow, nature is just so amazing!' And here I am, trying to understand it through a micro-pipette with RNAs. So, I just said [to his biology teacher], 'Paco, I have to leave, I have to stop this now. I'm really sorry, I understood something.' So, I put down the stuff and because it was very free, Paco was like 'OK, no problem!' And I went to join Friedrich in the garden. And I started working with him. And it was at that time that I discovered my guru, who is a Japanese farmer, Masanobu Fukuoka.

Fukuoka became, and to this day remains, McKenzie's lodestar. Leaving school aged nineteen, McKenzie came to Auroville.

Auroville

No doubt about it, the Farm in Tennessee was a very large hippie commune. Auroville, however, a township, a city even, dwarfs it. Situated in what was a desert plain, twenty square kilometres in the southern Indian State of Tamil Nadu, it was founded in 1968 by the French spiritualist Mirra

Alfassa (1878–1973), "the Mother", a collaborator with the guru Sri Aurobindo. The Mother articulated her vision of it thus: "Auroville wants to be a universal town where men and women of all countries are able to live in peace and progressive harmony, above all creeds, all politics, and all nationalities. The purpose of Auroville is to realize human unity."

The book *The Dawning of Auroville* (1994) by W.M. Sullivan is something of an official text of the Aurovillian community. Sullivan is known as "B" and is a neighbour of McKenzie's. My copy, set in dark orange ink, comes with an insert picture of Sri Aurobindo. It contains descriptions of how the land was brought back to fertility:

> And so, beginning consciously in 1972, Aurovillians took on the grass roots task of restoring the land, the land that was not theirs, the land that belonged to 'humanity as a whole.' It is hard to imagine, looking out on this slowly reviving terrain, that this region was once covered with rich green forests... The cattle and goats are left to graze wherever they will — wherever they can — ravaging the countryside, the tree is valued for its kindling, and the simple farmers, enamored of Western models of 'progress,' proudly whiten their fields and themselves with massive doses of DDT... and 'modern' farming methods implemented as compensation to squeeze out the last ounce of natural soil fertility, pump the exhausted earth full of chemical fertilizers and pesticides to artificially sustain a lifeless soil, forcing it to produce more.

The Aurovillians set out to restore the land:

> Such backing as is available (small grants, contributions, personal savings) allow freedom from acute economic angst, gives us choices village farmers ordinarily don't have. We use bullock teams instead of tractors, for example, but avoid traditional wooden carts in favour of steel-frame,

> rubber tyre, larger capacity vehicles. Besides lasting longer and carrying more, the rubber tyre carts escape a typical eco-surprise inherent in the village model: the traditional design uses narrow, steel-rimmed wheels, which cut deep ruts across dirt roads and fields which — in the context of deforestation and a general lack of erosion control — soon become small gullies, which — that spiral again — if unchecked become big gullies, gorges and canyons funneling tons of rainwater and topsoil off the land and are difficult and costly to bring under control...

They allude to grants, and it's interesting to notes that it would be through Point, a foundation set up out of the profits of *The Whole Earth Catalog*, that Auroville would receive its first American grant.

Very wisely, they set about planting trees:

> So we are learning to pay attention to the economics of afforestation, to let the forest become again what it has been throughout of most of the human experience: home, earth, larder, teacher, friend to human beings. The potential for this in India is enormous: literally everything seems to grow on trees. Food, fodder, fuel, shelter, clothing, cleansing agents, medicines, crafts materials, almost any human need can be met by a consciously developed forest in this climate... Planting trees as the basis for agricultural productivity makes sense here in many ways. Most species begin their productive lives within three to five years and continue to produce for decades thereafter. Once established, they are far more dependable producers — less susceptible to vagaries of weather and pests, less dependent on humans to survive — than are field crops.

In keeping, Sullivan puts the countercultural ethos of the importance to start change with yourself very elegantly:

> It's becoming clear that human beings are not only part of but have actually somehow invented the 'problem of the environment': our old game of seeking always outside ourselves for something to blame, study, work on, change... They are in essence and origin not problems of the earth, of the land or the whole environment but of human distribution and use, and ownership and greed, and fear and desire; problems of human psychology and quality of life; which can be dealt with nowhere if not within and among ourselves.

Johnny

I wanted to probe into the topic of the original, historic countercultural pioneers of Auroville. Krishna McKenzie spoke to me about Johnny, one of the earliest hippie-era founders:

> Without Johnny there would be no Auroville... Johnny is like a cult hero figure in Auroville... He's from Sydney. He's one of the early Aurovillians. More than fifty years here. But there's a number of people like Johnny. I mean, Johnny is really the epitome of someone who really was quite expansive in how he did things. Because at that time you had to build your own house... He made the first Cretan windmill in working order. He used the external combustion engine to power his well. You had to be hands-on and practical... You had to grow food. So, there's a lot of people with those colours... I would say those hippies [and the way they related to the local population in the villages], they gave Auroville its foundation...

Johnny Allen (his full name) had a remarkable encounter with countercultural icon and architect Buckminster Fuller (1895–1983) — who popularised the geodesic dome, the abiding motif of the back-to-the-land movement — at UNSW Sydney, Australia. Johnny had been about to qualify as an architect when Fuller, who was lecturing there, "convinced me and quite a few other people in the university that the whole thing was what he called a neo-Egyptian anachronism — it was consuming some of the most creative individuals on the planet". Johnny dropped out.

Johnny's young wife, who had written him off as a useless breadwinner, took off to Pondicherry and the Sri Aurobindo Ashram there in 1971. And he followed her there. He describes in an Auroville community interview on Facebook, how

> when I first came it was roughly 100 to 150 people and the collective ethic in those days was self-sufficiency. Although one of the understandings was that we were here to rehabilitate the land. The ethic that we were living by was as much as possible to be autonomous — to grow our own foods — to build our own houses — to educate our own children.

Johnny described how once he got to India, "I felt like I'd come home. I felt at ease, and I felt at ease in a lungi [a man's skirt]. I felt like this was my place. I let my beard grow. It just was where I wanted to be." Johnny had a head full of untried architectural ideas and set out devising structures which became icons of Auroville, like the "capsule". He described it in its instructions as "the simplest cyclone-proof one-man shelter to be built from local materials with village know-how".

McKenzie farming in Auroville

McKenzie showed up at one of the most durable and important of Auroville's farms, Annapurna, and told them he wanted to live there with no more reason than he was a devotee of the Mother and Sri Aurobindo. Tomas, a Dutch farmer who had trained at the celebrated agricultural college in Wageningen and still runs Annapurna, accepted him for a three-day trial. McKenzie worked as hard as he could, "at full power" to pass muster, and was allowed to stay:

> So, I lived in this tiny little hut with my mosquito net, with my meditations and my books, my guitar, and I started living there and working there. And I really look back at that as my apprenticeship time. It was a bit more than a year. And I learnt how to milk cows, and plough, and green manures, and the seasons, and the tools, and the language, and starting to get to grips with the [Tamil Nadu] culture, you know? And not knowing that that actually is the deepest thread of all my learning. And Tomas let me play around a bit here and there, with some ideas of natural farming.

Tomas, an excellent organic farmer, was not convinced of the value of natural farming in that context.

The work at Annapurna was very hard, but McKenzie wanted a greater challenge. He joined a fifty-acre reforestation project where no one wanted to live, within which there were a few acres of farmland. Returning from a trip to Japan, he found someone else had built a hut beside his own. Rather than fight the toss, in January 1996, together with a few friends, they set up the Solitude Farm that he now runs alone nearly thirty years later. This wasn't without one further detour. In 2003, after a couple of years pursuing a myriad of loose ends in music, Paris, education at the Brockwood Park School, romantically in California, and in meditation in the Black Forest in Germany, he had something of a reckoning: "And then I realised… why am I running around like everything? Everything that I could possibly want is here in Auroville." This time he was lucky that no one else had moved into Solitude Farm like on a previous occasion when he went AWOL. To double down on his focus, he drew up a list:

> I listed all the reasons why I'd come to Auroville. And the top of my list was Fukuoka… And I was like, 'Of course! What am I doing? That's my main focus!' And the next day someone gave me an invitation to go and meet him and I thought he was dead! And, you know, I was like, man, this

> is synchronicity if ever there was synchronicity! And I didn't have any money. It was at Vandana Shiva's Farm, the meeting. And they were all a bit, you know, 'There's no way to stay,' and 'You have to register,' and all of this. And I was like, 'Oh my god!' So, a friend of mine who is a really amazing Vipassana Yogi, he said... 'Oh no, I've got a tent. I'm not paying. I'm not doing that. Come and stay with me, we'll share a tent,'... then Tomas from Annapurna Farm gave me the money to go there. He'd just received an inheritance and he gave me some money. So, it was like five days with Fukuoka in Dehradun at Vandana Shiva's farm. That was in 2003.

What was it like meeting Fukuoka?

> Specifically, it was just like meeting your guru, getting Darshan from your guru. Being in the aura of this person that, when you read their book, you often cry. You know, you're often moved to tears. I mean, I've read his book, a hundred times at least. I'm endlessly reading that book... But I do specifically remember... this is very much part of my narrative when I teach, and I do a lot of teaching, is I say to people, you know, when I met Fukuoka, he said to us...'Only a fool will understand his relationship with mother nature.'

There's a special relationship within India to Fukuoka which is evident in the spread of another indigenous form of natural farming taught by the firebrand agriculturalist — and with India's Hindu Nationalist prime minister Narendra Modi's endorsement — Subhash Palekar. McKenzie reflects on the attraction of Fukuoka in India:

> Probably because of the inherent spiritual vibe of natural farming, it's profoundly Buddhism. It's profoundly non-dualistic, which is the very essence of the Advaita, which is the foundation in Hinduism. So, I think people just

vibe with that completely. And he looks like a little monk!

Since that time, McKenzie hasn't strayed from the path of natural farming.

> And you got to see over time, and what's happened in our farm, is a food forest has emerged, and because we've been very adamant like we never ever, ever, diverge from Fukuoka's non-tillage... Our soil has become very amazing. And so many plants have emerged on their own. So, what we've learnt is how to use those plants.

In practical terms, when he came away from one of Fukuoka's workshops, putting seeds in clay pellets right away, "we started looking at non-tillage rice cultivation by using things like *Mucuna pruriens*, the black velvet bean, as ground cover."

I ask McKenzie what form the volunteer plants which have sprung up unheeded at his farm have taken:

> So, I can give you some examples: like turkey berry, right? Turkey berry is a wild eggplant and it's like a little brinjal [aubergine]. It looks like peas on a big bush. So that's a volunteer plant... Tamil people use that, but traditionally it was used a lot more. Now, it's only known in one dish called *vathal kulambu*. With these peas that have been dehydrated and refried and it's in this curry. But traditionally it was also used as a vegetable dish, was made into chutneys. It was used in the sambar, that's the daily curry... I married a Tamilian, and we started a farm-to-plate cafe after we got married in 2007. And she started to point out that, 'well, oh, this we can use,' and, 'This we can use in this.' And the ladies in the field started to understand that that is the value that we wanted to learn. They started to point out, 'We can make a spinach dish from this, and this seed we can harvest and grind it and make that into a chutney. And you know, this resin from

this tree is added to this flour, it makes it soft, and we make a chapati with that.' And we started to see, 'Man, there is a cultural treasure here!' and industrialised agriculture in our very anthropocentric viewpoint, we belittle that to such a mind-boggling extent that people in our area, if you ask them what vegetables they like, they say: potato, carrot, beetroot, cauliflower, cabbage, but actually none of those vegetables have any relationship to the foundation of this local culture. They are all modern vegetables. So, we've been exploring all these traditional plants, and the more you go into them, the more you see, the ones that are really old, most of those are volunteers, like their air potatoes, the *Dioscorea bulbifera*. We introduced it to the farm. But now it just comes up everywhere and we have about two hundred edible plants in the farm. And we start to see the characteristics of local food... The first thing is that they grow easily, there's no expertise to grow them. Like, if you take *moringa*, the drumstick spinach, you break off a stick. You plug it in the ground. It germinates. You know, that doesn't make you an expert or me an expert. It's a collective knowledge and because it grows easily, it grows everywhere in abundance.

McKenzie talks about the non-exclusivity of these plants, and I asked him to elaborate:

Well, a rich person can have a pizza; a poor [person] can't afford a pizza, right? They can equally have moringa because it is in abundance, because it's everywhere. It's a very beautiful characteristic. What you do need is a relationship with the land to access that food, but you don't need money necessarily. And the more you go into that, well, *sundakkai,* the turkey berry, that's also everywhere, but people don't eat it anymore. Why? Because they eat things like potatoes, carrots, and beetroots. But that means those industrialised foods have eroded their cultural nutritional

> identity and the coin defines the sort of the nutritional profile of a society, and not the relationship with the land, and the seasons, which are inherently the foundation of our cultural identity. But the list goes on, and on, and on. And as you explore that community of plants that emerge in food forests, you start to see, well, they're also very high in medicinal and nutritional value. This isn't just a farm we have here, this is a pharmacy. This is the very essence of Ayurveda and the Siddha tradition. You have everything here [in the *farm-acy*], from [things for] your liver, for women's uteruses, to your brain, the eyes, the kidneys, you know everything! It's all here, and in Tamil we say, '*Uṇavu maruntu*', we say, 'Food is medicine', and you start to see that it's so connected. It's like in our cafe, we serve banana-stem juice. It tastes great, it's refreshing, it's yummy, and it's good for you.

A particular favourite of the Solitude Farm cafe is "the blue flower":

> the butterfly pea juice... *Clitoria ternatea*. So, as you go into the subject of that plant you see. 'Wow it fixes nitrogen! Oh, it's technical.' It's a ground cover. It suppresses weeds. We get seeds from it, that we sell. But then also, it has a beautiful nutritional medicinal value. We sell the juice, we make the blue ice cream, we sell the flowers. And use it extensively in our education. So, you know, it's very diverse and wide, the gifts of mother nature. I could literally go on for at least another two hours and explain and share with you all the little colours, the tapestry, of what has emerged here. It's extraordinary.

McKenzie and the wider Indian culture

McKenzie feels very grateful to be running the farm in Auroville:

> I can imagine that doing it elsewhere is maybe more challenging because, with the community… we attract a lot of people around us because of the nature of what Auroville stands for… But I don't believe that what we're doing is impractical. This farm is about five and a half acres. And we're probably farming about four and a half with irrigation. But my records show that there's about nine to ten tons of harvest in a year. That goes in the cafe. That goes in the basket service (like a CSA). Goes to local shops. And is sold on the farm directly. So, we're like, 'Wow, that much food!' Now, if you take something like a banana stem, economically, it almost has no value. A local farmer going to the market will spend more money on his petrol than what he gets to sell the banana stem. But you can create a community, to sell that banana stem to. To use that banana stem to feed people. So, you disconnect the economic value and look at its nutritional value. All of a sudden that banana stem has an incredible value. Our farm-to-plate cafe represents that, it symbolises in a practical way that idea… But if we can do this, why aren't colleges and schools and corporations and hospitals, why aren't they using their land like this? So, recently, I started to make the effort to put these ideas down on paper, in project proposals.

His first project is on a six-hundred-acre site near Chennai, a city that is committed to reaching zero emissions by 2035. McKenzie himself has become something of a celebrity, fielding calls from the government and invitations to hobnob with India's richest family, the Ambanis. In 2024, he had a remarkable 417,000 followers on Instagram.

Devoted to the Tamil Nadu culture and openly vocal about its wonders, a self-proclaimed "guy from Portsmouth", he thinks this has been the secret of his success on many levels. "All we have to do is honour our culture, and they love that, the Tamils, I tell you. That's why I've become famous because they love it… they are rightly proud of their culture and are so connected with it in many ways." Gary Snyder is another fan of that culture's vast and seamless interconnectivity. He writes in *The Real Work*:

> I sense South India to have been, for a period, one of those few totally solid, integrated civilizations in which for a time everything was moving together with great beauty and force, when minds were really dancing together. T'ang China was a place like that, Damascus in the twelfth century was another.

McKenzie credits local people with teaching him most of what he knows:

> You keep learning things. And at times it gets a little esoteric. I met this traditional doctor and he said when you eat the banana flour, eat drumstick with it because there's a connection on the sub-atomical level and it does this for the Nadis, these sort of energy channels. And I was like, 'Really!?!' I mean this guy is a hundred-year-old Siddha doctor. There's so much to learn here. Man, it doesn't stop... You start to see, 'Oh, we can make powder with the neem flowers and the neem leaves, and we can make oil from the neem seeds, and we can do this and we can do that.' And from the drumstick, the moringa, you have the flowers, and the leaves, and the stem, the resin, and the seeds and the fruit! It's literally endless... So, from a non-interventional agriculture, that's emerged on its own, you have endless wealth.

Refreshingly, McKenzie is up front about his interest in Vedic philosophy and its teachers:

> Of course, Ramakrishna, Vivekananda, my wife is from Tiruvannamalai, so Ramana Maharshi is considered a great, great teacher here. Nisargadatta Maharaj, who

> wrote the book *I Am That*, no? These are all teachers who point you into this direction of non-duality... Nisargadatta Maharaj is one of my 'guru devs', my very special teachers. And I've done a cross study, word by word, from him and Fukuoka, and there's times when I underline sentences from each book, and they're the same. What Fukuoka is doing is he's pointing out non-duality... He's pointing out that there's a oneness and that 'nature doesn't know economy.' Nature doesn't have a concept of opinion, a belief.

However, beyond this, and deeper than it, he sees locally grown food as expressing a more profound spirituality:

> This local food, which is the expression of this *shakti*, this mother nature, is the lowest common denominator for every man. So, there is an incredible depth of truth, and when you start to see that that food grows without effort, in many cases you know there's definitely engagement, but many things grow easily. But you start to think the new spirituality is [an expression of] enormous gratitude to mother nature. It's not just, 'Oh it's an ecovillage!' [Eating local food is] actually an act of love, an act of *bhakti*, of devotion to mother nature. I say to people, 'Man, stop waving incense at photos of the Mother and praying mantra and stuff. Eat the local food.' That *is* a puja. That is an act of love, and I think that if you go deeply into the subject, Ramakrishna, Vivekananda, Sri Aurobindo, Ramana Maharshi, they are all pointing to a oneness, they are all pointing to a non-duality. And the fact of the matter is we eat three times a day.

McKenzie thinks people need to work this message out: "We're in a particular time on this planet where it seems to be that we have to wake up to this really fast."

Sadhguru

In June 2023 I travelled to the far east of London to see the contemporary Indian guru Sadhguru talk at the massive ExCel conference centre. He has an incredible 11.8 million subscribers on YouTube, and there were an astonishing twelve thousand people gathered to see him talk in the hall. At the start, Sadhguru walked along a central elevated aisle into the crowd to greet people. Everyone was taking photos. If it had been me, I would have been completely rattled by the whole experience. When the talk began, we were instructed that there was to be no more photography. Sadhguru talked very engagingly about what he described as the stereotypical ideas of spirituality, about the problems of mental ill health, about people's maladaptive relationships with their phones, about school only testing your memory, about the need to be in the present, the mercilessness of time, and the brevity of all our lives.

Sadhguru is particularly interesting to us as he has made the plight of the soil a focal point of his work with the Save Soil campaign. In 2022, he rode a motorbike from the UK to India, a journey of thirty thousand kilometres, to raise awareness of the issue. His ideas relate to human interdependence with nature: "Whether you are aware of it or not, one half of your pulmonary system is hanging up there right now on a tree"; "What you call "death" is just Mother Earth reclaiming the loan that she offered to you."

Sadhguru was born Jagadish Vasudev in Mysore, India, in 1956. As a young man, he first ran a profitable chicken farm, but upon his family's criticism of his working with poultry, he set up a construction business, which also proved to be successful. However, aged twenty-five, a series of spiritual experiences led everything to change. In his *New York Times* bestseller *Inner Engineering — A Yogi's Guide to Joy* (2016), he describes an event which occurred when he was seated on a rock on Chamundi Hill east of Mysore: "But suddenly I did not know what was me and what was not me. My eyes were still open. But the air that I was breathing, the rock on which I was sitting, the very atmosphere around, everything had become me. I was everything that was." He believes that practicing hatha yoga since he was twelve years old was some part of the reason the experience alighted on him.

Sadhguru describes growing up in the 1960s:

> The era of the Beatles and blue jeans, read my share of European philosophy and literature — Dostoyevsky, Camus, Kafka, and the like. But here I was exploding into a completely different dimension of existence of which I knew nothing, drenched in a completely new feeling — an exuberance, a blissfulness — that I had never known or imagined possible.

He says that the best way to put it is that he "went up and didn't come down. I never have." He has a funny twist on this: "I have never touched any substance, but if you look into my eyes you will see that I am always stoned." But, as he points out, even then these states of mind miss the point:

> Most enlightened beings never stay in samahdi states. Gautama Buddha never sat and meditated for years on end after his enlightenment. Many of his disciples went into very long meditations for years. But Gautama himself never did this because he must have seen it was not necessary for him. He practiced and experienced all the eight kinds of samahdis before his enlightenment, and he discarded them. He said, 'This is not it.' He knew this was not going to take him to realisation. Samahdi is just a heightened level of experience, a kind of inner LSD without any external input, which causes altered levels of perception. The risk is that you could get caught up with it, because it is far more beautiful than the current reality, but even the most beautiful experiences, as we know, can become a drag with time.

Sadhguru has a very original and healthily *integrated* take on the typically disembodied *etheric* nondualist tradition of the Vedanta. He argues, not for dissolving one's consciousness (Atman) into the cosmic consciousness (Brahman), like the LSD-guzzling, meditation-fixated counterculture that I explored in *Retreat*, but rather for finding a harmony here on earth with the heavens. As he puts it, "The science of yoga is, quite simply, the science of being in perfect alignment, in absolute harmony, in complete sync with existence." An admirer of Gurdjieff, his perspective might be closer to Buddhism, although, of course, the Buddha himself was a yogi. Within this context, his passion for the soil makes total sense, and his advocacy for the subject gives it unprecedented global attention. I was delighted that he was happy to answer a few of my questions.

Sadhguru's answers

Was there a specific moment when you decided to concentrate on soil?

Sadhguru: This journey, in terms of experience, started very early in my life because I have always been outdoors, and I have a certain sense of the land. So, my engagement has been very long-term, but being action-oriented came in 1998.

In 1998, a team of experts predicted that by 2025, Tamil Nadu (a state in India) would become a desert. I don't like predictions. People make predictions based on statistics and cold figures; they do not take into account human aspiration and longing, and what beats in the human heart. I decided to drive around Tamil Nadu and take a look. I realized that we might not even make it to 2025! Small rivers had dried up and homes were built on riverbeds, and there was not enough soil moisture for even palm trees — desert vegetation — to survive. So, we started a project called Project GreenHands to plant 114 million trees, enough to bring at least 33% green cover to Tamil Nadu's land area, which was the national aspiration.

So it is not that we suddenly thought of the "Conscious Planet — Save Soil" movement. For the last few decades, we have been working on this. In many ways, whether it was Project GreenHands, or later initiatives of Rally for Rivers or Cauvery Calling, they are not different things — it has all been about soil.

What is the connection between the science of yoga and the soil?

Sadhguru: Soil is the very foundation of life. This body — not just ours, but that of all life forms — is just an outcrop of this soil. If soil is not alive, there is no way life can happen here. But unfortunately, human beings have lost connection with what is life and everything that nourishes and sustains life around us.

One simple way to look at this is, the very body that you are is just the food that you have eaten. The food that you ate is just the earth. So you are just a piece of earth, or earth is your larger body. Right now, our attitude has become like this, we take care of our little finger but we don't take care of our arm. If your concern is only the little finger and not the rest of the arm, you will anyway suffer.

The significance of yoga, meditation or the spiritual process is that they bring a sense of inclusiveness. The ultimate goal of yoga is to come to a state where you experience the whole existence as a part of yourself. When there is an all-inclusive experience, being concerned and caring about everything around you is very natural because anyone who looks into themselves, anyone who turns inward, naturally realizes that their existence and the outside existence are not different.

Human well-being and environmental care are not two different things. The preservation and nurturing of this planet is not different from aspiring for a good life for ourselves.

Care for the soil was part of traditional Indian agriculture. Do we need to go forward *to these techniques of stewardship?*

Sadhguru: In the world today, we have started referring to soil as dirt. If it is dirt, then we are all dirtbags! In most Indian languages, soil is referred to as Mother Earth. This is because there is a deep understanding in the culture that it is from Mother Earth that we are born. Our biological mother is only a representative; the real mother is the soil that we carry as our body. Even today, most farmers in Southern India bow down to the soil before they step on it because the culture taught them that soil is the basis of their life.

The 12–15 inches of topsoil is the basis for 87% of the life on this planet, including ourselves. But in the last 100–150 years, we have destroyed over 50% of this precious soil, which generates 95% of our food. Year after year, we are taking out the crop, and after that the land is empty. Modern machines are ploughing 12–14 inches deep, ripping the soil open, and leaving it open to the sunlight. The summer sun kills the soil completely because the first 12–15 inches has all the microbial activity. This is literally murder of the soil. A handful of soil can have eight to ten billion organisms. This life beneath the soil — all the worms, insects and microbial organisms — is not designed to survive in harsh sunlight; it is designed to survive in shade.

First of all, why do we plough? Ploughing is to oxygenate the soil. If it is hard packed, you want to open it up. But the best way to do this is to keep the organic matter high, so that the level of microbial activity is such that the soil becomes very porous.

Every farmer knew that land must always be under cover just fifty to sixty years ago. For example, in India, it used to be common practice during the summers to always have a legume or pulse crop. Everyone knew that they won't get much yield from it, but it was left there to cover the land. When the rains came, the crop was ploughed back into the land. This would easily put back two to four inches of organic matter, or humus, every year.

Right now, the Conscious Planet – Save Soil movement is aiming to bring about a global policy that there must be a minimum of 3–6% organic matter in agricultural land based on regional conditions. In consultation with top scientists in the world, we have prepared a soil policy document, which has hundreds of ways in which we can regenerate soil in the world, depending on the latitudinal position, region, soil conditions, economic conditions, and also the agricultural traditions of the nation, because agricultural traditions cannot be changed overnight. Every country can do it in their own way, taking all this into consideration.

As a generation of people, we have taken the largest bite out of this planet. Right now, we are consuming the soil that belongs to the unborn child. For me, eating up the food of the unborn child feels like a crime against humanity. We need to reverse this. Soil is not our property. It is a legacy that we have received from previous generations. It is our business to see that future generations have living soil.

CONCLUSION

In the negative light in which organic food has increasingly been cast, as the preserve of the rich and cranky, we can easily forget that the original pioneers of the natural farming movement in the early twentieth century were rebels striking a blow against the industrial complex. The story of the counterculture's engagement with natural, pre-industrial agriculture, mediated through the experience of those pioneers, should be a salutary reminder to us of that true rebel spirit.

Today, that spirit is now at a weakened ebb. It is buffeted on all sides by challenges, from the upstart regenerative agriculture, from technological solutions emerging from its own midst, from ecological initiatives which seek to remove people from nature, and from reductive science funded by billionaires. Too often, solutions to our problems proceed from panicked assumptions as to what is necessary in the face of population growth, without pause for thought. The worst kind of reductive science, seemingly only viable "in vitro" and rarely mindful of its holistic impact, is usually promoted above better, more thoughtful management of resources, the heir of indigenous peoples' sustainable land practice.

Most of us are not fortunate enough to own a piece of land to call our own. However, even if we don't have any outdoor space, we can still tend and water a seed to a plant on a window ledge. We can nibble on it, gather that plant's seeds, and sow another generation. The intrepid can fill a tiny wormery with the plant's now decaying organic matter and harvest its compost. The endlessly absorbing process of gardening tethers us, not only to the seasons and our immediate geography, but to the rotations of the wheel of life, and the true nature of universal harmony. We may not be lofty beings like these growers and farmers, carrying on their shoulders the responsibility of feeding thousands, but in conjunction with actions like buying biologically grown natural food, the grounding any such gardening brings its practitioner will serve as the fulcrum of a happier, simpler, and kinder life.

***

It was a dry Saturday in March with the faintest promise of spring in the air. Cycling up to Black Heath from Central London one tackles a steep incline. I'd discovered buried in amongst the organic literature, and given by Sir Albert Howard himself on 1st March 1945, an address for correspondence with him. I felt compelled to visit this, Howard's home, which was situated just on the edge of London.

Set in a road behind the heath itself, this was a large building, with a generous garden shielded behind a tall wooden fence. In the twilight of his great life, dying only two years after leaving the addressed paper I'd found, in 1947, Howard must have enjoyed gardening there. Leaning my bicycle on the wheelie bins, I rang the door's bell.

A brown-skinned gentleman came to the door, and I asked him if he was the owner. Naturally suspicious of me, he confirmed that, yes, he *was* the owner, and precisely what was my business? I asked him whether he was aware that the house had been the home of Sir Albert Howard, a pioneer of organic agriculture? He was, I insisted on the basis of his importance, worthy of a blue plaque.

No, the owner had never heard of Howard. I went on to explain a little of his history. As we were talking, the man looked up Sir Albert Howard on his phone, and saw that it listed him as having died in Black Heath. Slowly his attitude seemed to change. I said, "I can see that you are English", to which he replied with a smile, "I have an Indian heritage." I thought he might be interested to know that Sir Albert Howard is considered with the utmost respect in India for the praise he lavished upon his teachers, the Indian agriculturalists.

The man, who was now looking positively delighted, said that the previous owners did not mention anything of this to him, and that he was very grateful to me for my having brought this to his attention. We exchanged names, shook hands, and I promised that I would send him a copy of this book, which you have now finished reading.

BOOKS CITED

Abbey, Edward, *Desert Solitaire*, Touchstone, 1968

Abbey, Edward, *The Monkey Wrench Gang*, Dream Garden, 1975

Abe, Naoko, *"Cherry" Ingram*, Chatto & Windus, 2019

Asaṅga, *The Bodhisattva Path to Unsurpassed Enlightenment*, Snow Lion, 2016

Asvaghosa, *The Awakening of Faith*, Open Court, 1900

Aurobindo, Sri, *The Life Divine*, Lotus, 1949

Aurobindo, Sri, *Savitri*, Aurobindo, 1947

Balfour, E.B., *The Living Soil*, Faber and Faber, 1943

Bates, Albert, *The Biochar Solution*, New Society, 2010

Bateson, Greogory, *Steps to an Ecology of Mind*, Chicago, 1972

Bay Laurel, Alicia, *Living on The Earth*, Vintage, 1970

Bay Laurel, Alicia, *Being of the Sun*, Harper & Row, 1973

Bay Laurel, Alicia, *Sylvie Sunflower*, Ms. Magazine, 1973

Beeby, John, *Future Fertility*, Ecology Action, 1995

Belasco, Warren J, *Appetite for Change*, Cornell, 1989

Belgrad, Daniel, *The Culture of Feedback*, Chicago, 2019

Berry, Wendell, *The Unsettling of America*, Counterpoint, 1977

Berry, Wendell, *The Hidden Wound*, Counterpoint, 1989

Berry, Wendell, *The Gift of Good Land*, Counterpoint, 1981

Berry, Wendell, *The Need to be Whole*, Shoemaker, 2022

Berry, Wendell, *The Long-Legged House*, Harcourt, Brace & World, 1965

Bodhi, Bhikkhu, *In the Buddha's Words*, Wisdom, 2005

Bookchin, Murray, *Our Synthetic Environment*, Knopf, 1962

Borsodi, Ralph, *Flight from the City*, Harper Colophon, 1933

Bowdler, Jonathan A., *The Countercultural Back-to-the-Land Movement*, Washinton, 2021

Brand, Stewart, *Whole Earth Discipline*, Viking, 2009

Bright, Jean Hay, *Meanwhile, Next Door to the Good Life*, Brightberry, 2003
Bromfield, Louis, *Pleasant Valley*, Harper Brothers, 1945
Bromfield, Louis, *Malabar Farm*, Cassell, 1948
Brown, Dona, *Back to the Land*, Wisconsin, 2011
Brown, Gabe, *Dirt to Soil*, Chelsea Green, 2018
Buenfeld, Gina & Clark, Martin, *The Botanical Mind*, Camden Art Centre, 2021
Burbank, Luther, *The Training of the Human Plant*, New York, 1909
Butler, John, *Mystic Apprentice*, Butler, 2020
Caddy, Eileen, *Flight into Freedom and Beyond*, Findhorn, 1988
Caddy, Peter, *In Perfect Timing*, Findhorn, 1996
Callahan, Philip S, *Tuning in to Nature*, Devin Adair, 1975
Callahan, Philip S, *Paramagnetism*, Acres, 1995
Capra, Fritjof, *The Tao of Physics*, Shambhala, 1976
Carney, Judith A & Rosomoff, Richard Nicholas, *In the Shadow of Slavery*, California, 2009
Carson, Rachel, *Silent Spring*, Houghton Mifflin, 1962
Carson, Rachel, *On a Farther Shore*, Broadway, 2012
Carson, Rachel, *The Sense of Wonder*, Harper Collins, 1956
Carson, Rachel, *The Sea Around Us*, Penguin, 1951
Charles III, King, *Harmony*, Harper Collins, 2010
Chase, Alston, *Harvard and the Unabomber*, Norton, 2003
Cho, Youngsang, *JADAM Organic Farming*, JADAM, 2012
Clark Davis, Joshua, *From Head Shops to Whole Foods*, Columbia, 2017
Clark, Glenn, *The Man Who Talks with the Flowers*, Macalester Park, 1939
Clark, John, *Hunza*, Funk & Wagnalls, 1956
Cluitmans, Laurie, *On the Necessity of Gardening*, Valiz, 2021
Coleman, Eliot, *The New Organic Grower*, Chelsea Green, 1989
Coleman, Eliot, *The Winter Harvest Handbook*, Chelsea Green, 2009
Coleman, Melissa, *This Life Is In Your Hands*, Harper Collins, 2011
Conford, Philip, *The Origins of the Organic Movement*, Floris, 2001
Coyle, Stuart, *Protecting Cows*, Coyle, 2022
Crombie, R. Ogilvie, *Encounters with Nature Spirits*, Findhorn, 2009
Cullather, Nick, *The Hungry World*, Harvard, 2010

Curtois-Gérard, *Practical Handbook of Market Gardening*, Hetzel & Co, 1870

Daloz, Kate, *We Are As Gods*, PublicAffairs, 2016

Darlington, Jeanie, *Grow Your Own*, Bookworks, 1970

Das, Syamasundar, *Chasing Rhinos with the Swami*, Speerstra, 2021

Dawborn, Kerry & Smith, Caroline, *Permaculture Pioneers*, Melliodora, 2011

de Baïracli Levy, Juliette, *The Complete Herbal Handbook for Farm and Stable*, FSG, 1952

De Salzmann, Jeanne, *The Reality of Being*, Shambhala, 2010

Dickerson, Matthew & Evans, Jonathan, *ents, elves, and eriador*, Kentucky, 2006

Dominick, Raymond H. III, *The Environmental Movement in Germany*, Indiana, 1992

Dowding, Charles, *Organic Gardening*, Green, 2013

Dowding, Charles, *No Dig*, Doring Kindersley, 2022

Drake, Bill, *Marijuana The Cultivator's Handbook*, Drake, 1969

Duhon, David, *A History of Intensive Gardening*, Duhon, 1984

Ehrlich, Dr. Paul R., *The Population Bomb*, Ballantine, 1968

Elk, Black, *The Sixth Grandfather*, Nebraska, 1984

Evans-Wentz, W.Y., *The Tibetan Book of the Dead*, Oxford, 1960

Fairfield, Richard, *The Modern Utopian*, Process, 2010

Faulkner, Edward H., *Plowman's Folly*, Oklahoma, 1943

Faulkner, Edward H., *A Second Look*, Oklahoma, 1947

Federer, William J, *George Washington Carver. His life & faith in his own words*, Amerisearch, 2008

Felton, David, *Mindfuckers*, Straight Arrow, 1972

Fields, Rick, *How the Swans Came to the Lake*, Shambhala, 1981

Fisher, Mark, *Capitalist Realism*, Repeater, 2009

Freud, Sigmund, *Civilization and Its Discontents*, Penguin, 1941

Fukuoka, Masanobu, *The One-Straw Revolution*, Rodale, 1978

Fukuoka, Masanobu, *Sowing Seeds in the Desert*, Chelsea Green, 2012

Gampopa, *The Jewel Ornament of Liberation*, Snow Lion, 1998

Gaskin, Stephen, *Monday Night Class*, Book Publishing Company, 1970

Gaskin, Stephen & The Farm, *Hey Beatnik!*, Book Publishing Company, 1974

George, Nelson, *Hip Hop America*, Penguin, 2005
Gill, Erin, *Lady Eve Balfour and the British organic food and farming movement*, Aberyswyth, 2010
Godard, Dwight, *A Buddhist Bible*, Dutton, 1938
Goffman, Ken, *Counterculture Through the Ages*, Villard, 2004
Goldberg, Philip, *American Veda*, Three Rivers, 2010
Goodman, Paul, *Growing Up Absurd*, Random House, 1960
Graeber, David & Wengrow, David, *The Dawn of Everything*, Penguin, 2021
Gravy, Wavy, *The Hog Farm and Friends*, Links, 1974
Gudjieff, G.I., *Meetings with Remarkable Men*, Routlege & Kegan Paul, 1963
Gudjieff, G.I., *Beelzebub's Tales to His Grandson*, Harcourt, 1950
Hall, Stuart & Jefferson, Tony, *Resistance through Rituals*, Routledge, 1975
Hawken, Paul, *The Magic of Findhorn*, Harper & Row, 1975
Hawken, Paul, *Drawdown*, Penguin, 2017
Hawken, Paul, *Findhorn - a Center of Light*, East West, 1974
Heiney, Paul, *Country Life*, Doring Kindersley, 1998
Henderson, George, *The Farming Ladder*, Faber and Faber, 1944
Hesse, Hermann, *Siddhartha*, Peter Owen, 1954
Hobson, Jake, *Niwaki*, Timber, 2007
Holmgren, David, *Permaculture Pathways & Principles Beyond Sustainability*, Holmgren, 2002
Holmgren, David, *RetroSuburbia*, Melliodora, 2018
Holmgren, David, *Permaculture Pioneers*, Melliodora, 2011
Holthaus, Gary, *Learning Native Wisdom*, Kentucky, 2008
Howard, Louise E., *Sir Albert Howard In India*, Faber and Faber, 1953
Howard, Robert & Skjei, Eric, *What Makes the Crops Rejoice*, Little Brown, 1986
Howard, Sir Albert, *The Soil and Health*, Devin Adair, 1940
Howard, Sir Albert, *An Agricultural Testament*, Oxford, 1940
Hurvitz, Leon, *Scripture of the Lotus Blossom of the Fine Dharma*, Columbia, 1976
Huxley, Aldous, *The Doors of Perception*, Chatto & Windus, 1954
Hyams, Edward, *Soil and Civilization*, Thames and Hudson, 1952

Ingram, Matthew, *Retreat*, Repeater, 2020
Jackson, Wes, *New Roots for Agriculture*, Bison, 1980
Jeavons, John, *Biointensive Sustainable Mini-Farming Method*, Ecology Action, 2007
Jeavons, John, *How to Grow More Vegetables*, Ten Speed Press, 1974
Jenkins, Joseph, *The Humanure Handbook*, Chelsea Green, 1995
Johnson, Wendy, *Gardening at the Dragon's Gate*, Bantam, 2008
Jung Carl, *Letters Volume 1 1906-1950 [To Frau Patzelt on Rudolf Steiner]*, Routledge & Kegan Paul, 1973
Jung, Carl, *Memories, Dreams, Reflections*, Pantheon, 1963
Kaczynski, Theodore John, *Technological Slavery*, Fitch & Madison, 2022
Kat Anderson, M, *Tending the Wild*, California, 2005
Kennedy, Gordon, *The White Indians of Nivaria*, Nivaria, 2010
Kennedy, Gordon, *Children of the Sun*, Nivaria, 1998
Kerouac, Jack, *The Dharma Bums*, Penguin, 1959
Kesey, Ken, *One Flew Over the Cuckoo's Nest*, Viking & Signet, 1962
Kesey, Ken, *Sometimes a Great Notion*, Viking, 1964
Khan, Lloyd, *Shelter*, Shelter, 1973
Kimmerer, Robin Wall, *Braiding Sweetgrass*, Penguin, 2013
King, F.H., *Farmers of Forty Centuries*, Parrhesia, 1911
Kirk, Andrew G, *Counterculture Green*, Kansas, 2007
Kolisko, L., *Moon and Plant Growth*, Anthroposophical Agricultural Foundation, 1936
Korn, Larry, *One-Straw Revolutionary*, Chelsea Green, 2015
Krishnamurti, Jiddu, *The Penguin Krishnamurti Reader*, Penguin, 1970
Krishnamurti, Jiddu, *The First and Last Freedom*, Harper Collins, 1975
Kropotkin, Pëtr , *Fields, Factories and Workshops*, Allen & Unwin, 1898
Kushi, Michio, *The Book of Macrobiotics*, Japan, 1977
Lachman, Gary, *Rudolf Steiner*, Floris, 2007
LaConte, Ellen, *Free Radical*, Loose Leaf, 1997
Langer, Richard W, *Grow It!*, Avon, 1972
Leary, Timothy & Metzner, Ralph & Alpert, Richard, *The Psychedelic Experience*, Penguin, 1964
Leopold, Aldo, *A Sand County Almanac*, Penguin, 1949
Loomis, Mildred J., *Decentralism*, Black Rose, 2005

Lorde, Audrey, *The Cancer Journals*, Aunt Lute, 1980
Lorde, Audrey, *A Burst of Light*, Ithaca, 1988
Lovelock, James, *Gaia*, Oxford, 1979
Lymbery, Philip & Oakeshott, Isabel, *Farmageddon*, Bloomsbury, 2014
Maclean, Dorothy, *To Hear The Angels Sing*, Lorian, 1980
Maharaj, Sri Nisargadatta, *I Am That*, Chetana, 1973
Maharshi, Sri Ramana & Godman, David, *Be As You Are*, Penguin, 1985
Mann, Charles C., *The Wizard & The Prophet*, Picador, 2018
Mann, Charles C., *"1491"*, Vintage, 2005
Maraini, Fosco, *Secret Tibet*, Harvill, 2000
Margulis, Lynn, *Symbiotic Planet*, Basic, 1998
Markoff, John, *Whole Earth*, Penguin, 2022
Marsh, Jan, *Back to the Land*, Quartet, 1982
Meadows, Donella H & Meadows, Dennis L & Randers, Jørgen & Behrens, William W. III, *The Limits to Growth*, Universe, 1972
Merrill, Richard, *Radical Agriculture*, Colophon, 1976
Mitchell, John, *The View Over Atlantis*, Sago, 1969
Mollison, Bill, *Introduction to Permaculture*, Tagari, 1991
Mollison, Bill, *Travels in Dream*, Tagari, 1996
Mollison, Bill & Holmgren, David, *Permaculture One*, Corgi, 1978
Monbiot, George, *Regenesis*, Allen Lane, 2022
Montogmery, David R. & Biklé, Anne., *What Your Food Ate*, Norton, 2022
Moore Lappé, Frances, *Diet for a Small Planet*, Ballantine, 1971
Mungo, Raymond, *Total Loss Farm*, Pharos, 1970
Nearing, Helen, *Loving and Leaving the Good Life*, Chelsea Green, 1992
Nearing, Helen & Scott, *Living the Good Life*, Nearing, 1954
Nearing, Helen & Scott, *Continuing the Good Life*, Schocken, 1979
Nearing, Helen & Scott, *The Maple Sugar Book*, Good Life Centrer, 1950
Nearing, Scott, *The Super Race*, New York, 1912
Nearing, Scott, *The Conscience of a Radical*, Social Science Institute, 1965
Nearing, Scott, *War*, Vanguard, 1931
Needham, Joseph, *Science & Civilisation in China Vol II*, Cambridge, 1970
Neihardt, John G., *Black Elk Speaks*, Nebraska, 1961

Northbourne, Lord, *Look to the Land*, Dent, 1940
Ohsawa, George, *The Unique Principle*, Vrin, 1931
Ohsawa, George, *Zen Macrobiotics*, Ignoramus, 1965
Okada, Mokichi, *Health and the New Civilization*, Johrei, 1991
Oliver, Paul, *Hinduism and the 1960s*, Blooomsbury, 2014
Oluo, Ijeoma, *So You Want to Talk About Race*, Hachette, 2019
Ouspensky, P.D., *In Search of the Miraculous*, Routledge, 1947
Palekar, Subhash, *Philosophy of Spiritual Farming*, Palekar, 2010
Pascoe, Brude, *Dark Emu*, Scribe, 2014
Patanjali & Prabhavananda & Isherwood, Christopher, *How to Know God*, Vedanta, 300
Paulsen, Norman, *Christ Consciousness*, Builders, 1984
Penniman, Leah, *Black Earth Wisdom*, Amistad, 2023
Penniman, Leah, *Farming While Black*, Chelsea Green, 2018
Pfeiffer, Ehrenfried, *Introduction to Biodynamics*, Floris, 2011
Pfeiffer, Ehrenfried, *The Earth's Face*, Lanthorn, 1947
Philbrick, John & Helen, *Gardening for Health & Nutrition*, Rudolf Steiner Publications, 1971
Phillips, Michael, *Mycorrhizal Planet*, Chelsea Green, 2017
Pollan, Michael, *How to Change Your Mind*, Allen Lane, 2018
Pollan, Michael, *The Omnivore's Dilemma*, Bloomsbury, 2006
Prabhavananda & Isherwood, Christopher, *Bhagavad-Gita*, Vedanta, 1944
Ravindra, Ravi, *Heart Without Measure*, Morning Light, 1999
Reich, Charles A., *The Greening of America*, Penguin, 1970
Ridsdill Smith, Mark, *The Vertical Veg Guide to Container Gardening*, Chelsea Green, 2022
Rivers, Patrick, *Living on a Little Land*, Turnstone, 1978
Rivers, Patrick, *Living Better on Less*, Turnstone, 1977
Roberts, Hugh J., *Intensive Food Production on a Human Scale*, Ecology Action, 1981
Robinson, W., *The Parks and Gardens of Paris*, Macmillan, 1878
Rodale, J.I., *Pay Dirt*, Rodale, 1945
Rodale, J.I., *The Healthy Hunzas*, Rodale, 1948
Roszak, Theodore, *Person/Planet*, Doubleday, 1978
Roszak, Theodore, *Ecopsychology*, Counterpoint, 1995

Roszak, Theodore, *The Voice of the Earth*, Bantam, 1993
Roszak, Theodore, *Where the Wasteland Ends*, Doubleday, 1972
Roszak, Theodore, *Sources*, Harper Colophon, 1972
Roszak, Theodore, *The Making of a Counter Culture*, Anchor, 1969
Roszak, Theodore, *Unfinished Animal*, Faber, 1975
Sadhguru, *Inner Engineering*, Penguin, 2016
Sams, Craig, *The Little Food Book*, Alastair Sawday, 2003
Sams, Craig, *About Macrobiotics*, Thorsons, 1972
Savory, Allan, *Holistic Management*, Island, 2016
Schultes, Richard Evans & Hofmann, Albert, *The Botany and Chemistry of Hallucinogens*, Thomas, 1979
Schumacher, E.F., *Small Is Beautiful*, Abacus, 1973
Sender Barayón, Ramón, *Home Free Home*, Friends of Morning Star, 1977
Seymour, John, *I'm a Stranger Here Myself*, Faber and Faber, 1978
Seymour, John, *The Fat of the Land*, Faber and Faber, 1961
Seymour, John, *The Hard Way to India*, Eyre & Spottiswoode, 1951
Seymour, John, *One Man's Africa*, Eyre & Spottiswoode, 1955
Seymour, John, *Round About India*, Eyre & Spottiswoode, 1953
Seymour, John, *The Complete Book of Self-Sufficiency*, Doring Kindersley, 1976
Seymour, John & Seymour, Sally, *Self-Sufficiency*, Faber and Faber, 1973
Shankara & Prabhavananda & Isherwood, Christopher, *Crest-Jewel of Discrimination*, Vedanta, 1947
Shantideva, *The Way of the Bodhisattva*, Shambhala, 700
Sheldrake, Merlin, *Entangled Life*, Vintage, 2020
Sheldrake, Rupert, *A New Science of Life*, Blond & Briggs, 1981
Shepard, Paul, *Nature & Madness*, Georgia, 1982
Shi, David, *The Simple Life*, Georgia, 1985
Shiva, Vandana, *The Violence of the Green Revolution*, Zed & TWN, 1991
Shiva, Vandana, *Monoculture of the Mind*, Zed & TWN, 1993
Shiva, Vandana, *Stolen Harvest*, Kentucky, 2016
Side Door, *The Farming Ladder*, ecovillage, 2019
Skinner, B.F., *Walden Two*, Hackett, 1948
Skinner, B.F., *About Behaviorism*, Vintage, 1974

Smaje, Chris, *A Small Farm Future*, Chelsea Green, 2020
Smaje, Chris, *Saying No to a Farm-Free Future*, Chelsea Green, 2023
Smuts, J.C., *Holism and Evolution*, Macmillan, 1926
Snyder, Gary, *Turtle Island*, New Directions, 1974
Snyder, Gary, *The Practice of the Wild*, Counterpoint, 1990
Snyder, Gary, *Earth House Hold*, New Directions, 1969
Snyder, Gary, *The Real Work*, New Directions, 1980
Somerset Maugham, W., *The Razor's Edge*, Heinemann, 1944
St. Barbe Baker, Richard, *Man of the Trees*, Ecology Action, 1989
St. Barbe Baker, Richard , *My Life My Trees*, Findhorn, 1970
Steinbeck, John, *Of Mice and Men*, Penguin, 1937
Steinbeck, John, *The Grapes of Wrath*, Penguin, 1939
Steiner, Rudolf, *How to Know Higher Worlds*, Anthroposophic, 1961
Steiner, Rudolf, *Occult Science*, Rudolf Steiner Press, 1962
Steiner, Rudolf, *Theosophy*, Rudolf Steiner Press, 1922
Steiner, Rudolf, *Autobiography*, Steiner Books, 2005
Steiner, Rudolf, *Agriculture Course*, Rudolf Steiner Press, 1958
Stevens, Jay, *Storming Heaven*, Atlantic, 1987
Stevenson, Douglas, *Out to Change the World*, Book Publishing Company, 2014
Stiriss, Melvyn, *Voluntary Peasants*, Stiriss, 2018
Stone Barns, *Letters to a Young Farmer*, Princeton, 2017
Stout, Ruth, *How to Have a Green Thumb Without an Aching Back*, Exposition, 1955
Sullivan, W.M., *The Dawning of Auroville*, Auroville Press, 1994
Suzuki, D.T., *An Introduction to Zen Buddhism*, Black Cat, 1954
Suzuki, Shunryu, *Zen Mind, Beginner's Mind*, Weatherhill, 1970
Tetrault, Jean & Thomas, Sherry, *Country Women*, Anchor & Doubleday, 1976
The Findhorn Community, *The Findhorn Garden*, Turnstone & Wildwood, 1975
The Mother, *Agenda Volume 7*, Aurobindo, 1966
Thera, Nyanaponika, *The Heart of Buddhist Meditation*, Rider, 1962
Thoreau, Henry David, *The Duty of Civil Disobedience*, Lancer, 1849
Thoreau, Henry David, *Walden*, Lancer, 1854
Tilth, *The Future is Abundant*, Tilth, 1982

Todd, John, *The Healing Earth*, North Atlantic, 2019
Todd, Nancy Jack, *A Safe and Sustainable World*, Island, 2005
Todd, Nancy Jack, *The Book of the New Alchemists*, Dutton, 1977
Tolkien, J.R.R., *The Hobbit*, Allen & Unwin, 1937
Tolkien, J.R.R., *The Lord of the Rings*, Allen & Unwin, 1955
Tompkins, Peter & Bird, Christopher, *Secrets of the Soil*, Harper & Row, 1989
Tompkins, Peter & Bird, Christopher, *The Secret Life of Plants*, Harper & Row, 1973
Treitel, Corinna, *Eating Nature in Modern Germany*, Cambridge, 2017
Tucker, Mary Evelyn and Williams, Duncan Ryūken, *Buddhism & Ecology*, Harvard, 1997
Tzu, Lao & Mitchell, Stephen, *Tao Te Ching*, Harper & Row, 1988
Ungerer, Tomi, *Far Out Isn't Far Enough*, Methuen, 1984
Unknown, *The I Ching*, Penguin, -900
Van der Ryn, Sim, *The Toilet Papers*, Chelsea Green, 1978
Vivekananda, Swami, *Raja Yoga*, Brentano's, 1920
Vogt, William, *Road to Survival*, Sloane, 1948
Voltaire, *Candide, or Optimism*, Penguin, 1759
Von Goethe, Johann Wolfgang , *The Metamorphosis of Plants*, Biodynamic Faming Association, 1974
Wallington, Jack, *Wild About Weeds*, Laurence King, 2019
Walls, Laura Dassow, *Henry David Thoreau, A Life*, Chicago, 2017
Watts, Alan, *The Joyous Cosmology*, Pantheon, 1962
Watts, Alan, *The Way of Zen*, Pantheon, 1957
Way, Robert, *The Garden of the Beloved*, Sheldon, 1975
Weihs, Dr. Thomas J., *Agricultural Symbiosis*, Biodynamic, 1968
Whatley, Booker T., *Make $100,000 Farming 25 Acres*, Rodale, 1983
White, John, *The Highest State of Consciousness*, Doubleday, 1972
Whitefield, Patrick, *The Earth Care Manual*, Permanent, 2004
Whitman, Walt, *Leaves of Grass*, Viking, 1959
Whole Earth, *The Last Whole Earth Catalog*, Portola Institute, 1971
Wickenden, Leonard, *Our Daily Poison*, Devin-Adair, 1955
Wickenden, Leonard, *Gardening with Nature*, Faber, 1956
Williamson, G. Scott & Pearse, Innes H., *Science, Synthesis & Sanity*, Collins, 1965

Wrench, G.T., *The Wheel of Health*, Daniel, 1938
X, Malcom & Haley, Alex, *The Autobiography of Malcom X*, Penguin, 1965
Young, Rosamund, *The Secret Life of Cows*, Faber, 2017
Yunkaporta, Tyson, *Sand Talk*, Text, 2019
Zinn, Howard, *A People's History of the United States*, Harper Collins, 1980

ARTICLES CITED

-, *Blackfoot Valley Dispatch*, "An Interview with Ted Kaczynski", 1999

-, Book Browse, "Charles C. Mann Interview", -

-, *Farmer's Footprint*, "Meet Rick Clark", 2024

-, *LIFE Magazine*, "The Youth Communes", 1967

-, *Soul Fire Farm*, "Beyond Heroes: A Guide for the Media", 2024

-, *The Alan Chadwick Archive*, "John Cage Remembers", -

-, *The Daily Telegraph*, "Mary Langman Obituary", 2004

Allen, Johnny, *The Auroville Adventure*, "Bringing Flowers to The Mother", 2019

Banhart, Earle, -, "How New Alchemy was organized, operated", 2023

Barbour, Robert &Holden, Patrick & Fredenburgh, Jez, *Sustainable Food Trust*, "Feeding Britain from the Ground Up Report", 2022

Bates, Albert, -, "About Tempeh Lab", 2024

Bates, Claire, *BBC News*, "What happened to the self-sufficient people of the 1970s?", 2016

Bock, Emil, *The Golden Blade*, "The Search for Felix the Herb-Gatherer", 1958

Bradley, Kirsten, *Milkwood*, "Eliot Coleman's "Fertile Dozen", 2011

Brawley, C., *Journal of the Fantastic in the Arts*, "The fading of the world: Tolkien's ecology and loss in The Lord of the Rings", 2007

Brinton, Dr. Will, *Maine Organic Farmer & Gardener*, "The Roots of Soil Health in Organic Farming", 2021

Brinton, Dr. Will, *Acres U.S.A*, "The Great Humus Debate", 2024

Brinton, Dr. Will, *Maine Organic Farmer & Gardener*, "Tillage Effects on Soil Health Parameters", 2019

Brinton, Dr. Will, *Acres U.S.A*, "Will Regenerative Replace Organic?", 2023

Brown, David, *MIT Press*, "Inventing Modern America: John Todd Interview", 2002

Brown, Dr. Trent, *Permaculture Research Institute*, "The Philosophy of Masonobu Fukuoaka: Buddhism and Agriculture", 2020

Browne, Murray, *The Book Shopper*, "The Unabomber's Library", 2009

Butler, John, *Seed*, "The Changing Seasons", -

Coleman, Eliot, *MOFGA The Organic Farming Revolution Book*, "An Old-time Opinion from an Old Organic Farmer", 2021

Coppard, Sue, *Seed*, "Weekend Farmers weekend working on Organic Farms... or <<rent-a-serf>>", 1973

Coppard, Sue, *WWOOF Website*, "The History of WWOOF", 2024

Crosby, Lorber-Kasunic, Accarigi, *M/C Journal, 176*, "Value the Edge: Permaculture as Counterculture in Australia", 2014

Dasi, Devaki Devi, *Back to Godhead*, "Fifty Years of Hare Krishna in the UK London, Where It All Began", 2022

Denn, Rebekah, *The Seattle Times*, "Mark Musick transformed the way Seattle thinks of local, seasonal food", 2017

Dowding, Charles, *Charles Dowding Website*, "The advantages and recent history of no dig", 2018

Fairlie, Simon, *The Land Magazine*, "Monbiotic Man", 2022

Ferguson, Gary, *Los Angeles Review of Books*, "The Letters of Gary Snyder and Wendell Berry", 2014

Gidlow, Elsa, *The City of San Francisco Oracle*, "Notes on Organic Gardening", 1967

Grant, Dale, *Mother Earth News*, "Communal Life: A Vist to The Hog Farm", 1971

Greenberg, Peter, *Peer-to-Pier Interview*, "Sue Coppard", 2009

Greene, Wade, *The New York Times*, "Guru of the Organic Food Cult", 1971

Halfacree, Dr. Keith, *The Global Sixties*, "Revisiting 1960s Countercultural Back-to-the-Land Migration and Its Millennial Resurgence", 2022

Hochschild, JoshuaP., *Commonweal*, "Race & Anti-fragility: Wendell Berry's 'The Hidden Wound' at Fifty", 2020

Holmgren, David, *Holmgren Design*, "Permaculture in Japan", 2004

Holmgren, David, *Holmgren Design*, "The Counter Culture as Dynamic Margin", 2000

Holmgren, David, *Holmgren Design*, "Weeds of Wild Nature", 1997

Irwin, Aisling, *Nature*, "The 'Mother tree' idea is everywhere - how much of it is real?", 2024

Johnson, Nick, *EchoGéo*, "American Weed: A History of Cannabis Cultivation in the United States", 2019

Jones, James H., *The New York Times*, "A Symbolic Career [Washington Carver]", 1981

Jones, Melanie & Hoeksema, Jason & Karst, Justine, *Undark*, "Where the 'Wood-Wide Web' Narrative Went Wrong", 2023

Jones, Rhys, *Australian Natural History*, "Fire-Stick Farming", 1969

Lakhani, Nina, *The Guardian*, "'The food system is racist': an activist used a garden to tackle inequities [Karen Washington]", 2023

Leonard, Robert, *Journal of the History of Economic Thought*, "E. F. Schumacher and the making of "Buddhist Economics," 1950 – 1973", 2019

Lewis, Andy, *The Quackometer*, "The Insidious Pervasiveness of the Cult of Rudolf Steiner", 2012

Loomis, Mildred, *Christian Century*, "The Decentralist Answer", 1947

Maureen Decombe, *Garden Rant*, "Smith & Hawken is Dead. Long Live Smith & Hawken", 2009

McGrath, Maria, *The New Rebublic*, "The Bizarre Life *and Death* of "Mr. Organic", 2014

Mildred Loomis, *Green Revolution Magazine*, "The Life and Work of Ralph Borsodi", 1977

Mother Earth News Editors, *Mother Earth News*, "Biodynamic Farming Methods Lead To Bigger Harvests", 1976

Mother Earth News Editors, *Mother Earth News*, "Dr. E. F. Schumacher: Author Of The Book "Small Is Beautiful", 1976

Mother Earth News Staff, *Mother Earth News*, "Wendell Berry: Farmer, Ecologist And Author", 1977

Mother Earth News Staff, *Mother Earth News*, "Nearings "Leaving the City", 1979

Murphy, Kim, *Los Angeles Times*, "Self-Sufficient Loner Lived Life Montanans Understood", 1996

Musick, Mark, -, "A Brief History of Tilth", 2024

Penniman, Leah, *MOFGA The Organic Farming Revolution Book*, "African American Agrarian Traditions and the Foundations of Organic Agriculture", 2021

Pietsch, Bryan, *The Washington Post*, "Before he was the Unabomber, Ted Kaczynskiwas a mind-control test subject", 2023

Plewes, Rick *aka Horsedrawn*, *Resurgence*, "How I beat the system", 1978

Poux, Xavier & Aubert, Pierre-Marie, *IDDRI*, "An agroecological Europe in 2050", 2018

Rose, Steve, *The Observer*, "The Circle of Life [The New Alchemy Institute]", 2019

Roszak, Theodore, *SF Gate*, "When the Counterculture Counted 'Imagine Nation' Review", 2001

Sams, Craig, *Craig Sams Website*, "Carbon Farming — the Key to Reversing Global Warming", 2019

Sandford, Jeremy, *Seed*, "How to Win Friendship and Respect when you Move to the Country", 1976

Schnug, Ewald & Jacobs, Frank, & Stöven, Kirsten, *Seabirds*, "Guano: The White Gold of the Seabirds", 2018

Shaw, Janet, *Celebrating One Incredible Family Website*, "Lady Eve Balfour – An Introduction", 2023

Siegle, Lucy, *The Guardian*, "Patrick Holden: 'People's image of farming is a complete fantasy'", 2014

Smith, Chris, *The Press Democrat*, "Bill Wheeler, founder of famed Sonoma County hippie commune, dies at 77", 2018

Solovitch, Sara , *Modern Farmer*, "Meet Alan Chadwick, The High Priest of Hippie Horticulture", 2015

Specter, Michael, *The New Yorker*, "Seeds of Doubt [Vandana Shiva]", 2014

Sullivan, William, -, "A Grateful Being", 2022

Swann, Richard, *Star & Furrow Magazine*, "Interview with Biodynamic Association Patron Patrick Holden", 2011

Treadwell, D.D. & McKinney, D.E., *HortScience*, "From Philosophy to Science: A Brief History of Organic Horticulture in the United States", 2003

TSPTR, *Shindig*, "The Beach Boys and ecololgy– Counter-Cultural musings", 2023

Upton, Patrick, -, "Lauriston Hall Newsletter", 2020

Various authors, *Country Women Magazine*, "Spirituality", 1974

Various authors, *Country Women Magazine*, "Living Alternatives", 1973

Various authors, *Country Women Magazine*, "Food", 1976

Various authors, *Country Women Magazine*, "Farming Women", 1978

Various authors, *Country Women Magazine*, "Homesteading", 1973

Various authors, *Country Women Magazine*, "Women & Land", 1973

Washington, Karen, Green Dreamer Podcast, "Food security, justice, sovereignty", 2021.

Wee, Sui-Lee, *The New York Times*, "In China, Bill Gates Encourages the World to Build a Better Toilet", 2018

Wenner, Kate, *The New York Times*, "How They Keep Them Down on The Farm", 1977

Wheeler, Howard, *Mother Earth News*, "New Vrindaban: A Hare Krishna Community In West Virginia", 1972

Winkler, Elisabeth, *Biodynamic Association Website*, "Ten things worth knowing about biodynamic farming", 2018

FILMS CITED

60 Minutes Documentary, *A is for Alar*, 1989

Allen, Johnny, *The Small De-Mountable House Interview*, 2011

AP Archive, *RR7539B UK EXPERIMENT IN SELF-SUFFICIENCY*, 1975

ATTRA Interview, *Organic Pioneer Michael O'Gorman on Vegetable Production for Profitability*, 2023

BBC News, *A Billion Go Hungry Because of GMO Farming Vandana Shiva*, 2013

BBC Wales, *I, A Stranger - John Seymour anong his neighbours*, 1970

BBC Archive, *Crank Peasant. John Seymour on Self-suffiency. Living on the Land.*, 1975

Berry, Wendell, *Agriculture for a Small Planet Symposium*, 1974

Biodynamic Conference, *Karen Washington*, 2016

Brand, Russell, *Vandana Shiva Bill Gates's Book Is Rubbish!*, 2022

Brinton, Dr. Will, *Carbon Sequestration Is All About Plants, Not Soil*, 2023

Bush, Zach, *Dr. Zach Bush interview with Dr. Josh Axe "Revealing the Root Causes of Modern Illness"*, 2024

Carpenter, Ken, *George Washington Carver: An Uncommon Way*, 2010

Chadwick, Alan, *The Vision of Biodynamics*, 1/1/-

Chadwick, Alan, *An Introduction to the Biointensive Method*, 1/1/-

Chadwick, Alan, *Garden Song*, 1980

Chadwick, Alan & O'Brown, Norman, *Garden*, 1971

City as Nature, *Masanobu Fukuoka Natural Mind* - Larry Korn Interview, 2020

Coyle, Stuart, *Working Oxen for Milling or Rolling grains*, 2018

Democracy Now, *Vandana Shiva We Must Fight Back Against the 1 Percent to Stop the Sixth Mass Extinction*, 2019

Dogs Go Woof Films, *Permaculture The Documentary_ How it started_ original*, 2020

Entheogenesis Conference, *Permaculture stories celebrating floristic and fungal abundance*, 2024
Esalen Institute, *Growth!: An Evolution of the Farm & Garden*, 2023
European Ecovillage Conference, *Albert Bates on biochar, forest permaculture and climate change*, 2018
Festival of Faiths, *Distant Neighbors Wendell Berry & Gary Snyder*, 2014
Fleischer, Richard, *Soylent Green*, 1973
Florb, *Off Grid Homesteading in Wales Takes Simple Living all the Way Hoppi and Tao Wimbush*, 2021
France 24, *'Bill Gates is continuing the work of Monsanto', Vandana Shiva tells FRANCE 24*, 2019
Gardening Australia, *Extended interview with David Holmgren Co-originator of permaculture*, 2020
Gaskin, Stephen, *Interview with Swedish TV Summer 1973*, 1973
Guest, Jake, *The Antiwar Movement's Influence On Organic*, 2023
Hager, Steven, *High Times Saint Stephen Documentary*, 1/1/-
Haley, Alex, *Roots*, 1977
Happen Films, *David Holmgren Interview on Permaculture, Energy Descent & Future Scenarios*, 2016
Happen Films, *Legendary Australian Permaculture Garden Tour – David Holmgren & Su Dennett's Melliodora*, 2020
Hawken, Paul, *Paul Hawken Extractive Capitalism's Toll on Food, Farming + Life*, 2021
Hoffman, David, *Joni Mitchell Granted Us 5 Minutes To Ask About Her Early Influences*, 1989
Holden, Patrick, *Real-Organic Project: Organic Needs Top Down, Bottom Up, And In-The-Middle Action*, 2024
Holmgren, David, *Reading Landscape*, 2024
Hopper, Dennis, *Easy Rider*, 1969
Hoskyns-Abrahall, John, *Living the Good Life with Helen and Scott Nearing*, 1977
Iowa PBS, *George Washington Carver: An Uncommon Life*, 2018
Jeavons, John, *Circle of Plenty PBS Special*, 1987
King 5 Seattle, *An interview with Denis Hayes, the Seattle man who organized the first Earth Day*, 2020
Korn, Larry, *Fukuoka gets better soil with No-till Interview*, 1/1/-

Lopert Pictures, *Revolution*, 1968
Lorencova, Olina , *Eileen Caddy: the Story of Findhorn*, 2013
Lovelock, James, *How to save humankind according to James Lovelock* - The Economist YouTube, 2019
McKenzie, Krishna, *LOW EFFORT, Easy To Grow Plants in a Permaculture Food Forest, Circle Garden & Perennial Hedge*, 2021
Miller, Danny, *Opening Doors Within The Findhorn Film*, 1990
Mollison, Bill, *In Grave Danger of Falling Food*, 1989
Moore Lappé, Frances, *The 92nd Street Y Interview with Mark Bittman*, 2022
Our Ohio, *Malabar Farm*, 2006
Research Channel, *Lynn Margulis Interview With Jay A. Tischfield*, 1/1/-
Richards, Huw, *Amazing Tiny Vegetable Garden with Year-Round Abundance! | A Mini Permaculture Oasis*, 2022
Rodale Press, *The Close to Nature Garden*, 1982
BBC, *Ceres Grain Shop 1971*, 1971
Seymour, John, *Inaugural Meeting of the Academic Inn*, 1/1/-
Sidi, Alan, *Tribe of the Sun*, 1972
Soundings Mindful Media, *The Farm - Origin Story of the Stephen Gaskin Family Farm - 1975*, 2020
Stone Barns, *What is Agroecology?*, 2017
Sue Coppard, *The Origins of WWOOF Interview*, 2022
TED, *4 environmental 'heresies' Stewart Brand*, 2010
TED X, *Douglas Stevenson of The Farm Out to Change the World*, 2019
TED X, *On Leverage: Karen Washington at TEDx Barnard College Women*, 2013
Tell-a-Tale Studios, *Larry Korn on Philosophy of Masanobu Fukuoka*, 2020
The Giving Grove, *Rooted in Wisdom A Conversation with Karen Washington*, 2023
The Good Life, *Series 4 Episode* 7, 1977
Tickell, Josh & Tickell, Rebecca Harrell, *Common Ground*, 2024
Tickell, Josh & Tickell, Rebecca Harrell, *Kiss the Ground*, 2020
Todd Hénaut, Dorothy, *The New Alchemists*, 1974
Trumbull, Douglas, *Silent Running*, 1972
Evans, David, *dirt*, 1998
Warner Pathe News, *Louis Bromfield: Malabar Farm*, 1949

Washington, Karen, *Growing Diversity In The Farming Community*, 2022
Whole Village, *Albert Bates at Whole Village*, 2020

RECOMMENDED LISTENING

Alicia Bay Laurel, "Mandala": All the plants in the garden can heal you.

Bay Laurel & Sender Barayón, "Planting Day Ceremony": We will bring you compost, mulch, and posts to lean on.

Bently Boys, "Down on Penny's Farm": And when they went bust, Maggie bought it.

Bill Fay, "Garden Song": Planting myself in the garden... between the potatoes and parsley...

Billy Gault, "The Time Of This World Is At Hand": What our people really need is the land.

Bo Diddley, "Pollution": We got to keep America clean, honey.

Bob Dylan, "Maggie's Farm": Terrible working condtions.

Bob Marley & The Wailers, "African Herbsman": The old slave mill, might grind slow, but it grinds fine...

Bob Martin, "Midwest Farm Disaster": The bank took back the farm one day.

Booker T. & The MG's, "My Sweet Potato": Down South when you've had enough Green Onions.

Bukka White, "Parchman Farm Blues": I'm down on Parchman farm, but I sho' wanna go back home.

Buster Carter & Preston Young, "A Lazy Farmer Boy": The grass and weeds was up to his chin.

Captain Beefheart, "Safe as Milk": Written in response to DDT-contaminated breast milk.

Captain Beefheart, "Moonlight On Vermont": Lunacy in Vermont.

Carolina Tar Heels, "Got the Farm Land Blues": Gonna sell my farm, gonna move to town.

Charles Ives, "Concord Sonata": IV. Thoreau.

Charlie Ace & Lee Perry, "Cow Thief Skank": Upsetter implicates Observer in bovine larceny.

Creedence Clearwater Revival, “Green River”: I can hear the bullfrog calling me.

Dando Shaft, “Rain”: You’re the bringer of my comfort...

Dave & Toni Arthur, “The Barley Grain for Me”: The farmer came with a big plow, he plowed me under the sod.

Don Cherry & Penderecki, “Humus, The Life Exploring Force”: Hymn to the topsoil.

Dr. Alimantado, “Just The Other Day”: No man no want to be a farmer...

Gurdjieff & Hartmann, “Kurd Shepard Dance”: Gurdjieff recalling the music of his childhood.

Happy Mondays, “Country Song”: Smoke wild-grown marryjewana.

Hiroshi Yoshimura, “Sheep”: 1, 2, 3, zzzz.

I. Roy, “Water Rate”: When I wheel out me hose and I water she garden.

Iron Butterfly, “In-A-Gadda-Da-Vida”: Contains a musical quotation of the hymn “God Rest Ye Merry Gentlemen”

Jackson Browne, “Before the Deluge”: They would need to make their journey back to nature.

James Brown, “Funky President”: Let’s get together and get some land, Raise our food like the man.

Jefferson Starship, “Let’s Go Together”: Wave goodbye to Amerika, say hello to the garden.

Joan Baez, “Rejoice in the Sun”: From the movie “Silent Running” (1972).

Joe Dolce, “Hey Lou Gottlieb, He Opened Up His Land.”: Shaddap You Face!

John Cale, “Hanky Panky Nohow”: Cows that agriculture won’t allow.

John Martyn, “One World”: Holism.

John Prine, “Paradise”: The devastating ecological impact of surface mining for coal.

Joni Mitchell, “Big Yellow Taxi”: Hey farmer, farmer put away that DDT now...

Joni Mitchell, “Woodstock”: And we’ve got to get ourselves back to the garden.

Julie Anne, “The Gardener”: Hippie reggae.

Lal Waterson & Mike Waterson, "Child Among The Weeds": ...don't need no beads.

Led Zeppelin, "Bron-Y-Aur Stomp": Rockers visit Welsh Cottage.

Lee Dorsey, "Holy Cow": Zebu.

Lee Perry, "City Too Hot": I'm heading for the hills where the air is fresh and clean.

Lee Perry, "Soul Fire": Soul Fire Farm.

Leroy Sibbles, "Garden Of Life": We must forever hold our ground.

Marvin Gaye, "Mercy Mercy Me (The Ecology)": How much more abuse from man can she stand?

Mort Garson, "Plantasia": Garson predates Wonder.

Neil Young, "After The Gold Rush": Look at mother nature on the run in the nineteen seventies.

Nick Drake, "Harvest Breed": Wasted pollen.

Paul & Linda McCartney, "Heart Of The Country": Want a horse. Want a sheep.

Paul Horn, "Earth Sings": From Paul Horn's "Inside the Magic of Findhorn" (1983).

Prince, "Eggplant": The Purple One.

R.E.M., "Gardening at Night": Inspired by nocturnal piss-stop.

Ralph McTell, "Michael in the Garden": Proto-ecopsychology.

Randy Newman, "Burn On": Cleveland, Ohio. The Cuyahoga River Fire 1969.

Robert Johnson, "Milkcow's Calf Blues": Now, your calf is hungry... I believe he's outta luck.

Ron Geesin / Roger Waters, "Breathe": Savour the grass while it lasts.

Roxy Music, "If There Is Something": Bryan would do literally anything for her. Even grow potatoes.

Scott Walker, "Farmer in the City": You can take the boy out of the country...

Stevie Wonder, "The First Garden": From Wonder's Journey Through "The Secret Life of Plants" (1979).

Stravinsky, "Adoration Of The Earth": From the Rite of Spring.

The Band, "King Harvest (Has Surely Come)": "Vermont belongs to The Band, California to the Rolling Stones." Raymond Mungo.

The Beach Boys, "Vega-Tables": Cart off and sell my vega-tables.

The Beach Boys, "Don't Go Near The Water": Surfers protest runoff.

The Beatles, "Get Back": ...to the land.

The Beatles, "Mother Nature's Son": Born a poor young, country boy.

The Byrds, "Mind Gardens": One acre of mind.

The Fall, "Hard Life In Country": You get a terrible urge to drink.

The Grateful Dead, "Saint Stephen": Obviously Gaskin in spite of later denials.

The Grateful Dead, "China Cat Sunflower": Sunflower as icon.

The Groundhogs, "Garden": Like the distant past, before the days of agricultural land.

The Incredible String Band, "A Very Cellular Song": May the long time sun shine upon you.

The Incredible String Band, "The Half-Remarkable Question": What is it that we are part of?

The Move, "I Can Hear the Grass Grow": LSD affects hearing.

These Trails, "Garden Botanum": Hawaiian psychedelia.

Vashti Bunyan, "Window Over The Bay": Bunyan wishes she had a flock of white sheep.

Willis Alan Ramsey, "Boy From Oklahoma": Okie.

War, "City Country City": The band remembers their rural roots.

Woody Guthrie, "Talking Dust Bowl Blue": Woody's Wrath.

Yoshio Ikeda, "Whispering Weeds": Fukuoka-friendly Japanese Jazz.

URLS

Rudolf Steiner Archive
https://rsarchive.org/

Kirsten Hartvig at Emerson College
https://www.thehealinggarden.uk/

The Alan Chadwick Living Library & Archive
https://chadwickarchive.org/

Alan Chadwick a Gardener of Souls
http://www.alan-chadwick.org/

John Jeavons
https://johnjeavons.org/

Ecology Action
http://www.growbiointensive.org/

How to Grow Bibliography
http://www.growbiointensive.org/bibliography/

The Soil Association
https://www.soilassociation.org/

Craig Sams
https://www.craigsams.com/

John Butler
https://www.youtube.com/c/SpiritualUnfoldment/

WWOOF
https://wwoof.org.uk/

The Rodale Institute
https://rodaleinstitute.org/

The Real Organic Project
https://realorganicproject.org/

Eliot Coleman
https://www.fourseasonfarm.com/

Helen & Scott Nearing
https://goodlife.org/

Anne & David Sears
https://www.pantryfields.com/

Whole Earth Catalog
https://wholeearth.info/

Morning Star and Ahimsa Ranch
https://www.diggers.org/home_free.htm

Alicia Bay Laurel
https://aliciabaylaurel.com/

Tennessee's The Farm Commune
https://thefarmcommunity.com/

Michael O'Gorman
https://www.michaelogormanfarming.com/

The Findhorn Foundation
https://www.findhorn.org/

Findhorn Community Archive
https://celebratingoneincrediblefamily.org/

New Alchemy
https://newalchemists.net/

Rich Earth Institute
https://richearthinstitute.org/

The Humanure Handbook
https://humanurehandbook.com/

Sim Van der Ryn
https://simvanderryn.com/

Masanobu Fukuoka Natural Farm
https://f-masanobu.jp/en/

David Holmgren
https://holmgren.com.au/

World Permaculture Association
https://worldpermacultureassociation.com/

Malabar Farm
https://malabarfarm.org/

The Sustainable Food Trust
https://sustainablefoodtrust.org/

Albert Bates's The Great Change
https://peaksurfer.blogspot.com/

Rachel Carson
https://www.rachelcarson.org/

E.F. Schumacher
https://centerforneweconomics.org/

The Esalen Institute
https://www.esalen.org/

Steven Harper
https://www.stevenkharper.com/

Karen Washington
https://www.riseandrootfarm.com/

Soul Fire Farm
https://www.soulfirefarm.org/

Bhaktivedanta Manor
https://www.krishnatemple.com/

Ahimsa Milk
https://www.ahimsamilk.org/

Vandana Shiva
https://www.navdanya.org/

Krishna McKenzie
https://www.youtube.com/c/krishnamckenzie

Auroville
https://auroville.org/

Sadhguru
https://isha.sadhguru.org/

The author's blog
https://www.sickveg.com/

THANK YOU

John Jeavons, Craig Sams, Dave Chapman, Eliot Coleman, Barbara Damrosch, Anne and David Sears, Sally Seymour, Alicia Bay Laurel, Michael O'Gorman, Cornelia Featherstone, Roger Doudna, Hilde Maingay, Earle Barnhart, David Holmgren, Patrick Holden, Wendell Berry, Steven Harper, Albert Bates, Karen Washington, Stuart Coyle, Krishna McKenzie, Gary Snyder, Paul Hawken, Shyamasundar Das, Sadhguru, Bhagavan Das, Amulya Maa, Gordon Kennedy, John Butler, Mark Musick, Subhash Palekar, David Grinspoon, Greg Haynes, Randy Ryan, Michael Shaw, Caroline Shaw, Veronica Caldwell, Adam Powell, Craig Siska, Rebecca Holden, Rebecca Davies, Jacqueline Kluft, Susan Corl, Ron Corl, Ned Reynolds, Clara Coleman, Briana Alfaro, Danielle Peláez, Maya Hector, Meg Ulman, Catie Payne, Starlite Humphries, Henry Asplin, Phil Shankland, Douglas Stevenson, Vicki Montague, Linley Dixon, Jonathan Hawken, Kirsten Hartvig, Mike Hammer, Susie Kemp, Stephanie Miller, B.J. Bullert, Charles Dowding, Ed Hamer, Ian Wilkinson, Ninian Stuart, Rachel Phillips, Jason Warland, Tali Eichner, Sarah Watkinson, Kate Henderson, Mohammad Awthad Anees Mohammad, Jeffrey Mishlove, Jules Evans, Jeremy Gilbert, John Doran, Sam Kelly, Randi Fine, Pamela Peeke, Ron Purser, Sam Stern, Madeline Lane-McKinley, Amir Giles, Erik Davis, Rupert Sheldrake, Bob Thurman, Ramón Sender Barayón, Jon Leidecker, Ned Raggett, Lama Zangmo, Lama Yeshe Losal Rinpoche, Tariq Goddard, Carl Neville, Chris DeVeau, James Hunt, Josh Turner, Johnny Bull, Vicky Hartley, Jay Stevens,

Patrick Holford, Simon Reynolds, Ludo Hunter-Tilney, Jake Hobson, Mark Wallinger, Rafal Kaniewski, Charles Pryor, Sacha Dieu, Dom Tyler, Maggie Saunders, Simon Confino, Murray Partridge, Paul Gunn, Rosemary Lever, Carole Cox, Lulu Ingram, Sam Ingram, Catherine Ingram.

REPEATER BOOKS

is dedicated to the creation of a new reality. The landscape of twenty-first-century arts and letters is faded and inert, riven by fashionable cynicism, egotistical self-reference and a nostalgia for the recent past. Repeater intends to add its voice to those movements that wish to enter history and assert control over its currents, gathering together scattered and isolated voices with those who have already called for an escape from Capitalist Realism. Our desire is to publish in every sphere and genre, combining vigorous dissent and a pragmatic willingness to succeed where messianic abstraction and quiescent co-option have stalled: abstention is not an option: we are alive and we don't agree.